Making Peace with Your Enemy

Edouard Bustin
57 Columbine Rd.
Milton, MA 02186

THE ETHNOGRAPHY OF POLITICAL VIOLENCE

Tobias Kelly, Series Editor

A complete list of books in the series is available from the publisher.

Making Peace with Your Enemy

Algerian, French, and South African Ex-Combatants

Lætitia Bucaille

Translated by
Ethan Rundell

PENN

UNIVERSITY OF PENNSYLVANIA PRESS

PHILADELPHIA

Originally published as *Le pardon et la rancoeur. Algérie/France,*
Afrique du Sud: peut-on enterrer la guerre?
Copyright © 2010 Editions Payot & Rivages.
English translation copyright © 2019 University of Pennsylvania Press

Published by
University of Pennsylvania Press
Philadelphia, Pennsylvania 19104-4112
www.upenn.edu/pennpress

Printed in the United States of America
on acid-free paper

10 9 8 7 6 5 4 3 2 1

A Cataloging-in-Publication record is available from the Library of Congress
ISBN 978-0-8122-5110-4

For Dipuo, Nthabiseng, and Thabile Motshabi, in memory of Lebo

Contents

Introduction

The hostility one feels toward an enemy in arms and the political community he embodies only slowly abates. The political resolution of a conflict is not necessarily followed by the pacification of society and reconciliation among individuals. For the combatant who has engaged in or been subject to violence, the confrontation with the enemy is experienced in very direct fashion. Under what conditions can such a combatant be brought to forswear his enemy, understand the reasons that motivated him, see him as an equal, pursue cordial or friendly relations with him, and/or develop a new relationship with him on the basis of shared interests?

By comparing the accounts of veterans of the South African and Franco-Algerian conflicts, I hope to contribute to answering these questions. In South Africa, I consider the African National Congress (ANC) militants who opposed the apartheid regime between 1960 and 1994 as well as the members of the security services who defended it. In Algeria and France, I focus on the militants of the Front de Libération Nationale (National Liberation Front, FLN) and the Organisation Armée Secrète (Secret Army Organization, OAS). Where the former fought from 1954 to 1962 for the independence of Algeria, the latter opposed that project between 1961 and 1962.

The South African and Algerian conflicts were characterized by the clash of adversaries with antagonistic political projects. They were also colonial wars in which national liberation movements sought to destroy prevailing relations of institutional, political, economic, and social domination. Two issues are thus involved in relations between the former adversaries: in addition to (re)constructing a relationship based on trust, the former subjects and citizens of the colonial order must free themselves from the relationship of domination.

In this respect, the combatant's experience and perception of the enemy are inseparable from his position within the old political order. The majority of ANC members are thus black or nonwhite while the security forces who served under apartheid mainly consist of whites. In colonial Algeria, "Arabs" or "Muslims" joined the FLN while a minority of "Europeans" were active in the OAS. When Algeria became independent, the former became Algerians, and the latter, who had migrated across the Mediterranean, became known as "pieds-noirs."

In each of these postconflict configurations, I focus on the opposing actors. None of the "couples" studied here is perfect—both because the parties to these conflicts were not necessarily involved in direct confrontation and because their conflict was often complicated by the intervention of one or more third parties. It is also to be noted that none of the protagonists represented their entire community, even if they tended to claim otherwise. Nevertheless, in each case, my choice of ex-combatant categories has been guided by considerations of opposition, with each group of actors supporting a political project that excludes that of their opponents (the end of apartheid vs. the defense of apartheid, an independent Algeria vs. French Algeria). I have also chosen to focus on individuals whose involvement in the conflict was voluntary. In the case of South Africa, I thus consider only career soldiers, excluding conscripts from my field of study. For reasons of symmetry, it would have perhaps seemed logical to also take into consideration the French army soldiers who fought in Algeria. Their participation, however, did not necessarily reflect personal support for the conflict.[1] In the French case, engagement on behalf of the cause of French Algeria was embodied by the militants of the OAS. What's more, like the South African security forces who "shared" their country with ANC activists, the majority of OAS troops in Algeria consisted of Europeans living in proximity to their FLN adversaries. In each case, then, studying these groups allows one to identify the twofold nature of their relationship to their adversaries, a relationship that was at once colonial and conflictual.

Three considerations affect the evolution of the combatants' perceptions. The first is the belief that the conflict's resolution was fair or at least constituted an acceptable compromise. This condition must be fulfilled if there is to be support for peace. Next, representations of the past are shaped by the place that ex-combatants occupy in their societies—whether they are honored or instead marginalized—and, more broadly, the significance assigned to war by those in power and society at large. Lastly, the possibility or impossibility of forming contacts with former enemies plays a decisive role in the evolution of reciprocal perceptions. Whereas the absence of contact between former belligerents favors the persistence of negative representations, encounters between them offer new experiences of the Other and allow attitudes to evolve.

Spurred on by Comparison

It may appear bold to compare the subjective experience of South African, Algerian, and French ex-combatants. I do not attempt to make comparison an end in itself but rather draw upon it as a tool for understanding the cases under investigation. The present undertaking thus seeks to compare protagonist attitudes and narratives regarding transversal questions, not to systematically measure the gap separating them.

By treating comparison in sociology as the equivalent of experimentation in the hard sciences, Émile Durkheim set forth the requirements inherent in the researcher's work: sociological analysis is built upon the comparison of observed portions of reality among themselves. Yet few international comparisons adopt the actor's own point of view.[2] The reason for this may have less to do with reservations regarding the scientific validity of this approach than with the inherent costs of such an inquiry.[3] The resulting analyses demonstrate the value of comparing diverse fields for the purpose of understanding phenomena that are at once near and distant, commonplace and particular.

The comparative approach facilitates and accentuates the decentering of the researcher vis-à-vis his or her object, which is all the more necessary given that the researcher is not immune to the emotions of the individuals he encounters. These are particularly evident among individuals who have experienced or employed violence, some of whom are still animated by exclusivist political beliefs. By exposing him- or herself to several fields, the sociologist is opportunely led to adopt a proper distance vis-à-vis the object of inquiry. Another virtue of comparison: one may be surprised by the discrepancy in meaning produced by ex-combatants from one situation to the next. This feeling of surprise spurs on one's inquiry and acts as a vector of comprehensive sociology.

Interpreting such divergences is a difficult task, since one may suppose that the actors' differing attitudes are fully explained by the historic, temporal, and political particularities of the contexts they inhabit. Yet the temporal gap between the configurations under investigation shows that, for ex-combatants, the passage of time does not necessarily result in a process of distanciation relative to their former enemy or the cause around which they rallied. Cultural explanation would also offer a straightforward interpretive scheme, but I have ruled it out on the grounds that it risks locking us into static and erroneous perceptions.[4] One objective of the present work is to seek out divergences in order to shed light upon the meanings of each configuration as a political and social construction.

This effort of comparison does not concern the nature of the conflicts in question or the paths taken in exiting them, though I do, of course, attend to these matters in order to reconstruct my protagonists' trajectories. Rather, I seek to put the experience and discourse of ex-combatants into perspective: having become involved in the conflict, thereby exposing oneself to physical danger, how does one narrate that experience and assess the conflict's outcome? How does one regard one's former enemy? It matters little whether the cause one defended was "noble" or arouses our sympathy. The standpoint adopted here supposes that all engagement is equivalent to the degree that the individuals in question identified with values, acquired *convictions*, and subscribed to a political project, which they spent a portion of their lives defending.

The present work pursues comparison at three levels. First, I put the discourses and attitudes of veterans relative to their own group into perspective, underscoring the various profiles that thereby emerge. Second, I compare enemy pairs (ANC vs. police officers-soldiers, FLN vs. OAS), revealing the symmetries between protagonists and the effect produced by their reciprocal representations. The implications of their involvement differ depending on whether the combatants entered an illegal clandestine movement or rather joined the ranks of an institutional state structure. Such discrepancies of status, however, do not rule out mimetic phenomena or participation in shared discursive structures. Third, the comparison seeks to be transnational, bringing a shared perspective to bear upon the members of national liberation movements and defenders of the colonial order, though without conflating them.

The actors of these conflicts were, moreover, inspired by one another, with the transfer of skills sometimes taking place between them. The experience of the Algerian struggle, often referred to as "the Mecca of revolutionaries," aroused the interest and admiration of Nelson Mandela.[5] South Africa's apartheid regime studied and implemented the methods employed by the French army to put an end to "rebel" subversion in Algeria, including infiltration and torture.[6] The source of inspiration was subsequently inverted, with the dismantling of domination and the shift to democracy in South Africa in the early 1990s coming to be recognized as a model of pacific, viable transition. In France and Algeria, some regretted the failure to build democracy on the southern shore of the Mediterranean as well as the end of cohabitation between Arab and European communities. The work of the Truth and Reconciliation Commission (TRC) even led to calls for a comparable body to be created to come to terms with past violence between France and Algeria.

Violence and the Ex-Combatant

To define combatants—and, by extension, veterans—as a category, I have relied on three criteria: membership in a more or less formal structure, continuity of involvement, and participation in violent actions.

In liberation or resistance movements, the structures in question are generally of a clandestine nature. The ANC created a military wing. In 1961, the movement led by Albert Luthuli opted for a strategy of armed struggle, forming Umkhonto we Sizwe (MK)—literally, "spear of the nation"—which operated against South African soldiers from bases located in southern Africa. Some of its members were also sent to infiltrate the national territory to set up networks and carry out attacks. Created in 1954, the FLN immediately turned to violence as its main mode of action and formed the National Liberation Army (ALN). A portion of its troops were positioned in Morocco and Tunisia. In Algeria, FLN militants participated in the revolutionary war from within cities or joined up with the guerilla movement in the countryside (the so-called *maquis*). Created in Madrid in February 1961, the OAS for its part possessed a general staff and political organization. Operational structures—mainly, the "deltas" in Algiers and the "collines" in Oran—were created for urban combat.

Membership criteria for these three movements were sometimes loose. A combatant belonged to a group or network and participated in certain activities on the orders of his commander. Nevertheless, underground political movements are often characterized by local initiatives and occasional excesses on the part of activists.

For combatants who took part in institutional structures such as the army or police, voluntary enlistment constitutes the criterion of their membership in the organization. For South African soldiers, particular attention has been given to elite groups that fought the enemy in the field. In what concerns the police, I met with members of the Crime Investigation Unit—better known as the Security Branch—which was responsible for tracking down, imprisoning, and interrogating suspected terrorists as well as maintaining an intelligence network.

The second criterion is therefore continuity and intensity of engagement: participation in the struggle is a long-term matter and excludes one-off, isolated actions against the enemy, however effective they may be. For members of the security services, this criterion requires that they be career soldiers or police officers. For unconventional combatants, it also implies that their participation in the conflict constitutes the center around which their lives are organized. In the postconflict period, the combatant also generally continues to identify with the movement with which he or she fought.

Finally, combat entails recourse to armed force or another form of violence against the enemy. This third criterion covers a broad array of actions. Should the person who carries out an act of sabotage, the person who plants bombs, and the person who aids and abets them all be considered "combatants"? The answer must be sought primarily in connection with the second criterion: continuity of action. It must then be counterbalanced with the criterion of risk-taking. In clandestine movements, low-violence activity exposes those who engage in it to arrest, mistreatment, and even death. It thus qualifies them as militants or combatants. Is it not problematic, then, to compare them to security service members, who possess vastly superior technological and organizational resources? The moral and political meaning of their acts is of course distinct, but I consider the police and soldiers as fighting on behalf of a cause, that of apartheid. They thus also count as "combatants."

From this notion of the combatant, one may deduce that of the ex-combatant. For reasons of conviction, pragmatism, or a duty to obey group loyalty, the ex-combatant agrees to observe the peace negotiated with the enemy by his organization and gives up the struggle to which he has for several years devoted himself. He retains or cultivates a social (and sometimes political) identity linked to his wartime activity. Frequently, he participates in a (formal or informal) veterans network with his peers. The definition of the combatant developed here—in particular, the attention it gives to identification with the organization—takes the protagonists' subjectivity into account.

The manner in which the fight is pursued during a conflict depends upon the resources available to the actors. But it also reflects a political community's values, expectations, and relationship to the outside world. The members of a community engaged in struggle appeal to arguments of legitimacy and effectiveness to justify their use of violence. The passage of time affects the manner in which violent action is regarded. The 1960s were more favorable to revolutionary theories and a liberative vision of violence of the type set forth by Frantz Fanon. Thirty years later, the aura surrounding armed struggle and third-world causes had considerably diminished.

The processes by which societies are pacified may also result in the transformation of the manner in which violence is regarded. The suffering inflicted upon the other party may gradually come to seem unacceptable. Societies then distance themselves from violent repertories of action, sometimes condemning them. Perceptions change as political configurations are transformed. In peacetime, public opinion and ex-combatants are less inclined to develop arguments that justify attacks against civilians.[7]

Colonial System, Conflict, and the Enemy

There is a long-standing distinction between oppressive and liberating violence: philosophers and politicians legitimated the American and the French Revolutions, denounced their excesses, and examined the issue of proportionality.[8] I do not, however, seek to contribute to this discussion. Nor is my objective to construct a scale of violence or single out those cases in which it is legitimate. Rather, it is to identify a series of actions that seek to harm one's adversary by inflicting physical or material losses upon him in a framework of conflict, and study the discourse produced regarding these actions. There is much variation in the intensity of violence, the nature of the target, and the effect produced on it. The means that are employed are characteristic of the actors' position during the conflict. "Rebels" or unconventional forces employ sabotage against material goods, carry out targeted or indiscriminate attacks against enemy armed forces and civilians, or eliminate those they believe to be collaborators and traitors. Soldiers and police use legal violence, arresting and imprisoning the combatants they pursue. The latter are tried, sentenced to death, or sent to prison. The authorities present violence as a means to ensure respect for the law and rein in subversion. With fewer resources than their enemy, "rebels" sometimes seek to compensate for strategic inferiority with spectacular actions, which can include theatrical displays of cruelty. By contrast, the security services conceal their own use of illegal violence, sheltering behind a screen of legality, which supplies the basis for their legitimate use of force. Although dictatorships and authoritarian regimes are more inclined to depart from the rule of law, democracies sometimes dispense with constitutional safeguards and resort to illegal methods, including the mistreatment and torture of prisoners, extrajudicial killings, and setting what are sometimes mortal traps for armed militants.

The conflict in which South African, Algerian, and French combatants participated arose in a colonial context. Their use of violence was thus part of a historic *longue durée*. In order to examine the accounts of the various parties to these conflicts, one must take the position of all of them into account and, in particular, the fact that their relations were structured by an older system of domination. The use of torture was thus encouraged by the unequal relations that characterized the colonial system: the government used the security services to reaffirm state power over the rebels;[9] the fear of the Other and colonial racism led to the spread of torture as a practice.[10] Among other reasons, brutality was employed by turns to humiliate and to cleanse oneself of humiliation. During the Algerian War of Independence, it sometimes happened that one killed one's neighbor or "childhood friend." When this occurred, the protagonists condemned their adversary's cruelty and duplicity. But such murders, far from being gratuitous, brutally interrupted the fiction of friendly relations and exposed the racism of colonial Algeria.

In this book, I hold that the figure of the enemy is embodied by the ex-combatants' armed political adversary. This intimate relationship is characterized by the protagonists' attempt either to reduce to powerlessness those against whom they fought or to convince them to change strategy and attitude. The adversary was the object of combat, the target of violence; what distinguished him was his recourse to brutality. The experience of war did not exhaust this relationship between South African, Algerian, and French ex-combatants, all of whom were themselves part of colonial society. This configuration blurs the frontiers between the various combatant groups involved in the conflict and the community they represented. The adversary facing one may thus have formerly been a neighbor, a colleague, or an acquaintance. To the degree that it appears as a shifting social and political construct elaborated by protagonists inserted into a postconflictual, postcolonial configuration, I make no attempt to define a priori the notion of the enemy.

Narratives, Imaginaries, and Sources

This work is principally based on interviews carried out with South African, Algerian, and French ex-combatants. On four occasions between 2003 and

2006, I traveled to South Africa for a series of one- and two-month research trips. Based in Johannesburg, I patiently established contacts in order to meet former ANC activists, soldiers, and members of the Security Branch who had served under apartheid.

It was through intermediaries—in particular, NGO members—that I was first able to set up interviews with poor ANC militants in the townships (mainly Soweto). Some of these ex-combatants then introduced me to their comrades. Interpersonal networks also came into play in the case of black ex-MK who had benefited from social promotion, though access to this new bourgeoisie was sometimes difficult to come by. Altogether, I carried out around forty interviews with ANC members, most of whom had belonged to its armed wing.

I also conducted interviews with soldiers who served under apartheid, some of whom left the institution at the time of the political transition while others joined the new South African army. The task was a little more diffi-cult in the case of Security Branch members, in part because they had nearly all resigned from the institution and are now scattered among various pro-fessions, and in part because their reputation had been damaged by the ac-cusations leveled against them by the TRC. Whether genuinely guilty of the human rights violations committed by the regime or convenient scapegoats, police officers were stigmatized as a group. The greatest difficulty resided in tracking down contacts. After meeting with one of them, I was introduced to his former colleagues. As a result, I was ultimately able to meet around twenty members of the Security Branch and a similar number of soldiers who had served under apartheid. Most of these encounters took place in Johan-nesburg and Pretoria, with a few taking place in Cape Town or its environs.

In the case of FLN members, I traveled to Algeria in 2005, 2006, and 2009. The main limit of my survey sample was geographic, with all interviews con-ducted in Algiers or the surrounding region. Most of those with whom I met (though not all) were natives of the capital. Given their urban origins, they thus had contacts with the European population at the time of French Alge-ria and are in this respect not representative of the population taken as a whole. What's more, their proximity to the government overexposes some Algiers *mujahideen* and *mujahidat*[11] and contributes to shaping their remarks. The content of my interviews would doubtless have differed had they been conducted in a rural setting or in midsize cities.

Finally, nearly all of my interviews with OAS members took place in 2004 and 2005 between Cannes and Sète in southeastern France. Once initial contact had been made, I had little difficulty in convincing fifteen OAS members to speak to me about their experiences. I feared that many would not agree to meet with me, but in fact they were often willing to tell me about their careers. I no doubt began my OAS fieldwork at a propitious moment: the organizations affiliated with the group had recently launched what was to prove a rather successful campaign to promote their version of history. The timing thus helped my investigation. Though I conducted fewer interviews than with other organizations, the movement itself consisted of only a few hundred members and was active for fewer than eighteen months in Algeria.

In each group, I favored individuals who had fought on national territory rather than abroad; I also gave preference to militants or security service members who had "military" rather than political experience as well, as a first-hand experience of violence. Unless otherwise requested, I have changed my interlocutors' first names in order to preserve their anonymity. Nevertheless, those who are well known as a result of the offices they hold or their publications appear under their real name.

The accounts I gathered reveal specific modes of narration. They reflect the ex-combatants' subjectivity and represent a way for ex-combatants to affirm themselves in society or justify their failure. They allow the speaker to appropriate or challenge the dominant values of the postconflict context or the official version of the war. They also reveal a trajectory that runs from engagement to disengagement (or, sometimes, the transformation of engagement) and is linked to the evolving perception of the (ex)enemy. In each case, the account displays both moral and emotional dimensions. Their remarks reveal actors who are concerned to defend their interests and survive as well as their need for self-esteem. They are, in this respect, strategic. Through his account, the individual speaker seeks to appear "a decent or even worthy person in his own eyes and those of others." The interview is an "exchange [in which] the researcher represents a generalized other."[12] Self-heroization and victimization are the specific tropes by which the speaker seeks to achieve self-esteem. These two tropes coexist with others, including the "banalization of the self," which consists in demonstrating one's everyday (in)humanity and common sense.

French, Algerian, and South African ex-combatants have more or less mastered the techniques of this interaction. They may already have been interviewed by journalists or other researchers regarding the part they played.

Some are activists and seasoned speakers, and their discourse is often the product of a previously constructed interpretation. It remains a reconstruction by means of which the speaker experiences his identity. These performances, however, are not perfect; they vary from one person to the next, and the interviews offer glimpses of the speakers' contradictions and weaknesses. Moreover, repetition does not immunize against emotion or suffering when discussing painful and humiliating memories. For those telling their story for the first time, the interview can be liberating.

The interviewee's perception of the interviewer—who, he supposes, receives his account with a mixture of reservation, surprise, and disbelief—also plays a role in determining the techniques of persuasion and justification he chooses to employ in his self-presentation. Among ANC militants and security service members who defended apartheid in South Africa, the manner in which I was perceived was primarily determined by the color of my skin. This entailed feelings of proximity or distance toward me, feelings sometimes counterbalanced by calculations regarding my political leanings. In the case of mujahideen in Algeria, my French nationality was the most salient fact. Some of them seemed to view my nationality as a guarantee of empathy, while others underscored our difference. Above all, it was French-origin members of the FLN who most sought to distance themselves from me. It seems that our shared "ethnicity" required that lines be drawn between us. For OAS veterans, I belonged to a generation that had probably been indoctrinated regarding the Algerian War by the school system. The fact that I had been born after the war meant that I did not think of Algeria as a cluster of French *départements*.

My interlocutors' attempts to persuade me were thus crafted in keeping with the opinions they had formed of me. Some of the interviews lasted many hours. The fact that many of my interlocutors were retired or unemployed doubtless played some role in determining their availability. I began by asking my interlocutors to recount their personal trajectories, including a few questions regarding their wartime activities. I then asked them about their view of the conflict and its resolution and attempted to gather material regarding their various encounters with the enemy. The question of violence was raised only if my subjects themselves included it in their war narrative. I sometimes supplemented my interviews by meeting multiple times with a given ex-combatant. This allowed the relationship between researcher and interviewee to be extended and deepened, and the individuals with whom I met on two or more occasions supplied extremely rich material.

Their accounts allow one to reconstitute the facts less than to collect social representations and retrace political and symbolic imaginaries as individual and collective constructions. By way of their narratives, the ex-combatants assign meaning to the conflict and the actions in which they participated, and reinvent the meaning of the war and the violence with which it was associated. The difficulty resides in distinguishing between the role played, respectively, by the imaginary and the rational. Cornélius Castoriadis held that the real is rendered comprehensible by the imaginary. Indeed, he went so far as to claim that "[the] imaginary does not merely hold the function of the rational, it is already a form of the latter and contains it in an initial and infinitely fertile indistinction."[13] For my part, I hold that the actor's strategic intention and the production of his imaginary mutually feed one another and that it is always difficult to distinguish between what belongs to one register or the other, a task that I do not abandon for all that.[14] The aim here is to decode a narrative structure that allows for self-understanding via a narrative-based interpretation that mixes lived history with fictive history, biographical style with novelistic style.[15] The narrative identity that is thereby constructed seeks to procure a feeling of continuity and coherence with one's self.[16] And, like any imaginary, it is not only developed at the scale of the individual but also partakes of collective representations.[17]

The questions of conflict and the enemy are particularly propitious grounds for the operations of the imaginary.[18] If the Other is essential to defining the self,[19] this is particularly true of the ex-combatant, for whom the adversary fills this role. One's connection to the enemy resides in this exchange of violence, whether unilateral or reciprocal.

Individual narratives also constitute a way to experience one's relationship to the group. They simultaneously allow one to feel membership in a symbolic community and distinguish oneself from it. Each of my interviews simultaneously reveals this element of conformity and need to distinguish oneself. At times, the relationship established between interviewer and interviewee over the course of the exercise allowed the latter to stray from conventional discourse—that is, the official or public stance of the interviewee's peer group—and give free rein to his own subjectivity. By departing from the usual ways of speaking about their symbolic community, the ex-combatants reveal the degree to which they have moved away from it. In a way, each of their narratives may contribute to clarifying the place they occupy within their respective groups and political communities.

*   *   *

In gathering the narratives of ex-combatants, my aim was to understand their intimate experience of the enemy over the course of the war. From their remarks, I sought to extract a moral grammar embedded in individual subjectivity. While based on political beliefs, this grammar also draws upon ex-combatants' emotions—their feelings of loss, pride, and guilt. Moreover, it falls within a political configuration that delineates the frontiers of the political community and designates the outlines of the adversary.

My discussion is divided into four parts. I begin by putting the postconflictual order that characterizes South Africa, France, and Algeria into perspective (Part I). In what ways does past conflict shape or change the political order? In South Africa, the country's new rulers, the ANC, sought to reforge the nation on the basis of reconciliation and social transformation by including their former adversary in the new political pact. In Algeria, the FLN based its claims of historical and political legitimacy upon the fact of victory, raising the specter of the colonial enemy to ensure its continued rule. France, for its part, sought to forget the Algerian War in order to obscure the colonial dimensions of the Republic.

I then turn to study the manner in which each country extended symbolic and material rewards to its ex-combatants (Part II). In South Africa, little gratitude was shown ANC militants, and the financial compensation accorded former MK members for their participation in combat was limited. Access to wealth is determined by the laws of the market. Having suffered political defeat at the hands of the ANC, the security services that served under apartheid were prompted to transform themselves but retained the resources necessary to maintain their standard of living. In Algeria, the mujahideen were elevated to the status of a social group to which the nation was beholden. In France, OAS activists were tried and then amnestied; forty years after the end of the conflict, some of their claims are (once again) receiving a favorable hearing and their demands have increasingly been satisfied.

In the Part III, I concentrate on the narratives produced by ex-combatants. The narrative that emerges from each of the groups casts light on their relationship with the conflict and the violence that drove it. They appropriate or distinguish themselves from a state-sanctioned political reading of both past and present. Individual speech resonates with collective narrative, and studying it allows one to refine the comparison.

Finally, I once again address the question of the enemy and consider the ways in which ex-combatants may rid themselves of it (Part IV). To what degree is it possible to come to terms with the past? In the light of the specific experiences of South African, Algerian, and French ex-combatants, I explore the figures of forgiveness and recognition.

PART I

The Aftermath of Conflict: (Re)Forging the Political Order

IN SOUTH AFRICA, ALGERIA, and (to a lesser degree) France, civil and colonial conflict transformed the social and political order. War's winners—those who embraced victory as their own and invested it with meaning—emerged as the leaders of a new political community. In each of these countries, the postconflict order I seek to describe here consists of an institutional, political, and social configuration, the main symbolic foundations of which were laid on war and its outcome. The organization of power, the new frontiers of political community, the rules of peaceful coexistence, and the economic system are partly the product of a power struggle that takes place when warring parties settle a conflict. The reorganization of the political community is the most direct result of the conflict's outcome. In South Africa, the victory of the African National Congress (ANC) allowed this community to be enlarged. In Algeria, by contrast, the victory of the National Liberation Front (FLN) promoted a new, Arabo-Muslim political community from which the country's European population was excluded. In the French case, withdrawal to the "hexagon," or the territory of metropolitan France, meant redrawing the contours of the French national community to fit those of the community of citizens—a community to which the nation's former imperial subjects no longer belonged.

The use of the term "postconflict" is not meant to imply a clean break between the time of conflict and that of peace. On the contrary, it implies that the effects of conflict are so powerful as to still largely determine the present. I here define as "postconflictual" any period in which the languages employed by a political community continue to be determined by the conflict itself and in which the actors' efforts at legitimation are mainly or perhaps even exclusively constructed around the objectives for which the war was fought.

My use of the postconflict notion sidesteps the issue of what determines the shift from a logic of war to one of peace as well as debates concerning the reliability and durability of the postconflict peace. It is here taken for granted that the frontiers between wartime and peacetime are permeable and that the pacification of societies and minds is not a necessary and linear movement, but rather undergoes a series of what Paul Veyne described as successive "shocks."[1] In addition to the criminalization and brutalization of societies,[2] a form of symbolic violence emerges that consists in recalling the conflict and replaying it by brandishing the revived specter of the enemy. "War's end" is characterized by a "slow abandonment of violence" as well as the persistence of hostility and even hatred in societies.[3]

The decisive turning point occurs when war ceases to be the dominant tool of mobilization and is instead transformed into an object of pacified memory. Focusing on the interwar period in Europe and, in particular, the effects of Locarno diplomacy,[4] John Horne identifies the capacity of society or its leaders to ascribe positive meaning to the soldier's sacrifice as one of the factors that accelerates or impedes the process of "demobilizing minds" and sapping cultures of war.[5] For this reason, he claims, it is easier for a conflict's victors to pursue the demobilization of wartime culture. Defeated societies, meanwhile, are often tempted by resentment and rancor.

The cases studied here would seem to nearly turn Horne's claim on its head. In Algeria, where the FLN proclaimed itself victor, the war's meaning is clearly stated. Yet the process of demobilizing minds has made little progress. The sacrifices to which the combatants and martyrs consented continue to be mobilized for the purposes of legitimating the political regime and asserting the nation's vigilance vis-à-vis the colonial enemy. In the Algerian case, the conflict is overloaded with meaning, something that has proven an obstacle to moving beyond the postconflict context. In the French case, the nation's leaders struggled to redefine the meaning of its military involvement once Algeria had become independent. In order to conceal this loss of meaning, they sought to spread a veil of silence over the period. This loss and dissimulation of war's meaning blurred and obscured the figure of the enemy. In South Africa, the country's new democratic rulers opted for a project of reconciliation while simultaneously jettisoning the vocabulary of mobilization and confrontation. In so doing, they set about transforming the conflict's meaning.

According to Horne, moreover, the moral judgment regarding a war risks stigmatizing a nation and diverting it from the path to peace. The impact of moral and political prescriptions is quite apparent in the manner in which the groups involved in a conflict elaborate their respective narratives. The members of the FLN and, even more so, those of the ANC thus know that their struggle is legitimate in the eyes of the world. France, by contrast—and, by extension, the Secret Army Organization (OAS)—internalized the world's unfavorable judgment of its war. Official France is sometimes willing to recognize that its old adversaries had a legitimate cause. The stigmatization of the OAS, for its part, very clearly contributed to its representatives' retreat into ideological isolation and a static imaginary of the conflict.

*   *   *

The reconciliation project, which laid the foundations for a new and expanded political community, was thus the backbone of the South African regime that emerged in 1994. By offering to collaborate with their former oppressors, the country's leaders drew more upon the conflict's resolution than the conflict itself to legitimate themselves and lay the foundations for a shared narrative (Chapter 1). Algeria's rulers, for their part, emphasized the war and the victory over the colonial enemy in order to prop up the political regime and to ensure the cohesion of the political community. Converted into a constantly repeated collective duty, the task of national liberation became an alibi for depriving the country of political pluralism (Chapter 2). In the French case, General de Gaulle also counted on his role in bringing an end to the "events of Algeria" to enhance his authority and prestige. This period was then passed over in silence. To avoid creating rifts within society and also because France was loath to examine its colonial past, the adversary incarnated by the FLN tended to fade away, at least for a time (Chapter 3).

Chapter 1

South Africa: Sparing the Losers

The negotiations between the African National Congress (ANC) and the National Party (NP) resulted in the complete dismantling of apartheid and the creation of a nonracial democracy that included all of the country's inhabitants. Frederik de Klerk, the president of the Republic of South Africa responsible for formalizing the policy of openness toward the ANC, counted on constitutional arrangements to preserve a specific representation for the white minority. The ANC refused to yield on the essential principles of representative democracy and state unity. By contrast, the movement led by Nelson Mandela abandoned the socialist-type economic program it had hitherto defended and embraced liberalism. The end of apartheid thus did not result in a policy of massive redistribution or a drastic reduction of socioeconomic inequalities. While the white community lost political power, its dominant economic position was hardly called into question.

The new nation that Mandela hoped and prayed for required that hostility and fear subside or disappear between whites and blacks, between the forces of order and the members of national liberation movements. The ANC attempted to promote a spirit of reconciliation within the population. In becoming citizens, blacks were invited to forgive the beneficiaries of apartheid. The latter, seen as prisoners of a political, institutional, and social system, were encouraged to free themselves from the ideological chains that had hitherto bound them and lend their support to the rainbow nation.[1] This gesture toward whites was both a humanist choice on the part of Nelson Mandela and part of the power struggle that characterized the political transition in South Africa. As a political but not military victor, the ANC had to accommodate the military establishment that supported the apartheid regime.

The ANC and the Invention of the South African Nation

Sometimes described as a "miracle," the negotiated transition in South Africa brought an end to the confrontation between the existing regime and national liberation movements, resulting in the establishment of a radically new political system. The dazzling success of Nelson Mandela and the ANC in the April 1994 elections was a triumph for majoritarian democracy and the principle of nonracial citizenship.[2] Nevertheless, the ANC's victory cannot be reduced to a conquest of political power at the expense of former elites; the movement's project sought to create a new political community based on universal values. Rather than attempting to impose new rules of the game upon the political and demographic minority, Nelson Mandela tirelessly sought the path of compromise as well as the active consent of his former adversaries vis-à-vis the nascent social contract. The attitude of the country's new leaders was characterized by a policy of openness toward the leaders and beneficiaries of apartheid as well as a desire to make a place for them in the new South Africa.

This approach was written into law: the last paragraph of the Constitution, entitled "National Unity and Reconciliation," provided amnesty for the political crimes and offenses committed under apartheid and held that the treatment of past injustices called for "understanding but not vengeance" and "reparation but not retaliation."[3] The leaders of the apartheid regime therefore received a guaranty that they would not be put on trial once they left office. The 28 June 1995 law gave birth to the Truth and Reconciliation Commission (TRC). Presided over by Archbishop Desmond Tutu, the TRC sought to establish the "truth" regarding past abuses and thereby help initiate the process of reconciliation.

The rhetoric of reconciliation employed most prominently by Nelson Mandela constituted one characteristic of the South African democratic transition. Appeals to this notion supposed a return to an earlier state of understanding and harmony among the various communities that made up the country. However, no such state had ever existed.[4] The aim of achieving concord among South Africans and sealing a pact between them thus led to the invention of a new nation. The phenomenon of pardon, it was hoped, would allow one to envision this future harmony, affording the country's various ethnic groups the opportunity to move beyond their history of past conflict and harm—in particular, the white oppression of blacks. Though conceived of as a spiritual approach, reconciliation was meant to result in a transformation of identities, a reciprocal adjustment in the beliefs, representations, and emotions shared by the better part of society.[5]

Reality theater or shadow theater? For some, reconciliation embodied the redemption of South Africans. For others, it was no more than a petty political maneuver or, at best, a political necessity.

Interpreting Reconciliation: Mysticism, Cynicism, or Elite Pragmatism?

A romantic approach to reconciliation developed in South Africa. It included the notion that a fundamentally divine miracle had allowed the country's future to be saved. Reported as an almost mystical event, the meeting between negotiators from the opposing camps had, it was claimed, allowed the enemies to discover their points of convergence and common humanity, leading to the emergence of mutual complicity and profound understanding.[6]

This view of the transition was also embraced by some of the protagonists, particularly among the political and military leaders of the apartheid regime. By adopting it, they succeeded in ridding themselves of the racist garb of the old system and infused the process with a moral dimension. The narrative structure is nearly everywhere the same. They began by "discovering" their partners and ridding themselves of their prejudices. They next realized that they shared the same values and in this way sought to show that they, too, subscribed to the democratic ideal. They claimed to have discovered a common passion, what's more, in the love of nature.

Allister Sparks, a famous South African journalist, supplied the content of an interview he conducted with Roelf Meyer, a minister in the de Klerk government. In the course of a nocturnal safari in the bush with Cyril Ramaphosa, an ANC member and labor unionist, Meyer had a sort of epiphany: the spectacle of nature made him realize that they had "common values about what [they] wanted to achieve."[7]

The same structure is to be found in an interview conducted with General Leon, a specialist in counterinsurgency warfare in southern Africa.[8] Responsible for reorganizing the army and overseeing the institutional integration of nonconventional forces, Leon negotiated the form this was to take with the leaders of Umkhonto we Sizwe (MK), the armed branch of the

ANC. The mission of the group he formed with several ex-guerrilla leaders was to develop the foundations of an "integrated" military command structure. In the interview, he mentions the reciprocal distrust and palpable tension between the two teams. According to Leon, however, his desire to establish an atmosphere of trust and encounter with the enemy-become-partner transformed the confrontation between combatants into sincere and effective cooperation. The ex-combatants spent several evenings around the campfire, an experience that he claims favored exchange, openness, and rapprochement. It was at this time that Leon met Ronald, one of his MK partners, and the two became friends. Each recounted his experience of war, hardships, and suffering to the other. When the former member of the South African Defense Force (SADF) invited the ex-MK to join him on a catamaran, the boat capsized. According to Leon, the two men spent several hours in the water, where they continued to recount their stories as veterans. In the middle of the sea, Ronald, who did not know how to swim, is said to have declared: "Before, we said that unity was strength but today I know that diversity is strength." The general treated the ANC combatants as equals, embraced the project of nonracial democracy, and claimed for himself a role as prestigious and praiseworthy as that of the ANC leaders.

By pursuing an objective of emancipation without excluding those against whom they fought, Nelson Mandela's movement made it possible for the officials and supporters of the apartheid regime to support its calls for unity and reconciliation. The positive role that Leon played did not reflect a reasoned approach or personal conviction. Confronted by an unprecedented and difficult scenario, he was able to adapt and master the situation. One cannot dismiss the fact that, like others involved in negotiations with the ANC, Leon was disconcerted by their style and won over by their behavior. Leon reread his own trajectory in both present and future terms: he enjoyed fighting in Angola as part of the "first African army" but never felt racial prejudice or had an interest in politics. His "open" character predestined him to make peace. Once he had carried out his mission for the army, Leon joined the private sector and created a business in the security sector that sold its services across the continent. His socioeconomic success in democratic South Africa shows that he was able to take advantage of new opportunities. And he enjoys an international "rent" from his experience as part of the transformation. In Zambia, Burundi, and the countries of central Africa, he presented his method and concepts regarding reconciliation. "What happened in South Africa is a magnificent story," he declared. "It's the most incredible story in the world." It is also his story.

The romantic interpretation of the phenomenon of reconciliation mainly applied to members of the political elites. For members of the apartheid regime, it was a way to portray themselves in a positive light. It was also sometimes endorsed by ANC leaders, who thereby demonstrated their tolerance and kindness toward their former enemies. Conversely, some analysts have argued that the humanism of the new ruling party masked economic interests joining it with the new leaders to the white community. Reconciliation, they claim, was an artifact intended to ornament the political compromises and economic deals struck between the elites of the two camps to the detriment of most of the population, who were excluded from access to material benefits. Richard Wilson suggests that the new regime's use of human rights ideology sought less to develop a culture of human rights within society than to permit a fragile alliance to operate between white economic power and the country's new black leaders.[9] Other analysts support this thesis, referring to the transition as a "purchased revolution" and underscoring the manner in which the vast resources available to the state facilitated it.[10] By paying comfortable pensions to former officials and granting golden parachutes to some high-ranking members of the police and army, it is claimed, the ANC neutralized those capable of standing in the way of democratic change. Similarly, the absorption of members of the national liberation movements into a system that guaranteed their integration into a remunerative civil service and/or access to a lucrative private sector job is said to have co-opted those who might have been inclined to argue for pursuing the revolution.[11] Representatives of the left wing of the ruling alliance[12] rapidly adapted to the rules of capitalism: in joining the board of directors of large corporations, they abandoned egalitarian demands.[13] Former negotiation partners, military leaders, and the heads of rebel movements sometimes also formed business partnerships. Pooling their know-how, contacts, and access to information allowed them to achieve decisive advantages in the market.

Before coming to power, the ANC planned to nationalize the country's resources and redistribute them across society. Several years after the first free elections were held, the country's rulers, counting on economic growth and global market integration, adopted the principles of economic liberalism and postponed the project of redistribution. Macroeconomic equilibria were achieved, but unemployment and poverty increased.[14] Deepening social inequalities fed into the notion that the revolution had been betrayed. Now that they were themselves wealthy, it was argued, ANC leaders were willing to put up with the preservation of white economic dominance and continued poverty for the black majority. The discourse of reconciliation and forgiveness, it was claimed, sought to render legitimate the absence of significant change in the social structure. The leniency demanded of the black majority in this way concealed the fact that the social contract had been hijacked.

The third interpretation of the policy of reconciliation emphasizes the power struggles that were under way when the transition took place. As a political but not military victor, the ANC was obliged to moderate its demands for fear that the democratic process would otherwise be frozen. By establishing channels for dialogue that included the most radical forces, Mandela demonstrated his willingness to consider compromise and his desire to avoid a slide into violence. He thus met with Constand Viljoen, a former army chief of staff who since May 1993 had led the Afrikaner Volksfront (Afrikaner People's Front), a far right organization that sought to create a separate state for Afrikaners. He also met repeatedly with Mangosuthu Buthelezi, leader of the Inkhata Freedom Party (IFP),[15] which for its part demanded the secession of Kwazulu Natal.[16]

While Mandela's movement succeeded in imposing the principle of majoritarian democracy on the head of the National Party, he nevertheless gave essential guarantees to the party and its electoral base. On the one hand, legal proceedings were ruled out against the leaders who had presided over efforts to combat and repress the national liberation movements. On the other, the ANC abandoned the socialist-type economic program it had hitherto supported in favor of economic liberalism.

The interdependence of the negotiation partners was embodied in the formation of a government of national unity. In the domain of public administration, the "sunset" clause allowed reciprocal interests to be articulated. This clause provided for the smooth departure of civil servants, who were authorized to remain in their posts for five years following the election of the new government. For the ANC, this agreement dissuaded active civil servants from sabotaging the process and ensured that it would recuperate a functioning administration.[17]

One of the essential aspects of the compromise is to be found in the economic interdependence of the country's various communities. Their representatives are said to have pragmatically acknowledged the skills of their adversaries-become-partners.[18] Mandela noted the "useful" nature of whites. Addressing an audience of businessmen during a forum in Johannesburg, he replied to those who reproached him for letting them off too easily: "In putting aside quarrels of the past we have a country which has the opportunity to acquire education, skills and expertise in many fields. We want this. Let's forget the past. Let's put down our weapons; let's turn them into plough-shares. Let's build our country."[19]

As early as 1992, Mandela traveled to the World Economic Forum in Davos, where he underscored the importance of a market economy for South Africa and the need for foreign investment, while playing down the project of nationalizing the country's natural resources. Nevertheless, this conversion to economic liberalism must be seen not only as a concession on the part of ANC leaders to their negotiation partners. Allen has shown that international economic constraints had reduced the options available to the ANC, which was subject to the pressures of globalization. ANC negotiators, it is claimed, were converted to the virtues of the market over the course of their meetings with South African and international economic agents during the negotiation period.[20]

The Graciousness of the ANC: Moral Value or Political Ruse?

Beyond the prudence and skill shown by the ANC in negotiations, the policy of openness adopted toward the beneficiaries of apartheid corresponded to the ANC's nonracial ideal and its ambition to create a new political community.

The South African liberation movement did not aim solely to emancipate blacks and elevate them to the rank of citizens. The ANC's plan was to construct a new nation that would include the oppressors. Its objective was therefore not limited to dismantling the system of domination but also meant winning the supporters and beneficiaries of apartheid over to nonracial democracy. Mandela spoke of freeing whites from their own system of oppression.[21] The mission he set himself was colossal. And his way of formulating it showed he sought to invert the relationship of domination: the oppressed would not merely liberate themselves from their chains, but also reveal the chains that held fast their oppressor, providing the latter in turn with the means to free himself. The white community had to be persuaded to participate in radically reforming the nation. In exchange for its support for a transformative program that would provide new opportunities to those disfavored under apartheid, the ANC offered to forgive it.

The attitude of Mandela and ANC leaders corresponded to an ideal but also contained a strategic component, one that aimed not to undo the adversary, but rather to gain his support for the cause. Although his move-ment had failed on the field of battle—a failure he recognized—Mandela counted on a total victory in which the former enemy gave his support to the political project of what had until recently been labeled a terrorist organ-ization. He embarked on a three-pronged campaign of seduction that con-sisted in disconcerting his adversary by showing him in a surprising light, attempting to understand his adversary, and asserting his own generosity of spirit.

And it indeed seems that several ANC representatives succeeded in over-coming the reluctance of their counterparts. Thabo Mbeki possessed an ability to charm his adversaries. His refined, pipe-smoking manners, culti-vation, and very British reserve shattered white stereotypes regarding the primitive African. The Afrikaners he met, meanwhile, are said to have been impressed by his urbanity and self-confidence.[22] Over the course of his years of detention on Robben Island, Nelson Mandela studied Afrikaner literature and history and developed an understanding of the hopes and fears of that community. He wrote to the minister of justice to protest the absence of works by the Afrikaner poet D. J. Opperman in the prison library. The inmate naughtily revealed his cultivation, intellectual curiosity, open-mindedness, and curiosity about and interest in the Other. Shortly after his liberation, Mandela declared that Afrikaans is a "genuinely African language." He thereby extended the ANC slogan, according to which South Africa belongs to all communities that inhabit it. By shaking up linguistic and cultural cat-egories, he encouraged Afrikaners in the belief that the former prisoner sought to preserve a place for them in the South Africa of the future. By hold-ing that Afrikaans is a language "of hope and liberation,"[23] Mandela seemed to adopt an almost incantatory approach. If they were fond of liberty and hoped for a better future, the descendants of the Boers were welcome to back the ANC's project. By claiming that his own career as a freedom fighter was inspired by that of the Afrikaner combatants,[24] Mandela paid them unex-pected homage and invented a historic imaginary that bound the various communities together.

By supporting the Springboks rugby team, a symbol of Afrikaner nation-alism, Nelson Mandela made a start on overcoming racial division. When the Springboks team won the World Cup final against New Zealand in 1995, Mandela donned the team's jersey and hat. The stadium's white spectators responded with jubilation when he presented the national team's trophy dressed in this fashion, with many waving the new South African flag. In black neighborhoods, which tend to be keen on soccer and indifferent to rugby, the team's victory also gave rise to enthusiasm. On this occasion and a few others, it seemed that the new South Africa for which the ANC had fought had already been born.

Nelson Mandela repeated these gestures of openness and generosity toward his former enemies. For example, he invited the state prosecutor in the Rivonia trial to lunch, a man who, thirty years earlier, had wished to condemn him to death and is presented in anything but a flattering light in Mandela's autobiography: there, Percy Yutar is described as a man of limited honesty and professional qualities.[25] Mandela also held a lunch with women who had supported their husbands during apartheid, describing them as "heroines of the two sides," each of whom was expected to contribute "an essential stone to the new edifice." They included the widows of prime ministers J. G. Strydom and John Vorster, the wife of P. W. Botha, the spouses of the ANC leaders Walter Sisulu and Oliver Tambo, and the widow of Steve Biko, leader of the Black Conscience Movement, who was tortured to death by the apartheid police.[26] The new head of state also made a special visit to Betsie Verwoerd, the widow of the former prime minister and architect of apartheid who had made the ANC illegal. She was holed up in Orania, a sort of white colony, together with a few hundred Afrikaners who had decided to flee the new South Africa by establishing an embryonic *volksstaat*[27] in a remote corner of the Northern Cape.[28] Although these meetings presented psychological and ideological challenges for both camps, Mandela consistently behaved with ease and warmth. In this way he seemed to suddenly dispel the distance and deep divisions within society. Thanks to his daring, the principles and representations of his adversaries were rendered ineffective.

His speeches and writings as well as the testimony of many contemporaries give ample evidence of Mandela's generosity and indulgence, which extended to those who embodied the apartheid system. As he wrote in his autobiography, "In prison, my anger toward whites decreased, but my hatred for the system grew. I wanted South Africa to see that I loved even my enemies while I hated the system that turned us against one another."[29] Several of the ANC's white interlocutors noted the absence of bitterness or desire for revenge among its members and appreciated their willingness to listen and understand.[30] This generosity and open-mindedness exemplified the movement's values, which appeared superior to those embraced by apartheid's defenders. Indeed, this system had been morally and politically discredited. The good grace shown by ANC negotiators allowed the movement to score a moral victory in the eyes of South Africans and the world. Mandela became the most famous of prisoners, not only because he embodied honor, courage, and chivalry but also because he incarnated an ideal of liberation and antiracism that dovetailed with the emergence of a transnational anti-apartheid social movement.[31]

Nelson Mandela's popularity among the movement's militants and within the black population allowed the new president to convince them of the legitimacy of reconciliation. ANC officials and militants became aware that, thanks to Mandela's generosity of spirit and that of some other leaders, their political grouping had come to embody *grace*. Most of them (including those from disadvantaged backgrounds) adjusted their discourse and conformed to the style of their representatives, at least when interacting with a white, foreign interlocutor.

The stance adopted by the head of state charmed and even won over a portion of white South Africans hitherto distrustful or hostile toward the ANC. Most of them paid tribute to his courage and generosity. By pursuing an objective of emancipation without excluding those against whom it had fought, the ANC made it possible for apartheid officials and supporters to embrace its calls for unity and reconciliation. The latter became aware of the universal, humanist scope of the ANC's program. What's more, they realized that this man and the black opposition movement he led constituted the only option for reconciling ethnic group membership and national pride.[32] Following his victory in the April 1994 presidential elections, Mandela declared: "Never, never, never again shall it be that this beautiful land will experience the oppression of one by another, and suffer the indignity of being the skunk of the world."[33] By inviting whites to embrace the project of an egalitarian multicultural society, Mandela made it possible for them to appropriate the miracle and rid themselves of their stigma.

The Ambiguity of Reconciliation

The notion of reconciliation takes several forms. In its minimal sense, reconciliation refers to a foundational agreement regarding the rules of the new political pact and the appeasement of tensions between formerly opposing groups. As a dynamic process, reconciliation seeks to deepen the spirit of peace and concord. South Africa seemed to have taken this first step. In part, it did so by effectively reining in the threat of violence and division: the Afrikaner extremists failed to realize their political project, and no group developed a culture of revenge. But cooperation was equally important: although society remained divided, its two parts cooperated with each other. This was not merely because their mutual well-being depended upon it, but also because they recognized one another as legitimate citizens with different identities.[34] Although the electorate was polarized along racial lines, political parties sought to gain recruits beyond the confines of their traditional ethnic base. No significant political actor demanded a break with the social contract, and there was a consensus in favor of the political order, even if the manner in which that order's rule should be interpreted was a source of major disagreement. For whites, the advent of democracy and the rise to power of the ANC and the black majority were a source of apprehension. Over the course of the 1990s, between 100,000 and 300,000 whites left the country,[35] while others withdrew to a narrow private sphere. Yet a significant portion of the country's white citizens were convinced they had a role to play in the new South Africa.[36] For these whites, according to South African historian Tom Lodge, Mandela's ascent to the rank of national hero entailed the possibility of personal and communal salvation. Their support for this figure was a way of baptizing themselves in the new rainbow patriotism.[37] A number of former apartheid supporters thus began to display photos of themselves standing next to the former political prisoner, the image serving as "a talisman against the past."[38]

Yet if one examines reconciliation from the perspective of the development or reestablishment of relations between individuals—an indication of growing interpersonal and intercommunal trust—the process appears much more uncertain. The end of apartheid as an ideological and institutional system did not do away with mentalities that had been shaped by the discrimination and ethnic group compartmentalization inherited from the principle of separation. Socioeconomic divides partly took the place of or were superimposed upon barriers between communities. Thus, a profound imbalance emerged between a black minority who had attained commanding positions in government and business, and the great majority of blacks, who, standing on the fringes of the new South Africa, continued to experience difficult living conditions in the townships and suffered high rates of unemployment and intense social violence. Henceforth, upper-class whites and blacks could frequent the same upscale or hip places and live in the same neighborhoods on the northern edges of Johannesburg. They were partners in the business world and colleagues in the world of work. Some segments of the middle class also experienced this new proximity within companies or at the multiracial schools attended by their children. Despite the fact that the country—and, in particular, its urban component—had undergone genuine upheaval at the level of its ethnic references as well as in terms of everyday practices, society was still very compartmentalized. On the campus of the University of Wits in Johannesburg or that in Cape Town, for example, students tended to exclusively socialize within their own ethnic groups. The idea of living together was celebrated in minimalist fashion: while lip service was paid to the principle of respecting other cultures, the prevailing tendency was to stick with one's own kind. While the vast majority of South Africans adopted a politically correct discourse in conformity with the new rules of the political game and the antiracist ideal, the question of relations between blacks and whites still aroused mistrust, disappointment, and hostility. The fact that the racial question reflected a number of taboos made negotiating this relational issue all the more difficult. The advent of nonracial democracy coincided with silence and avoidance regarding the place of conflict in intercommunal relations. For the ANC, the nonracial ideal ruled out stigmatizing the beneficiaries of apartheid. The latter, for their part, spent a great deal of energy attempting to prove they had never been racist. Rather than indicating genuine change in terms of how one represented oneself and the Other, the scarcity of "racial" affirmations of identity reflected embarrassment.[39]

Nevertheless, both past supporters and opponents of apartheid looked favorably upon the aim of reconciliation. The content of reconciliation and its various forms were subject to conflicting interpretations. Thanks to his enthusiasm and grace, Mandela had paved the way for a warm and generous reconciliation that seduced the people of South Africa and external observers alike. Nevertheless, his message was not without ambiguity: was the aim to forgive or to forget the crimes of the past? Could the leaders and beneficiaries of apartheid be pardoned by those whom they once oppressed without asking for it or giving something in return? Was not the call for a "transformation" of society excessively vague, allowing everyone to project their own desires upon it? Mandela's stance gave the impression that the beneficiaries of apartheid had received a "free ticket" to reconciliation and that their support for the project did not require them to question the past or in any way change. The process of reconciliation thus collided with the meaning that individuals sought to give their trajectory, and with the conception of equality they thought should characterize the new form of citizenship.

Indeed, given their reconstruction of the past and refusal to accept any moral failing, a word must be said regarding whites' ability to adapt and willingness to accept the new regime. One rarely meets whites who admit to having supported the ideology of apartheid. It seems commonplace to reread one's trajectory so as to adjust it to the moral and political values of the new South Africa. The autobiographical account supplied by James Gregory,[40] one of Mandela's prison guards, is in this respect particularly revealing. The author recounts his rural childhood, presenting it as a sort of lost paradise in which he shared adventures with the black children who lived on his parents' estate. With the onset of adolescence, he was torn away from this free life in close contact with nature and sent to boarding school. Exposed to the institutions of apartheid, he gradually came to support it and embarked on a career in prison administration. Sent to Robben Island to look after the political inmates of the ANC, he felt deep hostility and contempt for the "terrorists" in his charge. His encounter with the prisoner Nelson Mandela, however, was apparently disconcerting. After discovering the latter's humanity and good manners, Gregory began to admire the great man and ultimately befriended him. With the passage of time, he claims, he became a sort of aide-de-camp to Mandela, for whom he sought to alleviate the harsh rules of prison life. By coming to know and love the ANC leader, Gregory claims to have in a way recaptured the innocence of his childhood and true identity. According to his biographer, Anthony Sampson, Mandela privately confided that, on several points, Gregory had "hallucinated."[41] The question of the former prison guard's honesty matters less than his skill in appropriating a narrative and inserting himself into his country's trajectory. His is a story of redemption: though corrupted by the apartheid system, which destroyed his deep connection to his native land, he ultimately rediscovered his own humanity and converted to democracy.

Since they were not obliged to recognize their collective guilt, many whites saw no reason to contribute to a form of restitution. Disagreement thus broke out regarding the content of the transformation. The policy of affirmative action became a flash point for the misunderstanding and frustration of all parties. In recent years, it has become a stumbling block for the process of reconciliation: for some, it is fair compensation; for others, it constitutes an unexpected punishment for an ancient wrong.

Among ANC supporters and the formerly disadvantaged, the objective of reconciliation clashes with the slow pace of social and economic change. The government's liberal policy allowed a small black upper class to emerge, while a somewhat larger group joined the middle class. Disparities in the standard of living nevertheless deepened: between 1994 and 2004, executive income increased from 37 to 48 times the minimum wage.[42] Flaunting its wealth, only a very small group has benefited from the policies of affirmative action and black economic empowerment (BEE). While the frontiers of capital are no longer exclusively racial, present trends do not benefit most blacks, who continue to live in poverty. The Reconstruction and Development Program, which aimed to supply universal access to water and electricity and provide free health care to pregnant women and children under the age of six, has achieved only some of its objectives. The government has failed to construct the 200,000 homes it promised to build in response to the housing shortage. There are long waiting lists for homes, and the results have been disappointing.[43] As the neoliberal agenda has gained the upper hand, this social policy has gradually been eclipsed.

Between 1995 and 2002, the unemployment rate increased in South Africa: defined broadly, it rose from 30.5 percent to 41.8 percent. Black Africans were the most severely affected group, their rate of unemployment increasing from 37 percent to 49 percent over the same period. The country's economic restructuring favored skilled jobs to the detriment of low-skilled or unskilled ones. As a result, the racial group hierarchy remains in place: whites are more likely to be employed than mixed-race individuals, Indians, or black Africans.[44] Most managerial positions continue to be occupied by white men, while blacks hold the largest number of semiskilled or unskilled jobs.[45]

For a large number of ANC activists, the business of liberation remains unfinished. To the degree that living standards and conditions have not improved, political equality has proven to be an abstract experience. Members of the organization who remain poor are more willing to attack the leaders of their own political grouping, who in their view have captured the financial rents of government and forgotten them. White reluctance to share economic power and make room for black elites is of greater concern to black members of the middle and upper classes.

Despite these frustrations, the ideal of reconciliation has remained intact. It is in a sense inseparable from the ANC's political victory, which is supported by a majority of the black community. For members of the new bourgeoisie, with their ties to the government, the imperatives of reconciliation justify the government's economic policy, from which they personally profit. Members of the middle class are often torn between their impatience to move up the social ladder and the attractions of multicultural sociability. For disadvantaged groups, meanwhile, rapprochement with other communities seems unattainably distant.

Despite this broad support for reconciliation, it remains an ideal to be attained rather than a profound transformation of social relations. After a period of euphoria that gripped the entire society,[46] illusions as to the advent of an unexpected fraternity once again subsided. Disappointment slowed the process of rapprochement and provoked a discursive shift on the part of the political leadership and population.

In his presidential address at the ANC's fiftieth national conference, Mandela changed his tone. He accused white political parties of seeking to keep their privileges and separate the objective of reconciliation from that of social transformation. He also criticized the NP for not having cooperated with the TRC.[47] The ideal of the rainbow nation faded from view. Political and intellectual elites with ties to the ANC were apparently irritated by the indifference shown by whites toward the TRC as well as by their reluctance to change.[48] Thabo Mbeki abandoned the notion dear to Desmond Tutu and promoted an "African Renaissance." By making South Africa a driver of economic development for the continent, the new president sought to promote Pan-Africanism. The use of this concept also entailed an affirmation of black pride and identity. It supposed a multicultural nation in which African identity predominated. It moved away from a nonracial approach to the nation, neglecting the question of harmony between the various groups in order to concentrate on a form of rehabilitation for groups that had been oppressed and disadvantaged under the apartheid regime. This turn to the "African Renaissance" project was evidence of the difficulty involved in reconciling nonracial national integration with the objective of reducing social inequalities.[49] It chipped away at the symbolic order of reconciliation[50] and put a damper on the process of deracialization then under way. This revival of ethnic and racial consciousness threatened to destroy the "non-racial dream."[51]

Memory and Legitimacy of the Combat

The struggle for national liberation was eclipsed by the desire to build a new nation and the efforts willingly undertaken to convince the various sectors of the population to reconcile with one another. The combatants—members of the MK—received little in the way of gratitude and were accorded scant symbolic or material recognition by successive governments. Although Nelson Mandela was behind the creation of the ANC's armed wing and had subsequently decided to transition his movement to violence, he hardly mentioned the armed exploits of the past. Nor did Thabo Mbeki do more to express the nation's gratitude to the combatants of the ANC. Three factors explain the discretion shown by the country's rulers in regard to the national liberation struggle: the influence of the discourse of reconciliation, the desanctification of the struggle, and the government's departure from the movement's original objectives.

In the first place, the objective of reconciliation supplanted the vocabulary of mobilization and confrontation. By establishing a model of forgiveness, the new elites committed themselves to a moral rhetoric that excluded the question of the value of physical combat. The members of the ANC proved themselves heroic, not so much by risking their lives against a more powerful enemy, but by extending their hands to him. Founding a nation requires that one forget certain events that are a source of division. Such was Ernest Renan's claim when he argued that every French citizen must forget or at least reinterpret the meaning of the St. Bartholomew's Day massacre and those of the Midi.[52] Nelson Mandela himself sometimes invited his compatriots to forget. For constructing the nation depended on setting aside certain historical events and underscoring others. By insisting on the sacrifices to which each had consented and avoiding excessive emphasis on past conflict, the country's new ANC rulers developed a narrative of the past that included its various communities. This was clearly expressed by the minister of education, Kader Asmal, in April 2004: "We need to construct a non-exclusive memory in which the heroes and heroines of the past do not only belong to certain sectors but to all. . . . Memory is identity and we cannot have a divided identity."[53]

The inclusion of Afrikaner history in the shared heritage of the new South Africa was part of this attempt. On several occasions, Mandela showed his respect for Afrikaner history and its protagonists. When he laid a wreath at the statue of the guerrilla fighter Daniel Theron, a hero of the Anglo-Boer War, Mandela stated that he "had been deeply influenced by the work and lives of Afrikaner freedom fighters."[54] When celebrating the hundredth anniversary of the war between the British Empire and the Boer Republics, Thabo Mbeki carried on in the same spirit: he paid homage to all who fell, underscored the price paid by black combatants, and asserted the need to use the past in a positive way for the purpose of constructing the nation.[55] Some Afrikaners profited from the occasion to assert their reading of the past: Afrikaners could free themselves from the guilt of apartheid by finding common ground with blacks in their struggle against British imperialism. Thabo Mbeki was not unreceptive to this approach.[56]

The Freedom Park project involved the creation of a single space that "does not only commemorate the recent struggle for freedom but gives an overview of the entirety of South African history."[57] It consists of a 128-acre area near Pretoria the various components of which pay homage to the heroes of the past and symbolize reconciliation and the path to democracy in South Africa. The project was launched on 1 June 2000 in response to TRC demands that victims be given symbolic reparation. One site symbolizes the suffering caused by past struggles and the unity of South Africans in sharing this pain. Ceremonies and rituals have been performed there to allow the spirits of fallen heroes to be put to rest. The names of the South Africans who gave their lives in combat have been inscribed on a wall. They include not only members of the national liberation movements, but also those who fell in the precolonial wars, the Anglo-Boer War, and the two world wars.[58]

Tokyo Sexwale, a former MK who became governor of Gauteng Province and subsequently reinvented himself as a successful businessman, provides another striking example of ANC efforts to invent the nation and its history. As premier of the province in which Johannesburg is located, in 1996 Sexwale had himself photographed by the *Sunday Times* at Voortreker Monument. Located near Pretoria, this structure represents a stage in the formation of the Afrikaner nation, which had moved northward from Cape Town in order to escape British control. In the Afrikaner national imaginary, this corresponds to the creation of a "white tribe" endowed with divine rights over the land and prepared for sacrifice and heroic struggle. The monument's doors are in the form of spears, symbolizing Zulu attacks against the Afrikaners. In the photo, Sexwale opens the doors and declares: "It was precisely the assegais at its height that turned the tide. Umkhonto we Sizwe, the spear of the nation, opened the path to civilization."[59] The former activist did not content himself with Africanizing the monument and disinvesting it of its first meaning; he inverted the relationship of domination by presenting the ANC as the agent of liberation and civilization.

Throughout the course of negotiations, moreover, the ANC's leader organized to limit violence and prevent any excesses that might jeopardize the democratic transition. Mandela sought to delegitimize recourse to violence by attempting to curb the zeal of the white far right and defuse the conflict between his supporters and those of the IFP in the regions of Johannesburg and Kwazulu Natal. He attempted to convince his supporters to set aside their conflict with the IFP. In a speech he delivered in Katlehong, a township in the region of Johannesburg—the epicenter of deadly clashes between the two factions—Mandela responded to his supporters' demands that they be given weapons: "It is difficult for us to say when people are angry that they must be non-violent. But the solution is peace, it is reconciliation, it is political tolerance. . . . It is also our responsibility. We must put our house in order. If you have no discipline you are not a freedom fighter. If you are going to kill innocent people, you don't belong to the ANC. Your task is reconciliation."[60] The father of the nation also intervened to put down a rebellion among MK who refused the conditions of their integration into the new South African army. He affirmed his authority over his militants, obliging them to bend to the rules of the new South Africa and thereby come to terms with members of what had been an enemy army.[61]

If the country's rulers proved reticent with regard to the national liberation struggle, it was also because the search for truth contributed to desacralizing the ANC's fight. Initially, the movement's internal investigative commission revealed the human rights violations committed by ANC officials against their own members in the camps in exile. The members of national liberation movements were subsequently treated in the same fashion by the TRC as former officials of the apartheid regime. Every individual who had committed acts involving human rights violations had to formally request amnesty and account for his behavior. By singling out victims and perpetrators in the ranks of the ANC, the TRC contributed to depoliticizing the combat of the MK.

Finally, the fact that ANC officials made little use of the theme of national liberation is explained by a desire among some of them to free themselves of this rhetoric. During their years of exile and military training, the MK were told they were going to liberate their country by force of arms. As soon as negotiations began between Nelson Mandela and the de Klerk government, resistance thus arose to what was seen an excessively conciliatory strategy.[62] In 1991, Operation Vula, which was secretly overseen by a portion of the ANC's armed wing, sought to prepare for an alternative to the ANC should negotiations fail. Mandela thus had to curb passions within his own camp.[63]

The desire to demobilize the armed militants of the ANC is also explained by the fact that some ANC leaders felt they had lost on the field of battle. The Marxist strategy of armed struggle had not succeeded in weakening the apartheid regime. Despite a few spectacular operations, particularly between 1980 and 1982, with attacks against the Sasol refineries and a South African army base, the ANC's insurrectional strategy failed.[64] Between 1969 and 1980, the ANC organized its action around four pillars: mass action and clandestine combat inside the country and armed struggle and attempts to isolate the apartheid regime abroad. During the 1980s, disappointing military results and growing support abroad led the ANC to refocus its efforts on the "international pillar."[65]

The ANC's meager ability to strike the Pretoria regime came as a hard blow to the militants. At an organizational level, the movement found it difficult to absorb the flow of young people fleeing South Africa in the wake of the Soweto riots. Most of those who joined its ranks in exile remained in the training camps, where they were confronted with malaria and extremely difficult material and psychological living conditions. While they dreamed of fighting their enemy, many never saw any action.[66] Demoralization made inroads among young MK. This was worsened by suspicions of infiltration, which led some officers to adopt authoritarian, summary methods. Mutinies erupted and were violently put down.[67] On the domestic front, a lack of organization and discipline, which resulted in many excesses, cast a pall over the militants' courageous clandestine actions.[68]

Although the ANC's policy of rendering the country ungovernable had been deeply embarrassing to Pretoria, it was thus difficult to supply a glorious narrative for the armed exploits of this period.[69] ANC leaders preferred instead to emphasize their engagement on behalf of human rights, democracy, and reconciliation. While Nelson Mandela, a political prisoner for twenty-seven years who converted to nonviolence, achieved iconic status, the death of military leaders such as Chris Hani[70] and Joe Slovo[71] contributed to weakening the voice of armed struggle. In paying them tribute, the head of state mentioned their status as combatants but also made sure to underscore their role in negotiations.[72] In his speeches, Mandela tended to insist on the need for reconciliation and economic development, merely alluding to those who sacrificed themselves and gave their lives for democracy.[73] Indeed, he hardly ever spoke of Umkhonto we Sizwe, an organization that he had himself created.

Finally, the principle of armed struggle was associated with socialist rhetoric that the ANC had abandoned. The creation of the armed wing of the ANC in 1961 was a response to the consistent failure of nonviolent action; it took place in a context in which many South Africans were inspired by contemporaneous armed struggles in Algeria and Cuba. By joining forces with the South African Communist Party, the ANC gained access to financial and logistical assistance from the USSR and the countries of the Soviet bloc. MK members thus received advanced training in guerrilla tactics, sabotage, and intelligence. By establishing this alliance, the ANC adopted a two-stage objective: the first stage consisted in reaching a democratic state, the second in building a socialist system. Once the ANC abandoned the socialist project, its representatives avoided a rhetoric that associated the national liberation struggle with building an egalitarian society. By skirting references to military and clandestine warfare, ANC officials attempted to defuse expectations of economic liberation. According to Dale McKinley, the ANC's abandonment of revolutionary objectives was an attempt to demobilize its base.[74] The effort of demobilization was thus not only military but also political. The liberal turn rendered obsolete references to armed struggle.

*   *   *

The creation of a new political community and the invention of a post-apartheid South African nation eclipsed the history of the fight waged by the ANC and the other national liberation movements. While the objective of the TRC was to contribute to allaying tensions and to lay the foundations of a new society, the institution could support only a necessarily imperfect and incomplete process. A successful transformation of society requires that a majority of the population have access to opportunities for economic mobility.

Algeria: The Victory over Colonialism

The struggle against colonial France is an essential part of the Algerian national project. By presenting their vision of the Algerian nation as an article of faith and regularly deploying the figure of the imperialist enemy, the country's leaders reject all critical discussion of the colonial period and the War of Independence. By making the people the sole hero of the Revolution, the government presents Algerian society as a whole as having participated in the fight against colonial France. The government's imposition of unanimity and the selective vision upon which its ideology is based are reflected in its authoritarian control over society and never-ending suspicion of what are perceived to be the agents and traces of colonialism within the social body. Partly reacting to the emphasis placed by France on its Latin and Christian culture as well as its disparaging attitude toward the "Algerian personality," the National Liberation Front (FLN) used Islam and Arab ethnicity as the basis for political and cultural cohesion. The Arabization of instruction and government and the Islamization of the country (particularly in the area of family law) have allowed Algeria to affirm its distance from the former colonial power.

The Algerian Nation According to the FLN

In opposition to colonial discourse, which set forth the various population categories residing in Algeria (Europeans, Jews, Kabyles, Mozabites, Chaouias)[1] and denied the existence of a nation, Algerian nationalism affirmed the continuity of the Algerian people throughout history. The preamble to the 1963 Constitution thus affirmed that "the Algerian people have waged an unceasing armed, moral and political struggle against the invader and all his forms of oppression for more than a century following the aggression of 1830 against the Algerian State and the occupation of the country by French colonial forces."[2] Such was the desire to anchor the Algerian state in a longer-term history that the National Charter of 1976 traced its existence to the Rustamid period—an Imamate founded around 776 near Tiaret by the Kharijite Ibn Rostem. In this narrative, Emir Abdelkader, who fought French troops between 1830 and 1847, figures as "the first builder of the modern Algerian state."[3]

According to Mohamed Harbi, the Algerian nation did not result from a social or a political process. In the early twentieth century, political relations were structured by local solidarities, whether occupational, tribal, or familial. Nationalism developed as a communal, not a social, project and was fueled by nostalgia for traditional ties, which it sought to revive. The influence exercised by the rural world, exported to the cities by migration, impeded the creation of a modern society.[4] Nationalist leaders developed an ideal vision of the nation in which all of its members were "brothers" sharing a common culture and common interests. They appealed to Islam and Arab identity as principles that promoted integration into the nation they hoped to create.

The confidence shown by Algerian leaders regarding the antiquity of their nation coexisted with a form of identitarian anxiety regarding the "Algerian personality."[5] This anxiety was produced by a fantasy of depersonalization. As Omar Carlier explained, the loss of identity was less a real phenomenon than one imagined and feared. For while the colonial conquest did give rise to trauma, Algerians lost neither their language nor their religion and the majority of the population had no doubt as to its identity.[6] The Algerian government thus remained a prisoner of this contradiction. Even as it asserted the continuity of the Algerian nation across the centuries, it mobilized the language of loss in its references to colonial aggression, the traces and consequences of which had to be erased via a restoration of the Algerian personality.

Islam was activated as a vector of national identity. In the fight against France, religion served as a powerful resource for mobilizing the rural population. The Algerian state kept to this dynamic, establishing Islam as the state religion. Its leaders attempted to reconcile the Islamic personality with the establishment of socialism and to arbitrate between these two contradictory currents.[7] While the Boumediene regime (1965–78) initially prioritized socialist revolution, it was later to set Marxist theories aside in order to experiment with its own form of socialism,[8] retaining only those aspects of Marxist theory that concerned developmental techniques, which were detached from their ideological foundations.[9] Whereas socialism was based on an analysis in terms of class, Algeria's rulers reproduced the myth of the Revolution, which denied social differences among the country's people.[10] The national project thereby collided with the contradictory desires of achieving material and technological progress while at the same time preserving or reviving the values and traditions of the group.

Since the country's colonial rulers had designated classical Arabic a foreign language and sought to divide Algerians by taking an interest in Kabyle and dialectical Arabic, the Algerian government chose classical Arabic as the national language and banished the population's mother tongues, just as it gradually did away with French. Little matter that most Algerians did not understand classical Arabic. It was *against* the French language that Boumediene made this choice, which was provoked by a French decision to boycott Algerian oil. Algeria adopted Middle Eastern linguistic norms for its model, although this meant dismissing locally established usage. Brandished as proof of authenticity, the importation of these rules actually had the effect of weakening Algerian culture.[11]

In regard to Arabization, the minister of national education, Ahmed Taleb Ibrahimi, reportedly declared, "It won't work but it must be done"[12]—eloquent testimony to the cynicism of Algeria's leaders. The Algerian school system absorbed ever larger numbers of students. In 1962, only 750,000 Algerians attended primary school. Twenty years later, 5 million students—or 90 percent of the corresponding age cohort—did so. In 1962, 32,000 students attended secondary school. By 1983, that figure had grown to 900,000, or 35 percent of the corresponding age cohort.[13] At first, the effort to Arabize instruction lacked resources. In the 1960s and 1970s, there was a severe shortage of secondary school and university instructors capable of teaching in the language. The country therefore imported instructors, most of whom were undistinguished graduates of Cairo's Al-Azhar University. Poorly trained and lacking pedagogical ability, they contributed to the failure of the Algerian school system, a result presaged by the meager resources invested in it.

In government circles, many continued to rely on French, sending their own children to a French school system and delaying or ruling out the Arabization of the most successful disciplines. The exact sciences and medicine thus continued to be taught in French. This situation was a source of frustration for those who favored the Arabization of instruction and helped fuel confrontations with Francophones in the universities.[14] Schoolchildren and students were sometimes victims of the incoherence and pace of Algerian linguistic policy. Educated in Arabic in primary school, some later pursued programs of study in French-language subjects for which they were ill prepared.

These contradictions—the result of conflicts between "Francophones" and "Arabophones" at the highest reaches of the state—gradually diminished from 1991 onward with the Arabization of all areas of study. Starting in 2005, President Abdelaziz Bouteflika distanced himself somewhat from the Arabic-only ideology, recognizing the need for multilingualism in Algeria and extending recognition to the Berber language.[15]

The promotion of the Arabic language was part of the process of inventing or affirming the nation. Imbued with the Jacobin model disseminated by the French school system, nationalist elites opted for a centralizing and homogenous model that dismissed any considerations of the country's organization or the question of language and culture.[16] Seen as a source of division, Berber identity was thus denied. This desire to construct a uniform nation met with failure, at least in part. This, however, was not due to the project's lack of authenticity. An authoritarian approach is often taken in inventing nations; when the process succeeds, its artificial nature fades from view. Consider, for example, the Third Republic's policy of imposing the French language and crushing regional languages, or the creation of Modern Hebrew in Israel. In the case of the Algerian national project, the model's flaws stemmed from its internal contradictions—the inability of elites to synthesize their various references, as well as their ambivalence and/or hypocrisy. The spread of poor-quality instruction revealed the leaders' contempt for the population and the unacknowledged attraction exerted upon them by the French model. The discrepancy between discourse and practices produced a schizophrenic society, one torn between crushing ideological constraints, on the one hand, and a more complex reality, on the other. This duality was also to be found at the economic level: while the government proclaimed a strategy of autarchy and self-sufficiency, the country's economy was in reality very open to the outside world, particularly Europe, the United States,[17] and, above all, France, which supplied technological and cultural cooperation as well as between 60 and 70 percent of the nation's trade.[18] Far from providing the means for its independence, in practice the country's leaders sought to personally monopolize the rents of this unequal relationship.[19]

Like their authoritarian counterparts elsewhere, Algerian nationalists and leaders drew upon a mythologized past to express culture and values. Theirs was ultimately a well-worn approach, but their inability to formulate a collective project for the future became a stumbling block for independent Algeria. Because of its systematic references to history and the Other, the obsession with self-definition stood in the way of the nation's invention and fed concerns about identity. After having maintained and exploited these concerns, the government lost control of them. Starting in the 1980s, the Islamist opposition exploited this anxiety regarding the "Algerian personality" for its own benefit.[20]

By asserting that the Algerian nation existed prior to colonization and drew its specificity from Arabism and Islam, the Algerian revolution ruled out the possibility of recognizing the European population as an integral part of the people.[21] According to the FLN, the Europeans of Algeria did not constitute a community but rather a minority that happened to inhabit the country alongside the Algerian people. While some Europeans provided ideological and material support to colonialism, others supported an intermediate solution to the Algerian question, and a few accepted independence. The FLN deemed that "Europeans who are willing to make the necessary adaptation may if they so wish remain in Algeria" and become citizens of the new state.[22] By contrast, it remained firm in its refusal to grant a specific status to this minority. After the blind acts of violence committed by the Secret Army Organization (OAS) and under the impact of the FLN's internal contradictions,[23] the Algerian stance in regard to the French of Algeria radicalized. In the program adopted in Tripoli in June 1962 by the National Council of the Algerian Revolution (CNRA), the French of Algeria were collectively designated as guilty: "Due to their colonialist mentality and racism, the overwhelming majority of the French of Algeria will not be capable of usefully serving the Algerian state."[24] That their privileges must disappear was a foregone conclusion. The nationality law of 27 March 1963 acknowledged the existence of European-origin Algerians but specified that they could possess Algerian nationality only by acquisition, as they were excluded from it by virtue of their origin.[25] Ultimately, few Europeans, including those who joined or helped the FLN during the war, were to continue living in Algeria.[26]

The Myth of Unanimity

According to the slogan disseminated by revolutionary rhetoric, the people are the sole hero of the Revolution (1954–62). The official history thus asserted that the entirety of Algerian society was united behind the FLN. It assumed that the whole population was driven by a national consciousness and desire for independence.[27] Those who sided with the French were seen as traitors and excluded from the national community. Although some Harkis—Muslim auxiliary troops who served in the French army—continued to live in Algeria, they were used as a foil for Algerian identity. In contrast to South Africa, where a form of compassion was expressed for ANC militants who had been "turned" by the apartheid police,[28] official discourse made no effort to explain and understand the Harkis' motivations or the reasons for their involvement. Thirty years after the war's end, Mohamed Saïd, the leader of wilaya 3,[29] still maintained that the Harkis deserve to die.[30]

In claiming that the Algerian nation antedated the onset of the Revolution and that the entire society was motivated by nationalism, the leaders of the FLN and independent Algeria refused to consider the modes of cohabitation linking colonial structures with the Algerian population, the ambiguous relations that developed between Europeans and "Arabs," or the manner in which French culture had come to imbue certain milieus. The Algerians had nevertheless entered the world of the French, even if, in most cases, they did so as servants.[31] The French colonial undertaking had imposed its institutions and rules, and these had structured Algerian society. According to Guy Pervillé, "in Algeria, cities were the only places where the two populations that considered themselves 'Algerian'—Europeans and Muslims—coexisted in large numbers."[32] Gilbert Meynier, for his part, holds that Algiers, in particular, was characterized by a form of "soft acculturation (school) for a relatively large number of people." According to him, this acculturation was even more pronounced in Oran among members of the elite and even workers.[33] Despite the inegalitarian nature of this system, in some circles relations of mutual interest and even affection were established on both sides. This relative proximity did not rule out conflict or, above all, situations of humiliation. It nevertheless remains the case that, far from being univocal in nature, complex relations at times existed between individuals from different communities.

Moreover, there was a small Algerian elite created and controlled by the French state and consisting of around 50,000 people. It included a very small number of landowners who had survived the advancing colonists, caids,[34] rich merchants, and a few members of the liberal professions. Of necessity, this Algerian elite became Gallicized. Those who sought to educate themselves did so in French. In the first half of the twentieth century, only a small number of Algerians attended the French school. After the Second World War, 15 percent of school-age Algerian children attended primary school, but only 6,200 attended high school, and just 600 attended the university in Algiers.[35]

What's more, France could count on the support of 263,000 people at the start of the Algerian War, including French army soldiers, civil servants, veterans, Harkis, and the members of self-defense groups.[36] Whether these men deliberately sought to keep Algeria within the French Republic, had been manipulated by French soldiers or village leaders, were prisoner to local conflicts, or sought protection from the French army, their large numbers show that support for the FLN was neither absolute nor immediate.

Thus, from the point of view of one of the actors in the independence struggle, the Algerian nation "only existed as a desire on the part of a minority of statists, the activists of the PPA (Algerian People's Party). Blocked in their development, a number of them decided to hasten the course of history and unify Algerians via the FLN—sometimes by persuasion, sometimes by violence—compelling them to see themselves as belonging to Algeria rather than to a party or a region."[37] There is nothing particularly unusual about the notion that violence and war should contribute to the process whereby a nation is created.[38] Resistance to nationalism did not discredit the national liberation project, but it must be noted that, in contrast to what the FLN claimed, not all strata of society unanimously participated in the same fight nor was the entire population permeated by an emancipatory national ideology. Local issues, family loyalties, and questions of honor sometimes worked against support for nationalism.[39]

While these communities were often violently split, rigid political commitments did not always determine the course of events. In some places, for example, Harkis were evacuated to France with the aid of local guerrilla fighters.[40] What's more, antirevolutionary participation was an ambiguous phenomenon: "Under intense pressure from the French army, some rural communities agreed to organize in self-defense without radically parting ways with the revolution."[41]

Official discourse neglected these gray areas, this ambivalence that one encounters among occupied populations and, even more so, within colonial societies. The ideology of unanimity portrayed the people as an indivisible whole, a representation that demands that everyone should have participated in the revolution. The official call for nationalist unanimity influenced personal narratives of the war in family and social circles. The FLN was even reluctant to mention the role of individuals in history, particularly when it came to paying homage to individual leaders. "It is as if history was solely the product of the group,"[42] and each individual embodied the community.

By generalizing the struggle's narrative and rendering it anonymous, Algeria's divided and contentious leaders found a way to maintain consensus. In setting the people up as the invisible hero of the Revolution, this simplification of history and politics also allowed the entire population to identify with the nationalist project and present themselves as participating in it. Nevertheless, a recurrent attitude of distrust and suspicion directed against the "enemies of the Revolution" supposedly hiding within the ranks of the FLN revealed the unease provoked by this official narrative. Jean Leca and Jean-Claude Vatin's discussion of the Tripoli Charter (1962) is revealing in this connection. Apart from the imperialist enemy—that is, the French of Algeria and their accomplices—"the internal enemy ('counter-revolutionary forces') is never named but everywhere denounced. He is everywhere and nowhere." The authors claim that "suspicion toward others as well as oneself" is "a deep undercurrent of the ideology of Tripoli."[43]

Several decades later, this discourse still reverberates. It is striking to note the strength of popular attachment to the War of National Liberation and the idea of the heroic Algerian people. Although the country's leaders appear to have lost legitimacy in the eyes of the public, the public nevertheless remains unwilling to give up on the foundational myths of the regime. Society's disaffection with its elites and politics does not prevent the revolutionary mold from continuing to shape representations. The failures of Algeria are not attributed to the contradictions or weaknesses of the revolutionary ideology; rather, they are seen as the fault of *usurpers*.

Moreover, the "people as hero of the Revolution" diktat obliged those who had lived through the War of Independence to conform to the official thesis and assert that they, too, contributed to the effort of national liberation. By stretching the truth and reinterpreting facts, some helped keep the national myth alive while simultaneously instilling in themselves and others an attitude of doubt and suspicion regarding war narratives.

In support of claims as to the group's absolute unity and cohesion, the leaders of independent Algeria glossed over present or past conflicts between individuals or clans. The party's assassination of Abane Ramdane, who insisted on the primacy of political over military action, was passed over in silence. According to the official version, Ramdane died in combat.[44] With no experience of democracy and loyal to a patriarchal model of the family in which expressions of individuality are relegated to the background, a large portion of Algerian society looks approvingly upon the ideology of unanimity.

Algeria's leaders succeeded in forging a consensus in Algerian society around the assertion of Arab and Muslim identity and the project of socialist revolution. The country's citizens, meanwhile, soon profited from the state's considerable efforts in the areas of education and health care. A large portion of the population put its faith in these leaders and accepted the creation of a one-party regime. Relying on the army and the legitimacy of its commanders, Algerian monopartism rejected factions and conferred upon the FLN the task of transcending all particular interests and working toward the national interest. By unifying the nation's various social strata, the FLN was to guide the socialist revolution.[45] Nevertheless, the central place occupied in official discourse by references to the past dictated a position that focused on defining "enemies" and had little to say about how communal life was to be defined.[46]

Internal conflicts did not disappear with independence but were rather managed behind closed doors. Relations within the elite were characterized by great mistrust as well as demands on the part of all parties that they be treated as equals and that decisions be taken collectively. In the generalized climate of suspicion and distrust that characterized the tenures of Ben Bella and Boumediene, the intelligence services flourished. In some respects, the government operated like a secret society, with statistics and the biographies of ministers treated as classified material.[47]

The Postcolony

This facade of unanimity concealed a tangle of social, ideological, and geographical divisions. Class differences were denied, but at the same time the bourgeoisie was vilified as retrograde, reactionary, and a threat to the country's socialist projects. Given the lack of cadres, however, the government had to continue relying on this elite to fill managerial and administrative posts. A portion of them had been cadres in the nationalist movement during the war. The bourgeoisie was thus not sacrificed on the altar of the socialist revolution. Although called upon to adopt a nonostentatious way of life, it was nevertheless among the social groups to benefit from independence. The bourgeoisie moved into jobs and homes formerly occupied by Europeans and frequented the same restaurants and cafés.[48] On this point, too, the profound contradiction between the leaders' discourse and social reality is apparent.

Moreover, the various groups that joined the fight against colonial France were characterized by diverse forms of political socialization,[49] and their visions for independent Algeria did not always coincide. While some counted on independence to revitalize Islam and Arab identity, others saw French culture as a link to modernity and technology. Most Algerians who had been educated in the French school system subscribed to nationalism not because they had "suddenly discovered the Algerian nation" but rather because "they had finally realized that assimilation was impossible and that revolution was the only way to escape from an intolerable condition of political and social inferiority."[50] For all that, a portion of them were more interested in attaining the citizenship and lifestyle of Europeans than in reviving a mythologized ancestral past.

This contradiction was even encountered within the regime and ruling elite. While charters and constitutions proclaimed Arabo-Islamism, the Gallicized elite continued to carry out its duties within the state, and French remained the language of government. One encounters the same divisions between village- and city-dwellers. As growing numbers of rural Algerians moved to the cities, the culture shock worsened. This rural exodus began during the colonial period and significantly accelerated during the war of liberation. It further increased with independence as hundreds of thousands of villagers left refugee camps. The urban landscape profoundly changed as a result. Contempt and misunderstanding dominated relations between longtime city-dwellers who had been exposed to European lifestyles and the newly arrived peasants.

In Aïn Benian, a small town located on the coast about twenty kilometers from Algiers, a portion of the population that had resided there since the time of French Algeria adopted a clearly standoffish attitude toward newly arrived country people and their families. Before independence, the town consisted of around 20,000 people. It was mainly inhabited by Europeans, and the Arab and, above all, Kabyle population that gradually settled there constituted around only one-third of all inhabitants. A few of them nostalgically recall their "pieds-noirs friends" and a time of easy living. In the 1990s, the expression of such feelings was certainly accentuated by the deterioration of the political climate and living conditions. They are nevertheless revealing of the persistence of social divisions in independent Algeria. In some families belonging to the small circle of the Gallicized petite bourgeoisie, men urged their French school–educated wives to don the veil on the grounds that the influx of "people from the East" and their rural mores no longer allowed women from this group to peacefully go about their business with heads uncovered. The new arrivals were accused of being backward and of upsetting the social equilibrium. Some lamented the departure of the pieds-noirs and displayed a distance and contempt toward the urban newcomers that was reminiscent of European attitudes.

The disintegration of the socialist, third-world ideology and the sudden emergence of the Islamists, who threatened bourgeois well-being, rekindled divisions and tensions between various groups and/or created new fault lines. A former *bombiste*[51] who had been raised in privilege and lived in Algiers recalled how, in the early 1990s, she was threatened by a young Islamist in her neighborhood, who told her she should wear the hijab. She claimed that she succeeded in silencing him by saying: "What business is it of yours?! I am a mujahida! When the French were still around, you wouldn't even have been allowed to wash my car!"

For another Aïn Benian family, it was less a matter of contempt for the rabble that had taken over public spaces in the town and country than an immense desire to cut their ties with what had become a foreign country to them. Children and parents alike had given up outings and excursions, concluding that they had lost the battle against the new city-dwellers, Islamists, and the women who even dragged their jilbeb to beaches and café terraces. The family lived hidden away in its rooms, the family circle serving as a warm refuge against what was perceived to be a backward and hostile environment. The children, meanwhile, planned their departure to study abroad. Gilles Kepel has underscored the sociocultural tensions that accompanied the growth of the Islamist movement, demonstrating that "the first consequence of the proliferation of moral prohibitions was to single out for opprobrium the Europeanized middle classes freed from traditional taboos."[52]

The adoption of a liberal economic policy in the late 1990s deepened—and, above all, made more visible—discrepancies of lifestyle and living standard. It was not unusual to encounter businessmen who had invested, for example, in select sports clubs that excluded insufficiently refined clients as a matter of policy. Without necessarily referring to the colonial model and French mores, a small number of Algerians adopted attitudes of differentiation and disdain toward their compatriots and thereby contributed to perpetuating mechanisms of social exclusion. These deepening inequalities were intolerable to those who suffered from them: the regime's embrace of egalitarian principles and the memory of colonial-era humiliations made many Algerians reject any situation that threatened to place them in a position of inferiority. Having felt or been subjected to this form of ostracism, some Islamic Salvation Front (FIS) activists supported the project of overthrowing the social and political order.

Violence as Rupture and as Legacy

The French military conquest that began in 1830 stretched over several decades, with Algeria under military administration until 1871. Facing organized resistance, in particular on the part of Emir Abdelkader, the generals repeatedly resorted to violence, destroying villages or towns and smoking out insurgents who had taken refuge in caves. Land was confiscated on behalf of colonists and the state. By 1919, Muslims had lost 7.5 million hectares.[53]

Although they acquired French nationality, the colonized became subjects of the Republic and were governed by the *Code de l'indigénat*, a truly exceptional penal regime. The Muslim population required a pass to travel within the country and paid a higher proportion of their income in taxes than did Europeans.[54] Finally, though the country's Muslims were subject to obligatory military conscription and participated in both world wars, "access to both civilian and military employment also remained discriminatory and relegated Muslims to a subaltern social order .... [The natives] lived like foreigners in their own country."[55] The violence of the colonial regime was thus both physical and symbolic. France saw the native as inferior. Sometimes, it allowed him to attend the school of the Republic, where he discovered the heritage of the Enlightenment and Revolution.[56] The Republic made promises of emancipation that it did not keep toward the colonized. Even if Gallicized and educated, the Algerian was confined to the status of a colonized subject; he was never the equal of a French person of similar skill and education. The relations he had established with European institutions and society could at any moment expose him to injustice.[57] The colonial regime was enforced by physical violence but was also distinguished by its racism and the exclusion to which it gave rise. The wounds of which these former colonial subjects often spoke generally had to do with experiences of humiliation, particularly in school. These painful memories reflected the ambiguous situation of some "Muslims" under French Algeria. Integrated into the French school system and encouraged by some teachers to acquire knowledge, they nevertheless sometimes noticed that they were valued less than European students.[58] What's more, these "emancipated" individuals—the colonial term used to refer to them—were not granted citizenship, a prospect that was endlessly postponed. "Wait, be patient, again and always, such is the fate of the 'young Algerian' eager to take the place that has for ages been promised him at the table of the Republic."[59]

As the voice of subject peoples grew stronger on the international scene, the blindness of the French government and the stubbornness of the colonists kept Algerians locked in this unjust system. Liberation-era France bloodily repressed the 8 May 1945 protests in Constantinois, betraying promises that colonial troops would be repaid for their contribution to the war effort with a revision to their political status. The Popular Front[60] abandoned its calls to extend "citizenship to a small social elite of twenty-five thousand people." The Fourth Republic subsequently hobbled the principle of universal suffrage, retaining the principle of separate electoral colleges[61] and attempting to smother Algerians' national aspirations by accepting the rigged elections of March 1948, thereby preventing the Algerian People's Party (PPA) from achieving parliamentary representation.[62] In 1956, the Socialists also yielded to the colonist party. By turning their backs on them, the French political establishment shattered the hopes for assimilation and equality that had been nursed by a portion of the Algerian elite, like Ferhat Abbas, who, before 1954, counted on a new Algeria tied to France.[63] At the same time, it led a number of Algerian nationalists to abandon the political route in favor of armed action.

The cowardly policy pursued by Guy Mollet following the "Day of Tomatoes" (6 February 1956) destroyed the hopes for negotiation on which Ramdane Abane, leader of the Algiers region, had counted and "led him to cross an important step on the route to systematic terrorism."[64] Colonial violence also distinguished the scale and methods of repression: sometimes carried out blindly to punish uprisings, it targeted suspects with the use of torture.[65] The violence of the repression and the duration of the war precipitated social change in the country and within the nationalist movement: increasingly, the movement's working-class supporters gained a foothold among those leading the war effort.[66]

For its part, "the FLN, it is true, more than any other independence move-ment, chose to take up arms, practiced terrorism, and even tortured its own people."[67] For the FLN, this was a matter of "shattering the political consen-sus from which the colonial system benefits," destroying the bonds linking Europeans and Algerians and eliminating political rivals.[68] Together with the escalating violence and the logic of war,[69] the massacres deeply and irrepa-rably divided these two communities. Military leaders received the order to increase repression by any means necessary. This only further polarized the two camps around their respective war parties, leading to severe punishment for those who expressed support for neutrality or appeasement. In Algiers, a similarly sequential logic of terrorism and repression was repeated, with similar consequences for social and political division.[70]

By opposing a political resolution that would have given center stage to reformist "politicians," the FLN sought to use violence to assert itself as the sole actor.[71] Indeed, FLN violence affected Algerians themselves. Accused of remaining faithful to Messali Hadj, of showing reluctance or hesitation toward the FLN and of supporting the French, Algerians were subjected to FLN terror.[72] The clashes that took place between Messalists and FLN supporters in Algeria and metropolitan France (among members of the im-migrant community) killed 10,000 in the two camps and wounded 25,000 more, leading to the description of the conflict as a civil war within the war.[73] Communist militants similarly paid a price for the uncompromising stance adopted by the FLN, which tolerated no rivals.[74]

Violence also erupted within the ranks of the party: purges eliminated intellectuals and figures seen as too moderate or who had wandered from the line decreed by those who had succeeded in clawing their way to positions of leadership. At the end of the war, violence again broke out among fellow com-batants as part of the struggle for power, pitting the Army of the Frontiers against wilayat 3 and 4, which supported the Provisional Government of the Algerian Republic (GPRA). Several hundred guerrilla fighters and soldiers died in these clashes. Finally, while the number of Harkis killed in the after-math of independence is uncertain, conservative estimates put it at 10,000 dead.[75]

This violence sometimes had a dimension of social vengeance:

Throughout the summer, the interior resistance substituted itself everywhere it could for the Provisional Executive. Characterized by a strong peasant identity and depoliticized, it only speaks the language

of force. . . . These are the beginnings of a system in which social revenge serves as incentive and cover for the creation of a new dominant
class. City-dwellers, when they are without protection, pay a tribute
to the masters of the day. They get called "children of France." Their
daughters, who are sometimes required to marry against their will,
are the "unveiled of May 13th" and "para girls."[76]

Targeted kidnapping of Europeans proliferated, as did reprisals against
Harkis.[77] These acts reflected a desire to prove personal involvement in the war
of liberation, take the country back from France, punish those who were too
close to the former colonial power, and seize the wealth of those who had formerly dominated. They are also evidence of the cultural gaps that separated
country people from city-dwellers in the waning days of French Algeria.

The leaders of independent Algeria glorified the sacrifice of the "one and
a half million martyrs" and the courage shown by the Algerian people during the conflict. The colonial enemy was reviled for his brutality and feroc-
ity, which was only overcome by the desire and self-abnegation of the
combatants, the mujahideen. FLN violence against Europeans or Algerians
themselves was not subject to critical evaluation but rather passed over in silence, obscured[78] or justified by political leaders. Seen as a necessary or just
defense against a more powerful enemy, their use of force conferred the status of hero upon the mujahideen. What was characterized as legitimate violence provided the basis for the new leaders' power and fueled the national
imaginary of Algerians.

The mobilization against colonialism and imperialism justified the demand for national unity. In the same way that the FLN used violence during
the war to impose unanimity around its leadership, its leaders demanded
unanimous support for themselves once in power. To that end, they did not
hesitate to employ brutal methods. These included the killing of protesters
(including members of the party), assassination (Krim Belkacem), forced
exile (Hocine Aït-Ahmed, Mohamed Boudiaf), and the violent repression of
popular revolts (October 1988, in particular) and cultural movements (the
Kabyle Spring of 1980, riots in Kabylie in 2001). Described as necessary and
righteous, this violence was a source of legitimacy for a dictatorship whose
leaders tirelessly clung to the legacy of the war of liberation.

The political, economic, and social causes that plunged the country into
civil war are many and complex. We shall not consider them in detail here
but rather examine the manner in which the actors' strategies and methods

were inspired by the cultural repertory forged during the War of Independence and under the FLN regime. "The idealization of violence"[79] and the desire to impose unanimity, which was reflected in the denunciation of traitors and external plots, supplied a framework of shared references for the government and the Islamists alike. Lacking social capital and the opportunities to which it gives access, the latter expressed a desire to rid themselves of a system that they perceived as unjust and even humiliating. The absence of critical work on the Algerian revolution and the taboo surrounding some of the FLN's actions facilitated a phenomenon of imitation and repetition. At the end of an interview regarding his involvement in the war of liberation, an FLN veteran revealed what are recurrent perceptions in Algerian society. "But I'm not a hero," he said. "I didn't kill anyone."[80]

A central argument offered by Luis Martinez in his book on the sources of civil war in the 1990s concerns the celebration of violence.[81] For the armed Islamists, violence was a vector of social ascension. In colonial Algeria, the figure of the caid represented a success story, an example of boot-strapping self-promotion. During the subsequent war of liberation, this role was occupied by the colonel. In the Algerian political imaginary, the use of force in political and social relations is perceived as proof of personal success.

The civil war's "political resolution," which took the form of the Charter for Peace and National Reconciliation that was submitted to and approved by referendum in September 2005, left largely unpunished those who had engaged in physical violence. Investigations concerning armed Islamists were dismissed, and those already in prison were pardoned in exchange for an agreement to cease their activities. The text of the Charter specifies that these measures did not apply to "individuals involved in collective massacres, rapes or bombing attacks on public places."[82] In practice, however, these individuals also benefited from the amnesty, as no investigation was ever opened into their cases. From a socioeconomic point of view, they often seem privileged members of their communities, either because the state allowed them to reinvest the money from illegal trade or because the law allowed them to seek compensation for loss of employment. The families of impoverished terrorists, moreover, benefited from "national solidarity measures."[83] An amnesty also covered police officers who had committed acts of violence. The families of "disappeared" people[84] and those who died in terrorist attacks were officially recognized as victims and could request reparations.

This state of affairs lent legitimacy to the idea that the use of violence is profitable and that one runs less of a risk in exercising force than in being subjected to it. One result of this was that, in the Algeria of the first decade of the twenty-first century people tended, even in the most trivial social encounters, to immediately resort to a type of rudeness, as if it were proof of the resources upon which they could draw in the event of a power struggle. Any expression of weakness, meanwhile, was seen as taking a risk. There was a patent hardening of attitudes in public places.

The Charter for Peace and National Reconciliation reaffirmed the unanimity of the Algerian people. No effort was thus made to explain the reasons for or origins of what is discreetly referred to as the "national tragedy." Through its various amnesties, the state ordained that this episode was to be forgotten. Indeed, totally forgotten: those who called into question its interpretation of events[85] or the role played during the conflict by the Algerian state's defenders (army, patriots, self-defense groups) could be punished.

Memory and the Legitimacy of the Struggle

The Production of an Official Memory

In producing a mythological history of the war of liberation, the Algerian government's main objective was to present the FLN as the sole actor in this struggle. In its narrative, the 1954 uprising constituted a break with the past—a portrayal that at once conferred revolutionary significance upon this event and allowed earlier nationalist organizations to be ignored. The leaders of the FLN declared themselves "historic leaders" and exercised "a sort of proprietary right over the 'revolution.'"[86]

The precursors and rivals of the FLN, like Messali Hadj's Algerian National Movement, were erased from this official history, as were the clashes that took place between them and the FLN.[87] Although the FLN's victory against the colonial regime was political rather than military in nature, the government asserted that the use of force and the heroism of its troops were what had caused France to give way. As a consequence, the People's National Army (ANP), the supposed embodiment of the people, became the rightful heir of the Revolution.

Beginning in 1966, the writing of history was nationalized: libraries and bookstores were overseen by the state, and historic research was monitored by official authorities. The government thus produced an "anonymous history since the names of the main actors of this 'war of liberation' disappeared from textbooks and public plaques. The dead, alone, had full rights."[88] "All that remained of nationalism was an impoverished and warlike representation," while the government claimed that France had been defeated in battle.[89]

In 1971, the Fonds National des Archives Nationales and the Centre National d'Études Historiques (CNEH) were created. The latter was "the only body tasked with directing and encouraging national historic studies,"[90] and a head of the criminal investigation services was appointed its director.[91] The powerful National Organization of Mujahideen (ONM), which is tied to the FLN and the state through the Ministry of Veterans Affairs, was called upon to participate in writing this history. Testimony was collected from the organization's members, thereby helping substitute "the memory of 'the Revolution and those who experienced it'"[92] for an intellectual and scholarly approach.

The school system—site of political transmission and socialization par excellence—served to convey a representation of Algerian history that centered on the war of liberation. History textbooks embraced a Manichaean vision that alternated between the horror of colonization and the heroism of the independence fighters. The divisions within the Algerian population remained hidden, with the figure of evil incarnated by foreign forces and the Harkis.[93]

Moreover, Algerian leaders asserted the glorious character of the victory over colonialism, emphasizing the paucity of the FLN's resources and the power of the French state, to underscore the remarkable determination, courage, and spirit of sacrifice of Algerian combatants. Houari Boumediene kept this spirit of resistance alive by adopting an anti-imperialist stance on the international scene; Algeria remained mobilized against the neocolonial temptations of France and the arrogance of the great powers. Now free, the Algerian was liberated from the subaltern position to which he had been confined for over a century. The Algerian pride that was asserted on the international scene was part and parcel of the national personality.

Permeation and Protest Within Society

To my knowledge, there has yet to be a study addressing the manner in which this memory constructed by the FLN state has been received in Algerian society. In the 1970s, the official anti-imperialist ideology seemed to "a powerful element for unifying the various sectors of society," winning support from business circles, students, workers, and peasants.[94] In the research I conducted in the early 1990s, I often encountered sharp criticism of the

Algerian leadership and system. These leaders were reproached for corruption, injustice, and their contempt for the people. Complaints were also heard regarding the lack of freedom, unemployment, the impossibility of procuring housing, and the absence of leisure. The state was perceived as at once stifling and ineffective.[95]

After dropping out at the end of middle school "because he did not get along with his professors," Kamel briefly worked as a taxi driver. Unemployed at the time of our interview, he remarked, "If Boumediene, Ben Bella, or Chadli were real Algerians, we wouldn't be in this situation. They couldn't give the tiniest shit about Algeria, so don't tell me they were Algerians."[96]

Although Kamel expressed an attitude of total rejection toward the country's leaders, in doing so he showed his affection for the idea of a pure Algeria, one faithful to the ideals of the Revolution. He agreed with the unanimist ideology and dismissed those he saw as usurpers by denying their Algerian personality or citizenship.

His friend Toufiq, who worked in the family shipping business, dreamed of emigrating. He said that he could no longer tolerate the country's lack of freedom or the administration's contempt, and preferred life as an undocumented immigrant in Europe, which he had already given a try.

"You don't care about Algeria?"

"I don't care, I couldn't give a shit," he said, before forcefully adding, "but I'm proud to be Algerian, of course!"[97]

It thus seems that, despite his desire to be freed of his family and the social straitjacket in which many young people found themselves in the 1990s, the issue of Algerians' dignity—a nationalist theme par excellence—remained as sensitive as ever. Even as Toufiq unambiguously disparaged his country and idealized France and Switzerland, he gave voice to it in an abrupt and visceral manner.

In a revealing survey of young people from the working-class neighborhoods of Algiers, Selma Belaala addressed their representations of the government, which oscillated between support for Islamism, an attraction to global culture, and an eagerness for consumption. The army, whose members are seen as country people, was thus seen as being for "bumpkins," while the members of the political elite were described as "outdated."[98] These young people seemed to have clearly given up on the ideals of the 1954 Revolution. Despite these various examples, it would nevertheless be wrong to see Algerian society as solely traversed by generational divides. While the Algerian youth of the late 1980s turned to protest, some of their more privileged members continued to support the FLN system.

Accusations that France had manipulated one group of Algerians against another were a commonplace of Algerian public opinion and could be encountered among FLN supporters, Islamist militants, and the detractors of both camps. The theme of the colonialist threat continued to be effective, as did the idea that only an external actor was capable of destroying the unanimity of Algerian society.

Although young people challenged the political elite, its privileges, and its determination to retain power, denigrating their own country and voicing a desire to emigrate, they had not, for all that, freed themselves from some themes of the FLN's ideology. Their minds were still marked by its representation of the national community, the perception of a French imperialist plot, and the idea of original purity. "Official cant [was] internalized by the subjects themselves, and it is this that rendered them so susceptible to the pressures of unanimity."[99] Although the success of the FIS was predicated on presenting itself as a radical alternative to the FLN, it nevertheless adopted some aspects of the revolutionary father's language. Algerian leaders were accused of betraying ideals, but the nationalist ideology was not for its part subjected to critical examination.

Appropriation by the Islamists

According to Luis Martinez, a monopoly on historic memory was among the issues at stake in the civil war.[100] The armed Islamists saw themselves as mujahideen. They claimed that their actions were in keeping with 1 November 1954 and sought to take possession of a memory and legacy that had been confiscated by the regime. The Islamo-nationalism of the FIS led its members to appeal to themes already used by the FLN.[101] In doing so, they presented themselves as returning to the authentic origins from which those in power had in recent decades strayed. The FIS official program reproduced the myth of the people's identification with the army: "Throughout history, the Algerian army has won a reputation envied by many of the world's armies. . . . The Algerian army has always been an army of jihad ever ready to ensure the religion's defense, the unity and glorious and invincible community of Islam. . . . The successive revolutions in our lands and, in particular, that of the liberation have demonstrated that the army is the people and the people, the army."[102] Like the government, the Islamists compared their adversary to the colonial enemy, evoking the figure of the Harki, the OAS, and the party of France to denigrate it.

*   *   *

While it allowed the silence that had shrouded the figures of Algerian nationalism to be dispelled, the regime's liberalization did not ultimately result in a genuine opening of national memory. The political actors competing for power chose to outdo one another in relation to the struggle against the colonial enemy—a recurrent figure of political discourse that continued to be mobilized as legitimating foil and diversion. The civil war of the 1990s and its resolution were not propitious for an examination of the political representations of the past. By setting interpretations of the "national tragedy" in stone, the Charter for Peace and National Reconciliation once again obscured the deep divisions within society and the responsibilities for violence.

Chapter 3

France and the Algerian War:
Forgetting or Endless Confrontation?

Little effort has been made to examine how the Algerian War has shaped the political and symbolic order of contemporary France. Far from constituting a peripheral episode, the war contributed to the collapse of one regime and the birth of another, that of the Fifth Republic. It also marked the end of a colonial period and ushered in a new French identity centered on metropolitan France. The postwar years were thus a postcolonial time. For several decades, however, the state refused to acknowledge France's moral and political defeat and ignored the "war," while French elites refrained from examining the Republic's colonial past.

With amnesty and the rapid economic growth of the *trente glorieuses*, the Algerian affair and its protagonists faded from view for a time. Nevertheless, the Algerian War had an impact on the political engagement, doing away with the traditional fault lines between left and right or tearing them apart from within. After a silence of more than two decades, positions on the conflict resurfaced with even greater force. Since the Algerian War was also a Franco-French civil war, its return to prominence has been accompanied by a clash of narratives. Are we witnessing the shift to a new political model that endeavors to satisfy the demands of particular memories? Today, the country's political class and government listen with indulgence to those who look back nostalgically upon French Algeria. The vanquished have shown skill in promoting their cause and interests.

Crisis of the Nation, Crisis of the Republic

The Algerian War and, through it, the colonial question tested the values of the Republic as well as the contours of the nation and its cohesion. According to Todd Shepard, "the Algerian Revolution was at the same time a French revolution" and posed "fundamental questions about who was French and how the country must be governed."[1] Could the French Republic retain its overseas conquests and operate as a democracy across the full expanse of its territory? While Algerian nationalists emphasized the fact that, in the framework of the Republic, they were granted neither liberty nor equality nor fraternity, the French were faced with three options: to enlarge the boundaries of political citizenship to include "Muslims," abandon the democratic spirit by maintaining a political body that excluded the colonized, or reduce the surface area of the territory and political community. By opting for the third, French society redrew the nation and its relationship to the Other.

The Nation Put to the Test: Speaking about the War and Interpreting Its Outcome

In contrast to the Second World War, with respect to which there was "instant unanimity on one point: those who suffered and died in the fight against the Nazis did not do so for nothing,"[2] it was difficult to give meaning to the French dead of the Algerian War. The roughly 24,000 conscripts who were killed in battle had gone to defend French Algeria, seen as an integral part of the nation. The nation nevertheless abandoned it: consulted by referendum, fully 90.7 percent of metropolitan voters (the inhabitants of Algeria were prohibited from voting) approved the Evian Accords. The Algerian nationalist struggle was tainted by the killing of civilians, whether they were victims of terrorism (2,788 Europeans and 16,378 Muslims) or had been disappeared (around 2,000 Europeans and more than 13,000 Muslims). Of the 125,000 Harkis who remained in Algeria, 10,000 were massacred, abandoned by France and killed for having served the Republic. More than 2,200 soldiers and civilians were murdered by the Secret Army Organization (OAS), while 40 members of the OAS were eliminated by the French secret service, and four were executed by a military tribunal. As these deaths show, the war also took place on a "Franco-French" scale. Assigning meaning to each of these categories of the dead would have meant acknowledging the vacillations of the French state and the wounds that had been inflicted on

French society. Unable to assign a place in the national pantheon to those who died in this multidimensional conflict, one avoided mentioning them. Meanwhile, the large number of "French Muslim" supporters of the National Liberation Front (FLN) who died in the conflict—somewhere between 150,000 and 200,000[3]—cast light on the inner workings of the French army's campaign of "pacification." However, as they were identified with the figure of the enemy and henceforth members of a new national community divorced from France, they exited the space of French memory—if, indeed, they had ever been part of it.

The question of commemorating the men who died in this conflict or giving it a name thus did not arise. For more than three decades, the state abstained from naming the Algerian War until the National Assembly recognized the term in June 1999. Efforts to dissimulate the nature and even existence of the conflict were primarily aimed at concealing a major reversal of French policy: the three Algerian départements had become an independent Republic. Might not one conclude from this that French Army conscripts had fought in vain, that those who had fallen in battle had died for nothing?

Silence was also a way to avoid examining the war's outcome. For while France had overcome the FLN in battle, it had been morally and politically defeated. Algerians and, more broadly, the dominated people who would soon make up the Third World, demanded citizenship and national emancipation; France had been forced to acknowledge these demands and their legitimacy. While the Algerian government endlessly proclaimed its victory, the leaders of the former colonial power dodged the question. General de Gaulle, in particular, invoked "historic determinism" to justify decolonization. This allowed him to "consolidate his reputation as a history maker"[4] while simultaneously rendering anonymous the actor of a historic movement directly confronting France. For the French head of state, Algerian independence was the result of an "act of French generosity."[5] According to Jean-Paul Sartre, this refusal to admit defeat was shared by the French people, leading him to remark: "In truth, this 'ceasefire' that everyone is in such a rush to declare 'without winner or loser' was imposed by the Algerian people. [They did so] alone, by virtue of their extraordinary resistance and discipline."[6] It is no doubt more fruitful to distinguish between the moral and physical dimensions of victory and defeat: despite the success of its army in the field, France lost to the degree that it had to abandon its initial project, that of preserving French Algeria.

Furthermore, the silence surrounding the conflict and the discomfort it provoked stemmed from the temptation to draw a veil over the fact that it was also a civil war and, as such, had given rise to major intellectual and cultural rifts in French society. Violence between French people took place on both physical and symbolic planes. In Algeria, OAS commandos attempted to kill liberals and the state's representatives; in France, they targeted intellectuals and then the president of the Republic. In December 1961, *barbouzes*[7] and members of Mission C (metropolitan police officers) were sent to Algeria to destroy the OAS, even if that meant resorting to brutal methods and summary justice. Several demonstrations were violently repressed: the peaceful protestors of 17 October 1961 paid the highest price for the police's fury;[8] eight of those who marched with the French left at Charonne on 8 February lost their lives; in Algiers, the police killed forty-six pieds-noirs as they demonstrated in the rue d'Isly.[9]

The questions of torture and war gave rise to foundational commitments[10] or extended older ones. The enmities formed during the conflict exploded older solidarities and created new fault lines that endure to this day. The generation of the Resistance, which occupied a central place in state and society in the years following World War II, was torn apart during the Algerian War.[11] The paths followed by its members speak to profoundly divergent interpretations of the Resistance's heritage. While some, believing themselves to be pursuing a patriotic project, championed a certain conception of the French nation and accused de Gaulle of incarnating the new Pétain, others were angered to discover the methods of "pacification" employed by the French army in Algeria, which in their eyes strangely resembled those used by the Nazis. Rifts also emerged within political parties, labor unions, the church,[12] and the army,[13] which on several occasions over the course of the war found itself divided into various factions.

The Republic Faced with the Colonial Question

In his book *The Invention of Decolonization*, Todd Shepard seeks to show how "a rewriting of the Algerian history of France took place at the moment of independence. Critical thinking about the formative role played by Algeria and the 'new imperialism' in the construction of the French nation-state disappeared. In its place there emerged the fiction that the 'Algerian experience' had been an unfortunate colonial detour, from which the French Republic had now escaped."[14] According to Shepard, this denial was accompanied by the exclusion and demonization of the French minority that supported French Algeria. Although no one went to the trouble of explaining the profound reversal of French policy and of the representations it entailed, the newly invented concept of decolonization established itself as an imperative, with de Gaulle presenting it as the inevitable movement of history.[15]

In reality, the "colonial enterprise" had been at the heart of the republican project. Benjamin Stora underscores the fact that French silence regarding the Algerian War is of a piece with its silence regarding colonization.[16] Emmanuelle Saada, for her part, maintains that the "Empire appears a 'nonsite of memory' in the history of the nation and, even more so, of the Republic, a social and political space of the nation separate from the metropolis from every point of view."[17] By showing the intimate relations between the republican model and the colonial project, as well as their ambiguities and contradictions, Nicolas Bancel, Pascal Blanchard, and Françoise Vergès' book, La République coloniale, contributes to filling this black hole in republican memory. "A dream of the colonial Republic existed, it inspired generations of colonial administrators, seduced colonized peoples, and fired the imagination of generations of French people," they explain. "Colonization is not only the site of a crime; it is also that of sincere hopes, indisputable humanist engagements, relations that were not solely structured by domination." In pursuing a secularized missionary enterprise,[18] the Republic sought to convert entire peoples to its values.

Drawing upon the universalism it saw itself as having invented, the Republic dreamed of greatness and of controlling the world. The Empire was thus to be the "'natural' expression of mankind's unity, of the universality of human nature." Trained by the French education system, the native elites of the colonies were, moreover, steeped in republicanism and sometimes turned "republican discourse against republican colonial discourse in order to develop emancipatory projects."[19]

While some believed that an original synthesis could be made of the Republic and its colonial project, in practice the effort to achieve overseas domination constantly contradicted the values of the Republic even as it appealed to them, thereby exposing the Republic to charges of hypocrisy. In its dealings with colonized peoples, France had long held out the prospect of a status and rights it never gave them. "The always postponed promise of assimilation" was a cornerstone of the colonial Republic, "this hybrid that simultaneously affirms the equality of all and institutes a hierarchy among the empire's inhabitants."[20]

This inability to apply the ideals of the French Revolution to the peoples of Africa and the Antilles stemmed not just from failures to implement the project or misrepresentations on the part of colonial administrators. It also stemmed from an original contradiction in the conception of French universalism. Even as they proclaimed that the values of liberty, equality, and fraternity were global in scope, the drafters of the Declaration of the Rights of Man and Citizen and their heirs were convinced that France and the French people had a specific destiny. As Pierre Bouretz explains, "France was long able to believe that the universal merged with the singularity of its national history."[21] A "belief in racial superiority" collided head-on with the principle of universality. In the colonial setting, the relationship to the foreigner was deeply ambivalent and marked by a primordial dissonance: the foreigner was simultaneously someone "who[m] one wants to usher into greater France" and the native "who[m] one refuses to integrate into the political body of the Republic."[22]

The violence of colonization thus made itself felt on three fronts. First, the brutality of military conquest and the social and political order imposed on the population was based on the material superiority of France. But the entrepreneurs of colonization sought to assert a moral point of view. To that end, they also employed the violence of assimilation, commanding subject peoples to familiarize themselves with the Republic and French history. The Republic's broken promises constituted a third form of (in this case, mainly symbolic) violence, a perpetual fraud entailing political, economic, social, and psychological implications for the individual. One of the main sources of Algerian nationalism resided in this humiliating experience: that of being called upon to support France while being denied the right to belong to it as a citizen. The desire for independence was stoked by the inability of the "nation of the Enlightenment" to apply its model to other races. After Algeria and France's other colonies had gained independence, it was easier for the French to appeal to the "movement of history" explanation than to say that the failure of the colonial project originated in France's inability to implement universalism when confronted with the racial question. The ethnic and cultural order was indeed used to exclude natives from citizenship and pervert republican principles.

The contradictions of French universalism and the relationship to the foreigner were once again on display when supporters of decolonization argued that the population was unassimilable by nature. The problem was in this way turned on its head: it was not the Republic that indefinitely denied citizenship to indigenous peoples, but rather the very character of those peoples, incapable of fitting into the French mold, that did so. Like Raymond Aron, who had also been converted to the idea of an independent Algeria, Charles de Gaulle was hostile to the idea of integrating "Muslims" and used this argument to justify his position. Todd Shepard claims that these approaches show that an ethnicized vision of the nation had imposed itself, with both right and left ultimately subscribing to the idea that a fundamental difference existed between the "French" and those who were to become the "Algerians."[23]

The treatment of the Harkis by successive governments over a period of several decades substantiates this claim to the degree that the issue of ethnic belonging took precedence over fidelity to the French Republic in the choice of public policy. Herded to the outskirts of cities, relegated to second-class citizenship, the Harkis once again found themselves excluded from the community of citizens. By remaining silent as to the Harkis' fate, by hiding them away and forgetting them, the Republic drew no conclusions from the errors and misdeeds of the colonial enterprise, which were indeed repeated.

The demonization of the pieds-noirs, on the other hand, helped assuage the republican conscience. Their resistance or opposition to Algerian independence singled them out as paragons of colonialism. Without calling themselves or the republican ideology into question, the French could thus blithely accuse the pieds-noirs of seeking to preserve an anachronistic system of domination.

To this day, the French conception of universalism clashes with the racial question. The Republic claims to so thoroughly ignore the ethnic background of individuals that it is rendered invisible. Its fiercest defenders, meanwhile, ultimately refuse to admit the partial failure of this system. "Universalists" vehemently denounce the positions of "particularists," whom they see as seeking to destroy the republican pact. One must of course take care "not to use the colonial issue to systematically parse all social questions." Yet it is to be noted that the republicanists, who oppose calls for taking racial considerations into account in order to reduce inequality,[24] resist critical examination of the Republic's action overseas and even tend to defend its colonial heritage. More than anyone else, Jean-Pierre Chevènement embodies this French vision:[25] he sought to revive an authoritarian version of the republican model, completely refusing to take ethnic or cultural particularisms into account and holding that the work carried out in Algeria, particularly via the French education system, requires that we "stop feeling ashamed."[26] This dependence on republican ideology prevents some from recognizing that, far from rendering color invisible, the French invention of universalism in reality sometimes obscures the nature of the discrimination to which a part of the "French" population is subjected, and has in the past underwritten a system based on ethnic difference.

Silence, Indifference, and Amnesty

The colonial nature of the war and of France's past relationship with Algeria as well as the civilian dimension of the conflict led the French government and political class to bury "the events of Algeria." Preoccupied with the delights of modernization and the growth of a consumer society, a large part of French society adapted to this policy of forgetting. Several amnesty laws were supposed to help put an end to this painful chapter of French history, which had divided the national community. Nevertheless, while the amnesties calmed tensions and resentments, they did not bring about reconciliation among the conflict's actors.

Embarrassment and Dissimulation

Contrary to expectations, de Gaulle accepted and oversaw Algeria's transition to independence. While he attempted to make the case that disengagement was both necessary and beneficial for France's future, the attitude he first expressed in his 16 September 1959 speech nevertheless constituted a dramatic departure from his earlier statements. According to Frank Renken, if this shift in Gaullist policy toward Algeria was subsequently banished from memory, it was because it indeed constituted a major (and very risky) about-face.[27] In the right-wing nationalist tradition, the colonial Empire was a power asset for France.[28] A segment of the right and of those who had supported General de Gaulle's return to power in 1958 found it difficult to accept his "abandonment" of the overseas départements. Some of them had counted on the hero of the French Resistance and the newly created Fifth Republic to save French Algeria and thus felt betrayed by the president's new stance. Others were persuaded by the arguments put forward by the new president and consented to decolonization, albeit sometimes reluctantly.

The Algerian War caused the inconsistencies and weaknesses of the traditional parties of the left—the French Communist Party (PCF) and the French Section of the Workers' International (SFIO)—to break into the open. What's more, they were caught short by General de Gaulle's strategy of negotiating with the FLN. The PCF, for its part, had been compromised by its decision to lend its support to a motion in the National Assembly granting special powers to the government, which was widely understood as a vote for a military solution in Algeria. At the same time, the PCF looked upon the FLN with ambivalence and clearly stated its support for Algerian independence only in 1960.[29]

The Algerian War was painful for the reformist left because it was the source of rifts within it. On the one hand, men such as Guy Mollet and François Mitterand, who were largely unreceptive to the Algerians' national aspirations, thought the FLN could be undone by a better application of republican principles, in particular via a program of political and economic reforms.[30] The image of the two men is associated with the war and government inaction in regard to the army's use of torture. The conflict also revealed another, more militant and moral left. It was led by intellectuals, young SFIO activists who rejected *national-molletisme*,[31] members of the new Unified Socialist Party (PSU), and political clubs that a few years later were to become the driving force behind the creation of the Socialist Party.

Having failed to take a clear stand in favor of independence, the better part of the French left overinvested in the memory of its "antifascist" struggle and focused on the OAS, identified as an enemy of the Republic. It purified its memory of the war to emphasize above all its anticolonial mobilization during the Charonne demonstration. The political significance of that day in February 1962 allowed the left to climb back in the saddle and portray itself as at the forefront of the "movement of history." It held that the threat that hung over the Republic had shifted: formerly incarnated by de Gaulle, this threat was now embodied by the leader of the OAS. Then a shift occurred, with the left distancing itself from and even expressing hostility toward the Harkis and pieds-noirs. It had long viewed the Harkis as collaborators, but then resigned itself to "silence, the only way to keep its credibility beyond the repudiations and rifts." The left soothed its conscience by making scapegoats of the pieds-noirs, blaming colonialism, fascism, violence, and racism on a well-defined group.[32]

For the various political forces in France, any reexamination of the Algerian War was thus a risky proposition. The actors had little appetite for reflecting on past sins, as that would further undermine their historical legitimacy. Society therefore acquiesced to the institutional silence that had been imposed upon it. It felt a "cowardly relief" at the end of the conflict and sought to close the wounds that had been inflicted upon it by the civil war, evading any examination of them the better to avoid revisiting those of Vichy and the Resistance.[33]

Les Trente Glorieuses: The Thrill of Consumption and Modernization

According to Jean-François Sirinelli, starting in 1962 France entered a period of unprecedented peace, with the baby boom generation the first not directly subjected to the experience of war. This age group and those that followed rid themselves of the imaginaries of the enemy, formerly characterized by the figure of the Prussian lancer and the enemy occupier.[34] Founded on rapprochement with Germany, the European construction breathed life into more pacific representations focusing on cooperation. As reconciliation with Germany proceeded, the decolonization of Algeria was expelled from the French mental universe.

Moreover, powerful social changes and the transformation of lifestyles in the 1960s led the French to turn away from the colonial and Algerian questions. Absorbed by prospects for social and economic progress and new possibilities of consumption, French society explored new practices and values linked to modernity. Henri Mendras showed how the peasant world contracted as cities grew. This phenomenon was accompanied by the advent of a middle-class society, as the middle class became ever larger and more central. Characterized by confidence in progress and the future, the values and lifestyle of the middle class spread throughout society.[35] An improved standard of living stimulated aspirations for comfort, consumption, leisure, mass culture, and hedonism. The music and practices of young people became ever more global in nature, and the young benefited from the liberation of mores that followed on the heels of May 1968.[36] The "new modern home" was based on the acquisition of a number of new, serially produced objects, including the refrigerator, the gas stove, the washing machine, the television set, and the family car. According to Kristen Ross, the modernization and Americanization of France had a close and complex relationship to the phenomenon of decolonization. Even as France got rid of one of its largest colonies, modernization and the invention of new hygiene became sources of social and racial differentiation. France distinguished itself from the newly independent Algeria; it was all the more modern for having separated itself from that traditional and backward society on the other side of the Mediterranean. Taking up a role that had formerly been confined to the "educated native," the housewife had to reinvent cleanliness and the home, which were seen as the foundations of national well-being. Comfortably ensconced indoors, the middle class occupied an ever-larger area of a renovated Paris. The "purification" of the capital led to the expulsion of 19 percent of its population on grounds of "hygiene" and "safety."[37] Most immigrants were pushed out to the *banlieues*, and the city was whitewashed with the sandblasting of most of the city's famous façades and monuments. Colonized or immigrant Arabs were relegated to the periphery of territories and imaginaries alike. The idea quickly took hold that France had carried out its modernization in a world undergoing transformation by ridding itself of its colonial burden. It was as if the colonial Republic had never existed.

Amnesties from De Gaulle to Mitterrand: Forgetting, Reconciliation, or Prolongation of the Conflict?

Amnesty policies serve two distinct but complementary roles: forgetting and reconciliation. By seeking to erase past offenses and convictions, the act of forgetting is intended to assuage the national community and close the wounds that have divided it. Amnesty is thus seen as serving the general interest, a way of finishing with the past and (re)constructing the nation via the forgetting recommended by Ernest Renan. This form of amnesty-forgetting is reflected in the 22 March 1962 decree regarding "acts committed in the framework of operations to maintain public order conducted against the Algerian insurrection." Presented as the counterpart of the amnesty granted FLN members under the Evian Accords, this presidential decision exonerated the soldiers and police implicated in acts of torture or disappearance in Algeria.[38] The authorities chose to bury state crimes for which they were themselves responsible. Herein lies the other dimension of amnesty-forgetting: the state's desire to protect itself and its agents. Unlike the Americans, the French did not try their war criminals.[39] Did the 1962 amnesty's attempt to decree forgetting succeed? While it initially provoked mobilization among opponents of torture,[40] it seems that the majority will of society to extricate itself from a distressing and destabilizing period allowed indifference to take root in the two decades that followed. Starting in the

1990s, however, the debate over torture in Algeria resurfaced. The forgetting had thus been only temporary; what had begun as the return of the repressed became an obsession.[41]

Moreover, the policy of amnesty sought to reconcile the divided community. The three laws of 23 December 1964, 17 June 1966, and 31 July 1968 took a gradualist approach. The first amnesty concerned the Europeans of Algeria who acted "in response to the insurrection," but excluded those who held commanding positions. The second extended state clemency to the authors of "subversion," which the government defined as any "undertaking tending to prevent the state from exercising its authority or to substitute an illegal authority in its place," but was applied only to OAS members who had already been freed or were sentenced to fewer than ten years of prison, with those on the run or in exile excluded. This amnesty also covered the "suitcase carriers" who helped the FLN,[42] and an article erased the excesses committed by the forces of order against OAS members, draft dodgers, and deserters. The third amnesty covered OAS leaders and putschists, finally resulting in "total penal and disciplinary amnesty."[43] With an attempt on the part of OAS members to assassinate the head of state in 1965, the return to civil peace was a real issue in the years after 1962. Amnesty was to be the "cement of reconciliation," allowing political conflict to be brought to an end in the interests of restoring harmony within the political body. It was to constitute a sort of "peace treaty" or even "armistice agreement"[44] among the parties. In this sense, the various amnesty laws helped allay fears and restore civil peace. With the exception of the Communist Party, all political parties supported amnesty. Various arguments were advanced: given that FLN activists had already been amnestied, the principles of justice and fairness demanded that the same policy be adopted in what concerned the opposing camp; some argued that the cause of the "lost soldiers" deserved understanding and indulgence; others thought that a policy of erasing past offenses would facilitate the integration of the pieds-noirs as a group.[45] For all that, there was to be no final reconciliation. Indeed, this would have required a form of exchange between rival parties—that is, forgiveness—or at least recognition of the enemy's suffering. However, most OAS veterans vehemently rejected this approach. They held that they did not need to be forgiven for having defended France.[46] In their eyes, the amnesty decisions that concerned them in no way commanded gratitude on their part. Moreover, the men and women involved in the fight against torture or in favor of Algerian independence also remained stubbornly resentful toward the "seditionists."[47] And so it remains to this day, as the vigorous debate provoked by the 23 February 2005 law—and, in particular, that law's insistence (Article 4) on the "positive role" played by France in the Maghreb—makes clear.

While the Algerian War amnesties failed to cement forgetting or reconciliation, they did reflect a process of negotiation and, indeed, bargaining between the government and some associative actors organized into pressure groups. The stakes of this negotiation were essentially symbolic and represented a prolongation of the conflict.

The first aspect of negotiation related to elections. According to Stéphane Gacon, "each law was used by the Gaullist government to consolidate a weakened political position on the eve of a major election."[48] In the same way, the 16 July 1974 amnesty can be interpreted as Valéry Giscard d'Estaing's "post-election thank you" to a portion of his electorate[49] as well as an illustration of the Union pour la Démocratie Française (UDF) candidate's sympathies for the ex-activists.[50] Finally, the bill to "erase the last consequences of the Algerian War," which was pushed through Parliament by recourse to Article 49, Paragraph 3 of the French Constitution, was in fulfillment of a promise made by the Socialist candidate to pied-noir associations.

The political benefit the president of the Republic hoped to draw from these measures constitutes a second aspect of the amnesty, one relating to the personal interest of the actors concerned. By appropriating to himself the right to amnesty by decree and by exercising his right of pardon, de Gaulle sought to portray himself as the nation's guide and reconciler,[51] above the fray of political conflicts and parties. Some of his adversaries were irritated at the thought that they owed their pardon to someone they saw as their enemy.[52] It is certainly possible that de Gaulle himself felt satisfaction at the thought that his adversaries' fate depended upon his will alone. Renken ascribed the same ambition to Mitterrand. In Renken's view, after having denounced the Fifth Republic as a "permanent coup d'état,"[53] Mitterrand sought to surpass de Gaulle in the role of "kindhearted reconciler."[54] According to Éric Duhamel, this stance reflected Mitterrand's loyalty to some friends as well as to himself. Indeed, the veterans of French Algeria shared Mitterrand's hostility toward the strongman of the Fifth Republic. Initially favorable to maintaining French Algeria, the victor in the 1981 elections had, moreover, testified on behalf of General Salan during his trial.[55]

The third aspect of this amnesty-bargaining is revealed in the particularities of the laws of 1974, 1982, and 2005, which introduced a form of reparation and even rehabilitation for members of the OAS. This type of amnesty-reparation was unprecedented in the history of the French Republic.[56] In 1974, the measures adopted on behalf of OAS veterans were simultaneously symbolic and material: the state restored their decorations, reintegrated officials into civilian and military structures, and reimbursed them for trial costs, damages owed the state and indemnities due to the victims of their attacks. The basis for doing so was the notion that amnestied individuals should be able to free themselves from the financial weight of their obligations. In 1982, the state made further amends, allowing soldiers and civil servants to benefit from the scheduled promotions they missed, a decisive factor in calculating retirement pensions.

In 2005, the material reparations granted OAS members from the private sector went unnoticed, eclipsed by the controversy over Article 4 of the 23 February law. However, Article 13 provided for OAS members and "suitcase carriers" to receive a sum proportional to the years they spent in exile. The decree specifying how the law was to be enforced provided for a payment of 7,323.48 euros for each trimester of inactivity.[57] In this respect, the 2005 amnesty departed yet further from the original aim of reconciliation, whether between French citizens or between the peoples of France and Algeria. It adopted a fundamentally partisan vision and took place at a time when the Algerian War and colonization were being actively debated. In doing so, it provoked outrage among former opponents of the Algerian War, human rights supporters, critics of the Republic, and academics who felt their freedom of expression was under threat.[58] Franco-French reconciliation demanded dialogue between the parties, that they recognize their excesses and try to understand their adversaries' point of view. Yet the 2005 amnesty made no attempt to lay the groundwork for a shared narrative. On the contrary, it reassured one camp at the price of deepening rifts with the others. If OAS were surreptitiously granted an indemnity, it was more with the aim of winning their political support than of healing old wounds and political rifts. In this respect, the deputies' gesture was evidence of the nimbleness and efficiency of OAS networks, which above all sought to change their image and even obtain an expression of gratitude for their action and rehabilitation in the eyes of public opinion.

By offering relief to a portion of the actors and their supporters, the first amnesties helped calm the postwar climate in Algeria. The indifference shown by French society toward this colonial conflict reflected above all the thrilling new phenomenon of mass consumption that had been ushered in by economic prosperity. Nevertheless, mobilizations and resentment did not cease to exist; they were merely toned down for a time.

Competing Narratives

The silence imposed by the state and society's apparent indifference in the years following the Algerian War sharply contrast with what today seems to be an overflow of memory, accompanied by a proliferation of demands on the part of victim groups and even the dismantling of the French republican model. Held in check for several years, vectors of identity originating in the conflict itself have since the 1990s once again burst into the public sphere. Under pressure from these contradictory demands for recognition, the state appears to be lagging behind in the debate over French Algeria and the Algerian War.

The Algerian War Is Not Dead

Continuing a movement initiated a decade earlier, the Algerian War once again became a subject of debate within French society in the 1990s. Several factors explain this "return" of conflictual narratives. Benjamin Stora mentions the emergence of a new generation of scholars and journalists too young to have lived through the Algerian War,[59] as well as the role played by the children of immigrants and the Algerian civil war, which inevitably revived memories of the earlier conflict.[60] As Éric Savarèse points out, the context was also marked "by renewed interest in the analysis of memory and the proliferation of calls to remember."[61] According to Frank Renken, the resurgence of Algerian memories revealed that the state was powerless to impose lasting silence on a period and set of events that meaningfully speak to the experience of multiple groups of French people. Starting in the 1980s, veterans, repatriates, and those nostalgic for the OAS all made themselves heard.[62]

Repatriate associations and those connected with the defense of French Algeria have long been mobilized. They first demanded amnesty for members of the OAS and called for state compensation. More recently, their efforts have focused on symbolic issues in an effort to impose their reading of history on French society and government. On the other side are to be found a collection of left-wing figures and intellectuals reaffirming their opposition to the Algerian War. This group revived the petition tradition to protest the

Courrière law, which had rehabilitated the putschists and members of the OAS. Pierre Vidal-Naquet and Laurent Schwartz, both members of the Comité Audin, were among the signatories and once again joined the fight on behalf of human values.[63] Another example can be found in the "Appel des douze," a petition signed by twelve prominent figures calling upon the government to acknowledge and condemn the practice of torture during the Algerian War.[64] The socializations and reciprocal grudges of the postwar years thus persist. The "suitcase carries," however, are notably absent from this debate. Their silence—or at least their failure to make themselves heard—is among other things explained by the loss of credibility that today afflicts postin-dependence regimes, particularly that of the FLN, which is seen as guilty for having seized power and led the country into civil war. In addition to condemning the French army's use of torture, in the 1990s a number of doc-umentaries also underscored the abuses perpetrated by the FLN.[65]

Since the 1980s, several conscript associations have also demanded a form of recognition. In 1974, veteran ID cards were granted to those who served in the Algerian War. In June 1999, Parliament endorsed what had become a matter of consensus: the "events" and "operations in support of the mainte-nance of order" were part of the "Algerian War." Establishing the exact date on which the conflict came to an end—a source of discord among the vari-ous veterans associations—proved more difficult. In 2003, on the first anni-versary of the inauguration of a memorial at Paris' Quai Branly dedicated to the soldiers and support troops who died in North Africa between 1952 and 1962, the date 5 December was finally settled upon.[66]

Of all the groups that participated in the war, the Harkis are doubtless the least vocal. At the same time, their descendants have been the driving force behind the various mobilizations to secure material and symbolic rec-ognition of their loyalty to France. It was the Harkis' sons and daughters who mainly protested, carried out hunger strikes, and spoke on behalf of their fathers. The debate was dominated by Mohand Hamoumou. The author of a sociology dissertation on the Harkis published in 1993, Hamoumou brought an academic and activist approach to bear on the issue. Among other things, he sought to put an end to French silence regarding the fate of French army auxiliaries.[67] In 1991, the children of the Harkis revolted. Although a law was passed on 11 June 1994 affirming that "recognizing the nation's moral debt toward these men and women who directly suffered on account of their ser-vice to our country is a priority,"[68] a number of them maintained that the au-thorities had not kept their promises. In the summer of 1997, they went on strike and, in the summer of 2001, took their grievances to court.[69] A day of homage for the Harkis was celebrated on 25 September 2001, and commemorative plaques were hung in various places. A 23 February 2005 law also paid homage to the Harkis.

The children of immigrants emerged as new actors in the 1980s. Some associations led an effort to win recognition and spread awareness of the 17 October 1961 massacre of Algerian demonstrators at the hands of the French police. Their action met with some success, as the event was brought to the awareness of the public,[70] and a commemorative plaque was hung on the Pont Saint-Michel. The responsibility of Maurice Papon—Paris chief of police at the time of the massacre—was of course noted. Papon's image had been tarnished by his conviction for crimes against humanity for his role in deporting Jews during the Second World War. In the eyes of the public, the guilty verdict handed down by the Bordeaux court was also confirmation of his responsibility for the October 1961 massacre.

In 2006, Jamel Debbouze[71] produced the film *Indigènes* in homage to the North African soldiers who fought in the Second World War. Directed by Rachid Bouchareb, the film was a form of memory activism and as such achieved some of its objectives: it was very successful at the box office and widely discussed in the media. Claiming to discover the tragedy of these veterans abandoned by France, President Jacques Chirac used the occasion to announce an increase in the pensions paid to overseas combatants— without, for all that, settling the question of back pay. This affair provoked little commentary in discussions of memories of colonization. It is to be remarked, however, that Debbouze adopted a distinctly consensual stance in his public appearances. Rather than emphasize conflict or the "colonialists'" exploitation of the "colonized," he used the occasion to pay homage to pied-noir combatants.

In the opinions voiced by particular groups and elsewhere, two subjects have structured public turmoil and debate regarding the Algerian War. The first of these is the issue of torture, which has been driven by the publication of new academic studies and first-person accounts on the part of the war's actors. In 2000, *Le Monde* ran an article by Louisette Ighilahriz detailing the torture to which she had been subjected. There followed responses by General Jacques Massu and Colonel Paul Aussaresses.[72] In public opinion, the issue of the torture of prisoners in the Algerian War made all the more sense as it resonated with torture in contemporary conflicts, particularly the war in Iraq, where American soldiers had been implicated in the practice. Though numbingly repetitive, these abuses were also morally intolerable, fueling calls for their perpetrators to be brought justice. At the same time, the focus on these acts diverted attention from attempts to assess the war itself and its broader, structural context: "In France, the central axis of remorse remains torture in Algeria from 1954 to 1961,"[73] which is presented as a shameful exception. This "sometimes masks a deeper examination of conscience regarding the systematic violence of the colonial system."[74] How to assess the history of colonization supplies the second subject of controversy. While a majority of the left is silent on this score, French Algeria activists defend "the French enterprise" ("l'œuvre française") in the colonies and have received a sympathetic ear from a growing segment of the political class.

Mixed with the defense of the memory and interests of a group involved in the war, the opinions voiced on these two subjects have resulted in confusion. The conflation of several levels of analysis—political, moral, historical—fuels crudely oversimplified representations in which only two camps exist: on the one hand, a French Algeria camp bringing together pieds-noirs, Harkis, OAS members, and the far right; on the other, an independent Algeria camp consisting of left-wing intellectuals, activists of immigrant descent, communists, suitcase carriers, and the FLN. Some narratives have congealed around a dramatization specific to the war. Trapped within the symbolic violence of confrontation, they accumulate without contributing to the development of debate or discussion.

In his various publications, General Faivre has thus sought to simultaneously defend the interests and honor of the Harkis and the French army during the Algerian War. He accuses the authorities, in particular, of having abandoned the Harkis. Underscoring FLN abuses, he also recalls "the French enterprise" on the other side of the Mediterranean.[75] In reality, these questions are distinct: the torture practiced by French soldiers does not excuse the violence of the FLN, and the supposed good conduct of French soldiers in Algeria supplies no information for assessing the colonial system. However, the actors tend to defend a continuum as if the alternative amounts to either subscribing to France's civilizing mission in the colonies or preaching repentance.

The State Assailed by Demands: Breaches in the Model

In French public opinion, the Algerian War produced no heroes, except for particular groups. French society today has turned its attention to identifying victims. Moreover, the French state has found itself besieged by the demands of the various protagonists. Would it seek to satisfy all of these overlapping memories?[76] Importuned by all sides, the authorities have felt their way forward, endeavoring to satisfy each supplicant without offending the vision of competing groups. According to Raphaëlle Branche, "for the state, it is not so much a matter of adopting a discourse regarding the past as of constructing a relationship with a given group for today and tomorrow."[77]

A memorial to the repatriated was thus built in Nice in 1987. In June 1994, a law affirmed France's moral debt to the auxiliary force veterans of Algeria, and 25 September 2001 was set as an official day of homage to honor the Harkis. On 11 November 1996, Jacques Chirac paid homage to the "victims and combatants who fell in North Africa, 1952–1962," dedicating a monument to their memory. On this occasion, he also took care to mention those who had suffered in Algeria: the Harkis and repatriated French people. This approach was crowned by the 23 February 2005 law. The repression of the 17 October 1961 demonstration was officially recognized by Paris mayor Bertrand Delanoë, though no mention was made of those responsible for the violence. In regard to the issue of torture, by contrast, the authorities sidestepped demands for recognition, calling instead for a commission of historians to examine the matter.[78]

The "one and indivisible Republic" thus ceded to particular demands for recognition. Some, such as the Harkis and the OAS activists, succeeded in shaking off opprobrium and donning the mantle of victimhood. The pieds-noirs, for their part, ceased to be exclusively seen as reactionary colonists by a segment of the metropolitan public. When compared to the South African scenario, the fate that forced the pieds-noirs to leave their native land may today seem a sacrifice on the altar of the FLN's uncompromising ideology, and thus an expansion of the "field of legitimate suffering."[79]

A greater receptivity to emotion and suffering was clearly illustrated in a 1992 decree allowing veterans of the Algerian War to receive the status of victims of traumatic neuroses.[80] The victims of this conflict thus appear to be mainly French. It is said that the republican model has been weakened by the crisis of the intellectuals and the ebbing of ideology, contributing to the rise of a society of victims.[81] Should one thus see the various acts of recognition performed by the national authorities as so many breaches in the republican model and part of a more generalized erosion of the French system? Does the "rise of the subject" threaten the French Republic? The perceived threat, in any case, troubles republicans and has caused them to dig in their heels.

The OAS-FN Convergence

Until the early 1980s, the far right was weak and OAS veterans seemed to have disappeared from the political landscape.[82] "Identified with the last partisans of French Algeria," writes Guy Pervillé, "the far right was isolated by its defeat but its convictions and certainty that it had been right all along were paradoxically reinforced." This also explains the three profiles that characterize members of the OAS: a first group was recruited among fascists "with a knack for violence and steeped in racial pride"; a second, larger group consisted of traditionalists with ties to Catholic fundamentalism and Pétainism; finally, a yet larger and more heterogenous third group can be described as nationalist and receptive to the ideas of decadence, France's honor, and the country's responsibility toward the inhabitants of Algeria.[83] These profound disparities among the movement's members were among the causes of its failure. Once the Algerian War was over, these disparities persisted, and many OAS veterans refused to rally under the banner of the far right. Nevertheless, bridges and affinities existed between the partisans of French Algeria and the National Front (FN) at the level of discourse and action. Moreover, if those nostalgic for the OAS made inroads in the public sphere, it was to some degree thanks to the resurgence of this political movement.

In 1981, the FN received only 0.8 percent of votes cast in the presidential election. Seven years later, it received 14.4 percent. Jean-Marie Le Pen succeeded in joining together the various families of the radical right: monarchists, Pétainistes, poujadistes, fundamentalists, Catholic traditionalists, and those nostalgic for French Algeria.[84] Did the resurgence of these currents indicate the return of the OAS and the celebration of its memory? Although the FN cannot be identified with those nostalgic for French Algeria, much less with the pieds-noirs,[85] former members of the OAS joined the movement and sat in the National Assembly between 1986 and 1988. Between the OAS and the FN, there is indeed kinship, even "osmosis."[86] Thus, "it is the only major party in which these characteristics [of being a repatriate or former activist or partisan of French Algeria] are more of an honor than a handicap."[87] This claim finds support in two considerations. First, there is the fact that leaders of the clandestine organization joined forces with Jean-Marie Le

Pen. This was the case of Pierre Sergent, who joined the FN in 1985. Later, Jean-Jacques Susini ran as FN candidate in Marseille in the 1997 legislative elections and, despite being defeated in the second round of voting, became a Provence-Côte d'Azur (PACA) regional councillor one year later. Moreover, Jean-Marie Le Pen was unfailingly solicitous toward those nostalgic for French Algeria.

Former OAS men and the far right shared the same vision of the colonial Empire, an aversion for de Gaulle and a rejection of the figure of the immigrant as incarnated by the Algerian. The belief that France had brought its civilization to a subject people had led these men to favor keeping Algeria under the authority of the French Republic. This turned into a "memory of revenge" against Maghrebin immigrants. Having thrown off the dominion of France, today's Algerians had lost any right to settle there. They were accused of invading the country, of not respecting its laws and mores. "Those whom one had imagined as 'peacefully dominated' at the time of the colonial system were transformed in the imaginary into newly triumphant victors, into 'colonizers.'"[88] In this, colonial racism found its continuation.

The success enjoyed by the FN in the 1980s was, among other things, due to its opposition to non-European immigration. By once again raising the issue of the integration of a Muslim population, this theme revived the memory of the Algerian War.[89] Nevertheless, according to Olivier Dard, the partisans of French Algeria were part of the FN's clientele, with younger cohorts largely indifferent to the theme of French Algeria.[90]

The Skill of the Vanquished

The veterans of the OAS and partisans of French Algeria lost their war: Algeria became independent, its leaders and some of its members were convicted by French courts, and French society overwhelmingly endorsed the notion that decolonization was the inevitable direction of history. Nevertheless, their defeat was not total, in particular because their vision of the world allowed them to find allies within the political class. What's more, the members of the OAS are particularly active militants and have proven highly effective in maintaining and expanding their networks.

The representation of Algeria as sick or devastated—proof of the failure of Arab and Muslim nationalists—supplied a posteriori justification for keeping the overseas départements within the Republic. The failures of independent Algeria and its plunge into civil war rendered French public opinion more receptive to the discourse of those nostalgic for French Algeria. Several political parties showed themselves receptive to this vision of history. The skill of the vanquished was revealed with the breakthrough passage of the 23 February 2005 law.

With this law, the Gaullist right showed some sympathy for OAS veterans. Breaking with a tradition of strict fidelity to General de Gaulle, the right revived a form of nationalism formerly defended by the OAS. As Romain Bertrand argues, this process of convergence is explained above all by reference to the evolution of the right itself. French Algerian nostalgia was mainly to be encountered among young deputies of the postwar generation who had recently entered politics and were located on the fringes of the Union pour un Movement Populaire (UMP) rather than in proximity to its centers of power.[91]

The political class, the left included, responded only timidly to this offensive on the part of a segment of UMP deputies, who had allied for the occasion with OAS networks. Quite apart from the changed perception of Algeria, the French left had not examined its conscience regarding the colonial system that had been championed by the Republic for nearly a century. As long as "the Republic's assent to the doctrine of inferior races"[92] was not recognized, the left will be poorly equipped to argue with the partisans of colonial France. Having long stigmatized "the fascists of the OAS" and the entire pied-noir population, a portion of its ranks today reacts only half-heartedly to assertions of the "positive aspects" of colonialism.

Yann Scioldo-Zürcher emphasizes the manner in which a colonialist ethos has permeated parliamentary discourse. He argues that "the vision of Franco-Algerian relations specific to the French of Algeria was not merely replanted in the metropole; it also spread to the point of becoming an official history of France." He thus observes that, since the mid-1980s, a number of senators and deputies have evoked France's "civilizing mission" without hesitation and without meeting resistance. The 23 February 2005 law, in his view, is merely the outcome of this consensus.[93]

Although they agreed on the principle of paying damages to the former inhabitants of Algeria, the various political formations allowed themselves to be dragged into political one-upmanship and rallied around the idea of the need for moral reparations. On both left and right, the deputies did not shy away from paying homage to France's "colonial enterprise." The sponsor of the 1987 law, RPR Deputy Claude Barate (Pyrénées-Orientales), thus remarked: "It is essential to show that this civilizing action did not infringe upon human rights, that on the contrary it constantly sought to expand them. Our repatriated brothers have reason to be proud of the work they accomplished in their country of origin and they can be proud today at seeing the entire French nation recognize its full value. Once again, Mr. Secretary of State, apart from the question of compensation, what matters is that you provide them the moral unction they need."[94] Kléber Mesquida, a Socialist deputy from Hérault who is himself a repatriate, did not hesitate to refer to France's "civilizing mission."[95] Scioldo-Zürcher notes that the debates that took place in the National Assembly preceding the law's passage on 23 February 2005 reflect a consensus on the issue of colonial memory; the Communist Party alone departed from this consensus, though it remained discreet and measured in its opposition. Today, the political, moral, and media defeat of the OAS seems much less absolute.

An allergy to "repentance" has in recent years assisted in spreading the ideas of the partisans of French Algeria. Divisions were deepened by the sudden emergence of the Indigènes de la République (Natives of the Republic), a group that argues that discrimination against the descendants of immigrants is the result of a reproduction of the colonial system.[96] Alarmed by this radical critique of France, the Republic's defenders on both right and left have adopted a defensive position. They oppose—indeed, dread—challenges to the republican model and have come out against a policy of "repentance," even if that sometimes means defending the colonial empire. Much like the polarization witnessed in France during the Algerian War, the debate once again became simplified, as if there were only two possible positions one might take: either one defended the colonial project or "repented" for the crimes committed by the colonial Republic. In an effort to calm tensions following the adoption of the 23 February 2005 law, Jacques Chirac stated that "official history does not exist in the Republic" and that it was "a matter for historians." In response, Nicolas Sarkozy published an editorial in the *Journal du Dimanche* to denounce "repentance." "Will we someday soon end up apologizing for being French?" he asked. "Our society is threatened by a baleful tendency for self-repudiation."[97] The same argument was employed by the deputies who refused to repeal the law,[98] as if refusing to pay homage to colonization was equivalent to admitting one's guilt.

The 23 February 2005 law produced additional confusion, further reducing the prospects for a calm and critical debate regarding the issue of colonialism. By juxtaposing an article concerning the indemnities to be paid to members of the OAS to assertions of "the work carried out by France in the former départements of Algeria" and "the positive role played by the French presence," the legislature further deepened a widespread tendency to confuse the action of a group of a few hundred people fighting to keep Algeria French with the colonial enterprise and the entire pied-noir population. This was hardly a favor to the pieds-noirs, many of whom suffer from their reputation as the allies of a terrorist organization that plagued Algeria and metropolitan France. Many hold that they were (or still are) scapegoats for a vilified colonial system. Others recall the poor welcome they received after crossing the Mediterranean, and to this day complain of being the object of unjust caricatures and prejudices on the part of their compatriots. Some, finally, deplore the fact that their contribution to the battles of the Second World War—and, in particular, the Allied invasion of southern France—have been forgotten. That said, many pieds-noirs would doubtless prefer to no longer be associated with the theories of the OAS or the ranks of its supporters.

After a period of dissimulation, embarrassment, and silence stemming from, among other things, a desire to shake off the colonial past, the 23 February 2005 law might be interpreted as grudging admission of the colonial Republic.

*   *   *

The three cases studied in Chapters 1–3 are exemplary of a type of postconflict scenario and its attendant consequences (see Table 1). The war that opposed the FLN and the French army ended in the Evian Accords, which "eliminated the conflict": an independent Algerian state was created that gave material form to a process of territorial secession, and the enemies were separated. The end of the apartheid regime, the establishment of a democratic regime, and the creation of the TRC constituted an attempt to "resolve the conflict" in South Africa. South Africa's rulers pursued a political project that sought to build a new nation on the basis of the principle of political representation—whites and blacks alike were invited to embody this new "rainbow" community.[99] The manner in which conflicts are resolved partly determines the subsequent relations between former enemies. "Peaceful coexistence" and "separation" have become the two terms that define the relationship between ex-combatants.[100]

Moreover, the nature of the political regime influences the nature of future relations with the enemy. In a democratic regime, politics endeavors to simultaneously address conflict and construct consensus. In South Africa, the former enemy is accepted as part of the political community; his defeat does

Table 1. Political order and perception of the ex-enemy

Country	Resolution of Conflict	Type of Regime	Relationship with Ex-Enemy
South Africa	Peaceful coexistence	Democracy	Appeasement
Algeria	Exclusion	Authoritarian regime	Mobilization
France	Disappearance	Democracy	Forgetting, displacement

not disqualify him as a citizen. The former beneficiaries of apartheid are called upon to participate in society's transformation, but most are under no real obligation to do so. In France, the FLN and the population it represented disappeared from the political landscape; the Algerian War was for a time expelled from the collective imaginary. After several decades, the war's return to the center of French debate shows that the terms of the confrontation had shifted to the interior of the French political community. Democracy allows only partial and imperfect consideration of the Republic's colonial past. In Algeria, the rulers' seizure of power is based on their anticolonial and "revolutionary legitimacy"; the threat supposedly still posed by the enemy justifies authoritarian practices. To this day, competition among rival groups for control of the state continues to draw upon the rhetoric of the War of Independence. The figure of the colonial enemy is not the driving force of the authoritarian regime; he is its alibi.

Postconflict political configurations are not static. In particular, the forms taken by the postconflict order are fueled by confrontation with the outside world: the models put forward by the international community play a decisive role, as do interactions with the former enemy. In France, controversies surrounding the Algerian War, the question of responsibility for violence, and the issue of "legitimate victims" once again came to the fore several decades after the Evian Accords were signed. The path taken by independent Algeria and the civil war that tore it asunder in the 1990s supplied new inputs, reinforcing or undermining discourse concerning the War of Independence. Requests for pardon or acts of repentance on the part of the pope and heads of state[101] kindled or stimulated other calls for recognition. These events transformed the ways in which memory and political history were approached and constituted a new language that other actors seized hold of. In Algeria, the signals given by France, in particular with Article 4 of the 23 February 2005 law, provoked nationalist escalation and calls for the former colonizer to recognize its crimes. In South Africa, the election of President Jacob Zuma, the former leader of the armed wing of the ANC who is reputed to have ties to the destitute and veterans, will perhaps modify the contours of the conflict's narrative.

These two postconflict configurations make clear that time does not necessarily heal all wounds. The place of veterans—the material and symbolic rewards they receive—sheds light on the meaning each society assigns wars past.

PART II

Ex-Combatants and the Nation

"THEY HAVE RIGHTS over us," said Georges Clémenceau of the combatants of the First World War.[1] "In the immediate post-war years," writes Bruno Cabanes, "French political authorities presented the entire nation as indebted to those who had defended it" and even children were not "spared [this] moralizing and guilt-inducing discourse."[2] As Antoine Prost has explained, French veterans positioned themselves in the interwar years as publicly spirited "keepers of truth and goodness," at once morally superior and motivated by a desire to serve the common good.[3]

The economy of recognition[4] was not limited to the symbolic sphere. The manner in which categories of legitimate beneficiaries were defined meant that it also affected redistributive policies. The criteria selected by the governments of the postconflict order determined the available, legitimate vocabulary within the political space, a resource to which individuals and groups appealed in (re)constructing their narratives in keeping with their objectives. Yet their approach cannot be reduced to this instrumental dimension; it also involved the advancement of sincere arguments that contributed to the development of categories of fairness within society.

By giving impetus to new figures of political legitimacy, the postconflict social and political order modifies opportunities for socioeconomic advancement. Whether one refused to participate in a conflict or had been a soldier, militia member, underground combatant, or "victim" can determine one's eligibility for symbolic and material resources. It can also regulate access to political power and positions within government or, on the contrary, constitute a more or less permanent handicap. The ex-combatants' individual trajectories and success in professionally reinventing themselves are evidence of their ability—or lack thereof—to seize upon a conflict's end to improve or maintain their position within society.

In what follows, I shall examine the reconfiguration of the symbolic and political order through the figure of the veteran.[5] The veteran's place in society—the role he claims or relinquishes—sheds light on a series of individual trajectories and the type of society that emerges from postconflict reconstruction. So, too, does the manner in which the veteran recounts or silently refuses to speak of his past as well as the prestige and rents he may hope to derive from his status.

*   *   *

In South Africa, the conflict that pitted the apartheid regime against the national liberation movements may be considered a civil war. Since it was linked to a project of reconciliation, the negotiated end to this conflict ruled out paying any too pronounced tribute to the victors. While the security forces that served under apartheid benefited from an open-hand policy, the combatants of the African National Congress (ANC) thus only sparingly profited from an economy of recognition (Chapter 4).

In Algeria, the legitimacy of the one-party regime is based on the permanent tribute paid the mujahideen and a condemnation of colonialism and all that smacks of it. The country's petroleum and gas rent sustains the political rent of the war of liberation and allows its heroic veterans to be rewarded. Yet the country's authoritarian regime has ultimately been caught in a trap of its own making, with veterans and other members of the "revolutionary family" engaging in a game of symbolic and financial escalation (Chapter 5).

In France, the combatants of the Secret Army Organization (OAS) find themselves in an awkward position vis-à-vis the state and the nation to which they belong. Initially prosecuted for their membership in a secret and violent organization, they were gradually amnestied and rehabilitated. Their trajectories demonstrate their skill at bouncing back, and their continued activism shows that the arguments advanced by them have (once again) found a place in contemporary France (Chapter 6).

Chapter 4

South African Ex-Combatants: The Constraints of Reconciliation and the Law of the Market

The fate of South Africa's ex-combatants touches many different sectors of society. Each of the country's liberation movements possessed an armed wing—Umkhonto we Sizwe (MK) in the case of the African National Congress (ANC) and the Azanian People's Liberation Army (APLA) in that of the Pan-African Congress (PAC). At the conflict's end, the members of these groups returned from exile or came out of hiding, presenting a large population in need of demobilization and professional and social reintegration.[1] Following the election of the country's first democratic government, meanwhile, many South African Defense Force (SADF) soldiers and Security Branch police officers left their jobs.

Two issues are involved in the reintegration of ex-combatants. The first is material in nature and concerns the ability of individuals to reinvent themselves in new careers. The second is symbolic: it concerns the veterans' willingness to accept the political order and hinges on their ability to become simple citizens content to live in peace under the new regime. These symbolic and material vectors of reintegration to some degree depend on the manner in which ex-combatants are perceived by their society. Although the MK are to be counted among the conflict's winners, the country's new leaders paid them no more than half-hearted tribute. They were granted only limited material rewards in keeping with restrictive criteria. Their integration within the new South Africa was a partial failure: a minority joined the small circle of the economic and political elites; somewhat less than half of them entered the ranks of the new army; the remainder often found themselves in situations of poverty and exclusion. Although the former guerrilla fighters have retained a strong political identity, their capacity for mobilization has been hampered by the fragmentation of their respective groups.

The apartheid-era civil servants who requested amnesty mainly consisted of former Security Branch police officers, a group stigmatized for its heavy involvement in repression. Nearly all of them quit their jobs and attempted to join the private sector. The military, by contrast, was spared: by limiting investigators' access to its archives, it succeeded in protecting its interests.[2] As a result, former South African soldiers were in a better position to protect their reputations, and some decided to continue their army careers after 1994. Their skills and connections made it easier for many former police officers and soldiers to get back on their feet in the labor market. Those who participated in negotiations and created ties with ANC leaders were particularly well-positioned from this point of view.

While some of these former enemies found a place for themselves within the new national army and thereby partook of the process of institutional and social transformation, others profited from their participation in the conflict to integrate themselves in very diverse ways within the new South Africa.

A Single Army for Enemy Ex-Combatants

As they prepared to take power, the leaders of the ANC sought to neutralize the army, fearing that certain generals would attempt to sabotage the democratization process. In April 1993, negotiations got under way between leaders of the SADF and MK to create a new armed force, the South African National Defense Force (SANDF). The country's new leaders sought to break with the preceding era, during which military leaders had interfered in the political decision-making process and South African society had undergone a dynamic of militarization.[3] They sought to put relations between soldier and civilian on a new footing and render the institution transparent—necessary conditions for the regime's democratic operation. To that end, they established a new code of conduct that made the soldier responsible for respecting the rights and dignity of individuals and obliged him to refuse orders involving illegal acts.[4] The ANC also wished to part ways with the apartheid era's aggressive foreign policy, under which the SADF and Special Forces had played a destabilizing role in southern Africa. By defining a defensive doctrine for its army and assigning it peacekeeping operations on the continent, the ANC sought to carve out a new role for the country in Africa.

The Creation of an Integrated New Army

The objective was also to establish a new armed force that represented the new nation while remaining modern and effective. The aim, in other words, was to maintain the high professional caliber of the 85,000-member SADF while adding 10,000 soldiers from the armed forces of the four Bantustans[5] and the former guerrilla fighters of the liberation movements (20,000 MK and 6,000 APLA),[6] whose skills generally fell short of military standards. Despite these disparities in point of professionalism, the country's military and political leaders believed that the integration of nonconventional forces would lead to the development of more creative strategic and tactical doctrine, introduce new styles of leadership, and assure the new institution's legitimacy. The country's new rulers also believed that the military's diversity could contribute to reconciliation and to creating a nation of citizens.[7] And the insertion of former enemies within the army did indeed constitute a significant concrete and symbolic illustration of the process by which national unity was to be constructed. The difficulties associated with the SANDF's creation and its internal transformations illustrate the conflicts and evolution of the new South Africa. In this sense, the army was a microcosm in which interracial and political tensions played out in a way that paralleled those affecting the larger society.

The process by which members of the nonconventional armed forces (MK and APLA) were selected excluded candidates who were too old or whose health or skill level disqualified them. Those meeting the eligibility criteria were assigned a rank by a commission consisting of SADF leaders, the heads of liberation movements, and British observers:[8] only 14,791 MK were ultimately given a place,[9] or merely half the total number of combatants demanded by the ANC.

In order to reconcile the need to uphold modern military standards and promote the former combatants of the liberation movements, the latter were given training to help them attain the requisite level. SADF instructors furnished them with a number of skills and instilled in them the characteristic attitudes and norms of a conventional army. The integration process was in keeping with the modern and institutional mold of the former army—the SADF—whose members continued to occupy a majority position. Former guerrilla fighters thus sometimes felt as if they were being absorbed into the army that had served apartheid rather than embodying a new structure.[10]

SADF veterans, meanwhile, maintained that standards were being sacrificed and the SANDF's combat readiness undermined.

More than 20,000 individuals thus resigned voluntarily or were ejected because of their inability to adapt. In any case, the government sought to reduce the number of soldiers and rejuvenate the ranks in order to increase combat effectiveness. Like South African society more generally, the army was affected by the HIV epidemic. Though no official figure exists for the SANDF, it is estimated that between 40 and 90 percent of soldiers had contracted the virus.[11]

Despite the difficulties engendered by ongoing transformations, the country's new leaders succeeded in remodeling the army. It was to prove loyal to the democratic government and came to be regarded by a majority of the population as a legitimate institution.[12]

The MK in the Army: (In)Patience and Frustration

In the space of a few years, positions within the high command had been filled with the MK and APLA leaders who had been promoted to the rank of general. The highest-ranking officers followed a series of training courses, allowing them to rapidly rise through the ranks of the military hierarchy. By 2000, all of the highest-ranking generals were thus black, as were 62.5 percent of all army corps generals. At this level, no racial problems arose. As high-ranking officers, they frequently commanded white SADF veterans—a collaboration facilitated by their complementary profiles. For their former enemies, these black commanders supplied much needed political and institutional legitimacy as well as distinctive military experience and, in some cases, negotiation experience.

Among the mass of ex-combatants, by contrast, the obligatory reviews of their intellectual and military skills were a source of significant frustration. Those not accepted challenged the selection criteria and felt they had been victims of injustice. Many found the endless waiting, lost files, bureaucratic delays, and their first contacts with SADF members to be exasperating. After several months without pay and weary of being confined to the Wallmansthal military post, 2,500 combatants—265 of whom never returned—left their barracks in a show of discontent in September 1994. In 1995, MK protests also took place in Durban and Cape Town. There was also much dissatisfaction among those who joined the new army. The question of rank particularly rankled with them. Each case was reviewed by a commission that consisted of SADF members and MK and APLA leaders, with assistance from British soldiers. For members of the nonconventional forces, the outcome of this process was nearly always to their disadvantage. Their status, salaries, and working conditions were all sources of misunderstanding and frustration among the new recruits.

When they discovered that they would have to obey orders from their former enemies and give up their wartime rituals—in particular, the chants that accompanied physical training—the MK who joined the subaltern ranks of the SANDF were shocked, even indignant. What's more, these former combatants had been socialized in a radically different manner, a fact that had left its mark on their habits and points of reference and clashed with the sense of hierarchy and respect for rules characteristic of a conventional army. Former SADF members in positions of command likely sought to discourage guerrilla war veterans from pursuing a career in the army.[13]

As Thami, a former MK living in Soweto, remarked, "It wasn't integration. I noticed that they told us: 'Now you MK are in a conventional army and can't shout these slogans anymore.' But we were the only ones who had to give up our habits. We had been absorbed. The structure of the SADF is still intact. In the training camps, the Boer calls you a kaffir. I decided not to go. I'll never wear that uniform."[14]

Between 1994 and 2000, the military careers of 3,216 former MK admitted into the ranks of the SANDF—or somewhat less than a third of the total—thus came to an end, either because they had given up or because they had been brought before a court-martial and expelled.[15] Former MK who mention their period in the SANDF express strong feelings of injustice regarding how they were treated and resentment toward a racist institution in which it was impossible for them to fit in. For many, the strict discipline of the army presented a particular stumbling block.

Gregory explained that he had been expelled from the army for having been "absent without leave."[16] "I was absent without leave but I was burying my father. These people were so white, they couldn't understand my situation."

It was among the subaltern ranks that interracial relations proved the most strained.[17] In September 1999, a black soldier fired on five of his white colleagues before killing himself. In the aftermath of this event, an investigative commission was created to study the transformation process within the SANDF. It concluded that the armed forces were being undermined by racism and demoralization among the soldiers. Black troops were subjected to harassment and attempts at intimidation on the part of their white superiors. A number of white commanders resorted to abusive language and attempted to curtail the professional duties of black members. The SANDF reacted to the report by stating that the army is merely a reflection of society and the state of relations within it. It underscored its success in integrating seven hostile forces within a unified military organization and declared that it would be naive to believe that such an undertaking could take place without incident.

For an entire category of former guerrilla fighters supplying the intermediary ranks of the SANDF, the prospect of career advancement, boosted by affirmative action policies, was a source of both hope and impatience. At the time of their integration, many of them felt they had been swindled in the assignment of rank. Integrated in 1997, Ronald had hoped to be given the rank of major but instead found himself assigned the rank of sergeant.[18] Despite an extremely difficult start, during which he was faced with the bad faith of the administration and his superiors' racism, Ronald chose to stay in the army, hoping for advancement and better working conditions. He was promoted several ranks and in 2003 became a lieutenant in the military police, where he received training in the areas of management and administration. Over a period of ten years, he observed considerable improvement in relations between the former enemy forces and between whites and blacks. He believes that the SADF veterans who remain in the army accept the new political order and have proven cooperative and eager to share their knowhow. Ronald also thinks that the South African Army's future resides in the arrival of a new generation. Indian, Asian, white, and black twenty-year-olds did not participate in the conflict and were less often burdened by political affiliation. Despite their difficulties and frustrations, former national liberation movement activists claim to be optimistic in regard to their future and the prospects for improvement within the SANDF.[19]

Resistance and Transformation Among the Former Soldiers of Apartheid

The most conservative members of the SADF generally left the institution at the start of or during the integration process. The arrival of recruits from the liberation movements created a cultural shock that some made no effort to overcome. Between 1994 and 2003, half of all SADF veterans left the army.[20] For some of these soldiers, the implementation of affirmative action undermined the institution and threatened to compromise its operation. ANC and PAC activists were seen as lacking experience of conventional warfare and as being recalcitrant to military discipline. Moreover, a number of whites found it unacceptable that black MKs were so rapidly promoted to the institution's highest-ranking positions. Having lost their dominant position and been forced to submit themselves to the authority of an enemy long seen as inferior, many members of the SADF chose to seek employment elsewhere.

Moreover, former beneficiaries of apartheid saw their careers blocked or slowed in order to make the institution more representative. Today, white soldiers know that they have almost no chance of ever achieving the rank of general.

What's more, the highest-ranking SADF officers had very enticing professional opportunities in the private sector and made careers for themselves in the security or military industries. The contacts they established during the period of negotiations guaranteed that they would have privileged access to the business world. By contrast, SADF veterans holding intermediary or subaltern ranks could not count on the same resources in starting a career in the private sector.

Hein is a captain in the navy.[21] He has mastered the politically correct language befitting a white soldier and South African. He specifies that he took the initiative of hanging a photo of the head of state, Thabo Mbeki, in his office, and that he was present for Nelson Mandela's inauguration as president. Witnesses are available to confirm the truth of these remarks, he notes. As further proof of his goodwill, Captain Hein tells of how he was in 1998 awarded the Military Merit Medal for his service on the navy's integration committee. While he alludes to cultural differences, he underscores the issue of skill level. The navy's demanding standards and the newcomers' difficulty in conforming to them allowed some former guerrilla fighters to be held back. While simultaneously asserting his loyalty to the new army and the new South Africa, Captain Hein worries about his personal future: "Do I have any chance of being promoted admiral? I don't know. A lot is uncertain . . . I am very well-disposed towards the new South Africa. I support Mbeki and I know his job is difficult but I don't think there should be a witch hunt against whites. Keep an eye on those who oppose change, yes." The navy captain personifies a generation that seeks to adapt to political upheaval but is aware of the negative effects that affirmative action has had on their own careers. In order to avoid being penalized by the new system, he seeks to integrate himself as fully as possible into the institution and society.

Other SADF soldiers insist on the process of personal transformation that was initiated in the course of negotiations with leaders from the military wings of the ANC and PAC. Colonel Bernard recounts how his conscience was gradually awakened over the course of the first years of democracy—a process that was at once intellectual, moral, and emotional.[22] His encounters with former enemies contributed to this transformation. A colonel since he was thirty-nine, Bernard knows that affirmative action makes it unlikely that he will be further promoted but continues to defend the institution he serves: "Although we have soldiers who are too old, and 21 percent of individuals have AIDS, SANDF has 10,000 more men than SADF, and we are deployed in RDC and Burundi, and it's the same number of troops as when we were at war between 1976 and 1988. Our capacity is a little bit weaker. We have to rejuvenate our army." Colonel Bernard, whose son recently joined the SANDF, is thus fully confident in the military's future. The South African Army has nevertheless scaled back its numbers and external intervention objectives. Formerly at the forefront of efforts to defend the regime and the country's security, it is no longer the central and essential institution it once was and has in the process lost some of its prestige. Yet, by refusing to absorb several thousand ANC militants and subjecting them to the standards of a modern army, South Africa's new leaders resisted the temptation to use the army as a tool of social reconstruction or for the purposes of containing violence. Former MK who now belong to the SANDF can for their part anticipate continued career advancement thanks to the operation of affirmative action. Yet the continued sway exercised by white culture and management styles requires them to reconstruct their social identities. As an institution, the SANDF does not live off of the rents of the ANC's victory now that the latter holds power.

The nation's police force has also been subjected to reform in order to inculcate the principles of human rights and transform it into a public service institution for the entire population. Sunset clauses apply to the police, but affirmative action policies have been established to ensure representativeness. In 1994, 55 percent of police employees were nonwhite, but only 5 percent of its officers. By 2002, the proportion of white officers had diminished to 48 percent. Since former enemies were not called upon to cohabit the institution, the question of transforming the nation's police thus assumed a different form. While a small minority of former MK joined the police, public policy did not encourage them to do so. Moreover, the police were seen in very negative terms by those who had fought inside the country—a fact that discouraged them from joining the institution.

From Guerrilla Warfare to Civilian Life: Poor Wretches and Millionaires

The ANC's rise to power aggravated socioeconomic disparities among its members. Only a minority of them were able to achieve professional success in the administration or private sector. Together with useful connections in the ruling circles, higher education represented the principal conduit for socioeconomic advancement. Some grassroots ANC militants never succeeded in making a place for themselves in the new social, political, and economic order and have been condemned to lives of poverty and idleness.

Demobilization and Veteran Status

The ex-combatants of the national liberation movements who were not admitted into the new South African Army for reasons of health, age, or educational level were demobilized, as were those who refused to join it or did not accept the rank assigned them. One's status as a demobilized soldier entitled one to receive a onetime departure bonus calculated on the basis of the number of years one served within the organization. An ex-guerrilla fighter with four years' service thus received 12,734 rands, or 1,554 euros. One with seventeen years' service received 28,721 rands, or 3,504 euros. If the ex-combatant served in the armed branch for more than twenty-two years, he received the maximum possible bonus—40,657 rands, or 4,960 euros.[23] Various criticisms were leveled against the conditions relating to the status of demobilized veteran. Combatants returning from several years' exile were accustomed to having their needs entirely provided for by their respective organizations and could find it difficult to manage such sums, which were paid all at once.[24] No thought had been given to the question of their professional future. Disoriented and lacking experience, many veterans found themselves at the mercy of a very tight labor market. Little use was made of the professional training opportunities offered by the army's Service Corps, which did not operate as it should and ultimately trained few candidates.[25]

The ex-combatants complained of not receiving advice or psychological support upon their arrival in South Africa. In their view, many of those who had spent years in training camps were incapable of adapting to peacetime society or understanding the political and professional issues confronting them. Some felt they had been abandoned just as the ANC was on the point of winning.

A special pension was provided for ex-combatants of the liberation movements as well as their wives and orphans. This was accorded to individuals who had served their organization on a full-time basis in South Africa or abroad, had participated in military operations, or had been banished, detained, or imprisoned. Of the 40,000 requests that were received, only 16,000 were approved, either because certain documents were lacking—in particular, evidence of combat or imprisonment—or because the candidates did not correspond to the stated criteria in point of year of service or age. Those who had not reached thirty-five years of age by 1 December 1996 were ineligible. Militants who had joined the armed struggle at an early age and not received an education thus found themselves without resources. Conceived as a sort of retirement, the special pension was not intended for the youngest veterans, who the government hoped would enter the labor market.

The amount of the special pension varies according to the veteran's age and length of service. Some receive it on top of what they earn from work or their retirement income. For those between thirty-five and fifty years old, the annual pension amounts to 6000 rands, or 736 euros. Ill or handicapped individuals can receive more but must provide evidence that their disability was caused by participation in combat. For those over age fifty, it varies between 12,000 and 84,000 rands per year, or between 1,464 and 10,248 euros, depending on their length of service.

Gordan, the Marxist Banker

The veterans who had had the possibility of following a university-level program of study in South Africa or abroad[26] were very rapidly absorbed by the new administration as it sought to fill staff positions. When negotiators began to realize they would soon be obliged to run the country, some were sent to Western universities in the early 1990s to deepen their knowledge. Black empowerment policies ensured them a career in the public sector. After a few years serving the new government, members of the ANC and its armed wing often quit their jobs to go into business.[27] Indeed, with the country experiencing rapid growth, the many prospects for enriching oneself seduced a portion of these former Marxists.

Gordan comes from an Indian family in Durban.[28] His father sold vegetables at the market, and he grew up in a neighborhood where he learned to fight and use a knife. He joined the ANC at the age of seventeen, received several months' military training, and joined an underground cell based in Durban. At the same time, he successfully pursued his studies. Gordan and the members of his group claim to have successfully infiltrated and spied on the Security Branch. Now forty years old, Gordan presents himself as a radical. A member of the Communist Party, he was opposed to the negotiations between the ANC and the National Party (NP) in the early 1990s and hoped that the leaders of the apartheid system would be judged by a Nuremberg-type tribunal. Today the former activist is a banker living in Johannesburg. He is unmarried and spends his time in the company of the new gilded youth who frequent the bars of Melville.[29]

In 1994, Gordan was integrated into the army as a brigadier general but instead opted for demobilization, since he did not feel like he was truly a solider. He joined a ministry as general director. In 1999, he left to study in England and returned to work in the banking sector. His social rise was meteoric. He had a large house with a swimming pool constructed for himself on the heights of Melville. Inside the residence, a two-way mirror allows one to observe the legs of the women who swim there.

Having sacrificed several years in the service of the nation and comported himself as a devoted and disciplined member of his organization, Gordan believes that the time has come to look after his own interests. This is what he means when he claims that his refusal to pursue a career in the army represented his first personal decision in more than a decade. He continued to assert his individuality when he entered the private sector. "I am still a member of the ANC," he says, "a critical member rather than militarily disciplined, but I live my life." Gordan still defines himself as a Marxist and oscillates between humor and rationalization in explaining the compatibility of his convictions and professional choices. He acknowledges that he has greatly benefited from the liberal economy and supports the notion that, once macro equilibria have been achieved, the country will be able to set about dealing with poverty. Gordan is one of the new South Africa's winners.

Thami, from Township to Township:
The Unfinished Liberation

Many ex-combatants found themselves relatively destitute in the new South Africa. For those who returned from exile or came out of hiding, the experience of returning to civilian life, reuniting with one's family, and accepting the new political pact presented difficulties.

Thami was born in Soweto, where he was raised by his grandmother. His first political socialization consisted of violent police raids targeting his grandfather, a member of the ANC. As an adolescent, Thami became aware of the arguments of the Black Conscience Movement and participated in violent actions against the township's black police officers, who were seen as traitors. A little later, he was recruited by the ANC and learned that whites were not necessarily his enemies. He soon joined the MK fighting structure, where he was placed under the command of Vincent, an older man trained in exile who secretly returned to South Africa to set up active cells in the country. This friend and leader was subsequently assassinated by a renegade ANC militia, which then turned its sights on Thami, who fled to Angola to escape them. There, he was assigned to intelligence operations and made responsible for unmasking infiltrators. Upon returning to South Africa, he was shocked by the operation of the new army and opted for demobilization. Although he became a father three times over, Thami was unable to remain with one woman. Today, he is emotionally unstable: lacking a regular source of income, he is troubled by the losses he has suffered and the violence he has inflicted.

A survey of 340 ex-MK conducted by the Center for Conflict Resolution found that 66 percent were unemployed—a figure roughly twice the national rate of unemployment.[30] Those who did not join the army and lack a diploma or connections are without particular assets in the labor market. Some are employed as security guards by private companies. For several months, this was Thami's case. His experience with one of these companies illustrates the manner in which harsh social relations can alter one's self-perception. Thami recounts that he outperformed the company's other employees in firearm exercises. His skill made him an object of suspicion and gossip on the part of his coworkers. "They said I was a killer," he complains. Initially active in the Johannesburg region before joining the organization in exile, this former MK thus takes no pride in his military skills. Unable to bear this perceived stigmatization, he quit his job. Forty percent of MKs believe that the labor market discriminates against them, and the least educated are the most vulnerable.[31] Thami maintains that the private sector is hostile toward them, claiming: "If we show up, they tell us to go 'talk to Mandela about it!'"

Many of those I interviewed felt rejected or mocked by their social set and believed their military past had put them at a disadvantage with employers. In a society governed by economic liberalism and marked by fierce competition between individuals for access to resources, the MK's bravery and skill were things of the past and of no social utility. Indeed, to the degree that such qualities are ill suited to the market, they are almost a handicap. The MK's disappointment and bitterness is all the greater given that they see political and economic liberation as going hand in hand. Without diplomas or professional experience and lacking a social safety net, some find that their situation has hardly improved since joining their respective organizations and may even have worsened.

Thami began a government-sponsored horticultural training program. Like many South African city-dwellers, he has fantasies about "returning" to rural life. The program was an opportunity to leave the violent life of Soweto behind and make a new start in a place where no one knew him. But Thami was unable to complete his training program and remained in Soweto, where he now lives with one of his sons. He tries to be a good father, sending his son to school properly dressed, with covers on his books and freshly shined shoes. His other son visits him from time to time. He hardly ever sees his oldest daughter, by contrast, and has the impression he has nothing to offer her.

The economic difficulties affecting these former guerrilla fighters disrupt their personal relationships. According to a number of them, their families were disappointed upon their return from exile, having expected that they would have become wealthy and well connected in the interim. Instead, they were penniless and a burden on their parents; once the demobilization bonus had been exhausted, their relations with their families sometimes significantly deteriorated.[32] Family pressure and disappointment fueled the activists' feelings of personal failure. In urban environments like that of the townships of the Johannesburg region, family and social networks had shattered. The apartheid-era policy of exploiting the black labor force by isolating men from their familial, social, and geographical roots and confining them to special peri-urban residential zones left deep scars. The social and familial fabric had been shattered by the dislocation of traditional ties of authority and lineage, and by brutal police repression and humiliating policies aiming to instill black inferiority. Single-parent families are commonplace, violence is an omnipresent fact of life in households and neighborhoods, and the uncontrolled spread of HIV further worsens living conditions and social relations.

The ANC militants whom I encountered expressed themselves as if the vertical and horizontal ties linking them to this party had disappeared. When mentioning ANC members who had succeeded, Thami condemned the disdain and indifference they had shown him: "There is conflict between the comrades because those who have a job do nothing to help us, to raise us up. They prefer to run us down. When you see them, you have to ask them for five or ten rands. They will never say to us: 'There's a job, you can come and work.' They'll take someone else, not you, their comrade." The impression that one has been hoaxed by one's own people reinforces this bitterness. Impoverished ex-MK today see themselves as losers twice over: losers for their suffering during the struggle and losers because abandoned by those in their camp who have done well for themselves.

At this stage, veterans associations appear insufficiently developed to support their members or effectively exercise pressure on the government. For MK veterans, conflicts among individuals and interests have weakened the organization's authority.[33] While the association partly covers the funeral costs when comrades die, a number of MK in the townships claim that the association is of little use to them and mainly operates on the basis of mutual acquaintance networks.

The country's black citizens have adopted new models of moral and/or social success that hinge on creativity, business acumen, and skill in manipulating networks. Incapable of understanding these changing values, some sink into alcoholism or madness. Yet upheaval in the nation's dominant values is a source of tension rather than rupture. Thami wishes to become part of the new South Africa. However, faced with his own weakness, psychological instability, and failure to complete his studies, he is once again tempted to turn to violence.

Indeed, Thami was sentenced to two years in prison for having taken part in criminal activities. The police confiscated a weapon from him, but he still keeps a revolver at home. According to the South African media, a number of MK have put their skills to work to attack armored cars. Together with their desire to exact social revenge and even avenge themselves against the leaders who abandoned them, the idleness of some veterans offers favorable soil for the development of criminal careers. Theft and violence allow these former activists to force their way into the society of consumption and destroy the tranquility of those who incarnate the new South Africa, seizing their wealth and threatening their lives. It is nevertheless difficult to determine how many have chosen this path, particularly as veterans sometimes serve as scapegoats. This widespread social fantasy must be taken into account. In the eyes of a segment of the population, the "criminal" has replaced the "terrorist" in stereotyped representations of the dangerous black man.

Still unemployed, in 2005 Thami said that he intended to form a group and name it Hamas. The reference to the Palestinian Islamist group was intended to make an impression and show that the comrades were prepared to do whatever necessary to obtain justice. As elsewhere, Thami's entourage has little prospect of becoming a protest actor. When he can, Thami works as a laborer on construction sites. Individualism and violence have become rife among underprivileged segments of the population, where all are tempted to count solely on themselves in dealing with harsh living conditions.

Apartheid Soldiers and Police: Room for the Vanquished

Many security force members quit their institutions once the democratic regime was established. They were eligible for severance pay calculated on the basis of their rank and length of service. No official data is available regarding the size of these payouts—the security force members I met were very often reluctant to talk about money—but they were considerably higher than those granted to the militants of the national liberation movement. The highest-ranking security force veterans were able to buy beautiful villas on the coast[34]—a police officer who reached the rank of captain, for example, received 400,000 rands after twenty-five years of service. To ward off any thought of protest or revenge, the leaders of the ANC decided to show generosity in their dealings with these former enemies.

Almost all members of the Security Branch, which specialized in political repression during the apartheid era, left its service in the months or years following the first democratic elections. Police officers and soldiers went into the security sector or became analysts with expertise in African politics and strategy. Seen as less effective than soldiers, police officers sometimes had more difficulty entering new fields of employment.

While some express anger and bitterness vis-à-vis the country's political transformations, few explicitly criticize the dismantling of apartheid, or the new black political elites. Even if they have strong reservations regarding the new South Africa, they strive to show that they are not racist, and rely heavily upon politically correct language.

Enthusiastic Oscar, Depressed Adrian: The New Democrats

Born into an Afrikaner family in 1950, Oscar grew up in the Eastern Cape.[35] His narrative resembles that of many of his colleagues. His family was poor and lived by working the land. With ties to the Dutch Reformed Church, it was heavily involved in Christianity but not especially politicized. As a child on the farm, he had African friends and even spoke their language somewhat— though he has now forgotten it—and he naively asserts that there was no difference between himself and his African friends. "We grew up together, we respected one another. And money did not enter into these relations. Each of us had their own house. Their homes were as clean as ours and sometimes their food was better because they had their own things and their own way of cooking."

Oscar claims to have rather casually joined the Security Branch. Like others, he was attracted by the prospect of having his studies financed by his employers, the police. "And I was young at the time," he notes, apparently by way of justification. At age twenty, he was offered a position in a department specializing in political repression. In the 1980s, he was promoted to the rank of brigadier and became head of intelligence for the Johannesburg region.[36] At the time, he was convinced he was fighting the forces of international communism that threatened his country. In a context marked by war and danger, Oscar saw himself as a soldier. In his view, the nonconventional nature of the conflict required that one use "all possible means" to combat the adversary. Without offering further explanation, he thus seems to justify the Security Branch's use of illegal methods to combat members of the ANC and PAC. Like all of his colleagues I interviewed, Oscar offered the following claim as a sort of certificate of innocence: "But I was never involved in politics or doctrine."

Starting in 1990, he became involved in the negotiation process with the ANC and participated in meetings with the ANC's political and military leadership. Oscar presents himself as liberal and pragmatic and claims to have supported Nelson Mandela's liberation:

"The South African economy was sinking. We were subjected to sanctions, and young people were emigrating because they saw no future in the country. Negotiating an agreement was in our interest because we couldn't pursue the conflict forever."

Oscar requested amnesty in two cases that concerned him, a move he presents as voluntary. When his daughter saw his name in the paper, she was shocked to learn that her father had devoted his life to repressing the movement of a man as "peaceful" as Mandela. In 1995, the new government nevertheless suggested that he remain with the police as head of the criminal division, but Oscar preferred to go into business. He tried his luck in mining concessions. Thanks to his travels over the two preceding decades, he possessed a network allowing him to operate throughout southern Africa. Oscar also became involved in the security sector at the national level, selling advice and equipment to companies. From his home in Johannesburg, he closely coordinated with companies owned by former MK.

Oscar claims to like the country's new rulers yet no longer votes. Like many other whites, he is able to maintain his lifestyle and standard of living and continues to occupy a high-profile economic role thanks to the orthodox liberal policy followed by the ANC government's Finance Ministry. He has thus abandoned any hope of taking an active role in the country's political affairs and has little interest in them. Like him, many Afrikaners who feel they were misled or betrayed by the NP see politics as an impure and repugnant domain.

The new political and social order does not necessarily require more than superficial displays of allegiance. To create a place for oneself in society, it is enough to master the new nonracial, democratic language while casting one's past behavior in an acceptable light. It is not necessary to fundamentally call oneself or one's group into question, recognize the legitimacy of one's former enemy, or acknowledge one's own involvement in an unjust system.

At fifty-six years old,[37] Adrian is Oscar's contemporary but strikes one as a tired, rather feeble, and entirely harmless old man. He organizes Afrikaner cooking competitions and sometimes gets behind the stove himself. He has also taken up painting and takes care of his little dogs. He is a quiet man and, in some ways, a budding artist. His remarks are sometimes surprisingly naive. Is this a tested tactic that allows him to evade the question of responsibility or a sign of a bewildered man's decline? Adrian is a retired police officer and has been married for many years, though he has no children. Every morning, he travels by car to a bar at the mall several kilometers from his home east of Pretoria. There, he meets some former colleagues, orders a few beers, and leaves what he believes is a generous tip for the waitresses he sees daily. For this Afrikaner without active employment, a dollar is a dollar, and he always expresses childlike joy when he succeeds in having others pay for his drinks. Adrian is glad to be interviewed, perhaps because he has so much time on his hands. It is also an occasion to once again feel he is a person of importance. For some Security Branch veterans, it has been quite a fall.

Adrian grew up in a small town in the country's interior and from his earliest years dreamed of becoming a detective. While performing his military service in 1968, he was sent to fight on the border with Rhodesia. The following year, he joined the police and began to work as a detective in Durban. In 1971, he was transferred to the Security Branch. Eleven years later, he carried out the same duties in Pretoria, but his department was now authorized to operate abroad. Adrian was subsequently appointed director of the African office and traveled extensively as a specialist in infiltration and espionage operations targeting the ANC.

Adrian passed himself off as a German businessman and in this way approached his prey. He sought to collect information and recruit members of the liberation movement as informers. With the help of blackmail, threats, and bribery, Adrian succeeded in turning eleven members of the ANC. He believes that four or five of them were unmasked and executed by their organization while working for him. Adrian regularly brought his wife on missions with him, where she served as a liaison agent. Starting in 1989, Adrian also participated in the psychological war unit that had been created to counter ANC and communist influence.

Adrian takes some pleasure in discussing this period of his life and his mastery of the tools of the trade. He accepted all of the missions assigned him, perhaps to avoid being "put on ice" but above all because he believed that "something had to be done for all these innocent people killed in shopping malls." In particular, he was part of the team that placed a bomb at ANC headquarters in London. On returning to South Africa, his team was amply praised by police leadership. While on mission with Eugene de Kock,[38] he once crossed paths with Joe Slovo, leader of the ANC's military wing. De Kock was of the opinion that they should liquidate him in the airport bathroom. In the absence of an order from his hierarchical superiors, however, Adrian preferred to pass up this opportunity and refused to take Slovo's life. Adrian sees himself as having loyally done his job and is to this day proud of having "defended the people of South Africa" and of having been the "most decorated captain in the history of the South African police, I had more decorations than the generals." "I lunched with P. W. Botha," he brags, "I was in contact with the highest levels and arrested the most dangerous criminals."

Adrian admits that he never thought apartheid was unjust: "In the townships, people had real houses, everyone worked, they made money, and they were happy. They loved the police. I was there to catch criminals. I could walk in the middle of a crowd . . . I took care of these people . . . They were happy. They had parties, they had smiling faces, they laughed all the time. They had vegetables, fruit, everything. I didn't think about politics," he claims. "I was too young." This "lack of interest in politics" did not prevent him from dreading the communists or fighting to defend the "capitalist system" and "Christendom." Fear was ultimately the driving force behind apartheid: "We were afraid of being invaded by these countries that had a way of life totally different from ours. Our churches and schools would have been destroyed. We needed apartheid to protect ourselves. The communist threat frightened us. All police officers would have been arrested, imprisoned, hung, our women would have been raped. Fear dictated that we keep what we had as long as we could. We told Botha that we couldn't hold on forever."

In Adrian's view, the end of apartheid was due to the international détente following the collapse of communism. Yet he only reluctantly accepted the idea of negotiating with the ANC, which he saw as a matter of self-interest. He subsequently decided to request amnesty from the Truth and Reconciliation Commission (TRC) in order to establish the facts regarding his personal case and thereby defend himself against the many people who were prepared to say "just about anything" regarding him. For Adrian, it was a painful ordeal: pursued by journalists, singled out for blame by his community, and obliged to acknowledge his role as "perpetrator" before the TRC, he could count only on his wife for support. Moreover, he was extremely disappointed by Frederik de Klerk, who refused to accept his responsibility for the repression and claimed to have never given an order in the cases in which Adrian was implicated. Adrian remarked in this connection: "Since that time, I have no respect for him. I knew that the politicians were using us. We were there to do the dirty work. I knew that if something went wrong, they would abandon us. I should have known it." According to one of his former colleagues, this was a period of tremendous personal decline for Adrian: a brilliant officer just a few years earlier, he today suffers from depression and abuses alcohol. It seems that his wife almost left him, and he has lost a great deal of money. When Adrian left the police in 2000, he succeeded in having an expert psychologist declare him "ill." On top of his monthly pension of

15,000 rands (1,830 euros), he thus left his job with the tidy sum of a million rands, or 122,000 euros. After one of the "terrorists" he had pursued became his hierarchical superior, Adrian no longer wished to work in his department.

He today counts himself among Nelson Mandela's many admirers. Adrian is critical of members of the white minority who reject the new regime and the transformations it has unleashed. He is unable to say, however, which system is best—the "old" one or the "new" one. Adrian says that he sees himself as "proudly South African."

Exiles

Accepting the new regime is more difficult for those who had no contact with ANC members and were under no obligation to account for their past behavior. Members of the elite units of the old South African Army violently reject the leaders of the NP, whom they accuse of having lied about the nature of the conflict and needlessly risked their lives. They also criticize their leaders' decision to negotiate with the enemy, their concessions to all of his demands, and their refusal to accept responsibility for the crimes of apartheid. Eager to distance themselves from politicians and their misdeeds, these veterans recount their personal biographies with an eye to maintaining their contacts with the new South Africa.

Nicolas was born into a traditional Afrikaner family in 1959.[39] Although he asserts that he "never supported apartheid," he claims to have been "brainwashed" by state, school, and army. "In this country," he explains, "you had no choice but to join the fight." Nicolas signed up following his military service and joined the prestigious Special Forces, commonly referred to as the "Recces."[40] He infiltrated behind enemy lines: "Disguised as a Cuban, I observed everything that could be seen and then had to make contact so that they were bombed. I had to escape as quickly as possible." Nicolas underscores the harsh conditions of combat and also speaks of the excitement of fighting, of risking one's life and rubbing shoulders with highly valued companions. In his eyes, the Recces were the embodiment of military excellence. Several years later, Nicolas says that he realized that he had been manipulated, that soldiers had lost their lives for the personal interests of cynical politicians who lusted for power. He thus quit the army, began studying business at the University of Pretoria, and got married. Since 1992, he has worked as an analyst in Cape Town. Nicolas says: "When the negotiations began, I was devastated.

There was no way to survive with a black majority. Before we fought, now we were giving up." Yet Nicolas claims that "apartheid didn't mean anything to me"—that, as a member of a "multiracial" unit, he was not "exposed" to it.[41]

Today, Nicolas claims that he has lost confidence in the country's legal system and complains of the injustice of affirmative action policies. He fears growing poverty, immigration, and crime. At the same time, he worries that the experience of Zimbabwe will be repeated and that the country will be invaded and conquered by Islam. Nicolas lives very comfortably in a property outside of Cape Town, surrounded by nature. He nevertheless is considering moving with his family to a boat in order to sail the world's oceans and seas and thereby become a "citizen of the world." This project is just one of many ways to protect oneself from unsettling social change. A number of whites have opted for internal exile, quitting the cities to take up residence on isolated farms. To justify this personal withdrawal and return to the earth, they often evoke their "love of nature" and old peasant roots. In this, they lay claim to a typically South African theme. Starting in the late 1990s, many urbanized whites began to turn their backs on public affairs, retreating to the safe spaces of the private sphere. This reflected the disappointment that succeeded the enthusiasm of the Mandela period. In a context marked by deteriorating security, whites who had grown distrustful of the government took refuge in the comfortable and relatively safe way of life that was available to them.

Although mercenaries were banned by South Africa in 2006, some veterans of the former security forces joined mercenary companies. Executive Outcomes, a famous mercenary organization, allowed them to continue fighting on the African continent without submitting themselves to their country's new social contract. A small number of South Africans are employed by security companies in Iraq.

Others chose the path of radical exile, leaving South Africa altogether. They of course had various reasons for leaving, but the degradation of security conditions ranks high among them. The perception of a dangerous environment sometimes echoes the failures and shortcomings attributed to the present regime and even nostalgia for the old order.

* * *

At a time of nonracial democracy, economic liberalism, and urban individualism, the South African ideal of sacrificing one's self for the nation—an ideal doubtless shared by many ANC militants and apartheid-era security forces alike—today seems obsolete. In its place, a new ethos has arisen cele-brating the "comrades," former soldiers and police officers who have mas-tered the language of democracy and profited from their networks to launch successful careers in politics and business. This new ethos penalizes those who, for lack of polish or diplomas, eke out a wretched life in the townships. The new system nevertheless makes room for former members of the forces of order who prefer to live at a remove from their rulers and the country's multiracial society. Some of them possess the economic resources necessary to withdraw to private, isolated spaces. Like the ex-combatants themselves, South African society remains deeply divided, with a portion of it exposed to the siren song of populism.

Chapter 5

The Ex-Combatants of the FLN: An Eternally Privileged "Revolutionary Family"

Scholarly research and official administrative sources do not supply precise data on the trajectories of Algerian combatants and their social or socioeconomic situation. It is common knowledge, however, that the number of mujahideen[1] significantly increased in the years following independence. On top of the phenomenon of those eleventh-hour combatants, the "Marsiens,"[2] there was a mad rush among the population to obtain a veteran's identification card, seen as the key that unlocks all doors. Usurpation of the status of veteran is not specific to Algeria; it is frequently encountered in connection with underground guerrilla movements, which do not keep official rolls. In Algeria, however, it took place on an unprecedented scale.

The absence of quantitative data does not prevent one from studying the inner workings of the Algerian army—the institutional successor to the mujahideen—or from considering the symbolic role played by the ex-combatant in the Algerian social and political system. Although now tarnished, the figure of the mujahid continues to occupy a central place in the national imaginary. Even as the government proclaims the unanimity of the Algerian people, elevating it as a whole to the status of hero, it grants specific advantages to members of the "revolutionary family." Today, frequent public denunciation of the manner in which this system is abused actually contributes to perpetuating it.

The People's National Army, Heir to the Fight for National Liberation

The creation of the People's National Army (ANP) from Army of the Frontiers units and guerrilla forces allowed the regime to confer legitimacy upon a central institution by associating it with the fight against colonialism. The army was thus able to lend moral support to the regime and, in this role, became its principal center of power and the guarantor of its continuity.

The Absorption of Guerrilla Fighters

Four years before the war ended, there were two distinct groups of Algerian combatants: guerrilla fighters (*maquisards*) inside the country, who were distributed between the commands of the various wilayat, and professionally trained soldiers on the ground in Morocco and Tunisia. The former are said to have numbered between 15,000 and 30,000 men, together with between 50,000 and 100,000 liaison agents, while the Army of the Frontiers contained 35,000 recruits, who were hierarchically organized in 1961.[3] Faced with the French army's new tactics, starting in 1959 internal organizations lost ground. Destabilized, dependent on external sources for arms and munitions, and sometimes weakened by internal divisions as well as enemy repression and attacks, these organizations were superseded by their counterparts in Cairo, Tripoli, and Tunis, which relied on diplomatic action to compensate for military setbacks. At the same time, the Army of the Frontiers was strengthened and professionalized: fitted out with modern equipment and heavy weaponry, its men received formal political and technical training and even benefited from the experience of career soldiers trained in the French army.[4] By increasing its capacity for action, the Army of the Frontiers acquired decisive political influence.

In July 1962, the struggle for power led to a confrontation between the Army of the Frontiers, supported by some of the wilayat, and the internal combatants of wilayat 3 and 4. Incapable of uniting, the wilayat lost the fight to Ahmed Ben Bella, who had the support of Houari Boumediene. Algeria's first president subsequently decided to fuse the various armies or, more specifically, to absorb the wilayat within the external army.[5] In doing so, he favored the soldiers of the Army of the Frontiers, and it was their leaders who assumed the main duties of command. The leaders of the internal army were integrated into the new formation or dismissed,[6] and most of its combatants were demobilized. Henceforth, revolutionary engagement and physical courage counted for less than efficiency and technical know-how.[7]

The military prowess of former guerrilla fighters was not rewarded via integration and promotion within the army. However, this did not prevent the new government that resulted from the 19 June 1965 coup d'état from asserting the contrary.[8] With the internal mujahideen who had seen the most combat shunted aside in favor of technical skill and unity around the government, the ANP served as the regime's moral and political guarantor. In order to make the army an efficient and modern tool of war, the best places were reserved for officers trained at Saint-Cyr, Saint-Maixent, or the schools of Prague and Moscow.

Yet by presenting the ANP as the sole heir of the National Liberation Army (ALN), Boumediene conferred considerable legitimacy upon it. The October 1963 war in Morocco strengthened the army, helped it win popular support, and demonstrated its importance to the country's defense. Attempts at "wilayism" failed and in so doing helped strengthen the fledgling institution. The memory of the deadly confrontations of the summer of 1962 and the the hostile takeover of June 1965 faded away, to be replaced by the heroic legend.[9] In 1967, the new army had 75,000 members,[10] though it is unknown how many of them were "internals," Army of the Frontiers veterans, or external recruits.[11]

The People's National Army, Guardian of the Revolution

The army of liberation was established as a model upon which a new society would be constructed. Under the presidency of Ben Bella, little distinction was drawn between soldier and civilian. The Algerian soldier was to hold a rifle in one hand and a spade in the other. He saw to the country's defense but also contributed to its reconstruction and to building socialism. When Boumediene came to power, the creation of a professional army—and the attendant specialization of military tasks—came to be seen as an imperative. The institution's autonomy increased accordingly. It developed a professional ideology that channeled social and regional loyalties and identities into one great military family. The military counted on specialization and internal cohesion to provide strong institutional foundations.

Starting in the 1970s, the APN no longer had anything to do with the ALN but nevertheless presented itself as the sole continuation of the latter. It represented the material guarantor of independence and a rampart against the neocolonial aims of foreign powers.[12] Its first test came with the war against Morocco in 1963. The dispatch of APN units to the Middle East during the Six-Day War supplied further evidence of its commitment to defending the Palestinian and Arab causes and its participation in the fight against imperialism.

In the 1970s, Algerian society subscribed to the vision of a protective army—yesterday fighting colonialism, today working toward economic development and modernization. The army embodied the nation and shouldered its hopes. Coming from the ranks of the army, Boumediene sought to base his power on a strong and effective institution united behind its leader, proof of the country's unity and the recognition of his authority. He encouraged technical training for its members and the recruitment of young professionals.[13] Starting in the 1970s, a new generation of students from the Cherchell military academy and foreign institutions embarked on careers as officers or NCOs. Their sense of mission and civic engagement were henceforth expressed in terms of profitability and specialization.[14] Significant financial resources were bestowed upon the army: from 1973 to 1979, military spending more than doubled.[15] At the same time, its numbers increased: by 1997, the army consisted of 140,000 men, 80,000 of whom were conscripts.[16] The military institution also became the regime's keystone. "In 1962, the army participated in power. In 1965, it seized it."[17] United behind Boumediene, it subsequently played an essential role in choosing candidates for the presidency and directly intervened in politics following the victory of the Islamic Salvation Front (FIS) in the first round of legislative elections in January 1992. "No regime change is possible against the army or without its participation."[18] The army's mobilization against armed Islamists during the civil war as well as its ability to mop them up and reduce the level of terrorist violence attest to its prominent political role. Thanks to the resources it deployed and the support of foreign partners, the APN was ultimately strengthened by this experience.[19]

The Army, a Tool of Social Promotion

The war impoverished entire groups of Algerians while enriching and promoting others. It led to changes in the relations between the upper and lower classes. In the aftermath of the war, the army appeared to be the main channel of social advancement for these newly social groups, whose ranks were mainly drawn from the rural world.[20] The army guaranteed stable employment for its members, possibilities for career advancement, and a decent salary—an entirely attractive prospect given the country's economic situation in the 1960s.

For all that, soldiers should not be seen as constituting a privileged group. There is relatively little distance separating the ranks from the top brass: there are neither field marshals nor chests weighed down with medals. Because of the manner in which they are treated and their position in society, however, soldiers nevertheless form a separate stratum; their prospects for social advancement undeniably provide them with a comparative advantage. "The army, the symbol of the nation, was set 'apart' from the nation." Access to the army offers the possibility of receiving excellent high-level training, and recruits are culled in advance by cadet, NCO, and officer schools. Moreover, science students wishing to pursue degree courses in specialties not taught in Algeria, or master an advanced technology, can sign contracts with the army and receive grants to study abroad. The Algerian army has become synonymous with professional careers, social promotion, enrichment, and prestige.[21]

The army also participates in economic life as a production and service enterprise, managing its own agricultural and industrial cooperatives. It wins a large number of government contracts in the public works and construction domains and has its own engineers, architects, and experts. It seems to be an efficient and profitable enterprise. The trans-Saharan highway was built under the military's direction, with labor supplied by conscripted soldiers.[22]

During the civil war, the enlistment of young cohorts in the ANP continued apace. The army was one of the only public enterprises that possessed the financial resources needed to expand its recruitment. Some recruits were persuaded by the government to defend the endangered state against the terrorist hordes. Moreover, the logic of the conflict radicalized commitments; in some zones, it became almost impossible for young people to avoid choosing a camp. For unemployed graduates, the status of officer still remains attractive.[23]

The Figure of the Mujahid: From Hero to Usurper

Celebrated by the government, which sought to legitimate itself by mobilizing the anticolonial struggle and to build or expand its social and political base, the figure of the mujahid has long been presented as the incarnation of heroism. Yet today this figure is also seen as the beneficiary of lifelong privilege and the symbol of a series of abuses. Despite its crumbling legitimacy, the myth that has arisen around this figure has not disappeared. Consequently, discourse has had to adjust to this contradiction: as its unnamed usurpers are stigmatized, the ideal has become all the more prized as a model. The "bad" mujahid is a blank canvas to be filled as one likes by the imagination, while identification of the "real" mujahid is lost in a perpetual quest for authenticity.

The Ideal of the Mujahid

The figure of the mujahid incarnates the war of liberation, made sacred by the government. Access to the title of "mujahid" confers a specific symbolic and social status. As Monique Gadant explains, though originally a religious term referring to participation in jihad against the infidel, *mujahid* nevertheless came to be secularized in nationalist discourse, where it was reassigned a moral and patriotic meaning corresponding to "steadfast will, concentrated effort, a spirit of total sacrifice until martyrdom in the aim of completely destroying the existing retrograde system."[24] The maquisard is the figure par excellence of the Revolution. He "incarnates the heroic model of the activist—his violence and courage are so many affirmations of *l'algérianité*."[25] In gestation during the war, this idealization is still to be found forty years later. According to Luis Martinez, the guerrilla warrior's underground struggle is a model for Islamists, who "confirm the authenticity of the combatant's faith by requiring that he break with his environment. . . . The underground struggle selects its own candidates to lead the war effort."[26]

The sociology of combatants in the war of liberation remains to be written. René Gallissot holds that the proportion of peasants in their ranks has been overestimated and that "the first guerilla fighters were most often former Messalists who had been politicized in towns and withdrew to the countryside to go underground."[27] The Algiers wilaya—on which the better part of my study focuses and which should not be taken as representative of all Algerian mujahideen—was in a number of ways distinctive: hierarchy was less pronounced there than elsewhere, and several young women played an important role in it, particularly during the Battle of Algiers.[28]

The Government: Patron or Prisoner of the Mujahideen?

As early as 1967, William Zartman wrote that the mujahideen "formed a sort of inchoate party or a political society-within-society and they attempt to occupy all possible positions of power, both as their reward for their exertions (jihad) and as a base from which to enact programs to continue these rewards." At that time he also asserted that they would "only slowly disappear for they entered the struggle at a very young age."[29] Forty years later, the mujahideen still wield considerable influence in the political class. The ability of some of them to co-opt political debate and claim the best economic and financial opportunities for themselves is a characteristic trait of the Algerian system. "Recognized as the country's creditors," these mujahideen constantly demand they be given more and "the state finds itself overwhelmed."[30]

In the aftermath of 5 July 1962, the mujahideen were well placed to profit from the rush to appropriate the homes and stores left vacant by Europeans and, in particular, acquired a large number of café operating licenses. They also used their influence to find jobs for civilian combatants. In the very difficult postwar economic context, these advantages constituted real privileges,[31] even if it is obviously true that not all mujahideen were quite so keen to profit from the opportunities that were offered them.

Rising to head of state, Boumediene sought to create a social base for his power among veterans. A year later, in 1966, the National Organization of Mujahideen (ONM) was created. Placed under the aegis of the National Liberation Front (FLN), it participated in party supervision of society and contributed to spreading the state ideology. The Ministry of Former Mujahideen was created to represent their interests. The Algerian president was also active on the symbolic level: he repatriated the bodies of martyrs fallen in France and arranged for the ashes of Émir Abdelkader—the mujahideen's foremost political and religious role model—to be returned. The anniversary of the 20 August 1955 offensive launched by Zighout Youcef in the North Constantinois became a national holiday to celebrate the mujahideen. Finally, Boumediene took care to cultivate veterans' prestige and increase their pensions.[32]

The nationalization of petroleum and gas resources in 1971 and the efforts made on the international scene to support increased hydrocarbon prices allowed the Algerian state to construct a petroleum rent and centrally organize redistribution.[33] Thanks to this godsend, the government succeeded in accumulating reserves and increasing household purchasing power—between 1967 and 1978, consumption increased fivefold. It ultimately mattered little that the country's food dependence had over the same period risen from 7 to 70 percent[34] or that state-run enterprises were unprofitable and practiced overemployment. Spurred on by the crises of the 1970s, its petroleum rent allowed the state to finance an unproductive system, pursue a policy of state aid, and pamper specific groups while simultaneously assuring a minimum standard of well-being for the population at large. In this way, it was able to ensure its continued legitimacy.

Former mujahideen are granted various types of advantage. All are eligible for a pension. The amount of the pension is calculated by reference to the veteran's level of disability. This is determined by a commission consisting of a doctor and a representative of the Ministry of Former Mujahideen. Thus, a 100 percent disability level does not mean that the mujahid is reduced to total immobility but concerns a vast array of physical and psychological afteraffects and takes the mujahid's deteriorating health into account. Blame for the latter is systematically laid upon the combatant's service record—even when his deteriorating health is the result of later accident.[35] The pension is increased if the disabled mujahid requires assistance from a third party and in accordance with the number of dependent children under his care. In 1969, 10,180 individuals received a disabled veteran pension. Also eligible for pensions were 101,200 widows of *shuhada* (martyrs) as were the descendants of combatants killed in action provided certain resource conditions were met.[36] Today, a mujahid who is declared 100 percent disabled has access to five different pension levels. The lowest is 10,000 dinars (around 100 euros), and the highest 68,000 dinars (680 euros), per month.[37] By comparison, the country's minimum wage was raised to 12,000 dinars (120 euros) in 2009. The mujahid may also receive a monthly payment of 9,000 dinars for his "guide"—typically, a member of his family who assists him in everyday life. The guide also benefits from preferential travel fares when accompanying the mujahid. A mujahid whose level of disability is assessed at 80 percent receives 5,500 dinars per month. The widow of a *shahid* (martyr) today receives 33,000 dinars per month. The unmarried daughter of a "martyr" for her part receives 5,000.

What's more, former mujahideen and state pensioners are treated free of charge in public hospitals, may receive medical attention abroad if necessary, and do not pay for medicine. Disabled veterans ride free or at half price on all public transportation (including airlines). Veterans and the widows of shuhada have priority in occupying state-owned residential facilities and benefit from a 40 percent reduction in their rent when this is justified by their resources. Moreover, veterans and war widows enjoy priority access to jobs and professional training, with posts reserved for them in business and state administration. Agricultural cooperatives are awarded them. Finally, they have been granted taxi and tobacconist licenses.[38]

Several years after coming to power, Boumediene authorized zero interest loans to be granted to young army pensioners in order to encourage them to become involved in business and start SMEs. Thanks to these easy terms, a number of billionaires were able to amass their fortunes. The mujahideen were also exempted from automobile import taxes. "Beginning in the 1970s and in a context of visible wealth and renewed austerity, it was no longer simply a matter of employment and housing, wages and pensions, but of currency, cars and educational grants."[39] In the 1980s, access to import licenses and land for construction became the gateway to wealth.

Thus, not only did veterans and their families benefit from a generous policy of state aid that did not take differences of revenue and wealth into account; gradually, a portion of them also attained a privileged status as economic actors and consumers. This policy created a very advantaged social group distinct from the rest of society. What's more, by systematizing this group's privileged status, the state contributed to undermining the value of productive labor.

By building a clientele for itself, the government sought to consolidate one of its main bases of support. Over time, however, this strategy turned the relationship of dependence against it. Some former mujahideen exploited their position to constantly increase their profits. Those who claimed to belong to the "revolutionary family" caught the government in its own trap by constantly playing upon the theme of the country's gratitude toward the martyrs and heroes of the fight against France. The political opening of 1989 led to multipartism and the creation of new associations. That year, the National Organization of Shuhada Children (ONEC) was established as was an association for the children of mujahideen. The mujahideen association and that of the Shuhada children demanded that their privileges be passed on to their children.[40] As Omar Carlier ironically remarked, "Soon, sons will inherit the status of veteran—and even that of [s]hahid—from their fathers."[41] To legitimate their financial claims, these organizations rely on nationalist one-upmanship. They roundly responded when polemic broke out in France over the 23 February 2005 law mentioning the "positive role" played by French colonization. Today, the powerful mujahideen organization calls upon France to apologize for its crimes in Algeria, while ONEC demands financial reparations be paid for the death of shuhada parents. Though it receives annual financial support from the state, the Association of Mujahideen Children has apparently not obtained specific advantages for its members. A breach may be opening, however, as one of its members informed me that, as the son of a mujahid, he enjoys a 50 percent reduction in his automobile insurance.[42]

There are many abuses, with each economic privilege susceptible to being misappropriated and monetized. Automobile import licenses are resold, as are those for taxis and cafés, fueling illegal speculation.[43] The vehicle import license exempts one from customs duties. Since mujahideen can repeat this operation once every five years, some have been tempted to trade in this preferential treatment. Once this phenomenon became embarrassingly widespread, a law was passed to forbid such transactions. Since then, the only people entitled to drive a car registered in a veteran's name are the veteran himself, his spouse, and his children. In the 1970s and 1980s, the mujahideen had privileged access to construction materials, which were at the time rationed. Here, too, some took advantage of their position to resell cement vouchers and in this way amassed illegal revenue. Millionaires receive veterans' pensions, and men who have acquired the title of "mujahid" retire early in the knowledge that they can count on it.

Not all mujahideen behave like profiteers, exploiting or misusing every privilege accorded them. Nevertheless, all are affected by the very broad advantages granted them. Moreover, the spectacle of businessmen amassing fortunes as "millionaires" in the 1980s and (especially) 1990s and revelations concerning the misappropriation of funds by the country's leaders convinced Algerian veterans that others were getting a much bigger piece of the pie. This, in turn, encouraged them to shed their scruples.

"False" Mujahideen

The political and ideological order produced the conditions for a system of corruption that was preceded and anticipated by the fraudulent award of veteran's status. Indeed, establishing the number of veterans is no easy task. At the August 1956 Soummam Congress, ALN numbers were estimated at 7,469 soldiers and 15,570 partisans. A year later, Abane Ramdane claimed that 50,000 soldiers and 40,000 partisans were active inside Algeria. According to Mohamed Harbi, these figures—totaling around 110,000 people—had already been inflated by FLN leaders during the war. All the more reason to cast doubt on the reliability of the mujahideen roster, which listed 336,000 names in 1974: "The distribution of emoluments increased the number of fictive actors and victims of the war of independence."[44]

Anticipating the symbolic and material advantages that the status of veteran would confer, some joined the FLN's camp in the final months of the conflict, when independence had already been won. In the aftermath of the war, access to the status of mujahid depended on obtaining a communal certificate attesting to one's political or military engagement. Social networks and membership in the single party were useful for obtaining false affidavits to that effect. Subsequently, "[as] the difficult years and the ethic of sacrifice faded into the past, the certificate became an attractive and marketable title."[45] Some former mujahideen denounced the manner in which dishonest opportunists trafficked in certificates and corrupted the system. The maquisard Ali Zamoun studied the lists of former mujahideen in eleven Kabyle districts and concluded that "nearly 50 percent of the communal certificates examined were false and illicitly procured, . . . with the complicity of people at all levels of government."[46]

Since 2000, the "false mujahideen" scandal has been a recurrent feature of Algerian political life. In 2002, the minister of veterans affairs admitted that the population of mujahideen—then numbering 300,000—had significantly increased over forty years.[47] An Algerian journalist for his part claimed that the number of "false mujahideen" totaled more than 2 million in 1989, or 150 times more than what it had been in 1962. According to this journalist, the material, financial, and symbolic stakes were such that false affidavits traded for several tens of thousands of dinars.[48] In 2007, Ahmed Benchérif, a former minister under Houari Boumediene, former member of the Revolutionary Council, and former head of the national police force accused the minister in charge of this portfolio of seeking to torpedo efforts to purge the rolls after the latter asserted that there were only 10,000 "false mujahideen." Benchérif pointed out that, "upon the death of Houari Boumediene, Algeria had 250,000 mujahideen, a figure that according to him [the responsible minister] rose to 500,000 during the Chadli period, ultimately reaching some 2,500,000 mujahideen."[49] Though perhaps inaccurate as to the scale of fraud, these estimates are revealing of the manner in which Algerian society regards the issue.

The at-once real and imaginary existence of "false mujahideen" is one of the mainsprings of the Algerian social and political system. First and foremost, it allows the regime to strengthen its social base by enlarging its client network, which enjoys priority in the distribution of the petroleum rent. "True" and "false" mujahideen receiving stipends from the state have an interest in supporting the regime that guarantees their privileged position. For a long time, moreover, the proliferation of veterans did not inconvenience the government to the degree that a large number of those involved in the war backed the regime's assertion of unanimity—that is, the claim that the Revolution's hero was none other than the entire Algerian people. An inflated number of mujahideen may well correspond to the authorities' policy of exaggerating the number of martyrs (1.5 million).

What's more, the "false mujahideen" issue reinforces another theory used to prop up the Algerian regime: that of the internal enemy. Discussion of the groups that usurped the title of combatant and sometimes even imposed themselves within the government evokes the idea of a traitorous presence in the social body, without, for all that, identifying culprits. Their existence thereby established, these enemies and profiteers nonetheless remain anonymous. As a result, everyone suspects one or several individuals or seeks to defend the authenticity of their own engagement, outdoing one another in displays of fidelity to the nation and the Revolution. Like the rest of society, former mujahideen subscribe to the rhetoric of the "false mujahideen" and the betrayal of the Revolution. These themes allow people holding widely divergent opinions to find common ground: whether Islamist, nationalist, Berberist, or democrat, all may proclaim that the anticolonial struggle has been compromised. This obsession monopolizes energy and obliterates other crucial social and political issues. After a fashion, the civil war further confused minds: Who was guilty of the massacres? What role did foreigners play in the violence? Was it not after all a matter of manipulation? Although Algerians may have different interpretations of the events and divergent political sympathies, all nevertheless rely upon the same vocabulary and type of reasoning.

Finally, the "false mujahideen" scandal also allows FLN clans to settle scores among themselves and pursue their strategies in the struggle for power. It allows one to identify those who are "corrupt" and attack the position of one's adversaries by targeting their moral and political legitimacy. Picked up by the press, the to-and-fro of these attacks regularly punctuates the news.

The Musical Chairs of the Mujahideen

The social and economic success of some mujahideen—their proximity to power—fuels feelings of injustice and jealousy among others. Accusations against usurpers are widespread in contemporary political discourse and take two distinct forms. The first of these targets an invisible and imagined internal enemy seen as responsible for the evils afflicting Algeria. The second is more personal: it identifies by name the individuals accused of profiting from the system or pushing themselves to the fore. In both cases, the accusations stem from the fact that various groups of veterans today seek to profit from their participation in the war of liberation, lobbying the state to increase their level of remuneration. In Algiers, the proximity of government and the media only amplifies this competition for resources.

Rachida, a former guerrilla fighter, combines the general accusation regarding internal enemies—portrayed as the infiltrated agents of colonialism—with a specific grievance concerning the amount of her pension.[50] In October 2004, the national press reported on a demand made by Rachida and several women from the same wilaya. Though recognized as mujahidat, they complained that they had not been included in the category of "cadre de la nation." Those holding this status are eligible to receive a very generous retirement pension: 72,000 dinars per month, or six times the minimum wage. Rachida also complains that, unlike the group of maquisards to which she belongs, those condemned to death under the colonial administration are eligible for the highest mujahid pension (calculated on the basis of a 100 percent rate of disability and corresponding to 68,000 dinars per month). In her view, some groups and individuals have monopolized the regime's favors at the expense of mujahidat such as herself, thereby calling into question the commitment and price paid by the women who fought in Algiers. She claims that she would be very satisfied if she were to receive the same amount: "It would be progress, and we would begin to clear out all and get rid of all the fakes, Harkis, and corrupt people."

Listening to these veterans, one sometimes has the impression of a game of musical chairs in which, in order to win, all participants must chant the same song. The emergence of ostentatious new fortunes in the 1980s and 1990s served only to intensify this competition. In order to capture the country's petroleum rent via veterans' and retirement pensions, the members of the "revolutionary family" had first to appropriate the "symbolic rent" of the Revolution. Divisions among mujahideen overlap with regional solidarities and coincide with political clienteles and practices of nepotism; they less often intersect with questions of ideology. Theirs is a shared discourse: everyone claims to be the embodiment of revolutionary purity, even if that means calling one's competitor a false mujahid, a counterfeit mujahid, or—worst of all—a throwback to the colonial system or even a neocolonialist. The civil war and the fact that much of its history has yet to be uncovered contributed to reviving conspiracy theories. Both those who support the government and those who support the armed Islamists accused France of colluding with the adversary and even of outright manipulation.

In Algerian society, the image of the mujahid has been tarnished. The diminished credibility enjoyed by this figure, however, has done nothing to render obsolete certain categories of language (mujahid, shahid, and harki) or the Manichaean vision of the world they describe.[51] Today, the obsession with counterfeiting in relation to the Revolution and the mujahid serves to preserve the idea of the Revolution's original purity. The issue of authenticity prolongs the revolutionary quest.

Portraits of Mujahideen

Louisette: Revolution and Purity

Louisa Ighilahriz was born in 1936 in Oujda, Morocco, where her father was a police officer.[52] Louisa's father, Said Ighilahriz, decided to retire early, and, in 1948, the Ighilahriz family, which included seven girls and three boys, moved to the Algiers casbah. Louisa and her sisters attended the French school, and their father opened a bakery in El Biar, a hilltop neighborhood in Algiers. Because she was bright and also in order to please her father, Louisa often was first in her class. The former police officer demanded excellence from his children and was inflexible with regard to how they should behave in the French school. Louisa had to bend to her professors' rules, even when they were unjust, and never express a political opinion.

In some ways, she was leading a double life: since the early 1950s, Louisa's father had been active within the national movement and drew his wife and children into the struggle against France. The El Biar bakery became a meeting place for militants. At her father's insistence, Louisa sat for both the BEPS and the CAP, which she received in 1954.[53] When she entered high school, she was one of the only "Muslim French girls" at her school. She then had her first experience of militancy, becoming a liaison agent. Transporting arms, messages, and militants, Louisette, as she was now known, played on her European looks to get through army checkpoints and cajole French soldiers. Several members of her family were arrested, and she was herself sought by the army in August 1957. It was thus decided that she should escape to join the guerrillas. The same month, she joined the forces of wilaya

4. In the eight weeks she spent in the Chebli douar, Louisette was the only woman among the combatants. She tended to the wounded and also carried a weapon. She was captured after a clash with the French army. Wounded in the leg, she was transported to the 10th Parachutist Division (DP), where she was tortured for two and a half months. Thanks to the intercession of a military doctor, she was freed from the clutches of her tormenters[54] and sent to prison. Louisette didn't recover her freedom and return to Algiers until the eve of independence. She attempted to regain her bearings. Her youngest brothers did not recognize her. Her father, meanwhile, had on several occasions promised her hand in marriage to a mujahid, but Louisette was no longer the obedient young woman she had been.

Her experience of war had led her to adopt an uncompromising attitude with regard to her personal liberty. She chose her husband for herself. A nationalist militant residing in France who subsequently joined the FLN's broadcasting service in Morocco, Ahmed was an engineer and fell in love with Louisette. The couple married for love, ignoring the traditional wedding ritual. The mujahida had found a true liberal who accepted her as she was and would support her throughout her life. They moved into a ruined apartment in a peaceful neighborhood of the capital, where they live to this day. The first years of independence were hard. Louisette worked at the cinema, began studies in psychology, and gave birth to a daughter and son. While she had won her liberty and autonomy as a woman, she knew that her lot was exceptional. Upon their return, women who had been mobilized during the War of Independence often found themselves once again cloistered at home by their brothers and father. The flow of country people into cities served as a pretext for "protecting" women from the mentality of "mountain dwellers" and village people. The regime gave in to the lure of the national-Islamists and abandoned any effort to pursue a progressive policy toward women. Moreover, a number of the women who had taken up arms in the 1950s ultimately divorced, a sign of emancipation sometimes at odds with the expectations of their family circle.

Louisette seems to criticize women themselves for their attitude of submission. Moreover, she makes it clear that she rejects the principle of parity, which she sees as "charity." For Louisette, women's freedom is like Algerian independence, and the mujahida employs the same vocabulary for both: "It has to be won, wrested away." Freedom, in other words, must be deserved. It may be that, in Louisette's view, Algerian women have not sufficiently fought for their emancipation. She thus embodies a type of exceptionality, one celebrated by the regime but severely limited insofar as women as a group must bear the costs of a retrograde policy.

Born into a family fully engaged in the struggle for national liberation, Louisette was the only one of them to join the higher ranks of government and the single party. In 1974, she joined the FLN-sponsored National Union of Algerian Women (UNFA) as a member of the executive committee and, four years later, was elected as its head. Her progressive ideas collided with the conservative projects of the political elites, the influence of social structures, and the authoritarian workings of the single party. When her mandate ended in 1978, she did not run again and was subsequently appointed to lead the FLN's external commission at the Government Palace. She was twice decorated under the presidencies of Houari Boumediene and Liamine Zeroual. Louisette wanted to fight to improve conditions for women and establish a democratic and socialist society. By her own admission, she has had little success. Yet she has remained at the center of power, split between her taste for freedom and her loyalty to the party.

Though critical of the system, the "Central Director of External Affairs" remains within it. She positions herself as an outsider, standing apart from her colleagues, obstreperous and ever out of step with the party line. Louisette Ighilahriz is no doubt an atypical figure: outspoken, stubborn, sometimes even obstinate, she nevertheless appears amenable to influence. Drawing upon her status as a mujahida, she speaks with some audacity. Does she or does she not have close ties to the government? Of Boumediene, she remarks, not without contradiction: "I never approached him. But I always discussed matters with him frankly. With me, discussion was frank. I could speak freely and was respected."

Louisette says that she has been marginalized as a result of her sharp wit and uncompromising attitude. In recent years, she has had little to do in her office but maintains that she deserves a retirement pension. She deems that, coming on top of the money she will receive for her retirement, her pension as a former mujahida (52,000 dinars) is just recompense. In her eyes, the state of her health and the psychological suffering that weighs upon her and her family will never be compensated.

In several respects, hers remains a conventional nationalist discourse. She lists the successes of independent Algeria in the area of public education, appears respectful or trusting of a portion of the country's leadership, and stands by the organizations of the "revolutionary family." She nevertheless inveighs against corruption. She is rigorous and honest by upbringing, traits she shares with her husband. Louisette and Ahmed perhaps belong to that small group of obstinate people who refuse all compromise, never straying from their moral principles. Given how commonplace string-pulling, resourcefulness, and skirting the law are in contemporary Algeria, those who resist can almost seem mad. At one time or another, everyone is obliged to compromise or is tempted to profit from the opportunities offered by the system—access to which, moreover, is far from open. Louisette made sure to return her official car upon retiring. She also displays the revolutionary inflexibility commonly encountered among apparatchiks. Despite her integration into the system, Louisette seems to have retained the purity of her original militancy.

The indulgence shown by Louisette toward the system is perhaps the product of naiveté or dogged optimism. For someone who has given so much of herself—someone who still lives with the moral and physical consequences of the tortures inflicted on her by French soldiers—calling into question the future of the Algerian revolution might simply be too painful to contemplate. Those who have accepted disappointment and turned inward are consumed by bitterness. In order to keep her spirit up, Louisette also speaks of the positive aspects of Algerian independence. Moreover, the quasi victory of the FIS in 1991 and the terrorist attacks perpetrated by Islamist groups in the 1990s led Louisette and those like her to throw their support behind the regime, the FLN, and the army. The former Marengo Street schoolgirl vigorously rejects an ideology she sees as retrograde and inimical to freedom.

In 2000, Louisette decided to speak out. There is the documentary by Florence Beaugé in which Louisette reveals her rape by French soldiers, the book written with Anne Nivat, the lawsuit she brought against General Schmidt for defamation. In France, her story has revived the debate over torture during the war in Algeria. Louisette's attitude is out of sync with the Algerian regime, which seeks to retain control over how the fight for national liberation is remembered. Yet when Abdelaziz Bouteflika demanded an apology from France in 2005, Louisette Ighilahriz became a torchbearer for this new Algerian cause. While history may be exploited by the regime for its own purposes, Louisette's quest—at once personal and political—is no less sincere for all that. For several decades, she concealed her trauma the better to appear a heroine in the eyes of her father and country.

Tahar: From Protester to "Patriot"

Tahar was born in Algiers in 1939, the youngest of five boys and two girls. His father was a day laborer in the city's port and sent his children to the French school. When Tahar was thirteen years old, his father died, and Tahar had to begin working. Two of his brothers became involved in the nationalist struggle: the first was sentenced to death and executed by the French authorities, and the second was killed by the Secret Army Organization (OAS) in 1961. When the war began, Tahar was not politically aware. He lived in the Fontaine-Fraîche neighborhood, adjacent to Bab El Oued. At the request of his older brothers, he delivered messages, served as a lookout, and carried out various small tasks. In 1957, at the age of eighteen, he was arrested and thrown in prison. It was in the jails of Algiers that his political apprenticeship took place at the hands of FLN members. Thanks to his denials and the intervention of a competent lawyer, he was acquitted in 1958 but nevertheless remained behind bars for two more years. Upon his release, in 1960, he attempted to join up with resistance fighters in Kabylie. Entering into contact with the leaders of wilaya 3, he was advised to pursue the struggle in Algiers. As part of a group, Tahar subsequently carried out attacks against Harkis and the French police. He obeyed orders and did not know his targets, except once when asked to kill a childhood friend, a European from Bab El Oued "who had nothing to do with it all." Tahar had won enough influence within his group to oppose this plan and prevent the murder.[55]

Upon independence, Tahar found a villa abandoned by its former inhabitants. He wanted to move in and showed it to his brother. The latter responded by slapping him: in his eyes, there was no question of appropriating the Europeans' property.[56] After being demobilized by the structures in which he had served, he was offered a job with the police. In the course of an intervention during which he entered a home with his colleagues to arrest a man accused of theft, Tahar became distraught over the attitude of the man's little daughter, who begged him not to arrest her father. When he got back to the commissariat, Tahar resigned from the police and turned down the pay earned during his three months on the force: "The army and the police weren't for me." It became difficult to make ends meet. Tahar explains: "At independence, we were demobilized. France had betrayed its commitments to Algeria. And it was a time of real misery. From 1962 to 1965, it was really miserable. Really miserable. We fed ourselves with donations from the UNO, which sent us supplies."

Despite these straitened circumstances, Tahar got married in 1964. Several months later, he joined former brothers-in-arms in a protest at the National Assembly to draw the government's attention to the problem of unemployment among veterans. Ahmed Ben Bella, who was present at the time of the protest, took offense and had the protesters thrown into prison. Freed a few months later thanks to the intervention of Houari Boumediene, Tahar was outraged about how he had been treated. He seized the first opportunity to express his disgust and his rejection of the regime, joining the rebellion led by Hocine Ait-Ahmed in Kabylie. The insurgents were undermanned and exhausted themselves in all-day marches. Tahar and the others were captured by the Algerian army as they slept. He returned to prison, where he was sentenced to death. After being postponed several times, his sentence was finally commuted when Houari Boumediene took power. Tahar left prison but was for several years unemployed. Through an acquaintance, he eventually found work as a truck driver and stayed with the job for five years. He was only "rehabilitated" in 1970 and finally received his pension as a mujahid. He subsequently found work in a national import company, where he first served as team leader and was later promoted to the role of department head. He stayed there for twenty-four years and was able to support his daughter and four sons. He eventually settled in a small town on the outskirts of Algiers. Tahar has voted in all elections to make sure he "has his say."

When he retired in 1994, the civil war had begun, and Tahar chose to become a "patriot." As the head of a local veterans association, he was twice fired upon in front of his home with real bullets and, at the age of fifty-five, decided to lend a hand to the army, the constabulary, and the police, with whom he conducted joint operations. He worked in intelligence-gathering and carried out operations against armed Islamists in the Algiers metropolitan area.

If he joined the ranks of the "patriots," it was partly for his daughter. She is his favorite. Of his children, she spent the longest time in school and later became a lawyer. The mother of two children whom Tahar adores, she today keeps a watchful eye over him, calling him twice a day. The ex-combatant presented his motivations as follows: "Do not forget, Mademoiselle, fifty policemen were dying every day. And all that for an Islamic republic we didn't want. I have a daughter who is a lawyer. She was threatened. She almost quit school. I refused. Because I love learning, I love school. I wanted her to have the opportunities I didn't have in my youth."

According to Tahar, the armed Islamists were defeated because, in contrast to the mujahideen who fought France, "they were abandoned by the people." He was personally in favor of eradicating the terrorists. Despite this, he ultimately accepted the regime's policy of reconciliation. In 2002, his mujahid pension was reassessed, with the result that he began receiving 32,000 dinars each month in addition to his 30,000 dinar retirement pension. Tahar has health problems, has received heart surgery, and sometimes suffers from depression. He hopes to be admitted into a higher pension category: a level 3 mujahid pension would bring him 52,000 dinars per month and, if he became a "cadre de la nation," he would be eligible to receive 70,000 dinars per month now that he is retired. He will try his luck for, as he not incorrectly points out, "everything is possible in Algeria." By contrast, he has always refused to request a "guide"—that is, to claim the 9,000 dinar pension paid to family members who care for mujahideen.

Gradually, the revulsion felt by Tahar in the immediate aftermath of independence abated. The regime sought to absorb and neutralize men like him. In a society dominated by the state and thoroughly controlled by the single party, Tahar found it difficult to survive without finding a place for himself in the cogs of the FLN. His status as a veteran allowed him to honorably join the system in both moral and pecuniary terms. Ultimately, Tahar risked his life to defend the regime in the 1990s. And yet, despite having volunteered, he feels as if he has been used. The civil war made his life bitter and fed his doubts. One Algerian observer claims he never met a mujahid who felt guilty for his activities during the war of liberation.[57] Tahar is perhaps an exception. He believes that some people were unjustly killed in the war against the French, and, for him, the memory of having participated in this violence has become "moral torture."

Mohamed: From Silence to Islamism

Mohamed was born in 1925 in Guyotville, a small coastal town located twenty kilometers from Algiers. Guyotville was a town of Europeans; "Muslims" were very much a minority there. The son of a fishmonger, Mohamed and his family shared a courtyard with their neighbors, all of whom were Europeans. He attended the French school, where he was a very good student. In the course of his studies, he was fortunate to meet a communist professor who encouraged him to pursue his education. Mohamed attended high school in Algiers but was unable to graduate: the Second World War was under way, and his school had been requisitioned by American troops. As a child and adolescent, he was best friends with Marco, a European inhabitant of the neighborhood. However, as he became aware of the injustice and contempt of most Europeans, Mohamed gradually withdrew from this childhood friend. Mohamed did not hesitate to throw a punch when confronted with the racist attitudes of young Europeans his age. He had the reputation of being a somewhat reckless brawler. His intellectual training and encounters lent political depth to his thinking. At high school in Algiers, he got to know some Messalist activists and came of age politically. At the time, he frequented the hair salon of a member of the Party of the Algerian People (PPA). When the war broke out, Mohamed joined a militant network. Mohamed's sisters chose a very pretty wife for him, a seventeen-year-old native of Algiers who had never attended school. In 1957, she gave birth to their first child. The same year, Mohamed was arrested by the French army; he remained in prison until spring 1962. When he returned home, his oldest son, Nacer, failed to recognize his father and hid in the arms of his paternal uncle.[58]

The return was painful. Mohamed was one of those who kept silent, crushed by suffering, guilt, and disappointment. He had been tortured but never spoke about it to anyone. The marks of his ill-treatment were strewn across his wasted body. Ultimately, his wife and children noticed his scars. Mohamed found it difficult to bear the death of seventeen of his comrades. Arrested the same year as he was, some Messalist militants died while in the hands of the third regiment of parachutists at the Salaison factory in Guyotville. Their mysterious deaths were never explained. Knowing that he could easily have shared their fate, Mohamed suffers from survivor's guilt. Finally, he noticed that, at the local and national level, those who assumed control of the country were not themselves nationalist combatants.

Mohamed subsequently became withdrawn—indeed, nearly prostrate. He began drinking. His wife bore him four more sons. As he himself says, he had to wait to become a grandfather for there to be a little girl in the house. Born in 1989, Rima is the daughter of his eldest son. She lives with Mohamed and his wife and has brought a bit of warmth to their lives. Despite his own feelings of disappointment, Mohamed was irritated that his sons talked about emigrating to France. Ultimately, two of them did just that. Their father succeeded in convincing his eldest son to return to Algeria, but another son still lives there.

Mohamed was appointed director of the Algiers slaughterhouses but retired as soon as he could, since his daily experience at work had done nothing to further reconcile him with independent Algeria. He was allowed to include the seven years he spent in prison as part of his working life and thus received both a retirement and a mujahid pension. He settled with his family in a pretty villa in Guyotville, which was renamed Aïn Benian at independence. The town council granted them this accommodation when their fifth child was born.

Following independence, Mohamed refused to vote. He nevertheless found new hope when the FIS was created in 1989. He admired one of its leaders, Abbassi Madani. One of his sons was actively involved in the new front. As he grew older, Mohamed gave up alcohol and became religious, finding some peace in asceticism and the practice of Islam. What if the FIS realized Mohamed's hopes for justice, which had vanished with independence? Its leaders seemed to hold to the same higher moral convictions as the former Messalist militant. Perhaps the movement presented an unexpected opportunity to throw out a corrupt regime. Perhaps the popular support they enjoyed was a sign that the Islamists were on the right side. In any case, this is what Mohamed chose to believe. Yet, once again, the years that followed brought their share of suffering. After the second round of elections was nullified in January 1992 and the FIS outlawed, Mohamed's son was arrested and sent to prison. The idea that his son was subjected to a fate similar to what he had himself endured little more than thirty years earlier came as a new blow. The country's descent into civil war and massacre troubled Mohamed. He found it impossible to believe that Abassi Madani was behind the violence, holding that certain usurpers would stop at nothing. By designating invisible and imaginary enemies, he doggedly attempted to keep the now flickering flame of the Algerian revolution alive: "These people are full of hatred, without faith or law. They respect nothing. They would like to have everything, money . . . They are a category of citizens who in my view do not deserve Algerian citizenship." Mohamed passed away in 2007 at the age of eighty-two, having never seen Marco again. The bitterness he felt toward the leaders of independent Algeria never diminished his feelings of revolt against the colonial system.

Despite the diversity of their trajectories and the fact that some of them have chosen disengagement, the veterans of the war of liberation constitute a pampered social base and a bulwark for the powers that be. Not all FLN militants have profited from the regime's largesse. Yet even among those who remain at a remove from the circles of power, the pride they feel in having participated in the anticolonial struggle continues to play a foundational role in their identities. Although these veterans complain of a lack of democracy, the neglect of public services, and the corruption of the FLN party-state, their criticism of the ruling elites and condemnation of the manner in which the external FLN and army seized power only rarely leads them to question their adherence to FLN dogma regarding the struggle for national liberation.

Chapter 6

The Ex-Combatants of the OAS:
From Exile to Overintegration

To my knowledge, no study has specifically addressed the experience of Secret Army Organization (OAS) militants and officials following the organization's collapse.[1] To reconstruct the trajectories of these men, I rely on interviews with eighteen of them[2] as well as studies concerning the pied-noir population to which they belong. In doing so, I do not seek to provoke or fuel confusion between this violent organization and the Europeans of Algeria. Only a few thousand of the latter joined this clandestine movement, and only a few hundred entered its ranks as combatants. The overwhelming—if rather passive—support enjoyed by the movement among Algeria's pied-noir population depended on the (temporary) belief that the OAS would allow them to remain in their homeland.[3] In depicting their struggle, the leaders of the OAS for their part like to draw upon "the myth of a new resistance in which the pieds-noirs become the anonymous heroes."[4]

Initially sought out for prosecution and repression, in the late 1960s the members of the OAS were amnestied. Like the pieds-noirs, they proceeded to socially and economically integrate themselves into a rapidly expanding France. Despite rivalries and ideological differences within the organization, OAS networks continue to thrive and today work to carry on and commemorate the memory of its struggle. At first, OAS militants militated within their associations while seeking support and go-betweens in the political world. Over time, they scored a number of victories at the local and national levels. The central goal of these (ex-)combatants is to transform national memory, legitimating their struggle and reclaiming its place in a heroic and patriotic tradition.

France, Cruel Mother

Between April 1962 and July of the same year, the members of the OAS quit Algeria. Some were arrested. Others succeeded in reaching France or Spain aboard ships. Before being pardoned or amnestied, they spent their time on the run or behind bars. Seen as extremists by a large segment of metropolitan society, they were stains upon the image of the entire pied-noir population. Successive governments nevertheless endeavored to lay the groundwork for their social and economic integration.

Surveillance and Repression

In Algeria and, later, France, OAS members paid for their action. Hunted by barbouzes, hounded by the police and gendarmerie, they were arrested and sometimes tortured.[5] The culmination of an intelligence-gathering and infiltration campaign, the wave of arrests that took place in March and April 1962 dealt a heavy blow to the Algerian branch of the organization. It was an illustration of the government's desire to be done with the last remaining illegal force in Algeria following the signature of the Evian Accords.[6]

Respectively apprehended in March and April 1962, General Jouhaud and General Salan were tried by a Military High Court created by presidential order a year earlier.[7] Initially sentenced to death, Jouhaud was pardoned several months later by General de Gaulle. Salan for his part was sentenced to life in prison. Displeased at the "leniency" of this verdict, in June 1962 the president of the Republic created a Military Court of Justice.[8] This decision seemed evidence of "government persecution" of the OAS and an abuse of power in what concerned the independence of judicial authority.[9] This exceptional jurisdiction ordered that the leaders of two Algiers "delta" commandos—Claude Piegts and Albert Dovecar—be executed for their role in the assassination of six social center members and of Algiers police commissioner Roger Gavoury.[10] Their sentences were carried out before summer. Roger Degueldre, an assistant to Jean-Claude Pérez and leader of the "delta" commandos, also received the death penalty. It took the firing squad that executed him that July several attempts to kill him. This twist of fate provided dramatic illustration of the condemned man's apparent invincibility and seemed to reinforce the legend surrounding the organizer of OAS violence in Algiers. Having directly served under the orders of this former legionnaire, three "delta" leaders express their great admiration for him.

Gabriel Anglade regards Degueldre as "an extraordinary fellow, a man who gave his life to France and who demonstrated such courage. Because when you know how he died—shot with four coups de grâce—you really have to be up to it." Edouard Slama holds that the lieutenant was of "exceptional uprightness and honesty because he got his hands dirty like the rest of us." Joseph Rizza for his part describes him as the "true boss" of the OAS. Whether for sentimental reasons or the love of beautiful cars, he managed to board the vessel on which he would flee to Spain with his leader's vehicle, a "Floride."[11]

Was Degueldre a cold monster and unscrupulous killer? A former resistance fighter or member of the SS Walloon Legion? The mystery surrounding him has survived the lieutenant himself. It seems that his willingness to accept responsibility for violence "as if he had unburdened all the others of it"[12] won him the esteem of the men under his command. For partisans of the OAS, the four men who "died for French Algeria"—Piegts, Dovecar, Degueldre, and Bastien-Thiry (responsible for the Petit-Clamart attack against de Gaulle)—supply a martyrs' pantheon. OAS activists regularly pay tribute to their memory.

Beginning in 1962 and continuing in subsequent years, the Ministry of the Interior requested that the nation's prefects "discretely place the activities of repatriates under surveillance in order to anticipate threats to public order." Militant repatriate circles received particular scrutiny, with the authorities relying on the C Mission inventory of OAS militants and sympathizers for this purpose.[13]

Of the sixteen OAS members I met, five were sentenced to prison in France, six took refuge in Francoist Spain, and one in Italy. The others were not troubled: as they had been less directly involved in the organization, their activities did not draw the authorities' attention. Among the men arrested, Gabriel Anglade was taken in for questioning as he moved into the Parisian apartment of a painter. The apartment had an unimpeded view of the Elysée Palace, and he planned to kill de Gaulle from this vantage point. He participated in operation "Chamois," which was originally intended to free Degueldre.[14] In 1962, he was sentenced to fifteen years in prison but was freed in 1967. Anglade holds that his incarceration was unjust, arguing that OAS prisoners should have received the same treatment as National Liberation Front (FLN) combatants: "The law of 19 March permitted all Arabs to leave while we had to stay for five years. In 1962–63, I thought that General de Gaulle could have amnestied everyone but he only issued the amnesty in May 68 when he was in danger . . . They amnestied the FLN. Mister Yaceef Saadi wasn't too shy to come to France. I will point out that in 1963—while I was in prison in Paris—he was cared for at the hospital in Monaco because he had had an accident on the Grande Corniche."

Edouard Slama was arrested just before he could reform his commando. Sentenced to twenty years in prison, he was freed in 1966 by presidential pardon. As he puts it, "Well, we paid. We were already glad that we haven't been executed—for one thing, it's what we expected. It's what we all expected. We had been warned." The others received sentences running from three to sixty years in prison. None lingered over the conditions in which they were detained.

Those who went into exile in Spain relied on Francoist support when not in hiding. The Spanish government was eager to maintain good relations with France, and its sympathies for the combatants of French Algeria did not necessarily take precedence over the state's interests. Faced with these precarious conditions and given the demobilization of their divided troops, Pérez and Jean-Jacques Susini realized that they were no longer able to carry on the fight.[15] Seen as an undesirable in Spain, Pérez found himself in Latin America, though he subsequently returned to Madrid, where he ultimately obtained official papers. Susini for his part went into exile in Italy.

For militants originating on the other side of the Mediterranean, there was no longer much reason to continue to fight once Algeria had been lost. Around 60,000 exiles, most of whom settled on the eastern coast of Spain or in Madrid, abandoned their political activities and longed for a degree of normalization.[16] Only one of those I interviewed spoke to me of having carried out a commando training course to join the Spanish foreign legion. His plan was to subsequently enlist alongside the Portuguese in Angola. Several thousand settled in Alicante, where there sprang up a pied-noir community with its own paper, church, school, and shops (170 of which were operated by Europeans from Algeria in May 1965).[17] Political, regional, and family ties operated as mutual aid networks. Some joined their loved ones and took whatever work they could. Others relied on contributions from the organization's coffers and well-placed friends. Such was the case of Marcel Ronda, a former Algiers industrialist and private secretary to Raoul Salan. Thanks to a friend with entry to the circles of Franco and Salazar, he had access to funds collected among employers who supported the OAS cause, and worked under a false name in an import-export company.[18] A former "delta," Joseph Rizza initially received financial assistance from Pérez and his family, who provided him with somewhere to live. Rizza was eventually expelled from the Province of Alicante as a result of the violent behavior of other pieds-noirs and took up work as a bricklayer. Athanase Georgopoulos for his part found a little corner of paradise in Torremolinos on the Costa del Sol. With help from a Francoist friend and funds collected by the OAS, he teamed up with another native of Oran to open a discotheque, the Eldorado. It proved a resounding success.[19]

Following contacts between Michel Baroin and Georgopoulos, Operation "Reconciliation" sought to neutralize activists who might once again take up arms, and persuade them to return to France. The former OAS leader recounts that Baroin demanded he cease all violent action in exchange. With no illusions regarding the influence he enjoyed over the organization as a whole, he nevertheless agreed to take the necessary steps.[20] Having received assurances that they would be acquitted or handed suspended sentences, between 1963 and 1965 250 individuals returned to France, appeared before the State Security Court and then resumed a life of freedom in France.[21] Those implicated in murder meanwhile had to wait for the amnesty of 1968.

Mutual Incomprehension:
Metropolitan France and the Pieds-Noirs

As Todd Shepard explains, the OAS attack that wounded young Delphine Renard[22] and the attempt to extort funds from Brigitte Bardot by blackmail helped cast the French of Algeria in a negative light as "violent males who attacked helpless women and children." While the partisans of French Algeria might still have seemed "lost soldiers" a little earlier, by the summer of 1962 they had come to be seen as merely "perverted men, men without women, who because of their perversions were not wholly French."[23] By way of a nearly logical but misleading shortcut, the "repatriates," now assigned the originally pejorative nickname "pieds-noirs,"[24] were put in the same category as the OAS. Perceived as colonists or colonialists, they were blamed not just for the war in Algeria, but also for more than a century of French policy overseas.

The material problems provoked by the massive arrival of the French of Algeria—precipitated but not anticipated by the authorities—the perception of their cultural specificities, and the desire to be done with the conflict and the colonial past reinforced their rejection by French society, which was ready to pigeonhole all of these overseas compatriots as fascists. Although this view was not shared by all, a representation spread of the pied-noir as boisterous, vain, racist, and incapable of engaging in logical discussion.[25]

In the towns in southern France where the vast majority of the newcomers disembarked, multiple conflicts arose between a population that felt suddenly invaded and another that felt torn from its homeland and despised by state authorities. Between May and August 1962, 670,000 French people crossed the Mediterranean from Algeria, with two-thirds of them arriving in Marseille.[26] Over the course of the year, the number of North African repatriates had reached 1.4 million, 930,000 of whom came from Algeria.[27] The deficiencies of their reception reflected the government's failure to adequately prepare: in 1961, the secretary of state's office estimated that 100,000 working-age adults were to arrive together with their loved ones, or a total of 350,000 individuals. The issue of housing presented particular difficulties.[28] What's more, a series of holdups in the region further tarnished the newcomers' image: in summer 1962, the number of armed robberies increased fourfold in the Côte d'Azur. Armed and possessing the necessary know-how, OAS members were responsible for some of these attacks.[29]

Society as a whole remained indifferent to the suffering of these newly uprooted people who had left their country in what were often traumatic circumstances. Some did not hesitate to profit from their distress. Many pieds-noirs recount being targeted for discrimination or abuse. This occasionally hostile reception became a focus of lingering—and sometimes permanent—resentment. For some, France was responsible not just for their departure from Algeria, but also for treating them like second-class citizens.[30] The humiliations suffered by the pieds-noirs in metropolitan France in some ways reinforced the narrative of a cruel France promoted by OAS activists. The demand for self-maintenance within the French nation formed a continuum with earlier demands regarding territorial integrity. Their anger was driven by the belief that they had been or continued to be expelled from France against their will. Hervé, for his part, is still furious and in our interview spoke as if the fight for French Algeria belonged to the recent past:[31]

> When we first arrived, we were constantly being stopped by the police to check our papers because we were pieds-noirs. When I showed my papers at the Evreux prefecture, I was told that I wasn't French. I ultimately saw the department head, who told me, "You know, with everything that is happening today, we no longer know who is French."

That was then, but it continues to this day. Our social security number is 99, that of foreigners! We're really second-class French citizens! I was born in France—in Oran—but on my passport it says I was born in Algeria. And in Arabic, what's more! If we go to the United States, we're held for hours at the police checkpoint.

For Hervé, the worst part of being assigned a non-French identity is that it puts him into the same category as Algerian immigrants. He is pestered by the police, considered part of the foreign population, and harassed when crossing borders.[32]

It is a widespread perception. Étienne, who sees things with a much calmer eye, is an exception.[33] After spending some time in Spain, he arrived in France in December 1962 and immediately decided to put his OAS past behind him. Of all those I interviewed, he alone refuses to see the nation as indebted to him: "I was well-received in France as long as I didn't interfere with their lives. For 30 years, I've lived a quiet life." As for the matter of compensation, he states: "France doesn't owe me anything. Anyhow, I've always looked after myself."

Policies in Favor of the Pieds-Noirs: From Subsidies to Reparations

According to Todd Shepard, integration policies targeting the pieds-noirs were designed to assimilate a population characterized by marked cultural and political differences. Economic growth and the population's dispersal across the national territory would soften its "Mediterranean" and "colonial" character. As Shepard sees it, this approach resembled that employed toward Muslims.[34] Ultimately, it was in no way exceptional but rather part of a deep-rooted republican tradition that, at another, not so distant time, sought to attenuate the cultural specificities of Basques and Bretons.

The Boulin law of 26 December 1961 established as repatriates the overseas French who, "as a result of political events, had or believed they had to quit a territory where they were settled and who had formerly been under French sovereignty, protectorate or trusteeship."[35] Apart from emergency measures, the central objective of government policy was to see to the newcomers' economic integration. The law mainly provided for a monthly living allowance to be paid for one year in order to allow the repatriates to seek employment corresponding to their skills. A policy of supplying credit as well as start-up subsidies and good-faith loans was instituted to encourage repatriate professionals to resume their activities. In some sectors, repatriates were given priority in hiring. Most civil servants were reinstated at the seniority and rank they had formerly held, even when that made them superfluous. Large companies such as the Bank of France and the Region Autonome des Transports Parisiens (RATP) were encouraged to take measures in favor of employing repatriates. Public housing quotas were also established on their behalf.[36]

A growing economy allowed France to devote 26 billion francs to integrating repatriates. Economic conditions and government choices facilitated the integration of the pied-noir population and in this way ensured a degree of social peace.[37] Documentaries broadcast on national television also contributed to pacifying representations and relations. News reports portrayed the pieds-noirs as pioneers whose dynamism contributed to economic development.[38]

It was only in 1970 that the former inhabitants of Algeria began to receive compensation for their lost property. Adopted under the presidency of Georges Pompidou, the "national contribution to compensation" law (15 July) allowed the most humble households to receive full compensation for the value of their goods, while the wealthiest ones were eligible to receive between 5 and 15 percent of their property's value. In the opinion of its beneficiaries, this law did not go far enough.[39] In a sign of growing discontent and radicalization, the Justice Pied-Noir movement was created in 1976 to denounce the slow progress of government policy and inspired a series of bombings. It was also in this period that the Recours association (Rassemblement et Coordination Unitaire des Rapatriés d'Outre-Mer) was created. In the 1981 presidential election, it supported the Socialist Party candidate.[40]

Another law, that of 2 January 1978, sought to improve upon its predecessor by giving priority to the elderly and impoverished while increasing the rate of compensation for the wealthiest. Under François Mitterrand, two other laws provided compensation to repatriates. These laws significantly contributed to reducing the debt of some pied-noir households by holding that their difficulties originated in the experience of repatriation and for that reason they could continue to lay claim to the nation's resources.[41]

Yann Scioldo-Zürcher identifies a "paradox of memory" among the pieds-noirs.[42] The latter explain their economic and social success by reference to their personal courage, dynamism, and abnegation, neglecting to mention the government assistance from which they have benefited. Dominated by the suffering of exile and the difficulties experienced upon their arrival in metropolitan France, the pied-noir narrative of victimization invariably portrays the French state as indebted to them.

Success: Dynamism and/or Useful Networks

The success of the pieds-noirs is common knowledge, with Alain Afflelou and Yves Saint-Laurent providing famous illustrations of it. In northern France— and particularly in the region of Paris, where many civil servants settled— the pieds-noirs were quickly integrated. Things went less smoothly in the south, where the capacity to absorb them was relatively weak: repatriates formed a larger share of the population, and, for small businessmen, artisans, and shopkeepers, the conditions were less favorable.[43] From a social and cultural perspective, their assimilation was also more profound in the north. Living in greater isolation from one another, the pieds-noirs chose to turn their backs on communal belonging and identity or resigned themselves to doing so.[44] It is mainly in southeastern France that the associations active in pied-noir circles recruit their members.

The pieds-noirs surveyed by Michèle Baussant are aware of their economic success and often prove "overadapted" and "overintegrated."[45] Clarisse Buono points out that none of those she interviewed "experienced notable social declassification relative to their life in Algeria." Indeed, several even benefited from career advancement. Some of them, she reveals, are also of the opinion, not just that they succeeded, but that they modernized France and perhaps even saved it from Third World status.[46]

Yet, despite the overall success of the pieds-noirs, the economic difficulties experienced by some of them—and, in particular, the elderly, the most vulnerable segment of the population—must be recognized. The establishment of prefectural Special Assistance and Exceptional Aid funds is evidence of the severity of the social problems that confronted a portion of the pied-noir population in the 1970s.[47]

The professional trajectories of the former OAS I met indicate that claims regarding the pieds-noirs' successful economic integration also apply to them. Their time as outlaws does not seem to have impeded their professional lives. Indeed, their ability to maintain networks suggests that, in some cases, their membership in the OAS worked to their advantage.

The leaders of two "delta" commandos, Edouard Slama and Gabriel Anglade, successfully launched new careers. A former parachutist who settled in Algeria and married a pied-noir after completing his military service, Edouard Slama spent four years in prison after arriving in France. While there, his wife and first daughter were assisted by Slama's former employer in Algiers, who continued to pay his salary. After he was released from prison, Slama worked in a real estate company, where the commission from his first sale "allowed [him] to get back on [his] feet." He subsequently became a salesman at Olivetti, a profession in which he excelled. He lived a comfortable life in Nice, where he had taken up residence. His marriage produced two more children, but, weary of his infidelity, his wife left him. In 1978, Slama created his own microcomputing company in Nice. The company was a success, partly because, the former "delta"-turned-entrepreneur explained, "I had very good contacts. I had contacts with Jacques Médecin and he gave me work—that is, his head of public relations gave me a lot of work."

Edouard Slama entered the Toulon city government on a Union pour la Démocratie Française (UDF, center right) list. He was responsible for computing and assumed leadership of a repatriate delegation. "I represented former prisoners, repatriates, and Harkis." During this time, he took advantage of the municipal and associative offices he held in Toulon to promote the memory of those nostalgic for French Algeria. In 1980, Maurice Arreckx, a Var deputy and mayor of Toulon, unveiled "the monument to the martyrs of French Algeria" in his town. A few days before the ceremony, the monument that had initially been constructed was destroyed by a bomb. Slama nevertheless brought roses for the occasion: "Everyone had their rose and laid it on the destroyed monument. After, with friends in the building, we rebuilt the monument as you see it today and that's where we commemorate the March 26th events—the March 26th massacres—and those of August."

Before devoting himself to the cause of French Algeria, Gabriel Anglade worked at the port of Algiers. He began at the age of thirteen and a half, first as a messenger and then as a transit employee. At seventeen, he became assistant to the quay supervisor. Following his military service, which he performed in Algeria, he became a section head and hired more than a hundred stevedores every day, nearly all of them Muslim. After a time in prison, Anglade became an operations manager with Renault. In this role, he principally traveled in Africa to set up garages: "Since these were high-risk countries, no one from Renault . . . because it's always the same in France, they have jobs as engineers and that sort of thing but, when they're asked to do something, suddenly it's too dangerous, and so us poor sods have to play mercenary for them." Since 1998, he has been the mayor's assistant in the

Cagnes-sur-Mer municipality. Today, these two former "deltas," who some suspect of having initially been tempted by a career of crime,[48] are retired.

In 1968, Joseph Rizza left Spain and joined his family in Nice. Thanks to the intervention of his "mates" and support from elected officials sympathetic to the partisans of French Algeria, he got a job as inspector in a company that oversaw the operation of red lights and parking meters. Reluctant to give up a good job, Marcel Ronda, for his part, only returned in 1969 when he was sure that he would be employed as an accountant at the hospital of Nice.[49]

Those who arrived in Spain in the late 1960s were promised that they would be amnestied, but efforts were also made to aid them. Athanase Georgopoulos, a former OAS leader in Oran who ran a café in his native town, recounts: "When I later returned to France, I became very close with Michel Baroin. And I entered the GMF [Garantie Mutuelle des Fontionnaires, a leading insurance company][50] and was later general director for all of southeastern France. I was the regional director of the GMF. I had 40 offices, 150 employees . . . And then after that I was in Paris, secretary general of the GMF group."

Georgopoulos is not alone in reporting that he benefited from "Gaullist" protection. Two other individuals claim that Gaullist figures helped them— one to obtain papers in order to return to France, and the other, an employee at the Naval Constructions Office (DCN), to secure a promotion after his career had stalled because of a military security report unfavorable to him. After a period sharing a tiny apartment with twenty-four members of his family, the latter succeeded in finding accommodation in Toulon with his wife, and his career subsequently advanced: "I'm happy here. I have my friends, I'm a club president . . . I'm in the AADEP [l'Association des anciens détenus et exilés politiques] et cetera. I have my friends. I go out. I have my family. I have my children. I have my grandchildren."[51]

From the Memory of the Defeated to the Reconquest of France

A multitude of associations exist in pied-noir circles, some of them regional or village-based. They seek to promote the cultural heritage of their community and preserve the sociabilities of the past. These associations hold an annual, one-day meeting at which the former inhabitants of Algeria get together to share a meal and celebrate. Larger, more socially and politically oriented associations were also created. In 1956, the ANFANOMA (Association

Nationale des Français d'Afrique du Nord, d'Outre-Mer et de Leurs Amis/ National Association of Overseas and North African French and Their Friends) was created to assist the repatriates of North Africa. The Recours association, created in 1978, sought to establish itself as a pressure group in order to influence compensation policy on behalf of the pieds-noirs. Some of those nostalgic for French Algeria were irritated by its leader, Jacques Roseau, reproaching his legalism, contacts with the RPR,[52] and excessive openness toward Algerian members of the Front de Libération Nationale (FLN). Roseau was assassinated in 1993 by men claiming to be members of the OAS.

In 1984, Joseph Ortiz, founder of the French National Front (FNF) and an OAS member who sought to continue the struggle for French Algeria, created the Federation for the Unity of Refugees, Repatriates, and Their Friends (FURR). This association, which disappeared with its leader's death in 1995, was suspected of being involved in attacks targeting immigrant workers in the 1970s.[53]

Jean-Jacques Susini created the AADEP (Association des Anciens Détenus et Exilés Politiques/Association of Former Political Prisoners and Exiles) in 1968. At the time, he hoped to launch himself in politics by uniting his troops around him. Though for lack of evidence no charges were ever brought against him, suspicion that he was involved in the kidnapping and disappearance of the former treasurer of the OAS, Colonel Raymond Gorel, sapped the revolutionary and unifying momentum he brought to his cause. He was later to be implicated in a number of armed robberies perpetrated between June 1969 and January 1970. After being remanded in custody for two years, in March 1974 he was acquitted by the Aix-en-Provence Court of Assises. He then resumed his medical studies, pursued a doctorate in economics, and launched a security consulting firm.[54]

In 1967, one of the 1961 putschists, Edmond Jouhaud, created the ADI-MAD (Association Amicale pour la Défense des Intérêts Moraux et Matériels des Anciens Détenus et Exilés Politiques de l'Algérie Française/Association for the Defense of the Moral and Material Interests of the Former Political Prisoners and Exiles of French Algeria). Jouhaud intended to devote his retirement to promoting veterans' interests with the authorities and personally assisting some of them. A large portion of the association's supporters consist of repatriates sympathetic to the cause of French Algeria—its mailing list contains 4,000 names, and the association's website speaks of 1,200 members.[55] Its bylaws state that it "seeks to defend, by all legal means, the memory of all of the martyrs and all of the victims of the enemies of French

Algeria. . . . The Association will devote all of its energy to ensuring that all
combatants of French Algeria killed in combat or murdered following exceptional Stalinist-Gaullist judgements are recognized as having 'died for
France.'"[56] Describing itself as a continuation of the OAS,[57] the association
honored the latter's combatants. At its website, photos of the four men executed by firing squad incessantly scroll across one corner of the screen. The
website features a regularly updated section concerning the passing of its
"enemies"—Gaullists, communists, "suitcase carriers," and FLN members—
with the words "good riddance" appended to announcements of their deaths.
The association defends the material interests of OAS members imprisoned
or in hiding abroad and seeks to increase the indemnities provided for by
the 23 February 2005 law. It takes great pains to erect steles in praise of its
"martyrs" and defends the right to commemorate its dead. The association
is today clearly aligned with the far right. Its president, Jean-François Colin,
is a member of the National Front (FN) and l'Œuvre Française, which has
ties to Pierre Sidos.

Despite Susini's difficulties, the AADEP was successfully launched. Taken
over by Edouard Slama in 1977, the association recruited only former OAS
and consisted of fewer than 300 members. It thus favored the community of
combatants, with "deltas" and "collines" preserving ties of friendship. In contrast to the ADIMAD, the AADEP made few public statements, though it took
care to avoid open criticism of the former. The two associations nevertheless
had several disagreements. The first stemmed from the OAS "loot" scandal
and the death of its treasurer, Raymond Jean Gorel. Jean-Claude Pérez was
a member of the ADIMAD, and the association apparently defended
Gorel's wife against Jean-Jacques Susini.[58] Moreover, some members of the
ADIMAD disapproved of the tolerance shown toward "Gaullists" by members of the AADEP.[59] Indeed, several active members of this organization
rejected the National Front and sought instead to develop relationships with
the right wing of the government. Yet, despite individual rivalries and disagreements regarding how the associations should position and present
themselves in the public sphere, the ADIMAD and AADEP pursued similar
objectives: to obtain additional compensation—both for pieds-noirs and for
members of the OAS—and to obtain recognition for their struggle. Each of
these associations was represented by one member at the interministerial
mission for repatriates. Following adoption of the 23 February 2005 law
providing for compensation to be paid to OAS veterans in the private sector,
a commission was created to apply the law and oversee payments. The

government chose the AADEP's sitting president, Athanase Georgopoulos, to serve on the commission. Thanks to the networks he had created since meeting Michel Baroin, and his talent for human relations, this former OAS leader was able to establish himself as an official interlocutor for his movement.

Clientelist relations have long existed between elected officials and these associations. As Scioldo-Zürcher has shown, every election since the late 1960s has been marked by promises of compensation and demands formulated by repatriate representatives.[60] At the National Assembly, deputies from all parties have acted as spokesmen for the pieds-noirs, and, prior to its election, each new governmental majority has promised to improve the manner in which the issue of compensation is handled. Scioldo-Zürcher also shows that, spurred by electoral jockeying and the persistence of a colonial vision, political discourse has increasingly lent the issue of compensation an air of moral reparation.[61] At a February 2007 speech in Toulon, the Union pour un Mouvement Populaire (UMP, right and center right created in 2002 and became Les Républicains in 2015) presidential candidate, Nicolas Sarkozy, denounced repentance and paid tribute to colonization, the pieds-noirs, and the Harkis. In letters sent to repatriate associations between the first and second rounds of the election, Sarkozy promised to create a memorial in Marseille to overseas France and establish the Foundation for the Memory of the Algerian War, which had been provided for by the 23 February 2005 law. Representatives of the repatriates would be tasked with overseeing it.[62]

The relations established between politicians and pieds-noirs, particularly in southeastern France, where the latter are heavily concentrated, may be explained in various ways. The alliance formed between those nostalgic for French Algeria and the mayors of Nice—Jean Médecin and, later, his son, Jacques Médecin—appears to have been based on genuine affinities, with all parties sharing a fondness for the lost empire and a hostility to Gaullism.[63] Such ideological promiscuity does not rule out, however, the possible role played by opportunism and a desire to use one another for political gain.

In his time as a representative on the Toulon city council and leader of the AADEP in the 1980s, Edouard Slama's career was characterized by the serial formation and dissolution of relationships. "I personally met Jacques Dominati and he became my friend. It's thanks to him that I made the monument to the martyrs of French Algeria." Slama also allied himself with Jacques Médecin and participated with "his mates" in providing security when Charles Pasqua came to support him. Slama may have overestimated his influence: "After I campaigned for François Léotard, we made him mayor, we made him deputy, we made him minister, and then after that I dropped him because he betrayed us. He was very good to us when he was a deputy, he defended us very well at the National Assembly. But later he changed, he changed course." This was not to be Slama's last disappointment: "I campaigned for Marchiani because I have a close personal friend who went to college with him, so I knew Marchiani . . . When I met Marchiani, he said to me: 'Can I count on you and your friends?' I told him: 'There's no problem, we'll help you out.' Well, I regret that now. There's one thing I realize: every politician I've met has been a thief."

The shifting, clientelist strategies are characterized by temporary alliances, bargaining between politicians and voters, favors for friends, and attempts to insert oneself into networks of power. Even though the former "delta" positions himself on the right, there is little evidence of political conviction. Although Slama worries over "the Islamicization of France," he refuses to be labeled far right. Both Slama and Rizza occasionally act as hired strongmen, carrying weapons and deploying their "know-how," which they have not lost despite the passage of time. Rizza thus recounts having supported Jean-Paul Claustres, a protegé of Jacques Médecin, when he ran for office in Draguignan. The former "delta" scrambled the socialists' radio programs and provided personal security for his candidate.

Of the sixteen-person sample considered here, four former OAS have become involved in politics and sit on city councils. Having spent forty years militating for their interests and to rehabilitate their past actions, these men have clearly become expert in political intrigue and the exercise of pressure and have mastered the techniques of public relations and lobbying within the associations in which they are active.

One result of these intrigues among politicians and OAS partisans has been the erection of steles in praise of the "martyrs" of French Algeria. Thanks to Jacques Médecin, this policy of commemoration first got off the ground in Nice in 1973. In 1980, it continued in Toulon in the presence of Toulon's deputy mayor, Maurice Arreckx, and the secretary of state for repatriates, Jacques Dominati. In 2002, a monument was constructed in Théoule-sur-Mer and was followed in 2003 by others in Perpignan and Béziers. In June of each year, the municipal government of Port-Vendres commemorates the landing of Charles X's first French battalions in Sidi Fredj.[64] These are all low-key affairs. In 2006, by contrast, the Marignane stele in the town's cemetery led to controversy. Although the monument was ultimately erected, the mobilization against it led the city to forbid its supporters from publicly inaugurating it.

Seeing themselves as defenders of the nation, those nostalgic for the OAS are persuaded that they have been excluded from national memory and treated like "second-class French citizens." They fight to win recognition for their cause and their dead. Frequently, they compare themselves to Second World War Resistance fighters: in casting aside legality, they see themselves as having remained true to patriotic legitimacy. Pierre Sergent claimed that his struggle would be over "when his comrades executed by de Gaulle were recognized as having died for France."[65] For his part, the president of the AADEP, Athanase Georgopoulos, states:

> For years, I have fought within my association so that the political will expresses itself—not to say "Bravo OAS, you were right," but to recognize the validity of our struggle, which was to keep Algeria in France. We don't want medals. The undertaking accomplished for France has been recognized, not just in Algeria but everywhere that used to be France overseas. That's good, that's a very good thing. . . . Indirectly, it's a way of saying that one can also understand the battle waged by some who had an ideal: to preserve French land.

The issue of recognition nevertheless requires official France to alter its vision of the war of Algerian independence. By endeavoring to rehabilitate their militants, former OAS members seek to shape France after their image. The adoption of the 23 February 2005 law recognizing the work accomplished overseas constitutes one step in this transformation. Should the partisans of French Algeria achieve their goal, they will lose the object of their struggle, and their memory will fade away.[66]

*   *   *

The individual trajectories of veterans illustrate rulers' political choices as well as their relative ability to negotiate postconflict dividends. Access to material reward is a political issue reflecting the legitimacy that the community accords to the combatants who defended it.

Nevertheless, symbolic reward is not always accompanied by material recompense, and conversely. The cases studied here thus show that a conflict's losers may sometimes lay claim to financial advantages even when they are delegitimated and marginalized by the new political order. In leaving their jobs, South African army and police veterans received large severance packages. In France, the members of the OAS, like the French population more generally, profited from the growth of *les Trente Glorieuses* to reintegrate themselves into the economy. Upon their return to civilian life, what's more, some profited from solidarity and support networks to get back on their feet. A form of material recognition may be established to dissuade the defeated from disrupting the new political order.

In what concerns the tribute paid victorious ex-combatants, South Africa and Algeria took opposite paths. In the country of Nelson Mandela, the project to radically remake the nation precluded repaying the sacrifices of former MK. The new rhetoric of legitimacy that had been adopted to promote reconciliation prevented the country's rulers from rewarding the violence associated with the struggle against apartheid. The decision to only slightly reward the armed militants of the ANC exposed the most destitute among them to extreme poverty. Socioeconomic discrepancies and the slow pace at which South African society was transformed thus ultimately came to be seen as the most significant obstacles to reconciliation. In what is perhaps a sign that this model is beginning to change, the new president of the South African Republic, Jacob Zuma, has recently transformed the Ministry of Defense into the Ministry of Defense and Military Veterans.

In the country of Houari Boumediene, the mujahideen became the regime's most important bulwark. In exchange for their continued support, the resources allocated to this ever-expanding social group were constantly increased. Founded on the revolutionary legitimacy of 1954, the regime survived the economic and political crises of the 1980s as well as the civil war that followed a decade later. It did so by consolidating and enlarging its base.

The summary offered in Table 2 shows that the absence or weakness of symbolic and material recompense prevents rapprochement with one's former enemy. Unemployed and discredited, impoverished ANC militants have no contact with their former adversaries. The significant stigmatization to which apartheid-era civil servants and former OAS are for their part subjected has led them to withdraw into a conflictual posture that requires them to keep the figure of the enemy alive. The prestige accorded ex-combatants can lead them to open up to their former adversaries. In the case of the mujahideen, however, a permanent threat is required if they are to maintain their legitimacy and status as heroes. In Algeria, the enemy is not an individual with whom one is at odds but rather an ideological construction underwriting a particular identity.

Table 2. The status of ex-combatants and their perception of the ex-enemy

Ex-Combatants	Material Recompense	Symbolic Recompense	Relationship to Ex-Enemy
ANC			
New bourgeoisie	Economic liberalism as means of regulation	Ordinary citizens	Open hand
The poor			Significant social distance
FLN	Privileged access to oil and gas rent	Heroes	Mobilization (against)
Security Branch	Job-leaving bonus	Killers	Suspicion
SADF	Job-leaving bonus and possibility of remaining	Reputation (relatively) intact	Relative openness
OAS	Access to economic growth	Violent reactionaries	Hostility

The place occupied by veterans within their nation influences the manner in which they develop their war narratives. The possibility of acknowledging violence and expressing pride or regret depends upon the manner in which particular political configurations structure the moral universe.

PART III

War Narratives and Imaginaries of Violence

WHEN AND HOW do ex-combatants speak about those they killed or tortured? Why does mention the violence of the past provoke feelings of regret, guilt, or pride? How is it possible to recall the past when doing so reminds one of the enemy's death as well as one's own suffering and that of fallen comrades? What is at issue here is not how the protagonists in a conflict behaved on the battlefield but rather the manner in which ex-combatants look upon violence.[1] According to Antoine Prost, the veterans who came back from the First World War were "silent on the subject of the soldier's fear." "The main experience" of the war proved incommunicable, and soldiers more willingly mentioned material difficulties than feelings of fear, compassion, or remorse. Moreover, "the combatants were the prisoners of civilians' expectations." As such, they were obliged to appear as they had been imagined: heroic fighters defending the fatherland rather than suffering men wondering at the war's absurdity.[2] Yet the absence of visible distress among former activists and soldiers does not preclude feelings of the same. And what is at issue here is less veterans' feelings of unease vis-à-vis violence than their ability to communicate these feelings. To what extent is one capable of evoking one's own acts of violence, and under what conditions does one acknowledge the disruptive effects they have produced on oneself? Why, in other words, are some individuals (but not others) prepared to acknowledge their weaknesses?

Narratives supply the meaning that protagonists subsequently confer upon action. Assembled one or more decades after the end of the conflict, narratives help distance one from the violence of war. In peacetime, once the conflict has been resolved or eliminated, the meaning of the violent act fades; it does not, for all that, fully disappear. This decline or loss of meaning reflects the dominant values of the postconflict order. As the gap between meanings deepens, it becomes all the more challenging to speak. In South Africa, the new elites' efforts to delegitimize violence have proven disorienting for ex-combatants who resorted to brute force. In Algeria, by contrast, the use of violence against the colonial enemy still has a place in a system of political justification. The manner in which the former enemy is perceived also impacts how one evaluates one's own violence. Today, former members of the OAS still accuse their enemies—the FLN and the French state—of barbarity and betrayal and only slightly distance themselves from the violent acts they committed.

In order to decipher the imaginary of violence among ex-combatants, I examine what they have to say about the conflict and the methods employed during it as well as their discourse regarding the former enemy. By comparing collective narratives, I show that, while the protagonists of the Franco-Algerian conflict celebrate or justify their own acts of violence, South African veterans disparage the use of force (Chapter 7).

After having considered the groups in question on a case-by-case basis, I take the opposite approach, focusing instead on the arguments that are used. Denial, rationalization, and a tendency to feel guilt for or boast of past actions characterize certain configurations. When the individual is placed at the center of analysis, however, the mechanisms that drive these configurations may be deciphered (Chapter 8).

Finally, the experience of torture is generally a matter of unspeakable suffering. In some cases, however, setting this suffering in the context of narrative allows victims of torture to achieve self-esteem. For these individuals, their past experience does not constitute an insurmountable obstacle to gradual rapprochement with the enemy (Chapter 9).

Chapter 7

Collective Discourse

A narrative postulates a subject capable of expressing an interpretation of distant or recent events and of relating it to a self-dramatization. It discloses a process of identity construction. It relates an ever-evolving collective memory to a vision of the present and a projection of the group into the future.

It is not always easy to reconstruct the framework of collective narrative, for it is simultaneously developed within the group and through interaction with the external world. Speech expressed at a given moment makes sense to the group; spokesmen take possession of it and diffuse it; it is appropriated by individuals who thus feel they belong to the group, the contours of which take form and are consolidated. Such speech includes the identification of heroic figures as models and the designation of former or still present adversaries. The narrative does not go without saying; its elaboration is just one option among others. Thus, the notion of "chosen trauma" developed by Vamik Volkan implies that the heritage of the past is selectively chosen and subject to ex post facto criteria of relevance.[1] The expression suggests the possibility that actors retain certain painful episodes from the history of their group while ignoring others. Their narratives do not systematically recall and include experienced suffering, because, among other reasons, one must assign it meaning and relate it to a grammar of injustice. Conversely, some facts are overemphasized in actors' narratives and thereby supply their basic fabric. Collective narrative also produces a system for justifying and legitimating the actions undertaken by a group: the recourse to violence and its renunciation, as well as the choice of alliance or enmity, are the objects of political and moral argument.

Collective narrative therefore allows one to redefine the contours of the group to which one belongs by stating criteria of legitimacy drawn from the war narrative. It allows one to establish a hierarchy among combatants.

At the same time, narratives open a "space of resonance" in the public sphere,[2] adapting to this space even as they contribute to shaping it. And they evolve over time, factoring in other narratives—the rival narratives of competitors and opponents as well as the official narratives of the authorities. As Jean-Michel Chaumont brilliantly points out in connection with Nazi victims' demands for recognition, several layers of discourse deposit their sediment, producing new power struggles.[3] These, in turn, give rise to new narrative content and style. Explanations and retorts to the accusations leveled against them are thus to be found woven into the fabric of the collective narratives produced by groups of ex-combatants. For the protagonists, these narratives serve as a system of defense and also intersect with issues of recognition.

The various groups of ex-combatants studied here developed narratives regarding their experience of war. Their discourse sets out justifications in terms both moral (the degree to which it is legitimate to resort to force) and strategic (the usefulness of violence in allowing us to achieve our objective). As one deciphers these remarks concerning the conflict, a representation of violence begins to take shape.

The narrative repertoires of enemy "couples" present similarities and reciprocally interact with one another. In France and Algeria, the war's violence has not been acknowledged and in many respects has been intentionally concealed, particularly by political leaders. Members of the National Liberation Front (FLN) and the Secret Army Organization (OAS) tend to play down the violence perpetrated by their groups even as they take a certain pride in recalling the blows they delivered against the enemy. In South Africa, the work of the Truth and Reconciliation Commission (TRC) brought violence to the attention of the public while at the same time subjecting it to a process of delegitimization. African National Congress (ANC) combatants, like those who defended apartheid, internalized what had become the dominant ethos.

Moreover, narrative construction also depends on whether one sees oneself as victorious or defeated. Victory and defeat can take various forms. The figures corresponding to these forms indicate the broad possibilities for post-conflict subjectification.

The FLN: A Heroic and Legitimate Conflict

Several decades after the end of the Algerian War, former mujahideen maintain that the humiliation of the colonial system and the repressive methods employed by the French army required the FLN to resort to violence. The moral stature of the combatant is thus illustrated by his determination in combat, sense of sacrifice, and willingness to give his life for the national cause. His status as a hero rests upon his use of violence, and he takes pride in the belief that he won the war. Meanwhile, the impression that the old enemy in some ways remains belligerent requires that he remain mobilized.

Faced with the Colonial State, a Necessary and Residual Violence

The ex-combatants present their involvement in the national liberation struggle as a personal revolt against an unjust and racist colonial system. Colonialism is identified as an initial violence that reveals itself through brutality—the brutality of conquest as well as that of the army and police who resorted to torture and napalm. This brutality continues to be embodied in the everyday contempt of Europeans. The theories of Frantz Fanon[4] have been internalized by the protagonists, who maintain that, faced with the systemic, structurally superior violence of the colonial system, the resort to force was necessary and legitimate: "[Colonialism] is violence in its natural state and will yield only when confronted with greater violence."[5]

The argument is itself contradictory: how can one deploy a force superior to that of an enemy endowed with massive means of coercion? Can determination and the recourse to new techniques of guerrilla warfare suffice to invert the power struggle? Yacef Saadi led an FLN group during the Battle of Algiers. He explains that the decision to detonate bombs in European public places was partly taken in order to convince Algerians and, indeed, FLN partisans that they had what it took to fight:

> The first bomb was planted in 1955 by what would later become the OAS. This was before the FLN's [first] bombing, which took place on 30 September 1956. The bomb exploded during curfew in the kasbah. It killed seventy-five people and wounded many more. We had to react to this. We had to say to the Algerian people—our people—that we had a weapon just as cruel as that of the enemy. We had to tell

them that we were capable of defending them; otherwise they would have surrendered their weapons. Violence calls for violence; it's a spiral.

Here one glimpses the liberating role of violence as Fanon conceived it: by employing equal or greater brutality, one demonstrates to others and, above all, to one's own people that one is capable of confronting the enemy and dealing him a heavy blow.

Nevertheless, there is an ambivalence to using violence for the purposes of self-heroization: in their remarks, the mujahideen seek to show both that they are capable of violence and that their violence falls short of the threshold of colonial brutality. Thus, their use of violence is always presented as paling by comparison to that employed by the French state; the enormity of the latter dispels any ethical reservations that might have been provoked by the death of European civilians. The FLN's responsibility for its actions is, as it were, mitigated by the position to which it was reduced by the enemy. When asked whether the decision to plant bombs was difficult, Yacef Saadi replied: "Very difficult. But, given the provocation, we were able to do it without remorse, despite the gravity of the act. The worst thing was not the people we killed but those we mutilated; we felt sorriest for them."

Nevertheless, while violence is acknowledged, few people narrate its use in the first person. Yacef Saadi and some of those who planted bombs in Algiers agree to speak about well-known actions. As we know from Fanon's work as a psychiatrist, some Algerian militants were troubled by the murder(s) they committed.[6] For many years now, they have perhaps been burdened by doubt and a heavy conscience; if so, it has been buried under a dead weight of legitimation and silence. Gaps in the historiography of the Algerian War have served to conceal some of its aspects, allowing the actors to conserve an untroubled discourse. Well-known episodes such as the Melouza massacre, meanwhile, are portrayed as an "Algerian affair."

The Moral Strength of the Combatants

The heroism of the Algerian combatant stems not only from his rudimentary resources, his way of excelling, but also from his willingness to sacrifice. The 1.5 million official martyrs are proof of this, and FLN veterans very often claim that they were ready to give their lives. Yacef Saadi exemplifies this type of discourse:

We didn't care about death because we were already committed to dying. We knew this wasn't a game of billiards or a tennis match. As soon as you get involved, you tell yourself: it's either liberation or death. You always have this hope, otherwise you would stop. And I had this idea that, if I died, as the partisans sing, "Friend, if you fall, another will take your place." So I told myself that if I died or was arrested, there would be others. The soldiers' reaction helped us a lot: by torturing us, the soldiers did us a favor, they became the best militants for the FLN and our cause. When you torture someone, when you kill someone, there's a great surge in recruitment.

Heroism resided in this dialectic between FLN combatants and the French army. When the latter was perceived as immoral, as a source of death and mutilation, it fanned moral and political revolt among Algerians. For the leaders of the repressive system and those charged with enforcing it, Algerian lives did not count; FLN combatants accepted this thoroughly colonial vision and inverted the stigma. Ready to give their lives and suffer with their bodies to defend the cause, the Algerians feared neither death nor torture. They supposedly signed up in ever-greater numbers. Indeed, the Algerians' victory is presented as residing in their ability to confront death and suffering, a moral strength that is said to have distinguished them from the French. In order to vouch for the idealistic and ethical nature of his engagement, however, Yacef Saadi takes care to appeal to a certain idea of France—that of the Resistance.

Another Fanonian theme of the Algerian revolution is that it was ultimately a humanist revolt to the degree that it restored dignity to the individual and people. The struggle for liberation brought out values of solidarity and generosity long buried under the reign of colonialism. FLN veterans often mention the atmosphere of fraternity that reigned among the men-at-arms, while *mujahidat*[7] speak of the respect shown them by their companions once the war had imposed a common life upon them. Despite the harsh living conditions characteristic of clandestine and guerrilla warfare, there is no trace in the interviews of conflict, egotism, or pettiness among the men. Even when recalling the FLN's internal purges, the battles fought against the militants of competing movements, or the clashes with the Army of the Frontiers in the summer of 1962, the ideal representation of the disinterested, disciplined, and courageous combatant remains intact.

Tahar also speaks to the purity of the combatants during the war of liberation. Once again, the trial of gender relations is overcome. This took place, what's more, in the context of a traditional society:

> At the time, women were veiled. As soon as they were fourteen years old, it was over for girls, they didn't go out anymore, not for school or anything else . . . But I remember that, after I escaped from prison in 1961, I was involved in a skirmish. When we fled, I found a woman, an old woman, standing in front of a door. She's the one who opened the door for me. She let me into her house. She hid me in the well. The soldiers searched everywhere and then left. I spent the night with them. And what did Algerians use to have? They had a bedroom, a family bedroom. Well, I spent the night there surrounded by four girls. For me, they were sisters. I didn't have any ulterior motive. You see, the . . . They trusted their combatants. The people trusted us.[8]

A Largely Uncritical Regard

The final characteristic of the FLN narrative is its very limited capacity for self-criticism. Doubts are expressed only in passing and are often followed by a discursive correction that serves to preclude any possibility of moral or political reconsideration. Once again, an extract from my interview with Yacef Saadi is revealing:

> —In any organization, some people make mistakes. You get your nose cut off for smoking a cigarette because you're accused of supporting the French economy, etc. There were mistakes on both sides, the French side and ours. So it was to be expected that errors would be made at the beginning. I made some, too, but it is hard to know which. Killing someone for nothing because someone misled me and accused that person of being an informer, even though he might not have been one. That's revolution for you. Revolutions are prepared by people who are very wise, but are carried out by barbarians and led by thugs.
> —Does this also hold for the Algerian revolution?
> —For all of them.
> —But this principle that you apply to revolutions in general, do you also apply it to the Algerian revolution?

—No, no, we won our independence, but what I'm talking about are revolutions like Castro's, etc. For us, the revolution had an extraordinary clarity.

These remarks from the leader of the Battle of Algiers might lead one to believe that he ranks himself among the "barbarians." But even as he tacitly acknowledges having killed people "for nothing," he clears himself of all responsibility and maintains that the Algerians' war was exceptional.

The ex-combatants are convinced of the righteousness of the movement in which they were involved. Possible misdeeds are blamed on elements outside of or marginal to the FLN, while violence is played down or justified by reference to the constraints that impinged on the clandestine organization. This refusal to speak of the misdeeds or errors of the fight for liberation suggests a certain inability to move beyond the stage of combat and the certainties with which it is associated. It thus comes as no surprise that the ex-combatants express hardly any guilt:

—Is there anything that you personally regret?
—No, personally I have no regrets, I have no regrets, personally I have no regrets. Because . . . I didn't harm people or my country. I did good by my country. I gave my life, you see. I threw myself into the great fight and thank God I'm still alive. I didn't harm people or anyone, and now I live *hamdullilah* [thanks to God]. When I travel around Algeria, wherever I go, they say hello Mr. G., they greet me.[9]

Social respect and the status accorded violence and war by the authorities serve as a moral guarantee. They relieve ex-combatants of potential problems of conscience. This allows them to smother any emotion or uneasiness relating to the perpetration of violence.

As reflected in the rhetoric of Algerian leaders since 1962, FLN veterans find themselves in the position of triumphant victors. Relying only on their determination, sense of sacrifice, and thirst for liberty and dignity, they confronted a fierce and militarily superior enemy who did not shy away from using immoral methods. In doing so, they became heroes. In Algiers, several women who fought in the war insisted on a point of semantics—"No one gave us independence, we seized it from France"—thereby underscoring the fervor shown by the protagonists in their struggle against a tenacious enemy, as well as the type of relationship that obtained between the colonial metropole and the people longing for independence. Denied the status of citizen during the colonial period, a new type of Algerian was born from this struggle: a free, independent, and proud being. Even among FLN militants who have not profited from the regime's generosity and remain outside the circles of power, pride at participating in the anticolonial struggle and adherence to the dogma of the struggle for liberation continue to inform their identities.

The ANC: The Moral Demands of the Struggle

For several decades, the ANC pursued a nonviolent struggle centered on civil disobedience actions. Repression by the apartheid regime and the absence of any prospect for change subsequently led the ANC to opt for armed struggle.[10] This change of policy was also driven by a desire to respond to popular anger. Yet the use of violence was limited, with Mandela placing himself as it were halfway between Gandhi and Fanon.[11] Despite the increasing brutality of the conflict in the 1980s and 1990s,[12] the ANC hewed to a conception of the struggle and its resolution that contributed to discrediting violence. Under these circumstances, heroism in South Africa mainly came to be defined as the capacity to forswear violence.

Morality as a Strategy?

Strategic considerations underlay the ANC's limited use of force. In a context in which the imbalance of forces favored the apartheid regime, economizing violence was a means of avoiding excessively heavy reprisal.[13] Moreover, the ANC's strategy sought to obtain international support and isolate the South African regime. This required the ANC—a signatory to the 1977 additions to the Geneva Conventions, to respect the human rights it advocated. Furthermore, it sought to preserve the possibility of future reconciliation with the beneficiaries of the apartheid regime. Finally, the moral stance adopted by ANC leaders precluded them from seeing apartheid's beneficiaries as their enemies. Indeed, several ex-combatants explained that, once they entered the fold of the ANC, they adopted its approach to the struggle, identifying the enemy as the regime rather than the entire white population and abandoning certain violent practices.

The use of violence was limited, and civilians were generally spared. In the early 1960s, Albert Luthuli already looked indulgently upon the "ignorance" of those who benefited from the apartheid regime with regard to the

fate of the black population, an "ignorance . . . increasingly desired and aggravated by the government."[14] The idea that whites had been misled by their
own political representatives persists to this day. ANC members also emphasized their own moral and strategic strength, which consisted in the refusal
to use violence. Some of them resolutely rejected attacks or assassination as
options, notably against the Security Branch police who captured and tortured them. According to these militants, it was by infiltrating the police
rather than taking vengeance against them or attacking strategic sites that
ANC combatants showed their prowess. Recourse to intelligence rather than
violence was meant to destabilize the adversary. For ex-members of Umkhonto we Sizwe (MK), the renunciation of violence was strategic but also
served as proof of their moral superiority over the enemy: "We did not try to
imitate the enemy; we tried to not learn the enemy's lessons of cruelty, harsh-
ness, and barbarity. We tried to turn the other cheek."[15]

Violence Against Oneself

However, the rejection of violence against civilians was not total and systematic. ANC structures were roiled by debate, and, on several occasions,
cells claiming to represent the movement attacked public places frequented
by white South Africans.[16] Few such actions took place, however. Indeed, the
principal victims of ANC violence were black South Africans. The deadliest
outbreak of violence occurred when militants from the ANC and Inkhata
Freedom Party (IFP), egged on by the powers that be, came to blows in
Kwazulu-Natal and the townships of East Rand.[17] As Fanon and Gandhi had
both intuited, violence against the enemy and violence against oneself were
inseparable.[18] In the case of South Africa, one may wonder whether the self-
control shown in dealings with the enemy did not have the effect of intensi-
fying the phenomenon of violence against oneself. Moreover, "collaborators"
and "spies" were summarily executed in the country's townships,[19] often by
being subjected to the ordeal of "necklacing." They were also killed in the
ANC camps scattered throughout southern Africa.[20]

Initially, the ANC's leadership rejected the principle of requiring its members to request amnesty from the Truth and Reconciliation Commission
(TRC). However, under pressure from the TRC's chairman, Desmond Tutu,
it resigned itself to participating in the process alongside the "perpetrators."[21]
In its report to the TRC, the ANC admitted having committed excesses
against mutineers and presumed collaborators, particularly at its camps in

Angola,[22] and expressed regret for several attacks that it carried out against civilians on South African territory. The ANC was more forthcoming than the National Party (NP) but remained reticent regarding its responsibility for the death squads that operated against the IFP.[23]

The extremely sensitive question of collaborators and what befell them at the hands of the ANC did not receive special attention from the TRC. Moreover, some commentators have argued that the TRC did not adequately address the human rights violations committed by the liberation movement against its own members. In the absence of a real investigation, ANC members implicated in these affairs were not inclined to criticize their own practices.

The TRC Effect: From the Status of Combatant to That of "Perpetrator" and "Victim"

By inviting perpetrators and victims to speak the truth and forgive one another, the TRC helped give new meaning to the conflict. As the authors or instigators of violence, the members of national liberation movements were obliged to request amnesty in the same way as the members of death squads.

Some ANC officials had little difficulty accommodating themselves to the requirement that they request amnesty before the TRC, grasping the commission's rationale for neatly categorizing all witnesses as victims or perpetrators. For many rank-and-file combatants, by contrast, doing so could be disconcerting.

Those who committed acts of violence or murder have found it difficult to adjust to the new categories of South African democracy. Confession and forgiveness have overshadowed the combatants' skill and daring. The policy of reconciliation delegitimized violence and, as a consequence, tended to arouse feelings of guilt among those who had employed it. While the struggle was still ongoing, their action had enjoyed moral and political backing. With its end, that backing disappeared. Today, the failure of ANC structures to offer social or moral support abandons ex-combatants to their solitude, financial distress, and memories. When the significance assigned past conflict fades away or is transformed, and the present nullifies the meaning of consensual sacrifice in combat, veterans lose their bearings.

Moreover, the proliferation of NGO initiatives to advance reconciliation and establish systems of psychological support has contributed to spreading the notions of trauma and victimization. In Soweto, most of those I interviewed had consulted a psychologist or a psychiatrist.[24] Both approach violence perpetrated or sustained from the perspective of the traumatic experience. While psychologists respond to real needs, it nevertheless remains the case that they encourage a particular reading of the combatant's ordeal, one that stresses the idea of individual suffering while obscuring the difficulty involved in supplying a political and collective meaning to one's experience.

The narratives of MK veterans differ depending on their trajectories. Those for whom liberation brought concrete political or economic benefits— whether in the form of significant economic and social promotion in the new South Africa or simply access to the middle classes—had no difficulty embracing the dominant discourse, rejecting violence, and experiencing self-esteem. They embody the figure of the magnanimous victor. Conscious of their moral and political victory, they subscribe to the stance of reconciliation laid out by Nelson Mandela. This attitude is proof of the protagonists' generosity and tolerance. Nevertheless, it also allows ANC militants to present themselves as liberators, not only in the sense of having secured citizenship for blacks but also in that of having freed whites from the dogma of the NP and the retrograde social system of apartheid. The magnanimous victors are future-oriented and believe in their project: the establishment of a multicultural society. Refusing to allow themselves to be overwhelmed by the past, they are resolutely optimistic and confident in future generations.

By contrast, a large number of the ANC's rank-and-file militants recognize themselves in the figure of the victim-victor. This group consists of former guerrilla fighters who, though aware of their enemy's defeat, nevertheless see themselves as losers within the new political order. Impoverished, unemployed, and socially isolated, they are exposed to the brutal social relations that characterize their environment. For them, the moral strength to be found in renouncing violence seems a little unreal. Their community is still scarred by the brutal treatment of real and imagined collaborators as well as by the extreme violence of conflicts between ANC and IFP militants. Moreover, since most of them have few if any dealings with whites, the reality of interracial reconciliation is beyond them. While these ex-combatants continue to proudly proclaim their membership in the ANC, they now associate their experience of combat with the idea of suffering. Feelings of loss have come to eclipse the more positive idea of self-sacrifice.

Their frustration is also stoked by unequal access to the privileges of power: in a context of growing poverty and socioeconomic discrepancies, their disappointment has been converted into a feeling of betrayal. The leaders are accused of hijacking their own political project. The legitimacy of the new political order is being called into question. As this happens, ex-combatants from disadvantaged backgrounds express greater hostility toward their leaders than toward the old enemy. The new black bourgeoisie—unfaithful "comrades" who made their fortunes by abandoning their companions-in-arms to poverty—are said to be a favorite target of criminality. Profiting from their military training and frustrated by the failure of political victory to result in material advantages, former MK combatants are slaking their appetite for social revenge in crime.

The OAS: Between Vengeance and Resistance

OAS veterans accept seeing themselves as the war's losers; they clearly failed to prevent the emergence of an independent Algeria, and some of them individually paid a price (via prison or exile) for their violent activities. As members of a minority that battled Algerian nationalists and the French state alike, they rarely call upon strategic arguments to explain their past violence, relying instead on emotional language. The moral dimension, for all that, is not lacking.

Vengeance, Honor, and Virility

Like their FLN adversaries, the members of the OAS regard their past use of force as legitimate. Moreover, they speak rather casually and freely about some of their military feats. For them, the OAS was justified in taking up arms for reasons of vengeance or the need to defend the group against constant threat and violence. They explain that they joined the partisans of French Algeria to avenge the death of "French people" among their relatives and acquaintances.

Like the combatants of the FLN, those of the OAS see their enemy as the more brutal party and present their own violence as lesser, necessary, and deserved by the adversary. They are less immediately forthcoming, by contrast, in what regards violence against liberals or the representatives of the state.[25] They only rarely admit to having assassinated Europeans: although enemies, it is difficult to present Europeans as a threat to the physical survival of the pieds-noirs or the OAS.

The use of violence is also seen as having been necessary. The enemy, it is claimed, understood only the language of power (a perception in fact shared by both parties); OAS violence was thus a matter of "teaching the Arabs a lesson." As a former activist colorfully explained, "They've got the idea of conquering the entire world for Islam stuck in their heads. But I don't follow Islam, I'm Christian. If you hit me, I defend myself. I'm not the sort of Christian who turns the other cheek when you slap me, not me, maybe you . . . If somebody slaps me, maybe I'll turn the other cheek. But if an Arab slaps me, I take a hammer and I hit him with it because I know why he did it."[26]

For the protagonists, the action taken to avenge and defend one's community calls for virility and a sense of honor. Their decision to become involved in this war is proof of their physical and moral courage. Sometimes, the stories told by these former armed activists underscore the gap separating them from other pieds-noirs, who are presented as big talkers incapable of action.

In contrast to Algerians, who consider the entire nation, one and indivisible, to be the Revolution's hero, the struggle of the OAS is seen in more personal terms. Its members recount their individual exploits or those performed with their closest companions. Individual pride is sometimes in evidence: one boasted of carrying out the first attack against General de Gaulle; another of becoming prefect of Algiers during the putsch while still only twenty-seven years old; yet a third of driving off with 250 kilos of explosives in his convertible to blow up the central government.

Feelings of self-satisfaction coexist with a form of competitiveness. Cutting remarks are sometimes made at the expense of companions who came late to the fight or "talk a lot." Struggles within the OAS over opposing political visions or the organization's treasury (which mysteriously disappeared) only rarely cropped up in these interviews. By contrast, while my interlocutors acknowledged that their organization may have committed errors or blunders, they lay the blame on other units or regions. There is nevertheless unanimity regarding the organization's "martyrs." Roger Degueldre is nearly systematically mentioned as a role model by the men of the "deltas."

Violence and Levity

Among OAS combatants, the war narrative reveals indifference with regard to the suffering and death of the enemy. The memory of murders seems lightly borne, as if the lives of Algerians and barbouzes did not count for much in their eyes.[27] This casual attitude doubtless relates to the feeling of omnipotence they came to acquire during the fight for French Algeria. The majority of pieds-noirs supported them (or at least did not dare contradict them), and a portion of the regular police force supplied them with assistance and information. One "delta" recounts how armed members of his commando accompanied him when he went to register the birth of his first child with the authorities—an anecdote that speaks volumes with regard to the atmosphere in Algiers at the time.

To listen to some of them talk, murder, bomb attacks, and torture are almost anodyne, indeed matters of routine: "So we picked him up, gathered intelligence, roughed him up a little, and then put a bullet in him; that's how it always went. And then there are the bomb attacks, but you know all about them already."

Moreover, in the eyes of some militants, there was too little violence, given the savagery of the FLN and the relentlessness of the French government. This stance also serves as a justification: OAS members claim to have peaceful consciences because they believe that they could have—or perhaps even should have—resorted to even greater violence. Some believe that their actions were not sufficiently large-scale or daring. According to Gabriel Anglade,

> Contrary to what everyone says, we didn't have much in the way of resources. There were very few of us, and we were very poorly armed. We didn't have much . . . On the other hand, I think that the OAS' political role should have from the outset been expanded in metropolitan France, since nearly everyone in Algeria supported the idea of a French Algeria. OK, there are always exceptions; you can't force 100 percent of people, but it was in France that we should have insisted and perhaps even immediately carried out a putsch in Paris, besieged the Elysée, did something. Now that would have been something because carrying out a putsch in Algiers . . . as General de Gaulle said, "a little group in retreat [en retraite]." It's true that they were all retired [à la retraite].

The Honor of the Defeated

Ex-combatants from the OAS draw upon French history for their rhetoric of political legitimization. They present themselves as patriots fighting those who would sacrifice national territory. As Todd Shepard has shown, the deputies who defended French Algeria attempted to set the Evian Accords in the context of a historical narrative centered on Alsace-Lorraine, territory lost to Germany in 1871 but restored at the end of the First World War.[28] OAS veterans, for their part, appeal to the resistance against Nazi Germany. As in 1940, the fact of having broken the law and resisted the established authorities is not seen as impeding their claims to legitimacy. The French Resistance and OAS veterans shared a similar conception of France, a desire to safeguard the national territory and their makeshift resources. As Gabriel Anglade put it,

> Let's not forget that the OAS was not an offensive formation; it was a form of resistance. During the 39–45 war, the Resistance was not constantly launching attacks everywhere in France; they carried out little commando strikes. [Our objective was] simply to keep Algeria French because, what's more, it was a French département. De Gaulle's the one who betrayed us with his promises. . . . He complained about Pétain but Pétain did exactly the same thing as he did. One day, he [Pétain] said, "I give up, I'm laying down my arms," and then he [De Gaulle] laid down arms without agreeing to an armistice. It was just like 19 March, exactly the same thing, maybe even worse.

While OAS veterans admit that they lost, they maintain that their failure merely reflected an uneven power struggle and in no way diminishes the legitimacy of their undertaking. They are still convinced that they fought for a noble and legitimate cause: defending France and their homeland while securing happiness for all of Algeria's inhabitants. They find proof that theirs was the right choice in the disaster that is independent Algeria. Despite the impossibility of ever building a French Algeria, some of them remain convinced that a historical error was committed. Others have adjusted their narrative, abandoning colonial discourse and subscribing to an independent Algeria, though they continue to regret that no place was made in it for the pieds-noirs. A few of them would have preferred a South African scenario based on the universality of political rights, multiculturalism, and reconciliation among the various communities; the evolution of these OAS veterans' political representation is real, even if they seek to establish logical continuity between their past positions and present discourse. They also reject the idea that they contributed to legitimating an unjust system, explaining that "laws were adopted in metropolitan France" without their approval and that, in any case, they were "never into politics." They deny having taken part in relations of domination and assert that "we were all the same." They embody the figure of the righteous loser. In their eyes, the contested "grandeur" of their struggle confers the status of unrecognized heroes upon them. Feeling misunderstood and the object of permanent historical injustice, they today find it tempting to borrow from the rhetoric of victimhood to demand symbolic and financial reparations from the French state.

According to OAS veterans, the conflict's resolution was in several respects immoral. Algeria was surrendered to the control of an illegitimate organization. The denial of jus soli for the Europeans of Algeria violated their right to freedom and equality. What's more, France deceived them. In rounding off their case, OAS activists appeal to the figure of the harki, which they brandish as proof of FLN barbarity and metropolitan treason. Finally, OAS veterans frequently complain of the loss of their homeland and the lack of consideration shown them by the national community. Some mention administrative humiliations or the everyday rejection they experience at the hands of French citizens. This profound feeling of injustice is the foundation of their identity and relationship to the world. A former member of the "delta" commandos thus claims that the pieds-noirs are "banished from history." Another activist, a native of Oran, confesses to deep-seated, all-inclusive anger: "I'm angry with the entire world because I was . . . I lived in a magnificent country, a country where I never had problems like that, we were self-sufficient."

In the system of representations of OAS members, the figure of the enemy is at once vague and multifaceted. Who was the true enemy against whom the underground organization fought: the FLN, General de Gaulle, the population of mainland France, seen as ignorant, defeatist, and full of contempt? Opinions differ among the militants. It is all the more difficult to make peace when one's enemy is not clearly identified. What's more, OAS activists have trouble identifying with a political community: as they were mobilized on behalf of France to safeguard Algeria, it is ultimately difficult for them to see themselves as part of a nation they consider treacherous, aggressive, and condescending toward them. This fragile bond with the national community acts as a brake on the evolution of how they see the Other. Thus, though forty years have now passed, few of them accept the cause of national independence as defended by the FLN. In a context marked by uncertainty and conflict over identity, the permanence of the enemy is at once formative and unifying.

The Apartheid Forces of Order: Violence Despite Oneself

The inversion of political legitimacy raises the question of what meaning is to be assigned to the past actions of former soldiers and police. Today, it is difficult to defend the apartheid regime's struggle against communism, in pursuit of which South Africa waged several wars in the region against national liberation movements. The communist threat has evaporated and is now generally acknowledged as having been exaggerated by the rulers of the time, serving as a pretext for the continued political exclusion of blacks. Faced with an inversion of values, members of the forces of order nevertheless believe that it was legitimate to use violence against their adversaries. Indeed, in seeking to confer meaning upon their trajectories, they even manage to draw upon moral categories forged by the new regime.

Loss of Meaning

Powerless, former apartheid officials looked on as power was transmitted to members of what had until then been considered a subversive political party. The conversion of their rulers abruptly abolished the meaning of their involvement and the violence they had inflicted upon "terrorists" and "communists." For South African whites, in general, and soldiers and police, in particular, the rapid disintegration of the political party[29] that had governed during apartheid, and the retirement of the era's political leaders, made it yet more difficult to find new forms of political expression. They could no longer rely on the moral compass of a profoundly discredited apartheid system. This ideological disarray explains why the collapse of the apartheid regime provoked so little resistance.

The political significance assigned violent actions in the past is further undermined when leaders seek to distance themselves from operations carried out at their behest. In South Africa, ex-police are thus unable to turn to political leaders, who have on several occasions disavowed them, claiming not to have known of the methods they employed on the ground.[30] With most individuals seeking to escape the disgrace that had befallen their institution, moreover, the peer group has tended to break down. Nor can they continue to count on support from their community, which disavowed them when their crimes were revealed in the course of the TRC hearings. Recalling a time when their merit was recognized and rewarded and their membership in the Security Branch a source of prestige, they experience their symbolic and social downfall as an injustice.

A Legal and Necessary Violence

Having taken the lead in repression against members of the ANC and the Pan-African Congress (PAC), police officers justify their use of violence. They insist on the legality of their past actions, presenting them as necessary, given the political and security contexts.

Employing the old vocabulary, they claim that liberation movement militants were "terrorists." Security service repression was a way of preventing illegal and illegitimate violence. After spending much of his career in the Security Branch, Lafras was appointed chief of South Africa's police force in 1990.[31] He claims that the security forces did their best to "maintain order and legality." Similarly, he presents the apartheid regime as having been a way to guarantee stability and civil peace. The meaning of the war is thus limited to a conflict between subversive forces resorting to illegal means and the official representatives of a legal political order.

All those who present themselves as mere underlings take refuge behind the duty of obedience. By making the award of amnesty conditional upon the fact that a crime had been politically motivated and ordered or tolerated by the hierarchy, the TRC encouraged former members of the Security Branch to claim some degree of bureaucratic innocence. They balk at the notion that they should accept individual responsibility, shifting it instead to political leaders and an entire society that passively acquiesced in maintaining the apartheid regime and its system of repression.

Several of them nevertheless present themselves as defenders of the free world against a communist threat then spreading at regional, national, and global levels. As evidence that South Africa was facing a severe threat, they cite Cuban military intervention in Angola, Soviet interference, and the alliance between the Communist Party and the ANC. While they acknowledge the sometimes illegal nature of the actions in which they participated, they maintain that theirs was a life-or-death struggle. According to them, their own use of violence merely sought to preserve the future of their group and the life of all its members. It was rational and proportionate to the outburst of brutal violence among the enemy. Some police officers are at pains to present the other side's crimes, offering an emotional account that refers to the cruel killing of innocents to explain their own plunge into violence. A sort of riposte to the TRC, *The Other Side of the Story*[32] is a short, self-published book that seeks to shed light on the crimes perpetrated by the national liberation movements. The text is accompanied by many photos of mutilated bodies.

The objective here is to present one's own violence as a defensive and necessary response to a "ferocious" adversary—in short, to legitimate it. Some admit to having participated in crimes or abuses but retain a positive self-image, underscoring the efficient manner in which they carried out the task, and their sense of duty.

Apoliticism as Proof of Innocence

Members of the South African Defense Force (SADF) and the South African Police (SAP) do not justify their engagement by defending the principles and objectives of apartheid, and the vast majority of them admit that non-racial democracy is a fairer system than what preceded it. In keeping with what is now a widespread opinion among white South Africans, the majority of former police and soldiers recognize that the old regime was unjust and oppressive for blacks and other nonwhite groups. They disassociate themselves from it, either by claiming that they never subscribed to the regime's values or by explaining that they supported them only because they had been fooled by political leaders, and are not responsible for this error. This stubborn avoidance of politics accelerates the disintegration of the political community. By refusing to take responsibility for the heritage of a political system and ideology, they abandon a series of values and principles that deeply informed the day-to-day operation of their institution. They thereby attempt to free themselves from collective guilt and preempt any suggestion of personal wrongdoing.

The individuals I met were at pains to present their family background, specifying the values and principles to which they had been exposed as children and adolescents. Their social origins seemed to be dominated by a single model: the family had little in the way of material resources and were members of the Dutch Reformed Church.[33] My interlocutors almost never mentioned the presence of politicized family members. By contrast, some identified their parents as "conservatives" who were nevertheless "open to political change." They were not racist, they told me, and had played with black children in their childhoods. Former officials claim that they had been "conditioned" by a series of institutions—school, church, and army—that, taken together, formed a sophisticated system. Their education had made patriots of them and apparently led a portion of them to opt for the defense of their community. Yet even as they described the grip exercised over them by the system, former members of the forces of order—and especially the members of elite units—attempted to persuade me of their apoliticism. They divorce their engagement on behalf of the fatherland from its ideological import, transforming it into an object of purity.

As the main perpetrators of human rights violations against activists and opponents, the police officers of the Security Branch represented a majority of candidates for amnesty among former representatives of the apartheid regime. The institutions of the military, for their part, were spared this. But while they successfully escaped investigation by the TRC and were not required to appear before it or confess to their crimes, military personnel cannot be unaware of the central role they played in the persistence of the apartheid system and the preservation of white hegemony within the country's political institutions. They nevertheless profit from the focus of public opprobrium on the police, distancing themselves from the horrors perpetrated by the regime, and contrasting these with the concept of "clean war." They even claim to be surprised or indignant regarding the methods used by the police as these were revealed in the course of the TRC hearings.

Each of the soldiers I encountered sought to dissociate his enlistment in the army from the ideological issues at stake in apartheid. While some described joining the military as a good opportunity for the son of a poor family, others insisted on their idealism and the purity of their patriotism, which rises above all political considerations. A number of them emphasized the tasks and maneuvers associated with the military life they had chosen—a true life of outdoor adventure. Here, the figures of the virginal soldier and the virile soldier dominate their self-presentations.

A retired general whose career mainly took place in the intelligence service sought to defend the purity of his engagement. He claims to have been completely unaware of the methods employed by the Special Forces: "You have to understand what it is to be an ordinary farmer, a simple soldier. That's what I am. I'm not sophisticated, I'm not a smooth talker or a politician. I'm an ordinary soldier who climbed the ladder, reaching the rank of general. Our values were the country, the flag, the land, the earth, animals and people, including blacks . . . We lived and we fought, we sacrificed our lives for these values. It's patriotism and, more than that, it's love, it's fighting for who you love, for the child."

This self-presentation draws upon memories of youthful convictions and feelings that, in their condensed state, supposedly form the general's true nature. Behind the uniform of a high-ranking officer with a career in the intelligence service apparently hides a romantic and idealistic adolescent who, remaining faithful to his education, never really grew up. His humble social origins in rural South Africa are presented as further proof of his innocence and sincerity. Rural origins—marginal or imaginary—root the Afrikaner in the land. In this vision, the state's servants signed up for a noble cause but were ultimately led astray by cynical leaders.

From Defeat to Victimization

Insofar as they recognize the legitimacy of the new political order, most South African soldiers and police officers openly or tacitly admit their defeat. Nevertheless, in both pragmatic and moral terms, they play down their status as misguided losers, which allows them to maintain a degree of coherence. Although members of South Africa's former army recognize that their camp lost the ideological battle against the national liberation movements, they insist on their success against the guerrilla fighters, thus giving proof of their competence. Soldiers and police continue to take pride in their experience of combat and thereby rescue themselves from collective defeat.

What's more, police officers, as well as some soldiers, responsible for putting down the opposition movements seek to show that, though they may have been misled into serving an illegitimate system, they were not at fault for all that. Each of them claims that he believed the speeches of the political authorities of the era, that he was prisoner of a familial, social, religious, and educational system or that he in fact favored political change. Supporting the new political order allows one to avoid retreating into the loser's stance. By elaborating upon the formative aspects of one's own personal evolution, one demonstrates a capacity for change. This is necessary if one is to abandon an identity rooted in defeat and become an active participant in the new South Africa. Some former soldiers thus appropriate the values that were extolled during the democratic transition. Others—ex-police—hold that they conformed to the norms of the new political order by stating the entire truth in the course of their hearing before the TRC. By adopting the rhetoric of forgiveness, yet others give proof of their desire to integrate the new political community.

Finally, former apartheid civil servants seize upon the figure of victim, which has made deep inroads in post-apartheid South Africa. Claiming to have been misled by the politicians they served, they present themselves as scapegoats. They have also picked up on remarks made by TRC chairman

Desmond Tutu, who at a TRC hearing declared that all acts of violence have two victims: the person who suffered psychologically and/or physically from the violence, and the person who inflicted it.[34] By depicting themselves as nonresponsible victims—even though this comes at the price of renouncing their free will and individuality—some Security Branch members thereby evade the category of perpetrator. At the same time, they subscribe to the stigmatization of past violence and see themselves as the equals of ANC combatants.

Most of the soldiers and police officers who served under apartheid concede that the new regime is more democratic than its predecessor and better guarantees the freedom of all. Yet, individually and as members of the white community, a number of them claim that the manner in which they have been treated is unjust (because of social stigmatization and/or their appearance before the TRC). Moreover, feelings of betrayal are widespread among former soldiers and police officers. Exposed to physical danger and distressed at the death of their comrades, they discovered that, despite their own sacrifices and prowess on the battlefield, politicians were negotiating with the enemy. Seeing themselves as conscientious handmaidens in a political conflict they did not understand, what's more, the police officers are often convinced that they were unjustly treated during the democratic transition. They believe themselves to have been abandoned, betrayed by politicians, and forced to pay as scapegoats for those they served.

Many also claim that affirmative action policies limiting their professional opportunities are unjust. Although they recognize the legitimacy of dismantling apartheid and moving to democracy, they find that they have individually and collectively paid an excessively high price for this transition. These discordant positions are difficult to manage: at the same time that they admit that these changes have resulted in a more just society, they argue that the loss of their status under the old system is unwarranted. What's more, former members of the apartheid regime's forces of order cannot unite around a collective identity, for their appeal to incongruous languages of justice reflects a desire to completely divorce their individual trajectories from the political history of their country. This stance often rests on a refusal to assume their share of the collective responsibility that would tie them to the apartheid regime or the white community of South Africa.

By accepting the new political system, former members of the army and police show a capacity for adaptation. By admitting the moral and political flaws of apartheid, they have embarked on a process of recognition. For all that, they do not carry it through to completion but instead bypass it in order to dispense with the question of their individual responsibility. The arguments advanced by apartheid-era soldiers and police attempt to reconcile three different objectives to preserve the coherence of their remarks, to maintain a positive image of themselves, and to create a place for themselves in the new system.

The figure of the victor comes in a variety of forms and fluctuates between two main extremes: the *victorious victor* and the *victim-victor*.[35] The *victorious victor* is embodied by the militant or wartime leader who, confident in himself, feels pride at the contemplation of his victory. The expression of victory may be characterized by reserve and modesty or instead brandished as the standard of an ongoing mobilization. These varieties of self-presentation are represented by the figures of the *magnanimous victor* incarnated by the ex-combatants of the ANC and the *triumphant victor* as it is encountered among FLN veterans. Alongside these classic figures of the victor, that of the *victim-victor* is to be found among a significant portion of rank-and-file ANC militants. They consist of former guerrilla fighters who, though conscious of their enemy's defeat, see themselves as losers in the new political order.

Calling into question the validity of one's violent action facilitates the adoption of an attitude of clemency toward one's adversary. The absence of critical distance, on the contrary, keeps enmity alive. On this point, as well, the ex-activists of the ANC and the FLN diverge.

Losers, for their part, do not abandon their efforts to construct a positive image of themselves. For former South African police officers—and, to a lesser extent, soldiers—identifying oneself as a victim allows one to compensate for a loss of social status and to shore up faltering self-esteem. Although victory escaped them, and they feel deprived of the recognition they believe they deserve, OAS militants have developed a heroic stance, which represents an intense form of self-esteem. This aptitude draws from the group's strong cohesion, notably maintained by the feeling that it constitutes a besieged fortress in a hostile world. This nourishes the combatant identity and prolongs the mobilization. The violence to which one was subjected is underscored as evidence of one's suffering, proof of one's courage, or an indication of the extent to which one has been a victim of injustice.

This feeling of injustice preserves a form of combativeness. Members of the OAS who perceive the conflict's outcome as illegitimate and their fate as unjust express resentment toward the FLN and General de Gaulle. Their refusal to accept defeat precludes their cultural demobilization.[36] Conversely, belonging to the victorious camp and feeling that one has received justice encourage calm spirits and a certain kind of clemency toward one's enemy. ANC members who have succeeded in the new South Africa advocate reconciliation. Former apartheid-era civil servants who admit that the new political order is fairer than what preceded it also exhibit a degree of open-mindedness.

Chapter 8

Perpetrating Violence

Antoine Prost claims that killing someone always leaves a "guilty memory" and that "the awareness of having transgressed a fundamental prohibition" presents a pressing moral question.[1] Why and to what degree do veterans talk about their past acts of violence? Is it not more rational to silently pass over the death and suffering one has caused? Until relatively recently, the violence of the First World War has been shrouded in silence, particularly as concerns rape and other atrocities.[2] In the case of the South African and Franco-Algerian conflicts, the relations between the combatants entailed a greater familiarity with the enemy. Killing or engaging in violence against the Other was often more directly experienced by the protagonists of these conflicts. Sometimes, the combatants knew those they killed.

But two distinct factors remove the impediments to talking about one's experiences in these cases. The first is the protagonist's belief that the violence he inflicted was "justified." By contrast, individuals rarely discuss having tortured their enemy, since the practice of torture is often associated with the idea of cruelty. The second factor that encourages combatants to talk about their experiences is the belief that publicly doing so will not result in legal proceedings. The astonishing confessions that Jean Hatzfeld collected among participants in the Rwandan genocide of the Tutsis are strikingly frank, for they come from individuals who have already been found guilty.[3] In a similar manner, the South Africans who requested and were granted amnesty for serious human rights violations know that they run no legal risk in speaking. The facts are known and available to the public. What remains is to confront society's judgment, particularly as it is embodied in the encounter with the interviewer. On both sides of the Mediterranean, by contrast, the political taboo regarding the Algerian War provides no incentive for the protagonists to undermine an edifice that still supplies the basis for the political community's identity.

The imaginary of violence is produced within a political, social, and symbolic configuration. Each group of ex-combatants is characterized by its own dominant narrative regarding the past conflict and the (ex-)enemy. We shall now invert the perspective to consider the analyses and feelings provoked by the discussion of violence. Collective narratives are always perceptible but do not exhaust the array of individual perceptions. Among those who claim to have employed force, three main stances emerge.

The first combines rationalization and denial: the ex-combatants demonstrate the necessity of their action, minimize it, or deny that it ever took place. This failure to call violence into question is favored driven by strong social and ideological cohesion within the group of ex-combatants or strong legitimacy within society. Nevertheless, the absence of collective moorings does not prevent the veterans from occupying the same relationship toward violence. Justifying and downplaying one's own violence is the most common behavior.

The second stance expresses pleasure. Veterans present their wartime deeds with a form of amusement, nostalgia, or bravado. The satisfaction that past violence procures reflects the warrior's excitement and forms of transgression. Historians have evoked the testimony of men who fought in the First World War and who admitted that brutality was a source of pleasure for them.[4] This tendency tends to express itself while a conflict is ongoing and is rarely encountered in the public sphere in peacetime.

In the third stance ex-combatants demonstrate uneasiness and doubt about the legitimacy of their past violence and sometimes display remorse and guilt. These feelings more readily appear among individuals who are not well integrated in social and political terms, either because the ideological references that had given them structure during the conflict have crumbled or because their membership in the group has been called into question.

These three stances are not mutually exclusive. The sense that one bears responsibility for a misdeed can be reflected in efforts to downplay it and,[5] in this sense, denial and guilt can go together. It is impossible, moreover, to externally determine when a veteran feels guilt. The effort to justify one's acts and the desire to present oneself in a favorable light can coexist in a single individual. And, paradoxical as it may seem, some ex-combatants express both guilt at having resorted to violence and satisfaction in recalling brutal acts.

Rationalization and Denial

The elaboration of moral and pragmatic justifications constitutes one way of addressing one's own past acts of violence. Such justifications, it has been claimed, are forms of denial, "an unconscious defense mechanism to manage guilt, anxiety and other disturbing feelings."[6] In peacetime, a dissonance arises between the moral precepts expressed by ex-combatants and their past actions, which include having killed, or worse yet, tortured their enemy (particularly when the latter is a civilian). To resolve this contradiction, ex-combatants deny their acts or the concrete or moral implications of those acts. Discrediting the enemy and denying his suffering make it easier to legitimate or minimize the abuses committed against him.[7]

Nearly all veterans employ the language of rationalization and/or denial to varying degrees. Yet, as the process of the Truth and Reconciliation Commission (TRC) obviated the need for denial, ANC members resort to this language less often.

Several forms of denial coexist, with some becoming established as privileged modes of expression for particular groups. All are tempted to appeal to the rhetoric of proportionality. The rhetoric of trivialization is more commonplace among the actors of the Algerian War. The argument of individual irresponsibility, for its part, is characteristically employed by the government forces that served under the apartheid regime. Finally, total denial is encountered among defeated ex-combatants, who are frequently preoccupied with winning recognition for what they consider to be falsehoods or injustices. Some activists of the Secret Army Organization (OAS) thus attempt to impose their version of the facts in the face of what they see as a biased official history.

Proportionality: "The Enemy Was Much More Violent"

The most commonplace way of rationalizing violence consists in comparing the acts of one's own group with those of one's adversary. Veterans explain that the enemy's use of violence was much greater than theirs, and that theirs is thus negligible or relatively minor. They subscribe to the rhetoric of proportionality to advance an argument that is at once strategic and moral. Since one's adversary employed such formidable methods, effectively countering him required that one respond in kind. Further, those concerned seek to prove that, if they are morally in the wrong, their misdeeds pale by comparison to those of their enemy. Through sordid anecdotes and illustrated publications, they offer evidence of the enemy's immorality while at the same time distinguishing themselves from those who would commit such terrible acts. This rhetoric appears to be shared by all of the configurations studied here, although it is less widely employed by partisans of the African National Congress (ANC).

The protagonists of the Algerian War of Independence employ this type of argument, with members of the National Liberation Front (FLN) referring to the practices of the French army to justify their own behavior. Tasked with planting a bomb in an Algiers café frequented by Europeans, Rym justifies her act in this way:[8] "I have no regrets because I did something useful for my country. You had to see all the massacres." Members of the OAS also appeal to this type of rationalization, since many maintain that their organization's actions were minor compared to "the FLN's atrocities." To this end, they refer to attacks against European civilians and what they claim was the FLN's common practice of slitting their victims' throats. Such depictions of the violence of one's adversary serve as an argument in justifying one's own use of brutality.

Another, contrary way of comparing oneself to one's adversary consists in placing oneself on an equal footing with him by claiming that the opposing combatants were at war and that each side had a hand in the violence that is inherent to any armed conflict. Security Branch veterans thus claim that their methods were necessary to foil the attacks carried out by the national liberation movements. Very often, they seek to show that, in their struggle against the ANC and the Pan-African Congress (PAC), all parties were soldiers in the service of a cause, that they were motivated by an ideal and sought to defend its interests. They thereby relativize their violent acts by asserting that such acts fell under the framework of a balanced and more or less fair fight. By inviting members of the apartheid regime and members of the national liberation movements to follow the same procedure in requesting amnesty for the violent deeds they committed, the TRC supplied former police officers with a precious resource for legitimating themselves.

Oscar[9] thus plays down the significance of his past actions by referring to the misdeeds of ANC members:

> I thought that I should work to help improve South Africa's security. And we believed in what we were doing. Whether we were right or wrong. I'm not saying that what we did was right but . . . But it's the same thing. I have a lot of ANC and PAC friends today, and if you ask them if they accept the bombs and mines [that the movements laid] because today a lot are parents and couldn't stand it if someone hurt their children. They didn't join the ANC to kill children or innocent people. But that was a consequence. It's the same thing for me. If someone asks me whether I joined the police to fight terrorism, not at all, I wanted to be a detective.

The rhetoric of proportionality places the theme of the violence to which one has been subjected at the center of the argument, where it is brandished to justify one's own brutality and implicitly evokes the notion of legitimate defense. To legitimate their behavior, the protagonists thus must constantly bring up the actions of their adversary, thereby prolonging a form of mobilization that centers on the figure of the enemy.

Trivialization: The Rhetoric of the Franco-Algerian War

Trivialization is first and foremost characterized by the choice of a certain vocabulary. Protagonists employ euphemism to neutralize the brutality of their acts. As Xavier Crettiez has shown, groups employing violence develop a "legal-rational language" to dissimulate practices that are "stigmatized as illegal and terroristic."[10] Indeed, the question of vocabulary gave rise to a debate within the TRC, with some politicians claiming that police officers overinterpreted the orders they issued on several occasions to eliminate the enemy. Among the operational forces of the OAS, a "one-off operation" referred to the assassination of an individual.

Trivialization also consists in explicitly stating the frequency with which the abuses in question have over the centuries taken place throughout the world. The veterans of the 1914–18 war, many of whom became pacifist activists, argued that war itself was the horror. They insisted on "condemning war as an atrocity rather than denouncing atrocities in war." This stance allowed them to free themselves of a form of individual guilt.[11] It is along these lines that Mehdi responds when questioned about FLN violence against Algerians and Europeans:[12] "Come on, all wars are dirty! Has there ever been a clean war? There's no such thing as a clean war. Mistakes, everyone makes mistakes. Everyone makes mistakes! Come on!" When Mehdi explained that the attacks he carried out during the war against European shops were not targeted, he let slip this conception of the adversary: "For us, all Europeans were the same, we didn't choose. Why? Why choose them? They looked alike, they were all, er . . ."

As an attitude that entails distancing oneself from the Other's suffering, trivialization can lead to a sort of ostentatious detachment. Rym flaunts her indifference: she knows that the bomb she planted wounded a lot of people, but still does not know, forty years later, how many people she killed. Her comments reveal the weakness of her political argument: "War is war. You don't make an omelet without breaking some eggs." Asked whether she had thought about seeking forgiveness, she answered: "No, not at all. I regret nothing. It wasn't much, just a bomb. It was war."

Some "deltas"[13] exhibit a similarly casual air when discussing the deaths they inflicted on their adversary. At the individual level, repeated murder results in habituation and a form of hardening.[14] "Man has the disturbing power to adapt to nearly everything," writes the German sociologist Wolfgang Sofsky, "even his own violence." According to Sofsky, "violence becomes routine, everyday life, work. The deed becomes a repetitive action. After the first metamorphosis, the perpetrator of violence has merely to imitate himself."[15] According to Quentin, a former "delta," this detachment was immediate:

—I think we did the first one-off—a "one-off" is to kill the person. He was a pimp.
—But why did you kill a pimp?
—Well, because he was dealing arms!
—And was he an Arab or a European?
—A European. And since we were there, we put ten bullets in him. That was the first operation.
—Was the first operation difficult?
—I don't think so, because, when your morale is based on French Algeria, you go into it like the Arabs went into the FLN. You can't be under any illusions, can you? I'm very Catholic, very much a believer,

but there are some things I don't let anyone do to me. If someone hits me, I hit back. If someone hurts me more, I know what to do. I've got plenty of opportunities.

Individual Nonaccountability: The Rhetoric of Apartheid-Era Soldiers and Police

Another way to minimize the significance of one's acts or supply proof of one's ignorance is to attribute one's acts and ignorance to one's "youth." The idea of immaturity—of passionate youth with little awareness of the consequences of one's acts—is frequently advanced in one's defense, particularly among soldiers who served in the South African Army and OAS activists. Nevertheless, while they seek to identify some attenuating circumstances, former OAS men more willingly acknowledge responsibility for the acts they committed. While members of the South African government forces seek to distance themselves from their contractual enlistment within one of the state's central institutions, the activists of French Algeria proudly lay claim to their rebellion, which was at once secret and antigovernmental. For the former, committing acts of violence was to some degree a matter of conformity. For the latter, by contrast, the outlaw nature of their operations required greater personal awareness, though this phenomenon was mitigated by group membership, position in a command structure, and institutional complicity.

Most South African police and soldiers seek to supply proof that they were neither racists nor supporters of the idea of white racial superiority. They underscore their distinctive identity vis-à-vis the system and/or downplay its discriminatory nature and implications. They oscillate between these various forms of denial, however contradictory.

South African Defense Force (SADF) veterans, particularly those who had belonged to the Special Forces, claim that apartheid did not exist within their institution. In their accounts, the fact that their units were racially mixed is proof of equality among blacks and whites. The missions they carried out (reconnaissance, intelligence, and targeted attacks) required coordination and trust and created strong ties between elite soldiers who risked their lives together. What's more, Recce veterans maintain that they did not grasp the social and political reality of their country, since they operated abroad and had neither the time nor the opportunity to wonder about the legitimacy of the political order. Nicolas, who spent nearly four years in the Special Forces, justifies himself in this way:[16] "Apartheid meant nothing to me, I wasn't exposed to it." Thus, the fact that the blacks under their orders cooperated and participated in combat and repression missions provides an alibi to exculpate the security forces of any racist feeling.

Although they strive to demonstrate the absence of racism and injustice in their professional environment, army and police veterans implicitly acknowledge the moral illegitimacy of apartheid. They constantly appeal to the notion that they were prisoners of their environment: socialized by a regime that imposed itself as a complete social and institutional system, individuals were deprived of alternative points of reference and were thus incapable of adopting a critical stance. While some soldiers and police admit that they had been wrong to serve the apartheid regime, they reject the notion that this constitutes wrongdoing on their part. Their ignorance, in their view, exonerates them.

Nearly all deny that their allegiance or consent to apartheid was political in nature. The political field serves as a foil; first, because veterans of the forces of order hold that their apolitical stance argues in favor of their innocence; next, because they claim they were manipulated—and subsequently betrayed— by politicians. A former police officer thus states: "Unfortunately, the Security Branch was perceived as an extension of the preceding regime. It's too bad because it consisted of excellent police officers, and we've lost their expertise. A political approach was favored, even though police officers could have adapted."[17]

After attempting to extricate themselves from personal wrongdoing, some attempt to minimize the collective responsibility of whites. They play down apartheid, either by denying its discriminatory nature or by comparing it to what they consider to be equivalent phenomena. In order to rule out the idea of a specific wrong committed by Afrikaners, soldiers and police who have moved on to other careers sometimes claim that the British and French—representatives of the world's foremost colonial nations—are the true inventors of racial inequality. Apartheid, they claim, was just a pale and belated copy of a model first conceived in Europe. Eager to rid themselves of their own guilt, Westerners revel in demonizing the South African regime.

Finally, a number of soldiers and police officers present themselves as avant-garde progressives. The highest-ranking among them claim to have alerted members of the government of the need to find a political solution and negotiate with the rebels. Their mission is thus presented as having consisted in laying the groundwork for the peace process by obtaining the most favorable possible conditions for their camp in the field. The soldiers, moreover, consider themselves to have been particularly effective. This leads some to particularly despise men like F. W. de Klerk. Guilty in their eyes of having deceived them, he also proved incapable of translating their military and security successes into political terms.

Their objective is to supply evidence of their "innocence" vis-à-vis the apartheid system. To that end, they seek to erase all signs of their past allegiance or entirely remove its ideological dimension. They claim to be individually nonaccountable for their participation in the conflict and the acts of repression with which it was associated.

Total Denial: OAS Militants Condemn a "Biased" History

A stance of total denial—what Stanley Cohen refers to as "literal denial"—constitutes one possible attitude toward the violence one has committed. Some former activists defend their integrity by claiming that theirs was a clean war, accusing opinion groups, the sitting government, and their adversaries of propagating a "biased" history with the aim of discrediting and demonizing the last partisans of French Algeria. OAS veterans react vehemently against what they perceive as the falsehoods indiscriminately spread by the French left, Gaullists, the FLN, the public education system, and historians. One of them thus refuses to believe that the OAS bomb intended for André Malraux that wounded a four-year-old girl on 7 February 1962 actually blinded her: "The little Delphine Renard brainwashing! They put a bomb on André Malraux's window, and the little girl was hit in the eye. She's blind and all that, they tell you. In reality, she's in the United States and lives like a queen. If I had the money, I would have gone there a long time ago to film her . . . That's what's called brainwashing. To make sure that everyone is against the OAS by presenting them as killers who blinded a little girl."[18]

Some of those formerly active on behalf of the cause of French Algeria admit that things got out of hand and mistakes were made in the spring and early summer of 1962. Others, by contrast, categorically deny the existence of racist attacks (ratonnades), claiming that such accusations seek only to discredit the OAS.

Auguste, a member of the "collines" group in Oran, is one such.[19] By once again appealing to the argument of violence suffered, however, he undermines his initial claim specifically, that cleaning women were not targeted for murder:[20]

No, it's false. That's their story, that's what they say. What were the cleaning women stories all about? They were women who were there and had come to spy. What did the FLN boys do when they carried out an attack? They were armed, they shot at someone who was waiting for the bus, and they gave the weapon to a woman because women weren't searched at first, and the woman hid the weapon, and that's how it happened. She made it through the checkpoints that way. The guy was arrested but didn't have a weapon. He couldn't be accused and the cleaning women . . . They're just stories, the cleaning women. You see, they're just stories. It's nice to be on the receiving end of these groundless accusations, because I don't remember . . . Your dad waited for the bus like mine, holding a newspaper in his hand, and was shot in the head and killed. What do you do, what do you do? You're going to try to avenge yourself because there's no reason for anyone to kill your father or your brother or, like me, my uncle. No reason. So, there you go, I don't believe we killed cleaning women. It's possible that cleaning women were killed, but you have to know the reasons.

Spared by their appearance before the TRC, South African soldiers for their part prefer to remain silent about events or practices that have yet to be revealed. In this way, they can preserve their reputation for integrity without being formally contradicted. In the case of FLN and OAS veterans groups, since these groups' representatives never acknowledged their "misdeeds" or "mistakes," nothing obliges their members to talk about these things. While various amnesty laws protect both groups from the legal consequences of new revelations, such protection may appear less than total to the degree that some parties have begun to explore legal avenues that would allow charges to be brought against those they see as the perpetrators.

The Pleasure of War

Psychoanalytical and anthropological approaches underscore the pleasure procured by committing violent acts, a phenomenon explained by sadism, the death instinct, and the need for power. Moral and social prohibitions are said to act as a check on these urges and prevent individuals from speaking about them. Drawing upon the testimony of British, American, and Australian combatants involved in the two world wars and the Vietnam War, the historian Joanna Bourke argues that pleasure is one of the dominant emotions among men who participate in combat. She quotes, among others, an American veteran who writes that, not wishing to be seen as bloodthirsty brutes, ex-combatants prefer silence to admitting the pleasure they took in waging war. For some, this pleasure is said to depend on a certain aesthetic of combat. The desire to kill, it is claimed, manifests itself in competition among the various units engaged on a given terrain and in phenomena of exaggeration and boastfulness. The practice of collecting "trophies" is said to attest to this morbid penchant in men.[21] Wolfgang Sofsky also mentions the pleasure involved in murder, which he relates to "the enthusiasm of survival" that is felt when a person contemplates another's death, discovering in doing so that he is still alive.[22] These two authors examine the emotions felt by combatants and killers as they engage in violence. The present material differs to the degree that it concerns veterans whose physical combat ended years or decades earlier. It is possible that my interlocutors felt satisfaction at the time they perpetrated some type of violence against their adversary, but the temporal distance separating them from such acts and the peacetime context in which they live has at least partly effaced this type of emotion.

Discussions of combat nevertheless evoke good memories among some ex-combatants. Some of them found themselves on the battlefield because they took pleasure in playing with death and taking risks. Making war is sometimes a choice of life. This was the case of the South African Special Forces who served under apartheid. Moreover, the detachment exhibited by a few of them, and the desire to underscore their own acts of violence, constitute transgressions and/or forms of provocation.

The Warrior's Excitement: The South African Special Forces

An unusual class of combatants, the members of a national army's elite formations present themselves as soldiers by vocation. Deployed in several southern African countries to combat the various guerrilla movements participating in the "communist assault" that had supposedly been fomented by the Soviet Union and its allies, the soldiers who served in the elite units of apartheid-era South Africa mention the pleasure they took in making war. Specialists of the southern African terrain, these professional soldiers engaged in nonconventional forms of intervention requiring technical mastery, guile, and excellent physical conditioning. While the members of the South African Special Forces insist on the risks they ran and the challenges they accepted, their adversaries are only ever mentioned in allusive fashion, as if the confrontation with the enemy was merely a pretext for the personal exploits of the Special Forces. Their combat narratives are mainly couched in virile, epic, and playful terms. The members of the Special Forces, whether Recces[23] or members of the 32nd Battalion,[24] claim they joined the army as a matter of personal taste: athletes tempted by adventure and physical exploits, they enjoyed living outdoors and discovering new countries. Having joined up at a young age, they were at once indifferent to the hardships of military life, carefree, and fearless. They are said to have possessed great human qualities: a spirit of comradery, solidarity in adversity, and an ability to surpass themselves. The members of the Special Forces known as the Recces incarnated this ideal soldier. They today continue to take great pride in their service and are convinced of their excellence and prestige. Now a computing consultant in Cape Town, Johann recounts:[25] "The Recces were known at the time for being the best soldiers. I wanted adventure. As strange as it might seem, it had nothing to do with the enemy. I was not particularly eager to fight the ANC or APLA [Azanian People's Liberation Army]. It was for the adventure. The selection began . . . Out of a hundred people, ten were finally recruited."

One tells the story of one's war experience by way of a few exploits. Reconnaissance missions, techniques of disguise and infiltration, and ways one succeeded in escaping enemy traps were all occasions for experiencing what these men sought: "the excitement of playing with death." They retain a rather happy memory of their service. In part, this is because they believe that theirs was a clean war. It is also due to the fact that, despite the physical and moral suffering to which they were exposed, the Recces never gave up they had also been chosen for their mental toughness. The wars were an opportunity for men to live powerful experiences in contact with nature. Johann recounts: "We did all of these amazing things, we jumped in parachutes, we handled mines. In Namibia, it was magnificent; there were wild animals and beautiful rivers. I have photos of myself with Teddy the lion."[26] The love of nature is a common theme in the experiences of these former soldiers. One's love for the bush is evidence of one's African identity: if one loves a land and respects it, one doubtless deserves it. Former soldiers also mention the strong ties that were formed in the field. And they emphasize a life among men, healthy and far from the scheming of Pretoria.

In his study of French veterans of the First World War, Prost discusses the apparent contradiction between their narrative of "the horror of war" and a kind of tenderness toward their own experience. The former soldiers made a point of saying that they "proved themselves worthy of respect" on the battlefield. Prost adds that "the combatant is not a soldier who glorifies war or the warrior virtues but rather a man who refuses to strike from his life an experience he had not sought out, one that mattered to him and of which he had no reason to be ashamed, as if it had never happened."[27] Prost's analysis concerns men who have not given up on investing past and present with political meaning. In the case of South African soldiers, particularly those who had belonged to the Special Forces, the absence of a political dimension accentuates their tendency to euphemize the violence of war: in their narratives, the adversary is often disembodied, and little mention is made of his death.

In somewhat less bucolic terms, a former "delta" amuses himself by recalling his participation in an operation that "blew up some barbouzes." Several interpretations may be advanced to account for his amusement in recounting this episode: the individual in question may have been concealing his embarrassment or seeking to show his detachment. I rather had the impression that he took pleasure in recalling a form of power that was all the more captivating given the skill and clever methods that it required. He recounts the struggle that pitted OAS activists and barbouzes against one another in the field—a struggle characterized by brutal and expeditious operations on both sides in the same way that he speaks of his skill at playing cat and mouse with the police. The former activist may consider this episode a good memory, particularly if it is shared with a group that remains united in its political and psychological stance. This lack of scruple is further explained by the fact that the members of the OAS saw the barbouzes contract workers hired by the government to carry out its dirty work as mercenaries and, as such, unworthy adversaries. Their brutal methods and the fact that they embodied the "treason" of a government that did not shy away from attacking French people fighting to "remain French" deprive them of any claim to respect today.

Acknowledging Brutality: The Case of an OAS Member

Ex-combatants do not generally claim and accept responsibility for the brutal and sometimes even cruel use of force. Rather than conceal their past actions or assign them new meaning, however, a few individuals tick off the list of those they killed, as if the moral prohibition on murder did not concern them. For these ex-combatants, such an attitude may also reflect a clear-eyed recognition of having given free rein to the dark side of their humanity. In contrast to the veterans described by Prost, these men recognize not just the horror of war, but also their own crimes.

In the case of Quentin, a former "delta," the experience of acting the killer for several years seems to have become second nature. He appears to have merged with the theater of war, in which all men who take up arms are alike and all equally "savage":

> Death was waiting around every corner. Grenades were indiscriminately thrown into tram cars. If you were nearby, you were dead, and that's all there is to it. Or you sat down in a bar, and someone blew the bar up. For example, the coastal road casino that was blown up [an attack carried out by the FLN]. It cut peoples' legs off; there was a pile of dead people. I don't believe that these guys . . . In humanitarian terms, we just copied them, you don't know what humanitarianism means when you make war. It was that way in this war; you have to realize there were only bad guys on both sides. You can't say to people: "No, I'm nice." It's not true. Because your head only gets hotter . . . Violence goes hand in hand with violence. The more you go there, the more aggressive and savage you become. And savagery is savagery; sometimes a man doesn't even recognize himself anymore.

Quentin wanted to keep his land and believed that the fight against the Arabs of the FLN was a fight to the death between "us" and "them." The violence he describes does not reflect an ideological program. In "playing" at war and perhaps aspiring to one of its leading roles, Quentin is aware that he crossed a point of no return. Indeed, should his side have won, Quentin believes that, with so much blood on their hands, he and his colleagues would not have been allowed to remain alive:

> —Among ourselves, we said . . . that if French Algeria was established, they would have shot us. We knew that.
> —Who?
> —Yes, they would have eliminated us; we didn't know who.
> —The leaders of the OAS?
> —Yes, we had them in mind.

Quentin recognizes in no roundabout way that he took personal initiatives, what he refers to as "extras." Whom did Quentin target?

> Oh, it didn't matter! At the end, we were doing things; we did whatever they did. They drove by in a car and fired machine guns into European cafés. We did the same thing; we fired machine guns into Moorish cafés.

Despite such excesses, Quentin claims that his conscience is in no way troubled. By contrast, he is not numb to the aesthetic dimensions of combat. And while he seems unaffected by the death of his enemies, his heart tightens at the mention of his old school:

> We went to the outskirts of Guyotville in the Arab neighborhoods where there are shacks, and I had some pretty big extinguishers full of explosives, with the fuses sticking out like that. Because, I'm sorry, but we didn't have any electric detonators or that sort of thing. It was still rudimentary; you had to light the fuse. And in the end we succeeded. It was a beautiful scene because the shacks rose up in the air and exploded . . . By contrast, I was given the order to burn schools. I couldn't do it. My school! It was stronger than me: it was a memory and I couldn't do it.

Despite his lack of restraint in pursuing the fight, his indifference in regard to his adversary's death, and his embrace of the role of warrior, Quentin still proclaims his humanity: "You shouldn't believe that we were just thickheaded brutes. No, we had feelings; I wasn't born like that. I was born to for a peaceful, stay-at-home life. Every night, I went to pick up my son. And then there was the war, the war."

Self-Dramatization: The Case of an MK

Laying claim to a degree of cruelty may also be part of an effort to persuade the interviewer of one's determination, tenacity, and virility. It may also be a form of provocation that is, an attempt to impress or shock one's interlocutor. This stance tends to be most often encountered among members of underground groups whose resources are inferior to those of their opponents. A veteran of the armed wing of the ANC thus told me of his pleasure in "neck-lacing" a collaborator. These remarks were particularly surprising given that this former armed militant had elsewhere expressed guilt for the people he killed in the course of the struggle. He was troubled by the memory of the black police officers and white civilians he killed. Although apparently at odds with one another, the various parts of his narrative are not mutually exclusive. His feelings of guilt coexist with an awareness of his capacity to use force. Beyond any ambivalent feelings that this ex-combatant may have had regarding his enemy's death, the knot of contradiction comes undone when one considers the complex relations that obtain between the researcher and the individuals he or she encounters in the field. On some occasions, this ANC militant thus acted out a particular role for the investigator: that of the cruel black man. Faced with a foreign white woman who seemed to correspond to the cliché of the timorous and distrustful racist, he took pleasure in embodying this frightening stereotype. By portraying himself in this fashion, he sought to provoke conflict and thereby test both his interlocutor and his relationship to her.

From Uneasiness to Guilt

Some ex-combatants speak of experiencing depression, of seeking psychological or psychiatric help, or mention the unceasing silence or suicide of colleagues. Some also describe other symptoms, including nightmares, alcoholism, and behavioral problems. The protagonists primarily discuss the consequences of their former actions in terms of inner turmoil and personal problems. They do not systematically address the ethical dimension of their actions. Indeed, psychological problems relating to the commission of violent acts do not necessarily lead one to display feelings of guilt,[28] but the fact that such feelings are not expressed does not mean they do not exist. The aim here is not to entertain conjectures regarding the subconscious mind of the ex-combatants I encountered. While feelings of guilt are often subconscious and can manifest themselves in various ways, I address such feelings only in cases where they are expressed.

The field of psychoanalysis took an early interest in war trauma. Following the First World War, Karl Abraham, a disciple of Freud, addressed this issue, referring to it as a very particular wound to the soul. Starting in 1929, the French state included neuro-psychiatric illnesses in the list of disabilities for which veterans had a right to compensation.[29] In the aftermath of the

Vietnam War, mental health professionals discovered that nearly a third of veterans suffered from psychological problems, and in 1978 this resulted in the elaboration of a new syndrome: Post-Traumatic Stress Disorder (PTSD). The veteran thus came to be seen as a victim. Dominated by the Freudian approach, military psychology saw guilt as a problem rather than as an appropriate—if painful—response to the past.[30]

Psychological and psychiatric approaches can help decipher the workings of trauma, but their contribution must not lead one to neglect the political significance of its expression and the forms it takes. In France, very few veterans of the First or Second World War thought to apply for pensions on the basis of the trauma inflicted upon them.[31] It was only after the Algerian War that veterans' rights associations began to refer to the combatants' psychic and moral suffering. A 10 January 1992 decree confirmed that psychotraumatic syndromes were to be recognized as "wounds" by the medical corps and compensated as such.[32] While the mobilization of Algerian War veterans may be linked to mental health developments, it perhaps above all reflected the difficulty of assigning moral and political meaning to France's "peacekeeping operations," a difficulty also experienced by American veterans of the Vietnam War. Moreover, the approach adopted by Louis Crocq makes trauma part of the victim's identity and therefore dismisses questions of responsibility and guilt.[33] What interests me here, however, are the conditions in which one speaks about suffering that stems from committing acts of violence, and the moral doubts and feelings of guilt with which they are associated.

In South Africa, there is nothing unusual about expressing this sort of discomfort. The heavy presence of psychologists within the TRC and the NGOs that emerged in the post-apartheid years certainly made it easier for the population to accept expressions of weakness on the part of "victims" and "perpetrators" alike. It is less common for other categories of veteran to acknowledge their moral wounds. Feelings of guilt, for their part, are only very rarely expressed.[34]

Anxiety and Piety: The Case of an OAS Member

Of Polish origin, Edouard Slama is a practicing Catholic and follower of Pope John Paul II. Born in the Ardennes to parents who had fled communism, he was the school "Polack." After joining the parachutists, he carried out his military service in Algeria, fought the war in the maquis and lost several friends. The European population of Algeria admired his uniform, and Slama was warmly received by them. He fell in love with a young pied-noir woman and, once demobilized, chose to stay in Algeria and marry her. Starting in December 1960, he became involved in "counter-terrorist" activities targeting the FLN and subsequently joined the OAS, where he became a "delta" leader. Although he made daily use of his sidearm until the very last moments of French Algeria, he had already begun to regularly attend church: "I prayed every night. I said my prayers and asked God to forgive me for all of the people I executed. That's how it was."

Arrested, tried, and sentenced to twenty years' incarceration, Edouard Slama did not experience his time in prison as unjust: "You pay. You are happy to not have already been killed by someone. Because you expected it. We all expected it. We had been warned." He explains that his time behind bars allowed him to break off his violent career: "It was the time I spent in the clink that saved me. It gave me a chance to think."

After receiving a presidential pardon, he remade his life, pursuing a career with Olivetti. At the same time, he became involved in former OAS networks and participated in the political scheming of politicians in southeastern France.[35] It was only once Slama had retired that he was overcome by anxiety, began to have nightmares, and decided to seek help. He admitted to some personal weakness, including emotional outbursts and alcohol abuse, but did not say much more. To allay this turmoil, he continued to rely on his faith: "I'm not sure whether I was right but I don't regret what I did. I think that if God forgave me, if I continue to pray for the executions that I carried out and for all of the people I killed. It's good, somewhere I am blessed. I succeeded in pulling through. I asked forgiveness but I forgave many things." Slama's conception of religion is self-centered: though he does not explicitly admit to feeling remorse, his personal arrangement with the Supreme Deity allows him to be absolved. He in this way dismissed the relationship with his former adversary and the debt owed his victims or their loved ones. At the same time, he seeks to position himself as a creditor and thereby asserts a form of equivalence: he, too, was made to suffer by the death of his comrades.

Slama is uncertain of the judgment that should be made of his past: "I'm proud of having been a parachutist. I'm proud of having been in the OAS but not really proud of what I did. I don't regret it but I'm not proud because perhaps there were other solutions after all. And it has to be said: I was a terrorist." Although he acknowledges the possibility of personal wrongdoing, he explicitly voices neither regret nor remorse. His various remarks sometimes contradict one another. Committing himself to the path of personal transformation would offer no guarantee of moral or intellectual support. He would run the risk of being disavowed by his companions, and his political adversaries would not recognize him as one of their own. The political and symbolic space does not encourage him to call himself into question any further. His doubts are stifled by fidelity to his identity and constrained by the consistency of his career and his loyalty to his peer group. Today a resident of Corsica, Slama takes comfort in walks in the scrub and offers his services as a magnetic healer and diviner, gifts he inherited from his mother's family.

Religious Redemption: The Case of a South African Police Officer

Since the belief that one has developed a private relationship with God offers a feeling of security, religious enthusiasm can assist in managing inner turmoil and solitude. By supplying a moral framework, religion allows individuals to reconstruct themselves on the basis of positive values. The South African police who found themselves obliged to supply a detailed accounting of the violence and humiliation they inflicted suffered a brutal loss of status and respect. Until then, they had been seen as protecting the nation from "terrorists," and their activities were implicitly approved by their departments. Suddenly, the revelations of the press and their own confessions made them the object of social and familial indignation. Stigmatized and rejected, some suddenly found themselves thoroughly isolated. Their newfound interest in religion helps makes up for their isolation and sudden fall in social status. It is also a vector of personal introspection and helps former police officers regain their moral bearings. For the partisans of apartheid, the moral framework of the democratic transition offers a possibility for rehabilitation.

Brian Mitchell is in his fifties.[36] In 1988, he was the commander of a police station in a small town in Kwazulu-Natal. After discussing the matter with Inkatha chiefs and his own hierarchy, he gave the order to blow up a house where an ANC meeting was to be held. Black police officers were tasked with carrying out the operation but mistook their target, killing eleven people, some of them children. None were activists of the national liberation movement. The police attempted to hush up the affair, which came to be known as the "Trust Feed Massacre," but Mitchell and his black underlings were nevertheless arrested. In 1992, Mitchell was sentenced to death. In 1996, this sentence was commuted to thirty years in prison. That same year, Mitchell formally requested amnesty from the TRC. Concluding that Mitchell had acted on the basis of political motivations and cooperated in the investigation, the TRC granted his request. He was the first member of the security forces to receive clemency from the TRC.[37] Less than five years after being incarcerated, Mitchell was thus freed, but his experience of prison had transformed him: "I gave my life to God when I was in prison."

For this former police officer, confinement came as a shock and fall from grace. He began to question his past and received visits from pastors, who rekindled his hope. Upon receiving the death sentence, he did not feel dejected: "I had this belief in me. I knew that two things were going to happen. I would be freed from prison before I was an old man. And my wife would divorce me . . . My wife had asked for a divorce and I knew that, after that, with the Truth Commission process, I would be freed from prison."

His redemption led him to make overtures toward the families he had plunged into mourning at Trust Feed. The TRC reparations committee organized a one-day visit to the township. After the commission's representatives had spoken, Mitchell addressed the victims' loved ones, asking their forgiveness. His remarks received an icy reception. Sometime later, however, a man named Thabani, the son of one of the women who had been killed in the bombing, had a dream: his mother appeared before him and ordered him to work toward reconciliation rather than vengeance. So Thabani decided to contact the white police officer and invite him to celebrate the national Day of Reconciliation. Mitchell was invited to a ceremony, where he spoke, promising to help the community. The ceremony was followed by Zulu songs and dances in which Mitchell participated to the best of his ability. In this way, his hosts showed him that they accepted his request for forgiveness. Another meeting took place the following year, during which a cow was sacrificed. The former prisoner remarked: "I think that the media missed a great event. It didn't really receive much attention. The media doesn't like to talk about happy things; they just concentrate on bad things."

Thabani and Mitchell decided to give more concrete form to their reconciliation. While Thabani wished to commemorate the past, Mitchell wanted to improve the living conditions of the people in the township whom he had plunged into mourning. Together, they set up an institution that was to house a museum as well as a job training center for young people. Five years later, the two partners were still seeking financial backing for the project. Mitchell saw Thabani as a friend and viewed his involvement as a kind of reparation.

He nevertheless considered it a onetime investment meant to repay his debt, not a calling to which he would devote the rest of his life. Once the institution had come into being, Mitchell reckoned that he would be able to withdraw: "If there are events that they would like me to attend, I'll attend them. But, yes, I need to succeed in life now."

A specificity of Mitchell's spiritual development is to have supplied a bridge between the former police officer and his victims' loved ones. Mitchell acknowledges his responsibility and does not seek to put the blame on politicians or his superiors. In contrast to his former colleagues, he declares: "I think that the country was governed by the security forces. The politicians did what the security forces told them to do."

He admits that he supported apartheid throughout his career as a police officer and never questioned it. Mitchell now lives in a small town, where he divides his time between his work for a car company, the church, home improvement, and his son. By acknowledging his guilt and seeking forgiveness, he is well positioned to integrate into the new political community. But Mitchell stands apart from it. He leads a secluded life, no longer drinks alcohol, never votes, and, when pushed to comment on his country's politics, chooses to position himself outside of it: "*They* have good leaders. *They* have talented businessmen. But *they* have a problem with corruption."[38] Mitchell's transformation is first and foremost internal: "[Giving one's life to God] totally changes one's direction in life . . . Before, I saw life—the way one lived in the police in terms of how you saw people, seeing blacks as evil incarnate. And I drank and went out with married women, all that." In placing all of his "sins"—a fondness for drinking, infidelity, racism, and, by extension, murder—on the same level, Mitchell dismisses politics and weakens the meaning of his transformation.

MK: The Ordeal of Treason

Thami joined the struggle at a young age and was subsequently recruited by the ANC.[39] He attacked black police officers in his township and threw grenades into public places but escaped arrest. In 1987, he teamed up with Vincent, a member of Umkhonto we Sizwe (MK) who had received guerrilla warfare training in Angola and been infiltrated back into South Africa to carry out operations. Thami felt great admiration and affection for his combatant-comrade. He had never known his father, and Vincent soon became a paternal figure for him. In November 1987, Vincent was run over by a car as he walked down a sidewalk in Soweto. Thami understood that his murder had been the work of a small group of ANC members involved in a violent spree. Realizing that he was next on their list, he fled the country. He traveled to Botswana, made it to Zambia, and then decided to join a military camp in Angola. There, he joined an intelligence unit, where he was responsible for monitoring his comrades within the camp in order to expose South African government agents who had infiltrated the ranks of the ANC. In doing so, his objective was to prevent the food supply from being poisoned and the sabotage of weapons. In the course of his duties, Thami identified four spies. In 1990, the ANC withdrew to Tanzania, where Thami served as a prison guard in a secret ANC prison. His memories of exile are painful, and he particularly recalls the harsh training regimen, the lack of freedom, and the fear of being mistakenly identified as a traitor.

More than ten years after returning to South Africa, Thami is still emotionally unsettled. He is on tranquilizers, sees a psychologist once a month, and has filed a request to receive a special pension for the psychological problems that affect him.[40] In Thami's case, the violence is palpable. He suffers from what was done to him as well as from what he did to others. He also feels abandoned by the ANC's leaders. Thami has never fully freed himself of his burden. Is this trauma or guilt? The anxiety that grips him seems to stem from the invasive experience of treason. A traitor for killing black police officers in Soweto, Thami was betrayed in turn by his comrades and was responsible for keeping a look out for traitors. He is overwhelmed by all of this and continues to perceive danger among those closest to him.

> It's said that only children are spoiled. But I wasn't spoiled. I didn't have this character, I was always smiling, but the struggle taught me something new about life: you can't trust anyone, not even your own comrade. You've always got to look over your shoulder. Who's behind you and what's that person doing? When people are ten meters behind me, I worry and wonder why they don't pass me. [*laughter*] And that sticks with you for the rest of your life. Until you are six feet under, you have to be alert and on the lookout because you don't know who's going to kill you. I'm not afraid of death. I know that I'll be taken out one day but I want to die knowing who got me.

The physical elimination of individuals who belong to one's political community but have been identified as collaborators is a source of discomfort.

Those who mention it exhibit feelings of guilt. Since it blurs the boundary between one's own community and that of the enemy and almost always entails taking the life of someone with whom one is to one degree or another proximate, one's neighbor or a member of one's national or ethnic group, this type of killing provokes considerable unease.[41] What's more, the confrontation with the traitor entails an awareness of the enemy's success in infiltrating one's camp, recruiting one's comrades, and thus weakening and dividing the side to which one belongs. Among other things, the violent measures taken in dealing with collaborators are to be explained by reference to the risk they pose for the political community and the fact that they call into question the meaning of its struggle. The very existence of a paid agent of the enemy constitutes a wound, one that his murder does not always adequately assuage. Finally, a lack of certainty regarding the guilt of collaborators may also be a source of anxiety. Recalling the summary manner in which justice is done in wartime—a matter of practical necessity—can rekindle doubts in the minds of the protagonists.

Two ANC militants told me of the persistent turmoil that affected them. Unemployed in Soweto, Thami is haunted by the faces of the black apartheid-regime police officers he killed. Michael, a former MK intelligence operative turned businessman, today questions the tactical choices he made during the struggle:[42] "One day, I learned that an MK hideout was going to be attacked by the Security Branch. I had the choice to warn them or let them die but safeguard the intelligence network I was working to construct. What would you have done in my place? I chose to let them die."

Thami and Michael felt a need to express the persistent anxiety that came with discussing their past choices. They seem to be sporadically assailed by a difficulty in accepting certain acts and by doubts regarding the legitimacy of killings for which they are partly or fully responsible. Doubts emerge and then disappear regarding their past behavior. It is a subject that they raised with me on only one occasion and then outside of the framework of our formal interviews. On a few occasions in the course of our exchanges, each militant relaxed and, for a limited time, revealed his feelings of guilt. Subsequently, these same individuals may shift to a discourse dominated by the rationalization or denial of violence. This phenomenon of relaxation is encouraged when one grows distant from one's peer group—either, as in the case of Thami, because that group has dispersed, or because one feels one has been sidelined, as in the case of Michael, who remains loyal to an ANC leader who had been marginalized. When the social and ideological cohesion of a group collapses or diminishes, its members are obliged to confront their moral doubts and questions.

*   *   *

Among ex-combatants, what positions encourage or prevent one from renouncing the figure of the enemy?

Denying or rationalizing one's wartime deeds tends to prolong mobilization against one's enemy. The perception that a conflict has yet to end encourages one to continue to wage battle to ensure the triumph of one's cause. Such ongoing mobilization discourages critical self-reflection. Such is the lot of a certain number of former FLN and OAS members. Yet justifying the brutality of one's group or side may promote acceptance of the other's violence. The expression "It was war" and the notion of natural proximity between combatants make it easier for the protagonists to have a drink together.[43] This form of conviviality does not entail recognizing the Other's political cause as legitimate.

The emergence of doubts and feelings of guilt may lead one to reconsider the Other. At the same time, the inner turmoil provoked by these emotional states threatens to dissuade ex-combatants from carrying the process through to its conclusion.

Chapter 9

The Intimate Ordeal of Torture

The social sciences have sought to shed light on practices of cruelty and extreme violence. In doing so, they have tended to focus on perpetrators, examining, among other things, their practices of torture, motivations (sadism, revenge, "reason of state"), the social and psychological conditions that paved the way for their action (perception of danger, submission to authority, group pressure, routine, and habituation to war),[1] political contexts such as the colonial situation[2] or American involvement in a "war of civilization" against terrorism,[3] and government efforts at justification.[4] Confessional memoirs written by torturers and witnesses alike have also been published.[5]

The issue of torture has received much less attention from the point of view of those subjected to it. In Algeria, the question has been passed over in silence. Christiane Chaulet-Achour notes that the testimony of veterans does no more than allude to the issue; in first-person accounts and novels alike, it occupies a marginal place.[6] It is above all in the writings of French intellectuals that the practice has been politically denounced.[7] In South Africa, the issue of torture has received particular attention from the victim's perspective, since it was publicly addressed in the context of the Truth and Reconciliation Commission (TRC) hearings. Accounts detailing methods, sometimes accompanied by exchanges between perpetrators and victims, were made public.

From the point of view of those who suffered it, discussing torture is an extremely sensitive matter. Shame, feelings of humiliation, and the suffering elicited in recounting painful memories are all obstacles to giving narrative form to the fragments of one's story. Nevertheless, the torture and abuse to which some activists were subjected can at times be a source of pride. Suffering, which crushes the victim, returns as a source of self-esteem. In South

Africa, some are willing to touch upon their weakness. In Algeria, the tra-jectory of a mujahida suggests that the Algerian dogma of heroism may now be changing.

Incommunicable Suffering?

It is not easy for the veteran to put into words the violence inflicted on his body by the enemy, for doing so can trigger psychic mechanisms of shame and distress. If such violence is referred to at all, it is thus only in elliptical terms. The question of shame is a primary issue in speaking out. As Numa Muraud has shown in connection with a French survey of victims of violence, individuals are more willing to acknowledge that they have been subjected to violence of a sexual nature when responding to self-administered ques-tionnaires than in the context of one-on-one interviews. In this situation, men are more reluctant to mention having been the victims of violence that have affected their health.[8] In a completely different context, Michael Pollak and Nathalie Heinich underscore the fact that survivors of Second World War concentration camps are reluctant to testify because "speaking up, far from 'making them proud' . . . threatens to trigger the traumatic experiences of events from this past that remain incompatible with their self-image or sense of identity."[9]

Sometimes, individuals avoid speaking of their ordeals. This avoidance can take the form of a refusal to individualize suffering in order to integrate it into a broader narrative of collectively experienced trauma. Vincent Romani shows that this attitude is commonplace among the Palestinians who were harassed by security forces during the al-Aqsa Intifada. The denial of per-sonal suffering is among a set of practices that serve to distance oneself from violence and its effects.[10] In discussing their lot, Palestinian men seek to avoid provoking an emotional response on the part of the interlocutor for fear of revealing their own fragility. If one is to preserve one's self-esteem, it is of fundamental importance to master the destructive effects of violence.

Although it is ultimately impossible to know what proportion they rep-resent, many individuals choose to pass over the question of torture in silence. The experience of torture reveals a particular situation: that in which a combatant has been captured, reduced to impotence, and dominated by a stronger enemy. Mohamed, a National Liberation Front (FLN) militant, never said a word about torture to me or his loved ones.[11] Covered in scars, how-ever, his body left his wife in no doubt as to the truth. The debasement and pain inflicted on him remained unspeakable. Among Algerians, the exposure of the naked body can provoke a profound feeling of shame.[12] This is all the more so when the unclothed body is handled by the enemy for the purposes of inflicting suffering and submission—an irreversible form of humiliation, impossible to express. In order to speak of this episode in one's life, it is necessary to change its meaning.

According to Marnia Lazreg, one reason for Algerian silence in regard to torture is that acts of physical cruelty were systematically accompanied by the rape of the men and women arrested by the French army. The stigma attached to rape prevents victims from speaking out and, Lazreg argues, limits its interpretation: even as they describe scenes of rape, some do not acknowledge it as such.[13]

Second, the question of torture raises questions about whether the captured combatant was compromised.[14] Did he talk? Does he feel like a traitor? Is he afraid of being accused of being one? These questions are a source of embarrassment for those concerned, political organizations, and commentators alike—all of whom are unwilling to explore the false choices of an individual in distress. It is nevertheless possible to touch upon the relationship linking torturer and victim when the latter characterizes himself in terms of the moral destabilization of the former, who has been seduced by militant ideals or seized by sudden compassion for his prey.[15] South African novels, for their part, have taken up the question of the combatant obliged to betray his loved ones.[16]

Third, individuals who have been severely abused are sometimes eager to retain or even emphasize their identity as combatants. They thus refuse to be considered victims and balk at describing the acts of physical cruelty inflicted upon them. Being a hero requires that one not feel sorry about one's sufferings.

Some of the individuals who spoke to me about the torture inflicted upon them told me about how much repeating their accounts—which they had already provided elsewhere—cost them. They nevertheless affirmed their desire to tell their stories. In this respect, they conceive of their approach in terms of what Pollak and Heinich refer to as "recounting one's life in the name of a general value." While the FLN militant Louisette tells her story in the interests of truth, Dipuo, an African National Congress (ANC) activist, seeks to show the way to forgiveness. This desire to serve universal values is not incompatible with a more personal reason for speaking out: self-liberation. This aim also informed Louisette Ighilhariz' decision to reveal her secret, which had been hidden for years. To the degree that speaking out allows one to invert the order of the dominant discourse, victim narratives of the experience of violence may in this respect sometimes be transformed into "reparative accounts."[17] It is an opportunity to leave shame and stigma behind and reaffirm categories of justice. Speaking out about one's own experience of violence while referring to universal moral categories also serves the purpose of denouncing an injustice that concerns not just oneself, but also a broader group.

The Ordeal Transfigured: The Heroes of the FLN and ANC

Veterans who found themselves in a position of structural weakness vis-à-vis their enemy feel pride in recalling the damage they inflicted upon him. Confronting a more powerful enemy force requires intelligence, skill, and physical courage. These qualities reflect an individual's determination and personal caliber. The inversion of the power struggle thus plays out on moral terrain.

The ordeal of torture entails a situation in which an individual who has been captured or arrested and lacks the resources necessary for defending himself is treated in a brutal, degrading, and painful way, enduring the sadism of his torturers. In this extreme experience, the physical and/or moral scars of which are carried for the rest of one's life, power relations are so unbalanced that they transform into a relationship of absolute domination. This relationship already characterized the colonial context in which the Algerian War and South African conflict took place. Torture is thus a form of interaction by means of which the security services remind rebels of their dominated condition. It is also an opportunity for the government's representatives to inflict punishment upon those dominated individuals who dare defy the political order, reminding them of their proper place, particularly by forcing them to cooperate. In South Africa, the practice of capturing national liberation movement militants and "turning" them so that they would work for the security forces was thus part of this larger desire to control bodies and minds, destroying the enemy's free will. In order to transform enemy combatants into *askaris*,[18] recruiters relied on coercion and corruption—complementary ways of subjugating one's enemy. For those subjected to torture, the stakes are significant: stay alive or die; talk or suffer; betray one's side or retain one's self-esteem.

If an ex-combatant who has been subjected to torture is to draw pride from it, he must reinterpret the facts and his relationship with the torturer(s). By telling his story, he supplies his experience with new meaning capable of sustaining his self-esteem. Among former FLN veterans, a number report that they were subjected to torture. They often bring it up in rapid, almost anecdotal fashion, maintaining that their choice to fight colonialism naturally exposed them to the soldiers' practices and that the rules of war made this experience inevitable.[19] Most do not linger over their stories, some keep silent, and a very small number discuss the matter in considerable detail.

Such is the case of Ghassan.[20] Wounded in combat in 1958, he was arrested, left without medical care, and tortured. He was subjected to beatings, burning, smothering, and electric shocks. Involved in a series of attacks targeting Algerians and a French soldier, Ghassan was sentenced to death and remained in his cell for over a year while waiting for the sentence to be carried out. He was pardoned in 1960, and his sentence was commuted to life in prison.

Ghassan recounts that the soldiers who captured him were so happy about taking him that they danced. They tortured him to obtain the names of his accomplices. Despite their brutality, Ghassan resisted, refusing to talk. His heroism derived from his ability to manage his torturers' violence through cunning and physical resistance to pain. The French soldiers injected Ghassan with a truth serum. He heard a man who presented himself as a comrade-in-arms speak to him in Arabic, encouraging him to supply the names of his accomplices. The mujahid claims to have seen through this trick and mocked the security forces: "I tell him: 'But you know very well, there was your sister, your mother, didn't you know? All you've got to do is ask them!' So, you see, I started being a little mischievous. And the captain saw that and he looked at me like this and then said: 'Take off this bastard's blindfold.'"

Ghassan's stamina was such that the equipment used to torture him failed before his body did:

—So they didn't get any information out of you?
—Nothing at all. The worst was my feet because of the electricity they gave me . . . They took wires and they attached them like this. And then they put the clamps on. So, when they turned the electricity on, it hurt. But when they kept going and kept going and kept going, the wires got red, and they had to stop the electricity.

After being subjected to torture for days on end, Ghassan decided to end his life by provoking an incident, attacking the captain tasked with interrogating him. Describing himself as "half dead," he claims that he nevertheless got the better of his adversary, and that his dogged attack was only overcome by the joint effort of eight men:

> I'm going to try to slit the captain's throat and they will shoot me. . . . When the captain came, I was nearly dead. I only had a few ounces of strength left. I was completely dead. He put a stool in front of me— like that, facing me. He said, "What is it, Mr. Ghoulam, you wanted to speak with me?" I told him yes and I did that because my hands weren't free; I did it so that I could throw myself on him. And since he saw that he was at the same level, when he saw that I did that, he raised his arms, and my hands passed behind like that, over the top, and that's what I did. I did that. I squeezed him like that against me, and that's all. There wasn't anything else I could do, I didn't have anything. It was all I could do so that they would shoot me. So he started shouting, "Let go of me! Let go of me!" He head-butt me, kicked my shins, but I didn't feel anything. So the guard came, held his rifle by the barrel, and began to hit me across the back with the butt. But I was half dead, half dead. I felt the blows, but it made absolutely no difference to me or almost. And there we were, turning like that, the desk, the chairs. We finally knocked everything over, spinning around the room. I was hitched to him. He could stand up, but I was hitched to him. My face was against his face, and he gave me head-butts. "Let go of me! Let go of me! Let go of me!" We were spinning around the room, spinning, spinning, and then this guy cracked. I could see that he was having trouble breathing. So he said, "Go find six volunteers!" They arrived, so there was the captain and six volunteers and the two guards who were standing at the door, all to raise my hands. And I was spinning. So they picked me up. When they picked me up, I was like a puppet. When they pushed me, I pushed him. We were going backwards; I was hitched to him. So when they pulled me, I took him with me, and we spun around the room. They kicked me, hit me with the butts of their rifles. Finally, they wanted to raise my hands. They broke my fingers one by one, lifted my fingers, and I held on, like a viper. So it lasted nearly an hour and a half from when I first got ahold of him until the end.

Ghassan's hand-to-hand fight began to resemble ballet. In this confrontation, which he had lost in advance, the FLN combatant led the dance despite the reinforcements' joint efforts. His determination allowed him to overcome his physical weakness and he gave up only once all ten of his fingers had been methodically broken one by one. This epic and poetic story reflects well on Ghassan. He nevertheless admits to being marked by a traumatic experience that affects him to this day: Ghassan was subsequently to spend more than a year waiting for his "turn" on death row, along the way becoming one of the oldest prisoners awaiting execution.

Marnia Lazreg notes the meaning that resisting torture had for Algerian combatants: "For the nationalist, going to his death without talking sealed his commitment to his cause and to his comrades in arms. Not only had he given them time to alter course and/or disperse but he had also defeated his enemy, their methods and their assumed knowledge of his being."[21] None of the individuals I encountered admitted to having cracked under the weight of physical abuse.

Captured in 1957 after she had joined guerrilla fighters, Louisette was sent to the 10th Parachutist Division, where she was tortured for two and a half months. Her account is in several ways similar to that of Ghassan. After learning that her companion-in-arms, Said, had been killed during the clash with the French army, she claimed that he was their leader and alone possessed the information the French were seeking. When her interrogators refused to believe this and insisted that she talk, she deceived them by suggesting that they allow her to confront Said.[22] Unlike that of Ghassan, Louisette's account reveals her suffering and impotence. But it is heroic all the same, and her great courage is an object of familial and political gratitude. Louisette states that she is her father's favorite child, especially since undergoing torture without revealing anything.

The veterans of the Algerian War of Independence thus hold that their capacity for physical resistance reflects their high moral standing. Their determination, sense of sacrifice, and thirst for freedom and dignity are the qualities that allowed them to stand up to a relentless adversary willing to employ immoral methods and possessing superior military resources. Through the ordeal of their opponents' power and cruelty, the protagonists' heroism is revealed.[23]

The ANC activists who fell into the hands of the Security Branch also ran the risk of being tortured. They frequently mention it. For some, making it through this ordeal is evidence of their moral stature, which impresses, destabilizes, and wins over their torturers. In this way, the power struggle is inverted. Not only do the torturers fail to "turn" their captive; despite his position of weakness, he impairs his torturers' ability to do their jobs, instilling doubt among some and sometimes even gleaning information from them. An ex-member of Umkhonto we Sizwe (MK) named Yunis recounts his experience thus:[24]

> My mom had died of a heart attack. But what all this did, you know the torture, my mom's dying, the way in which we handled the torture, it hung on to the sense of compassion amongst the Indian security guards people and the African ones. So they began to make gestures towards us, little things like, you know, get you chocolate, take a quick message clandestinely to your parents, to tell them you are OK. So in this way we grew a relationship. But also being in the headquarters, you got to see how the security guards function, you got very to close range of them. You began to understand their tension amongst themselves, their focus, their methodology of work. You also got rid of your own fear of them, because you had lived in their cells, you had endured the worst they could deliver to you and you found, amazingly, you lived. And it gave you a sense of how much he knows, what's his capability, what's the extent of his infiltration; you could make an assessment of his, his commanders and his officers. You just got to understand so much about his tactics, his techniques, the way in which they functioned. You know, so what it gave to us was this amazing confrontation with the enemy at close quarter, so that you could study him at close quarter and in the result, we began to find some cracks which we then sought to exploit. And that in turn now gave rise to us being able to infiltrate the security establishment. When I came out of detention we were able to recruit the Security Branch officers.

The activists' heroism is not limited to their capacity to endure abuse. Above all, it stems from the generous spirit of ANC members, who succeeded a posteriori in forgiving their torturers.

Popo was born and raised in Soweto. His first experience of political socialization took place in the context of a Christian youth group. After being noticed by ANC leaders, he joined the underground organization when still in high school. Sought by the police, he fled the country and joined the ANC's structures in exile. He first pursued his studies and then received military training in Angola. Popo was sent to the USSR and the German Democratic Republic to improve his military skills. Infiltrating back into South Africa to set up MK cells, he was arrested in 1984, tortured, and sentenced to ten years in prison. Popo ticks off the abuses to which he was subjected and speaks of the distress he feels each time he hears a key in the lock. Despite intense physical suffering and his torturers' attempts to bribe him, Popo kept quiet: "My wounds made me stubborn. It made no difference to me whether they killed me. [. . .] They asked me to cooperate and told me that they would free me and that I would have a nice house. I told them to go to hell and that I didn't know anything."

The MK was tried and sentenced to ten years in prison, time he served in the jails of Robben Island. In his account, the power struggle is spectacularly reversed:

> What moved me was when one of the guys who had tortured me came to see me on the day of sentencing and told me, "I have a lot of re-spect for you. You hung in there. What I did to you, I didn't do it because I like it. I acted under orders and I hope that you will forgive me." I shook his hand and smiled. But I was still angry. At Robben Island, I heard his voice again, I heard him saying, "You are a brave man," and, at that moment, I forgave him. It was like he was in front of me, like I was speaking to him and forgave him. My behavior changed, I became more easygoing with my comrades. It's such a re-lief to pardon the enemy who tortured you. I began to sleep well and smile.[25]

Popo's ability to forgive was particularly due to the recognition bestowed upon him by one of his torturers. After having denied his humanity and attempted to destroy his convictions, the cruel and determined enemy was ultimately moved and impressed by his courage. By revealing these feelings, the enemy restored the dignity that his abuse had denied. This episode was a significant moral victory for the activist: his adversary recognized him both as a man and as a political militant. This exchange between the torturer and the activist continued when Popo forgave him, a gesture that proved not only that he was deserving of his adversary's recognition, but also that his experi-ence had ennobled him. This allowed him to recover from his feelings of suf-fering and anger. Moreover, granting forgiveness inverted the relationship of domination. It was also a way for Popo to extricate himself from the position of victim and remain a combatant. In this connection, he refrained from testifying as a victim before the TRC and claimed to have no interest in his torturers' hearing, who for their part requested amnesty.

Popo's socialization and Christian commitment guided his approach, but his support for the ANC's aim of radically reforming the nation played a larger role. He embodies his organization's humanism and grace. The indulgence shown the agents of apartheid is also to be explained by the fact that the ANC believed they would be transformed as the ideal society they envisioned took shape. Popo acted in a pedagogical manner; he took the victims who testified before the TRC in hand and desires to live in a society characterized by forgiveness and reconciliation. His present lifestyle and standard of living cause him to socialize with white people. At the sports club, he sometimes tells his story to the white men who see the scars on his body: "Some say that they would not have forgiven in my place. One of them told me about what they were obliged to do in Namibia. They are angry for having been so naive."

Popo is aware of the global publicity surrounding the "South African miracle." His experience illustrates his country's exceptional character. He explains that he has recounted his story and experience and overcome his nagging wounds "in order to participate in understanding the human race." He conceives of his testimony as a way of mobilizing on behalf of a "general value":[26] forgiveness. The parallel he draws between his trajectory and that of the Jews during the Second World War reflects this ambition to serve as an example.

Admitting One's Failings: South African Voices

In South Africa, some members of the ANC are willing to admit their failings. Born in 1950, Dipuo was the daughter of an ANC militant in exile. After marrying and becoming a mother, she became increasingly involved in militancy. She was initially a liaison agent and then became an MK.[27] She was arrested by the Security Branch, who interrogated her in an effort to force her to reveal information regarding her chain of command. She realized that the police were acquainted with a number of her contacts:

> If they knew something, you had to tell them what they already knew because they are going to hit you, hit you and make you talk about things they don't know. You have to listen to understand what they already know and say, "Yes, I'm aware." . . . They put snakes around

my neck. They punished me. They beat me. But I didn't want to speak until Petro had time to go away. . . . My husband would warn him. If he hadn't, he would have had problems because they were going to hit me until I said his name. And I said his name the next day. By the time they got to the township, Petro had run away.

Dipuo took a strategic approach to managing her interrogation: to win time, she decided to resist for one day, assuming that this would leave time for the members of her group to pass on news of her arrest. Yet she was aware of her limits and acknowledges them as such: she knew that she would speak. Her account is short, pragmatic, and without lyricism.

Ex-MK Michael's remarks reflect the classic theme of the combatants' moral suffering.[28] Antoine Prost and Bruno Cabanes have discussed the solitude felt by soldiers returning from the front and faced with the representations and expectations of their family and community. Silence is thus a means for the veteran to avoid disappointing others, escape confrontation with those close to him, and continue to be esteemed by others. But the discrepancy between external perceptions and those of the combatant affect his self-esteem:

When you get out of prison, you're seen as a hero. You came from there and you stood up to it. But that's not what you yourself feel. You were broken, humiliated, tortured. You could have cracked. You don't feel like a hero at all. So you keep quiet. You have insomnia. Unable to sleep, you continue to work for the revolution and become even more of a hero. I've never talked about all that. My brothers and I were all in prison but we never talked about it together. Do you have to talk about it? Do you have to keep silent? My silence ruined my first marriage.

Even among combatants, feelings of incommunicability can arise. Having suffered the same ordeals as one's brother or comrade risks making his account all the more comprehensible. At the same time that one reveals one's own humiliation, one reminds one's companion of his. Acknowledging one's failings in recounting the ordeal of torture would thus be to inflict pain on oneself and this brother—so near and dear—whom one seeks to protect. If Michael chose to confide in me a little,[29] it was doubtless due to my status as a foreign woman, someone who disappears just as easily as she came.

That one may admit one's suffering in South Africa partly explains how I was able to interview an askari, a member of the ANC who was captured by the apartheid security forces and forced to collaborate with and join them. Christopher joined the armed wing of the ANC in exile in 1976.[30] Sent to the USSR, he specialized in the handling of explosives and in 1984 prepared to infiltrate South Africa to carry out an armed operation there. Captured in Swaziland before entering the country's territory, the MK received no trial. Collaborate or die was his choice: "You perhaps want to know, you are perhaps curious to understand, why I chose to join the South African security forces rather than die. I chose not to die. I didn't choose to die because, in my head, I thought at the time and still do that dead heroes don't fight, they don't continue to struggle for liberation. Dead heroes can't fight. If you stay alive, you have a chance to continue the struggle."

The turned MK spoke of the immense suffering and psychological exhaustion that his involvement with the South African police entailed. Although he was used as bait to catch former comrades and was present during torture sessions, his superiors doubted his loyalty and constantly kept an eye on him. Simultaneously victim and traitor, Christopher requested amnesty for the actions in which he participated in the South African police. He received it for various affairs and was simultaneously recognized as a victim.

Marginalized by the ANC, Christopher nevertheless still feels like he belongs to this organization and continues to support the movement. He states that he has no bitterness toward the former police but would like history to cast light on the meaning of his trajectory. If he became an askari, it was due to the infiltration of high-level collaborators within the ANC. The thorny question of collaboration was not addressed by the TRC. Christopher is nevertheless proud of what he accomplished: "I think I did my duty. I participated at my level. All of these people who are in the provincial governments, I trained them. They were MK, and I was the one who trained them. I'm proud of having participated. Some have become provincial governors."

Christopher seems to have overcome his tragic fate. Giving in to the Security Branch's blackmail is understandable. In a society in which the TRC has created a space for victims, some ex-combatants, freed from the imperative of purity, evoke the conflict's gray zones.

The Louisette Ighilahriz Affair: Heroism Reoriented

In June 2000, the testimony of a female Algerian combatant, Louisette Ighilahriz, appeared on the front page of Le Monde. It accused Captain Graziani of having tortured her between September and December 1957 on the orders of General Massu and Colonel Bigeard. In *Algérienne*, a book she published in 2001 in which she recounts her experience,[31] Ighilahriz alludes to her rape while in captivity, the particular circumstances of which she had discussed in a 2000 documentary produced by Florence Beaugé and at several public appearances in France.[32] Despite the distress this episode continued to cause her, Ighilahriz had passed over it in silence for more than forty years. It was only after becoming friends with the French journalist that she was willing to unburden herself of her secret. She explains what led to her decision to do so: "In 2000, I had a problem, a very strong tachycardia. That was when I decided that, since I was dying, I had to leave something—it's an obligation of memory against forgetting. It's true that we meet: we hold seminars, colloquia. But that doesn't go beyond the Mediterranean. And that's when Florence Beaugé came. She knew there was something. But it took seventeen hours of recording. She harassed me a little bit because she wanted me to let it out, she wanted me to free myself."[33] Ighilahriz insisted that the truth emerge, that the suffering and injustice to which she had been subjected be known. When she began to feel herself physically weakening and imagined her death, she wanted to speak of her past.

Her approach collided with the reactions of French soldiers. On a French television channel, General Schmitt did not content himself with denying her torture; he accused Louisette Ighilahriz of lying, calling into question the account that she had laboriously assembled. Indignant at being confronted with such remarks in response to her efforts to get her adversaries to acknowledge a series of facts, she took him to court: "One day, I was watching television and saw General Schmitt with an orchestra of torturers who had become generals. They accused me—me, little Louisette—of having written a web of lies. They called me an inveterate liar. And I couldn't accept that. I was not a victim, I was the guilty party! I didn't consider his rank, his past, or his experience: I called a lawyer in Paris to drag him to court. It was too much. Not only had I not got over it, but, on top of that, he calls me a liar and story-teller?!"[34] She fervently hoped that the torturers she named would recognize the acts that wounded her and "ask to be forgiven."[35] She links this approach to the fact that France presented its apologies to Algeria for its colonial policy and its violent acts during the war. Tormented by her traumatic memories, the mujahida thought that this approach would rid her of a portion of her suffering. She wondered about the South African experience and took an interest in the TRC. She wished to travel the path that led toward forgiveness. Several others have underscored the curative powers of forgiveness:

Vamik Volkan has shown that receiving an apology can change the course of mourning; Lee Taft[36] holds that the expression of regret and remorse on the part of the offender at his trial helps victims heal; Levy and Natan Sznaider claim that forgiveness is a way of freeing oneself from the past. Ighilahriz is upset that none of the soldiers with whom she dealt acknowledged the facts or expressed regret.[37]

In addition to a need for recognition and relief, her discourse reveals a desire to resume relations with her former adversary. Ighilahriz demanded an apology that she would like to grant. Would not repentance on the part of the French soldiers implicated in her abuse allow her to resume relations with those who were her enemies? Even though they retain a kernel of ambiguity—showing one's wounds requires one to insist on the other's cruelty—requests for recognition, apology, or reparations do not necessarily represent the intensification of a relationship of enmity. Rather, such a request here appears as an attempt to recreate the relationship. For Ighilahriz, it would come as a relief to receive and subsequently grant a request for forgiveness, but it would also be a means to show the path toward the Other. Her obstinacy seems to reflect a desire to rid herself of her enemy while simultaneously establishing new relations with him. For Nicholas Tavuchi, the request for forgiveness allows one to establish a bridge between the victim's need for recognition and the perpetrators' need to restore his humanity.[38] In the case of Ighilahriz, it is the victim herself who seeks to test the humanity of her former torturers.

Moreover, Ighilahriz' revelation in the French press was twofold: she recounted the torture inflicted upon her as well as her feelings of gratitude toward the military doctor who saved her from the hands of her aggressors. The militant accuses and thanks. To the French reader, she reveals a cruel French army that committed wrongdoings in Algeria. At the same time, however, the image she presents of France and its military is burnished by the figure of the "just man," who allows the prisoner to be cared for and live. She presents Doctor Richaud as a paternal figure: he affectionately calls her "my little one" and mentions to her his own daughter, whom he has not seen in many months. In Ighilahriz' account, Richaud appeared as a father-protector. Her story, what's more, was passed on by a French woman, and her autobiographical book was cowritten with another French journalist. Sylvie Durmelat insists on the feminine identity of the intermediaries who allowed the ex-combatant to construct intersubjective relations and move forward with her narrative.[39] And the nationality of these two intermediaries is hardly insignificant, suggesting that Ighilahriz expressly chose to confide in and speak with women involved in French public discussions.

In several respects, Ighilahriz' testimony departs from the dominant account and official Algerian discourse. The Ighilahriz affair portrays the experience of a woman who finds herself alone faced with the French army. The FLN, however, is reluctant to discuss the historical role of individuals or pay tribute to particular leaders: "It is as if history were the product of the collectivity alone,"[40] and each individual embodies the community. By individualizing her trajectory and making her private story public, Ighilahriz' account challenges the myth of the people-hero. As a media sensation in France and, later, Algeria, it provoked jealousy among her compatriots, which can be explained by the intense rivalry among Algerian ex-combatants who, particularly in the capital, compete with one another for fame and symbolic and material rewards.

What's more, Ighilahriz' revelations broke a taboo on rape. The pressure to remain silent primarily came from her family. Inferring that her daughter had been abused, Ighilahriz' mother made her promise to never speak of it. When she finally allowed herself to speak about the matter in 2000, her father had been dead for several years, and her mother had become senile. Both were thus spared her public revelations. Her husband had always supported and encouraged her. By contrast, her son believed that her mother should have kept quiet, and her daughter fell into depression. Ighilahriz also paid for her decision to speak out from a social point of view. She recounts that, after her interview was broadcast on a French television channel, she had the impression that passersby were pointing at her in the street. Affected by this reception, which struck her more as a matter of opprobrium or voyeurism than of concern, she shut herself away at home for a time, incapable of confronting the stares of others.

Finally, the Ighilahriz affair perhaps reveals an ongoing transformation in militant identities and their relationship to France. It foregrounds the account of a victim who continues to suffer from having been tortured and raped. This account challenges the received image of the revolutionary combatant, celebrated as a hero for his ability to withstand the confrontation with the colonial army. To speak of the "lost honor" entailed by forced intrusion into the female body is an acknowledgment of weakness to which the FLN hardly consented. The stance taken by Ighilahriz regarding the question of forgiveness departs from the official demands of the Algerian government, but neither discourse is impermeable to the other. Realizing that heroic voices are today losing their force, the Algerian government may have an interest in exploiting the Ighilahriz affair in its exchanges with France. It is now possible to reconcile feelings of victimization with self-esteem,[41] and the status of victim is today more effective in drawing attention to demands for recognition.

Louisette Ighilahriz, for her part, has herself been shaped by nationalist discourse and the FLN's "culture of war." One of her statements reveals the ambiguity she feels as a result of her various relations with the French and Algerian public. When addressing the latter, she sets aside the issue of forgiveness. Following her October 2003 victory in court against General Schmitt—who was sentenced to pay her 1 euro in symbolic damages—she told the *Soir d'Algérie* newspaper, "I took an oath to my deceased mother to avenge myself against those who committed these outrages against me."[42] On 3 November 2005, Schmitt was acquitted on appeal, the court accepting that he had acted in good faith.

Does the experience of violence, particularly in cases of torture, constitute an insurmountable humiliation and source of lasting enmity? The examples considered here would suggest that the violence endured by ex-combatants does not in fact constitute an obstacle to the idea of exchange and reconciliation. Is it possible that experiencing the Other's violence in one's flesh leads the individuals in question to support the need for peace rather than radicalism and rancor? This is a claim that must be advanced with care, particularly given that, as we saw above, many of those who were subjected to torture remain silent about this episode in their lives. If they are to be positively disposed toward their former enemy, ex-combatants who have suffered torture must be able to give meaning to their experience and transform it into a vector of self-esteem.

*   *   *

Putting these various accounts into perspective allows one to underscore the specificities of each group of ex-combatants (see Table 3). In the same way that the ex-combatants of the Algerian War barely call into question the violence they inflicted, they only rarely attempt to understand what motivated their adversaries. What's more, they are rarely exposed in any direct way to the discourse employed by their old enemy. Former FLN and OAS (Secret Army Organization) activists retreat into a heroic model that reinforces the legitimate grounds of their involvement: the feeling that one has satisfied the various demands of justice or, to the contrary, in every respect lost reinforces their exclusivist approach.

In South Africa, the heroic model applies only to a subset of ANC members and centers on moral rather than warrior values. In this postconflict society, it is the victim model that plays a unifying role. Involved in the struggle's most brutal episodes and today excluded from the economic benefits of victory, the former militants of the ANC's armed wing see themselves as victims. Former Security Branch officers also identify with this category. This stance allows the former servants of apartheid to rid themselves of the moral burden of the violence they perpetrated. Moreover, it makes it possible for them to find a place for themselves in the symbolic system of reconciliation. Their exposure to the new South Africa constrains them to acknowledge the illegitimacy of apartheid.

As elsewhere, the heroic voices of the Franco-Algerian configuration grow weaker as the status of victim increasingly asserts itself for the purposes of demanding recognition. It is now easier to reconcile feelings of victimization and self-esteem.

The combatants of the FLN and ANC see their victory differently. While the former are eager to proclaim and consolidate it, even if that means prolonging the ideological confrontation, the latter count on the transformation and allegiance of their former adversaries. This alliance is reinforced by the fact that shared economic interests unite white economic circles and the nation's new black elites.

Like the pieds-noirs who joined the OAS, the former members of the apartheid-era forces of order feel that they were betrayed by politicians, whom they see as responsible for their defeat and guilty of manipulating them. It is within the reach of the apartheid-era forces however, to create a new future for themselves by establishing relations with their former adversaries. OAS members, by contrast, amass grievances against the FLN and the French state and are unable to find a positive framework for political identification. Their mobilization in support of commemorations and demands for recognition ensure the group's perpetuation and, through it, the maintenance of self-esteem.

The belief that one has been betrayed and abandoned by one's own leaders is also encountered among the poorest ANC militants. Called into question for the acts of violence they perpetrated, they struggle to give meaning to their trajectory. Incapable of collective action, they find it difficult to obtain recognition as victims. Lacking education or skills, they do not possess

Table 3. Ex-combatants, their vision of peace, and their perception of the ex-enemy

Ex-Combatants	Position at End of Conflict	Self-Image	Attitude Toward Violence	Feelings of (In)justice	Ex-Enemy	General Portrait
ANC New bourgeoisie		Modesty	Justification	Just political order	Openness	Grace
	Victor					
The poor		Victimization	Guilt	Unjust personal situation	Social distance	Bewilderment
FLN	Victor	Heroism	Justification and denial	Just political order	Mobilization (against)	Certainty
SADF and Security Branch	Defeated	Duty and victimization	Denial and refusal of responsibility	Acceptable political order but unjust personal situation	Openness-Distrust	Accommodation
OAS	Defeated	Heroism and victimization	Justification, denial, bravado	Total injustice	Hostility	Eternal treason

the resources necessary to economically integrate into the new South Africa. The loss of meaning encourages them to call into question violent action and their militant past, but social marginalization prevents them from encountering the former enemy. For this fringe of the ANC, the feeling and benefits of victory are out of reach.

PART IV

The Demands of Justice and Recognition

MARKED BY THE settlement or separation of belligerents, war's end does not guarantee that societies or individuals are reconciled. The concept of reconciliation, moreover, is imprecise or at least used in a polysemous manner. While some authors favor a structural approach that limits reconciliation to a series of conditions guaranteeing a modus vivendi, others assign it considerable spiritual and emotional significance. There is also divergence among the necessary criteria that are seen as essential to achieving a state of reconciliation: truth, justice, and forgiveness.[1]

South Africa, Algeria, and France have also taken divergent approaches to the question of reconciliation. In South Africa, the former beneficiaries of apartheid would like to be absolved of responsibility for the past, a subject they wish to put behind them. Yet black South Africans can support the national project only to the degree that their new status is accompanied by real progress. An ever-growing number of Algerians—some of whom desire rapprochement with France—demand that the former colonial power apologize for its past violence. Attached to their shared history with Algeria, many French, including the pieds-noirs, reject the idea of colonial guilt. A priori, no one rejects the aim of reconciliation, but each party wishes for it to take place on the terms that they define.

In the cases studied here, the wounds left by conflict only add to the baggage of the colonial situation. To dispel enmity, distrust, and resentment, it is necessary to come to terms with the violence of war and colonization. Reconciliation entails the establishment of relations of trust and reciprocally freeing oneself from relations of domination. Ultimately, the issue has less to do with the harmony, trust, and friendship that is associated with the new political pact than with the question of recognition. If they are to extricate themselves from the past, it would appear necessary that ex-combatants avow past acts of violence as well as the consequences these had for their adversary. They must also attend to the reasons their enemy chose to fight them. For ex-combatants and their society to construct relations based on equality, moreover, it would appear essential that they acknowledge the colonial situation.

*   *   *

In South Africa, the establishment of the Truth and Reconciliation Commission obliged a portion of those involved in past violence to publicly avow the acts for which they were responsible. The protagonists were encouraged to express their regrets and forgive their adversaries. In Algeria, there have in recent years been calls for France to officially apologize. The nature of this demand and the form it takes doom it to failure (Chapter 10). The accounts of South African, Algerian, and French ex-combatants constitute a source for exploring the processes by which one attempts—and sometimes fails—to move beyond relations of domination (Chapter 11).

Chapter 10

Offering Forgiveness/Demanding Apology

Despite the remoteness of the conflict between France and Algeria, the wounds of the past have yet to fully heal. In South Africa, the process of reconciliation, though not always smooth, has firmly begun and permeates society.

Created in 1995, the Truth and Reconciliation Commission (TRC) was central to the South African policy of forgiveness. This body sought to shed light on the most serious human rights violations[1] committed between 1 March 1960 and 10 May 1994.[2] Compensating for the absence of a legal process, it aimed to establish a just order by revealing past crimes and their authors and providing some consolation to victims. By seeking to establish the "truth" regarding past abuses, the TRC hoped not just to relieve victims, but also to initiate a process of personal transformation among perpetrators and (re)build relations between the two groups.

The president of the TRC, Desmond Tutu, was a former opponent of the apartheid regime within the South African Council of Churches. Drawing upon the language of psychology and an Anglican Christian orientation, Tutu wielded the TRC as a tool to promote interpersonal reconciliation.[3] As a component of political life, religion contributes to shaping the manner in which the past is represented and the present legitimated.[4] In South Africa, a country in which 80 percent of the population describes itself as Christian, political leaders do not shy away from displaying a religious sensibility.[5]

In contrast to South Africa, where the chosen political model required a new political contract allowing for peaceful coexistence among all peoples, the separation of French and Algerian populations and institutions excused the two countries from the need to make arrangements for their coexistence. No efforts were thus made to establish policies of justice, forgiveness, or shared memory. On both sides, the rulers maintained a stance of denial or silence regarding the violence committed by their camp during the war. Each country embraces a divergent narrative of the conflict, something that continues to be an obstacle to reconciliation between them. In recent years, the Algerian government has demanded that France apologize to it for its crimes in the War of Independence and the colonial period. This demand may be interpreted as a need to settle accounts, a search for recognition, and ultimately a desire for rapprochement. Yet acknowledging the misdeeds of the past and expressing regret for them in no way guarantees reconciliation between these formerly colonial and colonized societies. In contrast to the approach undertaken by the African National Congress (ANC), which offered forgiveness of its own volition, the Algerian demand that France apologize requires that the latter first confess.

The TRC in South Africa: Toward the Construction of a Shared Discourse

The question of justice collided with the constraints of the pact negotiated between leaders of the old apartheid regime and those of the ANC. The former received a guarantee that they would not be tried after leaving power. A concession to the very principles of democracy, forgiveness and forgetting constitute necessary conditions of political change.[6] Amnesty for the crimes committed under the apartheid system was therefore included in the interim Constitution of 1993.[7] In its operation, the TRC thus lacked a punitive dimension, though individuals who failed to request amnesty nevertheless faced a potential threat of subsequent criminal punishment. By according a central role to victims and individually questioning the authors of human rights violations, the TRC proved bold in design. The public nature of the hearings and the presence of the media were intended to ensure that the process was a therapeutic and educational experience for the entire society.

Victims at the Center of a Political and Therapeutic System

In December 1995, the TRC got under way with hearings before the Human Rights Violations Committee (HRVC), where victims and their loved ones recounted the abuses they had suffered. Altogether, 21,297 South Africans recounted their suffering, whether to investigators who had traveled to record their testimony or in the course of public hearings that were held throughout the country. Of this number 86.9 percent were black, with a majority consisting of women testifying in regard to the death or disappearance of their husbands or sons.[8]

On the basis of the protagonists' accounts, the HRVC investigated murders, disappearances, and acts of torture. Establishing the truth made it possible to break with the culture of secrecy that prevailed under the apartheid regime. By publicly speaking out, oppressed parties stood up to their fears[9] and sometimes rid themselves of social stigma.[10] Publicly speaking out about one's traumatic experience was intended to liberate and heal. Whereas a victim's remarks are, in the context of a criminal trial, restricted by procedural rules and must abide by a series of requirements, those testifying before the HRVC were allowed to freely relate their personal misfortune without interruption. Psychologists were on hand to lend support to victims before, during, and after their appearance before the HRVC. Individuals could subsequently attend the hearings of those implicated in their cases and question them.

The respectful hearing given victims, the rituals invented to demonstrate respect and compassion for them (e.g., songs and prayers), and the fact that TRC members stood when witnesses appeared all sought to restore the victims' dignity.[11] Yet, while these were remarkable and inventive efforts, their psychological and political effects are unclear. For victims, speaking out can initially come as a relief. But, by reopening old wounds, doing so can be a source of further distress over time. For victims who have been cared for at a given moment, it can be a devastating experience to subsequently find themselves left to their own devices.

In collecting the testimony of individuals who had been subjected to torture or lost loved ones and giving them a national audience, the TRC initiated a process for recognizing victims. For a number of them, however, the process proved incomplete. Some families received no response to their questions concerning the death or disappearance of their loved ones.[12] In the first decade of the twenty-first century, the government nevertheless established a special unit to search for missing persons and find the bodies of those who had been murdered.

The TRC has also been criticized for having deprived victims of the opportunity to express their resentment. The hearings were organized in such a way that it seemed inappropriate to express a desire for vengeance. The victims were even sometimes guided beforehand to integrate the idea of forgiveness into their account.[13] Yet, though they were stifled by the TRC, hatred and resentment are legitimate emotions—indeed, they are essential to the victim's process of reconstruction.[14] Moreover, the expression of anger sometimes serves as a vehicle for morally more robust demands of the enemy. As such, it can supply a better foundation for constructing a new community.[15]

An approach centered on compassion also risks weakening its intended beneficiaries. By confining them to the role of victim, it highlights the duty to assist them but threatens to destroy their capacity for action, underscoring their suffering rather than their heroism. By embracing a binary distinction between perpetrators and victims, the TRC distorted the political meaning that national liberation movement militants had assigned to their struggle. This threatened to imprison survivors and ex-combatants within a victim identity and thereby deprive them of the fruits of their own victory. Though they had been tortured by the men of the Security Branch, some MK, moreover, refrained from testifying as victims. This was particularly the case among former activists who had successfully integrated the political or economic world of the new South Africa and succeeded in conferring a heroic meaning upon their trajectory.

A portion of those who testified before the TRC believe that it did not go far enough or employed unsuitable methods, on the grounds that their status as victims did not receive the attention and/or compensation it merited. An ANC militant in his fifties who was arrested and tortured, Michel testified as a victim before the TRC and confronted the four police officers who had physically abused him.[16] Despite his recognition as a victim and the prospect that he would be paid reparations, he holds that the balance had not been restored: "The President of the Commission asked me if I recognized them and I said that I did, that I was sure of it. When someone hurts you, you don't forget, even after all this time. He asked me if I was willing to forgive them and I said, 'No, I can't.' They said they were sorry. They're sorry and they quietly drive away in their car. But I stay poor. It's because of them that I lost my job. I would have agreed to forgive them if they had paid me reparations themselves."

The government did not follow the TRC's recommendations[17] and downwardly revised the amount of compensation.[18] The reparations corresponded to a fixed sum of 30,000 rands[19] and were the same for all categories of victim. The public authorities, however, were slow to pay them. This lack of alacrity demonstrates the leaders' reluctance to financially compensate the sacrifices of activists or the population. The former minister of justice, Dullah

Omar, stated that victims should not be transformed into beggars and that freedom was the combatants' only reward.[20] In the absence of remuneration, the individuals who had been designated as victims seemed condemned to this stance without any prospect of significant rehabilitation. As a process, however, restorative justice requires that victims receive financial and moral compensation.[21] It was only morally acceptable to grant amnesty to apartheid's "perpetrators" on the condition that their victims were paid reparations in compensation for their suffering. Yet this implicit transaction was realized only on a very small scale. The fact that those responsible for abuses were absolved of their wrongdoing so much more rapidly than victims were paid reparation only worsened the feeling of injustice. Since the ANC wished to neutralize them, what's more, members of the police received compensation upon leaving their jobs. These payouts were at least ten times greater than the reparations paid victims or the demobilization bonus received by combatants belonging to the nonconventional forces. In financial terms, it is undeniable that the "perpetrators" of the "losing" side came off better.

Victors and Defeated on an Equal Footing

Thabo Mbeki, president between 1999 and 2008, rejected the notion that the ANC's official policy had been to deliberately kill civilians, but admitted there had been abuses, particularly in the training camps in Angola, and conceded that it had been increasingly difficult to maintain discipline among the militants and limit the use of violence.[22] Initially, the ANC's leaders tried to obtain collective amnesty for every action their members carried out as part of their struggle for a just cause, but the commissioners of the TRC refused. Perpetrators of violence within the ranks of the ANC and the Pan-African Congress (PAC) thus had to request amnesty in the same way as members of death squads. Moreover, 60 percent of the requests for amnesty concerned ANC activists, while only 18 percent concerned the security services and the apartheid government.[23] In its final report, the TRC underscored the fact that, though the violent acts perpetrated by the national liberation movements were from an ethical point of view in no way equivalent to those committed by the security forces of the criminal regime, the "just means" to which one turns during a conflict are a matter of universal principle.

Cognizant of the rules that had been laid down by the new democratic order, a number of officials and militants decided to play along. Following a stint as a general with the South African Defense Force (SADF) and within the Ministry of Defense, Abu Bakr Ismael is director of the South Africa Central Bank. He belonged to the ANC's military command and, as such, was responsible for several operations, including the 1983 Church Street operation against an army building in Pretoria.[24] Ismael takes care to distinguish his approach from that of his adversaries.[25] Unlike the police and politicians who had served the apartheid regime, who very often cast blame on one another, Ismael assumed responsibility for the acts committed by the members of his organization. He also maintains that he acted of his own free will, an indication of his pride. He thereby transforms the meaning of his appearance before the TRC. While he admits that there had been abuses and miscalculations, he says that he used his hearing as a forum to pay tribute to the ANC's struggle.

Surveys of the South African public demonstrate that the TRC contributed to propagating the notion that anti-apartheid militants and members of the segregationist regime alike fought for their ideas. According to surveys conducted by James Gibson, the TRC contributed to South African reconciliation by reducing the distance between the way blacks and whites each saw the past, forging as it were a shared collective memory regarding apartheid.[26] It is also interesting to note that, just before the TRC report was scheduled to appear, the country's sitting president, Thabo Mbeki, attempted to delay its publication because certain of its conclusions tarnished the ANC's image. The investigation of human rights violations also concerned violent acts committed by the victors.

The Ritual of Confession: A Promise of Amends?

One of the TRC's major innovations concerned the forms of amnesty. Provided that they cooperated with the institution and were forthcoming regarding their past actions, individuals who requested amnesty and appeared before the TRC's Amnesty Committee were eligible to receive it. A further condition concerned the nature of their crime, which had to be politically motivated rather than criminal in nature. Individuals thus exchanged their future freedom and tranquility for the "truth." Altogether, 7,116 requests for amnesty were submitted, only 1,764 of which were judged admissible, the rest having originated among common-law prisoners. Amnesty was thus at once individual and conditional:[27] the issue of responsibility was raised by the naming and public exhibition of those who had committed violations. It concerned specific acts of flagrant human rights violation and allowed—indeed, required—individuals to submit a particular request for amnesty for each act of brutality they perpetrated.

Among other reasons, the principles of restorative justice and conditional amnesty were defended for their effectiveness. In contrast to a criminal trial format, it was claimed that defendants would be more disposed to cooperate and testify as to the acts they committed. Tried for having created death squads and authorized their practices, the former minister of defense, Magnus Malan, was ultimately acquitted for lack of evidence after eighteen months of proceedings. He proved more forthcoming during his appearance before the TRC.[28] The institution's limits were nevertheless clearly on display in its inability to oblige high-ranking apartheid leaders to account for themselves. Former presidents Frederik de Klerk and Pietr Botha both refused to request amnesty. Only a few underlings and police chiefs revealed the acts in which they participated; ministers and the highest-ranking officers claimed to know nothing of the methods that were employed to "eliminate" the regime's opponents. Responding to questions asked during his hearing, de Klerk claimed that he had been shocked to learn of the security forces' methods of operation. He held that most of the actions were illegal and that he could not be held responsible for them.[29]

Full disclosure was among the conditions for obtaining amnesty. The perpetrator of violence had to acknowledge his acts, supply a detailed account of them, and explain his motivations. For the police officers of the Security Branch—at the forefront of the fight against the national liberation movements and their networks and source of the apartheid regime's largest contingent of candidates for amnesty—this confessional account meant coming to terms with the loss of their omnipotence.[30] For some, appearing before the TRC was a humiliating experience.[31] At the hearings, they were encouraged to inform the victim or his loved ones of the circumstances in which the events took place and of their outcome, which was sometimes still unknown. They were obliged to confront the abuses they had inflicted and the suffering they had caused. Moreover, their remarks corroborated those of the victims and helped preclude or limit forms of denial within South African society. Through their statements, the perpetrators at once acknowledged the facts and recognized the victim.[32] Concealing some of the facts ran the risk that others would speak for the perpetrators and thereby expose them to prosecution. To a certain degree, their interest coincided with that of the TRC—that is, to bring out the truth and construct a shared narrative regarding the past.[33] Recounting the murders one had committed was less a matter of bringing moral opprobrium upon oneself than of initiating one's integration into South African democracy.

The perpetrators frequently accepted this system, not out of conviction but as a matter of personal interest to escape legal proceedings. Some candidates for amnesty approached the matter strategically and sometimes cynically. Many refused to accept their share of individual responsibility, instead blaming their education and the social and institutional system that had, they claimed, conditioned them. This attitude does not exclude the possibility that those guilty of serious human rights violations had absorbed the principles that guided the TRC. Yet though their transformation—or that of their discourse—was perhaps no more than superficial, it had nevertheless begun.

Jan was one of the only member of the SADF to request amnesty. He claims that he did so in order to fulfill his duties as an officer. When the proceedings began, he was annoyed and distrustful. Yet he found satisfaction in testifying, for the TRC supplied a rostrum, not just for victims, but also for perpetrators. They, too, could present the grounds of their past actions:

> I was very nervous. I spent five days sitting in the witness box. I was asked questions and had the opportunity to clearly explain [myself]. On the fifth day, I told the judge, "I came here with a negative attitude, I was almost afraid of what would happen. I had been advised against coming here. I can now tell you that I've been fairly treated. I am happy to have had the opportunity to present my case and, whatever your decision, I will accept it." I had an opportunity to explain our actions, plans, and ideas in detail. I was able to explain the ANC's atrocities in detail. They didn't stop me. I was able to explain the murders, the ordeal of the necklace.[34]

This former intelligence corps chief received amnesty. The TRC's leniency reaffirmed his clean conscience: Jan sees himself as a soldier with a pure heart who was manipulated by politicians. His interaction with the clergyman Desmond Tutu led him to redraw the lines of demarcation within South African society and see himself as belonging to the ranks of the just:

> Tutu played an enormous role in reconciliation. . . . I think Tutu feels the same way I do. With Tutu, there is the same love, the same concern for the country and its people. The same goodness. I don't think

the others have that, especially the politicians. Their values are different than ours. . . . I never want to see another one of them for the rest of my life. I don't want to see Botha or de Klerk. I no longer want to talk to them. I'd rather deal with anyone from the ANC than with de Klerk. I can't understand their values and don't believe they understand mine. Tutu understands my values much better than de Klerk.

By kindly hearing out regime officials and allowing them an opportunity to explain their motivations and ways of thinking, the commissioners reassured some of them. Some then adopted the values of the TRC and its president. By claiming that he fulfilled his duty as a candidate for amnesty, Jan sees himself as embodying a part of the South African miracle: he was able to make peace and accept change.

The ANC's attitude of tolerance and grace toward the old regime's stalwarts and beneficiaries was characteristic of the democratic transition. The effort to understand the other's reasons reflects the protagonists' tolerance and magnanimity but also their belief that the partisans of apartheid could be morally and politically transformed. A portion of the candidates for amnesty were able to alter the significance of their participation. But the sincerity of their adherence was less important than their absorption into a process that aimed to transform individuals, almost despite themselves.

The Uses of Forgiveness in South Africa

"The language of forgiveness has emerged as a 'grammar' that structures discussions regarding justice, leading even the most reluctant protagonists to modify their arguments," writes Sandrine Lefranc.[35] In South Africa, this "grammar" is omnipresent. As president of the TRC, Desmond Tutu encouraged blacks to accept whites as brothers in the family of God.[36] The archbishop linked the Christian conception of forgiveness and radical reform of the community to the reinvention of a traditional notion. Tutu argued that South African blacks are full of *ubuntu*, a form of humanity that disposes them to welcome back into the community those who stray from it and encourages them to show indulgence toward those who had formerly abused and exploited them.[37] He further believes that the trauma of apartheid affected the entire society: blacks whose human rights were denied for centuries as well as whites who, subject to obligatory conscription, were exposed to the horror of war and made to bear the guilt of privilege.[38] The TRC attempted to help all heal their wounds and encouraged the protagonists to forgive one another. Churches and the ANC's local structures diffused this message of forgiveness.

The state's forgiveness, expressed in the form of amnesty, neither entailed nor required forgiveness on the part of victims. Nevertheless, forgiveness was sometimes exchanged over the course of the TRC's hearings and the meetings arranged between perpetrators and victims. Together with their desire to be absolved, the reluctance of apartheid-era officials to apologize shows that they required their former opponent to grant them an unconditional form of forgiveness: the offended party was to forgive them without demanding anything in return, not even that they show signs of remorse.

Forcing Forgiveness

The highest-ranking leaders were excused from presenting their apologies regarding apartheid. Pietr Botha intended to justify himself only before God.[39] Frederik de Klerk admitted that apartheid was a mistake but refused to consider it a sin or ask for forgiveness on behalf of the state or his political party, the National Party (NP). Apartheid was "an honorable conception of justice" intended to allow the country's various ethnic groups to develop separately; it was only when the system no longer functioned as it should that it became unjust.[40] When he appeared before the TRC, the last apartheid president nevertheless expressed profound regret. He maintained that blacks should forgive whites in the same way that Afrikaners forgave the British for the death of women and children in concentration camps. Describing forgiveness as "the essence of Christianity," he portrayed its absence as "a new form of racism."[41]

Members of the Security Branch adopted the same discourse: they admitted to having made "mistakes" but balked at apologizing for them. For "those who had been privileged their entire lives"—men who, what's more, had been responsible for exercising "legitimate violence"—the act of asking forgiveness could be seen as a humiliation, a renunciation of the superiority they saw themselves as embodying.[42]

Oscar is a former Security Branch member. In charge of intelligence for the Johannesburg region, he participated in negotiations with the ANC. Presenting himself as a liberal in favor of change and comfortable with the new South Arica, he established good social and professional contacts with ANC members.[43] During his time in the police, Oscar was not a field agent but rather gave orders. He requested and received amnesty for two cases, one of which he discussed with me: the preventive assassination of an MK team abroad as they prepared to infiltrate the country in order "to kill policemen." Oscar supplied an account of his encounter with the mother of the one of the MK killed in this operation, a meeting organized by the TRC in the context of its hearings:

> I said who I was and that I was the one who took the decision. And I said that I could not ask forgiveness for what I did because that would be to admit I was wrong at the time. Because I believed in what I did and thought I was just. I said, "I would like to apologize to you as a mother because I'm a father today, too. I also have children. Today, I think that I was a tool in the hands of a political order that manipulated us for its own interests. . . . I cannot ask forgiveness for something in which I believed at the time. But if you ask me whether I would do the same thing again, the answer is without a doubt no. I will never do it again."

Oscar admits that he gave the order to assassinate the MK. While he gives the impression that this decision was a mistake, he acknowledges no wrongdoing, citing his good faith at the time and claiming to have been manipulated. The empathy he felt, faced with the mother of one of the MK, came from his own status as a father. Parental love allowed him to feel this woman's pain and draw her attention to their common humanity. But faced with the negative reaction of the eliminated activist's mother, he reversed the situation and attacked:

> She was very abrupt and accused me, she said that I was a murderer and other things. And so I told her, "I can also accuse you of being a very bad mother. . . . You didn't know where your kids were, you didn't know what your children were doing. If you had known at the time that they had already been trained in how to use an AK-47 and grenades, would you have congratulated them?" She said no. I said, "Exactly! So you were a bad mother." So then we got into a discussion. But at the end I told her, "You have to decide. Bitterness is a personal feeling. If you feel bitterness, that affects your health. Keep that in mind! No one is going to share your bitterness. You will be alone faced

with your bitterness. It's your choice. If you ask me if I'm bitter, I will say, 'No, I made peace with my Creator.' I'm also ready to take a step toward you and tell you, 'Mother, I am sorry for what happened.'" I said and I insisted, "I don't ask forgiveness for my action. I'm sorry about what happened and I have to live with my conscience." I said, "You have to live with your conscience. Give me your hand. Mama, it's your choice: you can hate me and all police officers till the end of your life or you can say, 'Let's all move on.' At least we have testified and we have said what happened to your child, Mama. No one forced us to come here, there was no legal action against us. We came of our own free will and put all of our cards on the table in order to promote a process." She came, took me by the shoulders and hugged me, she was crying. And she told me, "Let's both of us go forward in the new South Africa."

Oscar used several devices to force the mother of the assassinated MK to forgive him. He first accused her and then addressed himself to the victim, the woman whose child was eliminated by his decision, inverting the order of responsibilities. By criminalizing the activity of the MK, Oscar transformed the "freedom fighter" into a violent young man in possession of weapons. On this view, the mother was doubly guilty—first for having done a poor job raising her delinquent child and then for losing control over him. Oscar thereby took advantage of the feeling of parental guilt. Another argument consisted in a warning: Oscar told this woman that she would suffer if she insisted on holding a grudge against him. However, he assured her that he deserved her forgiveness, since he had shown courage and honesty in requesting amnesty from the TRC. Finally, the last device employed by Oscar consisted in appropriating the national rhetoric of reconciliation. The violence of his speech paid off: the mother of the young man he had killed embraced him with her forgiveness.

In principle, it is up to the offended party to grant forgiveness. Several interactions nevertheless show that the exchange of forgiveness between victims and perpetrators reflects relations of power within South African society. The offender seeks forgiveness in order to be freed of the violence he perpetrated, and can bring pressure to bear on the victim or his loved ones to acquire it. By appropriating the discourse of the political and spiritual elites in regard to reconciliation and the promise of a better future, some demand that they be pardoned even though they refuse to apologize.

On the other hand, there is what the psychologist and TRC member Pumla Gobodo-Madikizela has called the "forgiveness of the weak," in which victims forgive perpetrators before the latter have shown any signs of repentance.[44] This attitude cannot necessarily be reduced to a situation of domination. The TRC's calls for *ubuntu* and forgiveness, and the strength of the new symbolic order, have imprinted their meanings on the South African space and support those who show leniency.

Misrepresenting Forgiveness

Kobus is the associate of a former soldier who runs a business selling security services on the African continent. After joining the police in 1971 at age nineteen, he quickly distinguished himself and joined the Security Branch. First sent to Southwest Africa (a protectorate that in 1990 became an independent state, Namibia), he was subsequently based in Durban, where he fought ANC cells. With the establishment of the TRC, the public learned of a series of crimes committed by the security services, including some in which Kobus had a hand. After learning of his crimes from the newspaper, his wife immediately demanded a divorce. A candidate for amnesty in thirteen different cases of murder and torture, this zealous police officer sought to redeem himself with the help of Christianity. In contrast to his colleagues, Kobus acknowledges his personal responsibility for the crimes he committed:

I was implicated in some atrocities. I fully cooperated. It's not simply a matter of saying it; it's also a total change in one's heart and one's head. I found peace by developing a personal relationship with God. Just before appearing before the TRC, I wrote down all of the atrocities in which I had participated. It was like confessing my sins. Some did this because they were afraid, but it was out of conviction [in my case]. I was ready to change. I wanted things to change so that they never happened again. I explained this to my children. What needs to be done so that it never happens again, here or elsewhere. I can contribute to this by telling my story, by offering my testimony.

Nevertheless, his conception of forgiveness does not include an exchange between offending and offended parties: "I never asked their forgiveness because that was not the aim of the TRC. For me, it was more of a healing process that allowed me to speak freely while telling the truth. I never asked their forgiveness. If they wanted to forgive me, they could have."

Invited to a conference in the United States to speak about his experience of reconciliation, the former Security Branch member shared his spiritual journey. His conception of justice, which confuses the perpetrator's discomfort with the victim's anger, is revealed in this exchange with a Guatemalan woman:

—When I spoke about my experience in the United States, there was an Indian woman whose husband had been taken by the army in 1993 and whose whereabouts remain unknown. I told her, "You won't find peace if you do not start by forgiving yourself. You have to return to your religious beliefs." And she wanted to know how one forgave oneself. . . . Her problem was that she is unable to forgive herself. She felt guilty.
—Why did she feel guilty?
—She hated these people; she didn't know who kidnapped her husband. So she doesn't know who she should direct her anger against. One forgives oneself by saying, I forgive myself for thinking about what they did to me. I don't know who they are but I forgive myself for this thought. As soon as you do this, it no longer matters who you are dealing with or what they've done.
—And you mean that it's the same process for you?
—I couldn't expect anyone to forgive me; I have to do it myself. It makes no difference whether they forgave me; that's not the point.

The meaning of forgiveness is here misrepresented. By reasoning from the experience of this Guatemalan woman, Kobus inverts the relationship between perpetrator and victim. The latter becomes guilty for her resentment. In a way, this is the same type of moral pressure that certain members of the old regime exert over blacks who are reluctant to absolve the leaders of apartheid. The path to inner peace is presented as requiring the same process for offending and offended parties alike: both must begin by forgiving themselves. In constructing an analogy with this widow, a victim of political violence, the former apartheid official thus absolves himself of his wrongdoing.

He concludes his explanation in this way: "If I can forgive someone, I put myself in the position to receive forgiveness." By this assertion, Kobus probably means that he no longer feels any hatred for his former adversaries. Once again, he has inverted the relationship to the offense: whether an enemy combatant or victim, the Other is indebted to Kobus. What's more, his "granting" of forgiveness is, as it were, virtual: it requires neither that he meet with nor that he address those concerned. Directly coming to terms with God is a way of moving beyond human judgment and thereby avoiding confrontation with one's former enemy. In asserting that he feels no guilt and continues to take some pride in his work as a police officer, he nevertheless makes use of the language of reconciliation. In this way, he is able to attain a moral status consistent with the values of the new South Africa.

Granting Forgiveness

Among the ex-combatants I met, several members of the ANC say they have forgiven their former adversaries. This is the case of Yunis, an MK who was arrested by the Security Branch in 1985, tortured, and held for eleven months in solitary confinement. After having worked for the new ANC government, he set up practice as a lawyer in the Johannesburg bar and had no intention of presenting himself before the TRC, whether as victim or perpetrator. But one of the men who tortured him ten years earlier is also a lawyer and submitted a request for amnesty for having physically abused him. Yunis assesses his motives as follows: "He didn't want to be subsequently caught for not having avowed his crimes. It could create problems for him as a lawyer. He wanted to acknowledge his acts and avoid having a complaint lodged against him."

Yunis attended his colleague's hearing. He did not discuss the feelings inspired by once again seeing the man who had tortured him, and instead spoke in moral and political terms:

> I forgave his offense. Looking back, we were all caught up in a war, a war with the hatreds that came from our parents and three hundred years of racism and colonialism. People couldn't see things any other way. My own torturers were victims of this tradition, of this idea that Africans and all those who are not white cannot be their equals. Their churches confirmed it. Their lawyers, jurists, writers, and actors— their entire society was an endorsement of racism. Why just hold a police officer responsible for acting like a brute when his entire community tells him he's doing right? I think that he's a victim of his people's prejudices. And his violence against me is just an example of

the way in which his community dehumanized and demonized us. He was just the tool of torture. And I think that all human beings suffer when they harm someone.

Even in his evaluation of his torturer's offense, Yunis proves lenient. He adopts the arguments employed by the men of the Security Branch, who accuse the system of having indoctrinated them, and society of making them do its dirty work. Yunis does not merely find extenuating circumstances for the lawyer; he discharges him of responsibility for having dirtied his hands. He even displays compassion for him on the grounds that he has suffered. Yunis takes up a theme developed by Mandela: that the transition to democracy does not free just blacks from servitude but also whites from a system based on fear and prejudice. This magnanimity is closely linked to the belief that one is acting as a liberator. By following the path laid out by the ANC's leaders, Yunis safeguards the moral stature of his organization.

As to whether the lawyer and former Security Branch officer feels remorse, Yunis says that he has "chosen to think he does." He has no recollection of his torturer asking his forgiveness. Is the forgiveness granted by Yunis unconditional and absolute? Is his a totally disinterested act, equivalent to the love for one's enemy preached by the New Testament?[45] "Even when absolute, generosity is an object of doubt."[46] Does it not reflect his will to power? By presenting the other side of his cruel and barbaric enemy and illustrating the victors' undeniable grace, the ANC militant demonstrates his moral superiority.

This interpretation does not exclude the possibility that Yunis' forgiveness is also a sort of gamble on the future. The offender is granted pardon in exchange for a promise of transformation: the former servant of apartheid would be won over by the democratic and multiracial ideal of the ANC. In this way, forgiveness not only liberates the guilty from the harm he has done but also constitutes a gesture on the part of the offended party indicating that he believes the offender capable of change. The act of forgiveness, in this sense, ushers in a new future together.[47]

When I ask about his view regarding Kobus' "commitment" to reconciliation, Yunis confessed to having mixed feelings. The memory of this man inspired disbelief, but he had faith in the prospect for transformation: "Kobus H.? My Kobus? He was one of my torturers! Kobus H.? He goes to the United States to talk about reconciliation? Damn, I'm impressed! Human nature never ceases to impress me. He was such an insensitive bastard and one of those who tortured me who never requested amnesty for it. But despite all that I'm very happy he understands reconciliation and nonracial democracy. As a human being, we have a real capacity to change. That's good, and I try not to be cynical about these things. I try to understand his struggle against himself with compassion and without disdain."

ANC members are not alone in this understanding and willingness to forgive. Beneficiaries of the apartheid regime also forgave ANC and PAC members responsible for attacks against civilians. This is the case of Beth Savage, who was wounded during an attack by the Azanian People's Liberation Army (APLA), the armed wing of the PAC.[48] Ginn Fourie, whose daughter was killed in an attack carried out by the PAC, also met with the operation's leader, Letlapa Mpaphele—a man who had refused to participate in the TRC and thus did not request amnesty. Not only did Fourie forgive this man who had never asked for forgiveness, but she teamed up with him to create a foundation that supplies aid to the people of his village.[49]

Despite its limits and the perverse effects it sometimes produced, the TRC changed South African society. In this connection, James Gibson's study shows that each part of society discovered the injustices committed by its camp and abandoned a Manichaean vision that divided the country between "good guys" and "bad guys." Sharing feelings of responsibility and victimization allowed for dialogue.[50] This optimistic analysis no doubt requires qualification, primarily because the politically correct discourse now in force allows little latitude to those critical of or disappointed by reconciliation. Moreover, the reconciliation process continues to be hampered by the assessment of debt and credit among the beneficiaries and victims of apartheid, particularly in what regards the issue of affirmative action.

France and Algeria: Moving Beyond Denial?

French and Algerian accounts of the Algerian War of Independence never seem to overlap. In contrast to the South African scenario, each party contents itself with denouncing the other's crimes, never calling into question their own past actions. The remarks of a former chief of staff of the French army, General Schmitt, are representative of this way of thinking: in the course of a television broadcast, Schmitt reacted to Louisette Ighilahriz' revelations regarding her torture at French hands by describing her as an "inveterate liar." After the TRC, the Security Branch's former members would not dare deny its record of abuse and summary execution. By contrast, some

French soldiers still cling to the notion that theirs was a clean war. Article 4 of a law adopted by Parliament on 23 February 2005 similarly illustrates French blindness regarding colonialism. In Algeria, the officials and former combatants of the National Liberation Front (FLN) also show little inclination to examine the violence and abuses committed by their movement during the war. Given the vastly inferior resources at their disposal, Algerian combatants never matched the French army's capacity to repress and eliminate. In their eyes, it is thus obscene to compare any wrongdoing committed by the FLN with the crimes that accompanied the actions of the colonial power.

Impossible Justice?

This posture of denial sustains efforts to initiate legal proceedings on both sides of the Mediterranean. These efforts collide with the amnesties provided for by the Evian Accords. Complaints are filed, particularly by Algerian families who were victims of the Battle of Algiers and by the families of Harkis massacred following independence.[51]

Legal steps have also been taken by the loved ones of missing persons, whether French or Algerian. The example of Chile has shown that a new generation of judges can restrict the interpretation of amnesty: holding that, when bodies have yet to be located, cases of disappearance constitute lasting crimes, the Chilean justice system brought charges against several high-ranking soldiers, among them Augusto Pinochet. In what concerns the Algerian War, however, the passage of time and the absence of evidence make it unlikely that charges will be brought.

Although some lawyers and human rights activists obstinately seek an opening that will allow them to circumvent the Evian Accords, and count on the growing supremacy of international law over domestic law to bring about changes in French jurisprudence, to date no one has been charged with crimes against humanity for acts committed during the existence of French Algeria. At present, the only possible way to obtain symbolic condemnation for those who carried out violent acts is to criminalize their speech. In 2001, General Paul Aussaresses was tried[52] for "complicity in justifying war crimes" in connection with his book, *Services spéciaux Algérie (1955–1957)*.[53] In 2002, Aussaresses was sentenced to a 7,500-euro fine. Several months later, General Schmitt was taken to court by Louisette Ighilahriz for his remarks about her. Found guilty in the first instance, he was acquitted on appeal in 2005 on the grounds that he had acted in good faith.

Given this desire to settle accounts with the past and the law's inability to respond to it, a few historians have suggested that a Truth and Reconciliation Commission be established along the lines of the South African model. Doing so would allow the parties to advance the cause of "historical truth," initiate a process of reconciliation, and fulfill a number of moral obligations. Yet, in addition to the fact that French protagonists (soldiers and conscripts, Harkis and OAS [Secret Army Organization] members) would be unlikely to go along with such an exercise, it would require painful concessions on the part of Algerians.

For while suffering and victimization were effective in creating consensus in South Africa,[54] in Algeria there has been no attempt to construct victims as a category. The actors of the war of liberation are called upon to be heroes, while the loved ones of missing persons or those who were executed are raised—and confined—to the status of children or wives of *shahid*. Hardship and pain are only rarely individuated; in general, the suffering provoked by colonialism and armed conflict is recounted in collective terms. In the eyes of some, moreover, the combatant's skill and triumphant status stem directly from the violence of the French state during the war. As one FLN ex-combatant put it, "I got involved to die and to liberate my country. The goal was achieved. Before achieving it, I knew that those I was fighting would harm me. And they did harm me, and I reacted to that harm. It's entirely normal. I won. What is the point of saying, Sorry, I tortured you, etc.? Where does it get you to say, Sorry, I fucked up?"[55]

In France, a few militant associations tend to the memory of the conflict's European victims, but their memory has not stamped itself on the nation's collective consciousness. Furthermore, the operation of the TRC was based on the observance of its rules by all parties. For many FLN partisans, however, the notion of following the ANC in an approach that involves confessing to and admitting one's excesses and misdeeds remains unthinkable.

France Apologizes to Algeria?

Though inspired by numerous examples on the international scene, the Algerian demand that France apologize is rooted in a lingering representation of the symbolic enemy. With the wounds of the civil war years still fresh, the

Algerian government seeks to legitimate its policy of reconciliation with the armed Islamists. In this context, recalling France's various crimes in Algeria and demanding that it apologize for them seem to be a way of reaffirming national pride and uniting a society divided and exhausted by the crimes of armed Islamist groups and the violence of the security services. Having grown distrustful of its rulers, the Algerian people nevertheless continue to be motivated by a form of nationalism in which the figure of the colonial enemy remains the driving force. Adopted while preparations were under way for a treaty of friendship between France and Algeria, the law of 23 February 2005 was seen as a provocation. The Algerian government seized upon it to sustain its rhetoric, with President Abdelaziz Bouteflika denouncing "a mental blindness verging on negationism and revisionism."[56]

Since competition among the various clans vying for control of the state draws upon this shared language, the Algerian government is captive to this combative nationalism. Political disagreement often assumes the appearance of a struggle to defend revolutionary integrity, concealing other issues. Created by former minister Bachir Boumaza, the 8 May 1945 Foundation seeks to shed light on the crimes perpetrated by France and represents a call to order directed at those who might be tempted to betray the Revolution. The Foundation was "born in a dangerous political context. That of the insidious revision of colonial history by some nationals, including some with ties to the government. Proceeding little by little on the pretext of 'moving beyond' a dark chapter in colonial history, some politicians have encouraged the 'normalization' of relations between the former ruling power and its former colony."[57]

While it is true that recognizing its crimes and apologizing for them would put an end to France's denials, it would not contribute to developing a common narrative or allow for reconciliation. Diplomacy cannot be substituted for work that must take place within societies. In a context marked by persistently antagonistic and conflictual visions of the past, the act of apologizing could further strain public opinion in the two countries. On one side of the Mediterranean, certain groups would perceive such an apology as a betrayal; on the other, it would be considered insufficient.[58] Moreover, although the declarations of France's ambassador to Algeria[59] and Nicolas Sarkozy's remarks[60] during his visit to Algeria were first steps toward recognizing French crimes and abuses, they received a mixed reception in Algeria, where expectations remained unsatisfied.

It is unlikely that France will apologize to Algeria, Sarkozy having set the tone by stating that, while one should "not deny the past," "the future is more important."[61] This is in part because it is difficult for the French people to acknowledge wrongdoing relating to their colonial past. The country's rulers, meanwhile, have proven incapable of managing conflicting memories. Yet the extreme form in which the Algerian demand is expressed in itself precludes its realization. For the policy of apologies is based on an effort to find a shared language with the opposing party.[62] Hyperbole, particularly in the choice of terms, forces Paris to harden its stance and obstinately reject "repentance." Ultimately, however, the Algerian regime has an interest in not receiving the apologies it demands. This unsatisfied demand helps preserve the spirit of anticolonial struggle. If France pursued a policy of apology or restitution, Algiers would lose its main source of legitimacy, and its revolutionary identity would further crumble. Such is the paradox of Algerian demands regarding France.

Rebuilding Franco-Algerian Relations

Apart from the issues of power relations and political maneuvering, the Algerian demand that France apologize also indicates a need for recognition and a desire to reconcile with France. This demand seeks to make France acknowledge the injustice and absurdity of a colonial system based on excluding "Muslims" from citizenship.

This demand for equality is sometimes awkwardly expressed in terms that call to mind the "competition of victims."[63] After French president Jacques Chirac expressed regrets during a trip to Madagascar in July 2005, President Bouteflika stated that "Algerians deserve France's repentance more than the Malagasy."[64] But the ultimate comparison involves the Jews. As Boumaza, director of the 8 May 1945 Foundation, declared, "The colonial phenomenon entails certain values that must disappear. They have yet to do so. And its most successful expression is this term 'crime against humanity,' which is reserved for a special category of the population. . . . Crimes against humanity are applied and recognized in regard to Jews but not Algerians, who, it is forgotten, are also Semites."[65] While these remarks are tinged by an obvious Judophobia, the point here is less to render moral judgment than to deconstruct the speaker's reasoning and understand his relationship to justice. The Jewish community is a source of fascination to the degree that, more than any other group, it has succeeded in being recognized as a victim and obtaining the West's acknowledgment for the crimes committed against it. This discourse thus swings between minimizing the Jewish community's status as a victim and underscoring the degree to which it has won recognition as such. Certainly, this is often an occasion for expressing racism against the Jews, but referring to their situation serves above all to provide a benchmark against which one's own situation may be measured. Ultimately, the recurrent question concerns whether the life of an Arab or Muslim is worth as much as that of a Jew. This doubt had already arisen with adoption of the Crémieux Decree, which unconditionally granted French nationality to the Jewish inhabitants of Algeria while excluding Muslims from these integration measures. By reiterating that Algerians are also Semites, Boumaza underscores his misunderstanding: the French have shown themselves unfair by not according the same value to Algerians and Jews; since both groups ultimately have the same origin, the French have also shown themselves to be inconsistent or ignorant.

Moreover, the question of equality reflects civilizational judgments. When the French refer to the "positive role" of colonization, it is implied that they brought enlightenment to the inhabitants of Algeria. They give the impression that the Algerians did not have a civilization and were incapable of achieving progress on their own. Revolutionary rhetoric has thus endeavored to counter this vision by demonstrating that the Arabo-Muslim culture that preceded the colonial system was rich and fertile and, what's more, that the colonizer was miserly in sharing his knowledge.

For a number of people, a kind of reparation is to be found in achieving with words the equality that was denied one when one was still a child or adolescent. In their eyes, this past humiliation would be less painful to bear if France admitted to the injustices it inflicted. In the wish expressed by Mehdi, one senses that the equality denied under colonialism particularly played out in relations with Europeans:[66]

—But what exactly does France have to acknowledge, in your view?
—What it has to acknowledge is how the pieds-noirs lived, how they saw themselves as natives here.

Memories of past contempt do not preclude a desire for rapprochement with France. Comparison with Germany is also a way to formulate a demand for equality in relations with France. By underscoring the profound enmity that formerly separated the two European neighbors, Mehdi raises the issue of the choice of partners: "Between Germany and France—well, with all the wars, all the horrors [that took place], they ended up with the same flag. I don't see why Algeria . . . Why not?"

To demand equality with France is to demand that France recognize the value of Algerians, not just by admitting its crimes against them but also by becoming aware of their ability to embody capable autonomous subjects endowed with reason and equipped for progress.

*   *   *

In South Africa, those who had formerly dominated recognized that apartheid was an unjust system, and contribute to the collective narrative regarding reconciliation. The victorious ANC and black people victimized by apartheid granted formerly dominant parties forgiveness without requiring that they show contrition. The road to peace thus required involvement on the part of those who had formerly been oppressed. If socioeconomic inequalities continue to be so flagrant, however, the state of mind promoted by the TRC cannot take root and last. The poverty that still affects a portion of the population threatens to become the breeding ground for a form of populism that makes use of the themes of social and ethnic revenge. The criminal violence that is rife in South Africa is part of a larger challenge to what is perceived as an unjust social order.

The colonial question remains the main point of disagreement between France and Algeria, with the former reluctant to revisit the Republic's past exploitation of its overseas territories and the latter still waiting for its common humanity to be recognized. In these two postconflict configurations, perceived or experienced relations of domination constitute an essential issue in representations and relations between former enemies.

Chapter 11

Extricating Oneself from Domination

In the South African and Franco-Algerian contexts, seeing the Other as one's equal is doubly distressing: on the one hand, the enemy in these conflicts tended to be demonized, as in any violent conflict; on the other, the ideologies of apartheid and colonization were based upon the supposed inequality of racially defined groups. The issue thus does not only concern the combatants of these wars; it also calls into question the experience of individuals as black or white, pied-noir or Algerian.

Equality is almost always adopted by the protagonists as an abstract and universal principle. Yet they do not always consent to this or successfully rid themselves of the hierarchical vision of society inherited from the past. Extricating oneself from relations of domination is a laborious process. Feeling the Other to be one's fellow man is a new experience for those concerned, an experience that they must embrace and perpetuate. The evolution of these relations is facilitated by a change in lifestyle or standard of living. The process by means of which one frees oneself from an alienating relationship is nevertheless often imperfect, fragile, and ambiguous and sometimes takes place over the course of several generations. For the sociologist, what's more, perceiving domination or the process of emancipation presents specific challenges to the degree that these phenomena are mainly unspoken or denied by those concerned. The researcher must trust to the evidence she encounters as an observer or participant over the course of her interactions. The resultant observations are often haphazardly gleaned from the situations in which this investigator took part as a white woman in South Africa and a French woman in Algeria. Words, hesitations, and gestures are all subject to interpretation.

In South Africa, the spirit of reconciliation has disrupted the interracial representations that formed during segregation. Apart from obstacles stemming from the social and political system—for example, the absence of contact between populations and persistent spatial barriers—the main impediment to reconciliation is the laborious work of self-transformation that it requires. The separation of 1962 significantly limited opportunities for Algerians and pieds-noirs to experiment with ways for moving beyond relations of domination. Despite these difficulties and impediments, however, Algerians and black South Africans have not given up.

The present chapter explores the issues involved in moving beyond domination from three perspectives. Memories of the colonial era reflect the ambiguities of the colonial relationship among whites, blacks, pieds-noirs, and Algerians. The legacy of a relationship based on domination, these memories have been transformed into an interpretive account of one's relationship to the Other. The postcolonial present is also marked by tensions. While newly emancipated citizens seek to experience the principle of equality in their own lives, their formerly dominant counterparts attempt to contain its effects. Finally, recognizing the wounds and injustices inflicted upon the Other is a painstaking process and generates friction and resistance. And is it not precisely recognition—an at once human and intellectual journey—that is needed to dismantle the colonial relationship?

Colonial Memories

Relations between Europeans and Muslims in French Algeria or those between whites and blacks during apartheid in South Africa cannot be fully reduced to the relations of domination engendered by the colonial structure or the enmity and fear that the conflicts inspired. Patterns of sociability jostled against situations of colonial domination.[1] Neither the injustice of the social and political order nor the exploitation, contempt, and humiliation that accompanied it precluded friendly relations and ties of affection from developing between individuals of distinct political status. In their refusal to be taken for "colonialists," it is the formerly dominant parties who most often speak of their "friendships" and "excellent relations." Childhood, in particular, is presented as a possible sphere of equal exchange that partly escaped the dynamic of ethnic and cultural subordination. Their accounts have been in large measure reconstructed. Nevertheless, ties of affection did indeed exist. In colonial Algeria, such ties were above all established in school. In South Africa, institutionalized racial distance limited the possible spheres of exchange to professional relations.

Natives at the School of the Republic

Some Muslim students attended the secular and mandatory public school system. The accounts of Algerian ex-combatants show that they themselves or their parents relied on French schools for instruction and social advancement. Their gratitude toward the teachers who supported them and encouraged them to pursue their studies is evident. But the republican institution was also a focus of profound disappointment: its promises were often betrayed by the racist behavior of teachers and principals. At school, racism took the form of enforced physical distance and suspicion of the native body, which was seen as dirty or diseased and a source of contamination. Distrust and rejection served to remind Muslims of their inferior status and were a means for precluding possibilities for social and intellectual advancement and for perpetuating conditions of domination.

After acting as a liaison agent for the National Liberation Front (FLN) during the war, Nadia became a nurse following independence[2] and recounts her experience of the colonial school. Her father enrolled her in nursery school. Three months after she entered it, she was expelled by the headmaster because of her warts; he feared that the little girl would contaminate "the children of caids and colonists." Her family used every medicine available to rid her of her pimples. Nadia lived across the street from the school. For months on end, she got dressed in the morning, did her hair, and stood at the classroom windows to watch the other children. Nadia claims that she could "forgive France for everything" except for having deprived her of an education.

Tahar, whose own academic career was cut short, hoped that his children would be able to pursue their educations. All of his offspring attended college. He is particularly proud of his daughter, who became a lawyer. Despite Tahar's exemplary behavior, his teacher decided that additional precautions had to be taken in regard to Tahar's hygiene.[3] The resulting humiliation continues to be a source of shame for the mujahid. One gathers that the teacher was particularly obsessed with lice: "I had beautiful hair and was fond of it. It was always well combed. The schoolmistress put a pencil in my hair to examine my scalp. She said I wasn't clean. I protested, saying that my mother had washed me the night before. I was clean and well combed. The mistress had my mother called. My mother, who spoke hardly any French, swore that I was clean. But they still shaved my head."

A few years later, it was the school principal who humiliated Tahar's father. The result was not long in coming: Tahar was taken out of school. Tahar recalls:

The principal asked him, "Are you Kabyle?" My father told him, "Yes, I'm Kabyle." And he told him, "You know, Arabs aren't good people, they don't like you." . . . And then he said, "Are you a Muslim or nonpracticing?" My father said to him, "No, I'm practicing." He said, "How can you be a Muslim and leave your son at the French school? He'll become a Christian!" My father gave me a real dressing down, my mother cried. He said, "Can you imagine, a Frenchman gives me a lesson in morality, leaving my child in a French school! Do you know how to speak French?" "Yes." "Do you know how to count?" "Yes." "Well, that's enough, that's enough!" And at age thirteen I began to work.

Mohamed, another ex-combatant (see Chapter 5), attended high school in Algiers and mentions a dedicated and fair professor who encouraged him to continue his studies. Since his school was requisitioned by the US Army in 1943, however, he was prevented from graduating.

Friendship, Treason, and Rescue

A native of Oran who took part in OAS (Secret Army Organization) activities, Lucien interrupted my interview with his brother:

May I speak about a friend of mine? His name was Tchitchi. He was an orphan, and his [European] adoptive parents were bakers. They took him and adopted him. And he was always with us, even when the events were taking place. We went out dancing together. He danced rock, he was a great rock 'n' roll dancer. I remember him. He was very nice. He was always flashing his gold teeth like this. He danced, but I asked him, "How do you manage to pick up chicks?" Because he was really small and I'm tall, I'm a good-looking guy. I teased him a bit; we were always good friends and all that. One evening we were talking about what was going on and all that, and do you know what he said to me? He said, "If the FLN enters Oran someday, you're the first person I'll kill. I'll cut your head off." I was just amazed. I said to him, "How can you say that to me?" I said, "Have you lost your mind?" And then I said, "But before you get near me I'll punch you and flatten you against the wall." He said to me, "No, I'm joking, Lucien, I'm joking with you!" You know what he did when everyone left? He called his parents, who had brought him up, and said, "If you don't leave, I'll kill both of you."

His brother added:

He was Arab. He didn't know how to speak Arabic. He only spoke Spanish and French because he had been brought up by these people. We spent so much time looking for him. We weren't able to kill the bastard; our feelings got the better of us.

Lucien continued:

Because I had him there, I had a revolver in my pocket and I asked myself, "Do I kill him or not?" I didn't kill him. He was my friend; I couldn't do it and I could have. We were both talking. I said to him, "I know what you did. You threw a grenade at that guy with his arm in the cast; we saw you do it." "No, Lucien, I swear it wasn't me! What are you doing?" "Nothing. It's because I have money in my pocket." I had the firepower to kill him but I didn't do it because he was my friend. So we hesitated. But they didn't worry themselves with these scruples, and then afterwards he left with them, and we weren't able to catch him. He knew us all.

Tchitchi is not a name, just a nickname. This raises doubts as to his communal membership. An Arab taken in by Europeans, he spoke French and Spanish, knew nothing of Arabic, and hung around with a group of Europeans. As the war continued, and the gulf separating Arabs and Europeans deepened, it became impossible to sustain this sort of in-between state, which was not so much a matter of dual belonging as of not belonging at all.

Was Tchitchi really Lucien's friend? The former wasn't there to say, and the latter presents him as such. The anecdotes regarding Tchitchi's talent for dancing and seduction show that, while there were indeed bonds of comradery and affection, they did not preclude envy and even contempt. In this account, it is difficult to distinguish between run-of-the-mill competition between young men and the irresistible urge to put an Arab in his place. In any case, the sudden tension that clouded relations between the two Oranais is evidence of a form of biased communication. Tchitchi had formerly given no sign of anti-French feelings or support—actual or sentimental—for the FLN. Nor did he state his involvement with the nationalist side. Rather, he expressed this frightening threat against Lucien—a threat, moreover, that he very quickly withdrew, claiming it had just been a joke.

Dialogue regarding the question of Algeria's political future seemed impossible. Most interviews with former FLN and OAS combatants have this in common: political subjects, the issue of inequality, and the injustice of the colonial system never came up between European and Muslim "friends." Since each party was more or less vaguely aware that it would degenerate the situation, conflict was nearly always avoided. Tchitchi and Lucien, for their part, also appear to have been incapable of sharing their opinions regarding the "events." It was doubtless already too late: by this time, the OAS had already been created, and the escalation of violence significantly reduced possibilities for exchange between individuals from different communities or holding divergent convictions.

In his autobiography, *Black Boy*, Richard Wright lists the many subjects that were impossible for white and black Americans to discuss with one another at the start of the century. Among them were "American white women; the Ku Klux Klan; France, and how Negro soldiers fared while there; . . . Communism; Socialism; the 13th, 14th, and 15th Amendments to the Constitution; or any topic calling for positive knowledge or manly self-assertion on the part of the Negro."[4]

The OAS militant never had the impression or even imagined that Tchitchi harbored resentment toward him. This perhaps indicates a lack of judgment or sensibility in regard to what his Arab friend might feel. Lucien thought he knew his friend, but had in fact never understood him. He was shocked and disappointed and felt betrayed. For those in a dominant position, there was no advance warning of the colonized subject's revolt or desertion.

In a study of the experience of housemaids in Rio de Janeiro, Dominique Vidal underscores "the friendship" linking household employees and their employers, which "reflects a shared demand for consideration and affection."

Given the vastly different and even contradictory expectations of each party, however, such relationships are based on something of a misunderstanding. While the housemaids hoped for "recognition of their common humanity," their mistresses conceived of the friendship "as a way to maintain a relationship of mutual trust without for all that abandoning the idea of radical difference between the two parties."[5] As an expression of gratitude, gift giving is similarly based on the divergent perceptions of the dominated and dominant parties: while the former see it as a mark of recognition, the latter use it as a means for reaffirming their superiority and in return expect additional signs of loyalty and devotion. The sudden severing of relations by a mistress or her employee causes surprise and indignation for the person who thought she could count on the other's "friendship."[6]

In both Rio and Oran, this misunderstanding regarding the content of friendship transforms desertion into treason. Tchitchi's subsequent choices led Lucien and his brother to perceive him as a cruel and ungrateful traitor. Evidence of this is found in his threats against the couple who raised him. We know nothing about relations between Tchitchi and his adoptive parents, of course, nor what would have led the son to demand their departure. Nor do we know anything about the circumstances and motives for his belated or hidden involvement with the independence movement. Tchitchi was perhaps obliged to choose camps or change sides. Eric Savarèse deciphers colonial ambiguity thus:

> During the Algerian War, it was impossible for French citizens to distinguish between a fellaga acting "in the shadows" and the familiar Arab integrated into the network of warm inter-individual relations. . . . The French of Algeria were incapable of imagining that the Muslim who was part of their daily lives participated in the illegal activities of a population summarily described as a "bunch of terrorists." . . . Muslim French who "betrayed their masters" oscillated between resistance to the colonial domination orchestrated by the French state and affection for the French of Algeria with whom they established inter-individual ties across ethno-cultural barriers.[7]

Marie Cardinal, a writer born in Algeria, reports an exchange between her mother and her family's Arab employee. In contrast to Tchitchi's remarks, a cruel and gentle threat immediately casts a pall over the servant's words: "If the fellagas order me to cut your throat, Madame Marcelle, you don't need to worry about it—I know, Tounsi, I trust you—You can trust me, Madame Marcelle, I will cut your throat while you nap and you won't feel a thing at all."[8] How to interpret this? Behind her apparent naiveté, is the servant taking pleasure in frightening his mistress, in giving an indication of his power? Is he seeking to alert her as to the proximity of danger? Or do his remarks instead hint at the violence of his inevitable emancipation, which will sweep away relations based on an order that is on the verge of disappearing? But this does not rule out genuine affection to the degree that Tounsi promises to save Madame from terror and physical suffering.

Sometimes, the friendship between Europeans and Muslims—or what remained of it as the war separated their communities—saved lives. In these cases too, however, the political involvement of Algerian nationalists remained taboo. The revolt against the colonial system, the fact of risking one's life for the independence of Algeria, never seem to have led individuals to challenge the convictions of their European friends. For clandestine militants, discretion was a question of survival, and dissimulation was sometimes a matter of strategy. In Assia Djebar's novel, the narrator recounts how he learned of the existence of the Algerian flag while still a schoolboy. He did not understand why it had to remain "hidden." After he proudly drew it during class at the French school, his father, a nationalist militant, went to great lengths to convince the school's principal to keep his son.[9] Even though it might mean reinforcing the contemptuous stereotypes of the dominant party, the dissimulation or tricks upon which the dominated party had to rely could be a source of satisfaction—that of playing upon the gullibility of individuals incapable of doubting the effectiveness of their control.

Discretion and silence perhaps also reflected an inability to smash the ties of sociability with which they were held fast in the colonial web, though the national liberation movement militants sought to destroy the latter. The inability of Europeans affiliated with the OAS to converse with their Arab friends partly stemmed from their lack of interest in political matters when they concerned the "natives." Moreover, by keeping or maintaining relations of affection, they preserved the fiction of a French Algeria based on the consent of all populations.

One of the leaders of the OAS in Oran, Athanase Georgopoulos, recounts:[10]

At the time, I still hadn't become involved in clandestine activity. One morning, a Muslim who was a taxi driver and whose father had been a friend of my father came to see me. He said, "I've come to see you, Tassou, I don't know what to do. You know that you need permission to leave Algeria. I have eczema and would like to have myself treated in Spain." I knew him well; we embraced when we saw one another, and he said, "Can you do something for me?" I told him to come with me. I took him and went to police headquarters. I knew the chief of police. He said, "I'm not going up there, I'll stay outside."

Georgopoulos gave assurances of Mourid's good conduct, and the latter received authorization to leave the country that very afternoon. The next day, an inspector from the criminal investigation department criticized him for having helped a "terrorist" escape. A few years later, Georgopoulos was living in Torremolinos in Spain. Mourid came specifically to see him to express his gratitude: "He threw himself into my arms, kissed me, and said, 'If I made it here, it's thanks to you!'" Mourid promised to lay flowers on the grave of Athanase's father and to send him photos. On a later visit, he brought them.

As Savarèse underscores, the fact that the French of Algeria wished for greater repression against FLN militants even as they frequently intervened to protect Muslim acquaintances illustrates the ambivalence of colonial relations.[11] Relations of protection were part of a system of domination. Nevertheless, there is hardly any doubt as to the affection or loyalty between the two men; later to become an OAS leader in Oran, Georgopoulos allowed his spontaneous fidelity to take precedence over his interests and reflexes as a political militant. Did he really believe that his taxi-driver friend traveled all the way to Spain to be treated for eczema? Was he not alerted by Mourid's suspicious behavior in refusing to accompany him to the police station?

Other accounts from Algerians mention Europeans who intervened to shield Muslims from OAS arrest or assassination, and pieds-noirs recount having been saved by Muslims.[12] OAS members and sympathizers are said to have protected "their Arab." So recounts Azzedine:[13]

I had friends, good relations with people who were nearly members of the OAS. Maybe Jeannot wasn't actively in the OAS but he was on their side, he was on the OAS' side. I'm sure of it. Once, he saved my life, mine and Ali's. We were working at his home, and the OAS boys came to do us in. They were armed. Ali and I were holding hammers, but what can you do with a hammer against guns? And then bang! He appeared from nowhere and as soon as he saw them he said, "It's

French Algeria here!" He stood in their way and took them like this: "There's nothing to do here; it's French Algeria!"

Why did Jeannot follow the OAS? Azzedine protected him in his turn, explaining that it was Jeannot's wife (whose father had been killed during independence) who was "racist": "Jeannot wouldn't have left if there hadn't been the events with his parents-in-law. He wouldn't have left because he knew all of the young Arabs here. He rubbed shoulders with them. He didn't feel any hatred towards them. It was what happened to his father-in-law. He was afraid and ran away."

Without ever explaining themselves or quarreling, Mohamed[14] and Marco—inseparable friends—stopped spending time together as they became more deeply involved in their nationalist causes. Both men were later to become militants; never did they discuss politics together. Mohamed explains:

Marco was not in the habit of attacking those weaker than himself. Although things degenerated later, he became an OAS leader. I don't believe he ever came back from that; he couldn't. But I'm above all talking about him when we were children. It's when we were children that we became friends in the best sense of the word. It was something healthy; there were values. We didn't draw any distinction [between ourselves]. We were two boys, and that's all there was to it. There really wasn't anything wrong with it. But people criticized us ... It was because of his political opinions. When we learned that he was one of the leaders [of the OAS]. We were giving Marco all this attention, but there were some who were much worse than him. We had lived together, we had grown up together, and our friendship was really sincere. His mother told my mother, for example, "My son can't do without your son." She came to our house to tell me that Marco wanted ... It's when we were adults that it all blew up. And it was the time that was to blame. The nationalists' idea began to take hold, to produce a certain climate. That aggravated things, as it were; things got complicated, and that's it.

Mohamed seems to be suggesting that group pressure played a role in his break with Marco. He takes particular care to underscore the authenticity and innocence that characterized their friendship, as if it needed retrospective justification in light of his subsequent nationalist involvement. He also suggests that, through his mother, Marco had attempted to resume their friendship. But in becoming involved and as a result of the war's violence, Mohamed and Marco had no choice other than to give up their innocence and the feeling of fraternity that had united them. Mohamed was not liquidated by the OAS when he left prison a few months before independence. He knows that Marco had something to do with it.

The Barriers of Apartheid

In the course of my research in South Africa, I heard far fewer anecdotes regarding interracial friendships. Those that were forthcoming were unilateral in nature: only a few white Afrikaners mentioned childhood memories featuring blacks. These were generally individuals who had grown up on rural farms. The biography of Nelson Mandela's prison guard, James Gregory, typifies this kind of romantic narrative, which combines a love of nature and close relations with black children.[15] It is with feeling that Gregory discusses his adventures in the forests, guided by his friend Xhosa, who possessed extensive knowledge regarding local flora and fauna. He also presents his traumatic transfer into the world of whites—shortly after reaching adolescence, Gregory was sent to boarding school. It was thus inevitable that Gregory would be integrated into the apartheid system. It was only when he met "his prisoner," Nelson Mandela, that he was able to recall the lost innocence of his childhood.[16] In my interviews with white former police officers and soldiers, such ties of comradery and friendship remain vague: their accounts omit given names and offer little evidence of an effort to remain in contact.

Among the black people I interviewed, only one offered an account of this type: "I had a little experience of apartheid as a child because I recall that one day I had to go with my grandmother, who worked in town. I was innocently playing with a white child and kissed him. I then saw that this had caused serious conflict between my grandmother and her white employers. So I realized that something wasn't right in this society."[17] The ex-member of Umkhonto we Sizwe (MK) spontaneously recounted this episode after I asked him to present himself at the very start of our interview. Nor were stereotypes absent: the black servant had no choice but to bring the little boy to work with her. He was open and affectionate toward the white child, but the white family rejected such physical contact. Little David became aware of the absurdity and injustice of the world in which he lived. A Pan-African Congress (PAC) militant told me the same story.

This discrepancy between the handful of positive memories of interracial comradery among whites and the negative experiences (or absence of experiences) among blacks is a reflection, among other things, of my survey sample. While some apartheid-era police officers and soldiers were from a rural background, most MK were city-dwellers. Life in the countryside centered on agricultural work and the running of farms; as such, it entailed close, unequal relations between whites and blacks. In towns, the strict separation of residential areas limited interracial contacts to those between servants and their employers' families. The black children of the townships were generally absent from these interactions.

In his autobiography, Richard Wright describes this tendency among the white employers of blacks in the American South: they "took themselves for the negroes' friends."[18] By persuading themselves that they harbored humane and affectionate feelings toward those they saw as their inferiors, those in a dominant position partly unburdened themselves of their bad conscience. This attitude may also be conceived as a tactic on the part of whites to win the trust of blacks, whom they saw as naive and gullible. Such ambiguous friendships are also encountered among individuals who find themselves in a status of inferiority. Jim was a black soldier who served under the apartheid regime and one of the only blacks to succeed in reaching the rank of captain. No longer able to abide the racism of his "comrades-in-arms," he left the army in 1989. Jim's realization that his situation and professional relations were in no way affected by his promotion to the rank of officer only aggravated his feelings of injury and disappointment. After describing the noxious atmosphere to which he was exposed within the South African Defense Force (SADF), Jim nevertheless observed: "I made lots of white friends. In fact, I was one of the most popular black soldiers in this country. I am . . . we were the first blacks to become officers. We made history in this country." This need to say that he was liked or appreciated even by those who behaved in a racist manner toward him reflects Jim's desire to avoid being reduced to the inferior category to which he was assigned. Instead, he seeks to show how he succeeded in freeing himself from it as an individual.

When I questioned soldiers involved in the integration process within the new army, this discrepancy once again reared its head. While former members of the SADF displayed some emotion in narrating their discovery of their black interlocutors from the African National Congress (ANC), ANC members who settled into commanding positions within the military institution hardly mentioned their former adversaries.

As he chose to remain in the army at this time of political change, Colonel Bernard's meetings with his new colleagues and superiors were a source of intellectual and emotional distress. When the World Veterans Federation held a farewell dinner in Pretoria, he suggested that an MK veteran bring his wife to the meal. He arranged to drive his car to Soweto to pick up the freedom fighter's wife. This show of consideration, it seems, provoked much emotion: "He took my hand. You know black people are very sincere. They take you by the hand if they are grateful. He took my hand and thanked me. That's all he did, and I wanted to cry. I cried. I felt so humble. This old man, who had fought so many wars against me, told me, 'Thank you for bringing my wife, I really appreciate it.' He nearly cried because he would never have thought that a white would do such a thing."[19]

Bernard also mentions a general he liked and respected, a founding member of the MK. In 1997, the general brought him to Soweto. Having been there a decade earlier to maintain order, the white soldier was to deliver a speech to a group of black school students. Colonel Bernard was also "lucky" to be taken to a burial and invited into a home: "They had prepared a separate plate for me. Everyone tried to talk to me, to put me at ease, because there were only blacks. They began to speak to me and have a normal conversation with me, talking about work."

When I subsequently interviewed the general to whom Bernard referred, he did not mention the names of his colleagues from the old South African Army or offer anecdotes that would testify to profound changes in relations between blacks and whites or between former enemies. The fact that he knew white South Africans within the ANC partly limited any feeling he might have had of discovering the Other. Nevertheless, the man's indifference was perhaps not as total as he let on. Above all, the general seemed preoccupied with asserting his new position of power. Perhaps he thought that recounting a warm or moving encounter with a white SADF soldier—in conversation with a white female interviewer, what's more—might detract from his image as a leader.

Police and Army: "Good Black Colleagues"

In South Africa, colonial relations most often tend to be described in the framework of working relations. During my interviews, former police officers and soldiers very often seized upon the opportunity to discuss their excellent relations with their black subordinates.

In two respects, the discourse employed by the Europeans of Algeria and South African whites involved in professional and hierarchical relations with the "natives" overlapped: both groups judged their subordinates' behavior as if the latter were entirely free and could genuinely make their own choices— as if Muslim employees, the Angolan recruits of Battalion 32 and *konstables* (black police officers) could quit their jobs, challenge their leaders, or question orders. The consent of the dominated is presented as if it amounted to support for the system, its values, and its leaders. The second respect in which colonial representations overlap is the belief that one knows black or Muslim culture. While the experiences of those who employ this discourse affords them some understanding of the "local population," their tendency to present themselves as experts is often based on a series of clichés allowing them to legitimate a form of behavior based on force.

To cite one example, an associate of Raoul Salan, Marcel Ronda formerly managed a factory in Algiers with 180 Muslim employees, none of whom, he assured me, ever complained.

A former chief of police, Lafras is convinced that relations between blacks and whites in the police were unusually good: "We served together, we protected one another, and we made sure to take care of one another." For their system of domination, infiltration, and repression to properly operate, the beneficiaries of apartheid required a portion of the black population to collaborate.

The account supplied by a black police officer complements the former police chief's description. After being hired by the police at the age of twenty, Karl joined the Security Branch. He explains that he preferred the company of his white superiors:[20] "Us blacks, we didn't want to see one another get promoted. There was jealousy. . . . Relations were very good with my white colleagues. I preferred to work with the whites because when a white sees you make a mistake, he doesn't keep it to himself. He tells you: 'Listen, Karl, I don't like that. Don't do that.' But a black will keep it to himself."

Karl internalized some of the stigma to which he was exposed, claiming, in particular, that blacks were jealous and hypocritical. As Albert Memmi explains, "constantly confronted with this image of himself, which was assigned and imposed by institutions and all human contact," the colonized subject ultimately appropriated it. "Weren't we a little guilty after all? Lazy because we were so idle?" "[This] mythical and degrading portrait was to some degree ultimately accepted and inhabited by the colonized subject. It thereby acquired a certain reality and contributed to the real portrait of the colonized subject."[21]

Like the black man who served in the army of apartheid, Karl claims that his behavior allowed him to escape the black "personality." All of his black subordinates—the askaris—thus respected him because, "if they did something wrong," Karl "frankly told them so." Karl thus possessed the same qualities as the white police officers.

Karl never thought that apartheid was unjust. He believed that if everyone became a millionaire, "there would be no one left to wash cars." "Domination above all proceeds from the dominant party's ability to legitimate his representation of the social order."[22] He sees as natural the fact of separation, which reflects a hierarchy of bodies: "If I work in the mine and come home covered in dust, grease, and oil, I shouldn't sit on a white chair." Yet Karl approves of the new political order. He holds that "everyone has a right to a better life," and is delighted that his children have escaped the sometimes absurd instruction of white masters. Even though he votes for the ANC in every election, Karl remains proud of his certificates for twenty years of "good and loyal service" to the police and has had them framed.

After discussing the South African Army's use of extortion to recruit men from Angola and Zimbabwe, a former member of the South African Special Forces asserted that military life in southern Africa had nothing to do with apartheid, since whites and blacks shared the same daily routine:

> At first, it was bizarre. We had no choice but to trust one another. We depended on one another. We trained to be sure we were capable of doing everything that the enemy soldiers did, used the same weapons as they did, ate the same food. We were trained by our former enemies who had been captured or who voluntarily joined us. They also adapted to us: they started to eat well and drink alcohol, which they weren't used to. They put on weight. . . . It was wonderful to live with them; they were skilled. They spoke several languages. . . . Relations were excellent as long as we kept them away from alcohol. With alcohol, they fell apart. When sober, they were aggressive; when drunk, they fought one another. You couldn't joke with them. For a joke or a push, they could draw their knives. With alcohol, they became savages.[23]

His perception of the black recruits' latent violence, their touchy character, undermines the representation of a harmonious multiracial military life.

Richard Wright explains black touchiness in this way: incapable of challenging the entire system of domination and exploitation, they seize upon minor injustices to express feelings of indignation and revolt.[24]

Jan Breytenbach was the soldier who conceptualized counter-guerrilla units to combat revolutionary movements in southern Africa, and brought blacks into the South African Army. In his view, this undertaking was a great success:[25] after receiving extensive training, the black recruits became excellent soldiers. The loyalty and respect they showed for their white leaders stemmed from the fact that, unlike African commanders, South African officers themselves took part in battle. The Afrikaner Breytenbach boasts of his knowledge of the bush and the mores of its inhabitants. He depicts the personality of African men and appeals to a view frequently expressed by whites living in the colonies: the native is fundamentally good-natured but has been corrupted by poor leadership. This perspective justifies domination over local populations: the savages give their best when commanded in accordance with the civilized rules of Europeans:

> The African is a type of person totally different from the European. They have good qualities and bad qualities: once they've accepted you, they are extremely loyal. If they respect you, you must not let them down. You are therefore obliged to do things that you wouldn't do for others. When I led Battalion 32, I had to get involved in family problems. For example, when a man left for war, and another man moved in with his wife. The guy bitterly complained to me, and I had to take care of the problem. If his wife went too far, we thus had to give her a thrashing. Because that's what they do in their culture.[26]

Corporal punishment is part of the arsenal that is used to discipline colonized peoples. Its legitimacy is said to stem from the fact that those concerned themselves employ this type of justice. Once again, the dominant party asserts that the exercise of his authority is a matter of consent on the part of the dominated. A former resident of Philippeville claims that it was a mistake to apply the law to French Muslims: "You arrest an Arab for stealing. You try him six months later. The Arab has forgotten why he's there. In my factory, it was a lot simpler and more effective: whoever was stealing got a head-butt."[27]

The dominant parties often laid claim to cultural expertise within the colonial system. Those responsible for carrying out repression studied the

Other's culture in order to better identify its weaknesses. Once the conflict was over, this knowledge of the other community's culture—formerly used to argue for black inferiority—came to be flaunted as proof of openness and tolerance. Culturalist clichés confine the dominated parties within a representation of the backward native. A former South African police general in all seriousness explained the "immense cultural difference between whites and blacks."[28] After long observation of Zulu customs, he claimed to have finally succeeded in "understanding" them. Thus, the Zulu man who butts his way in front of white women waiting for the elevator is in reality looking out for them by verifying that no lion awaits them inside! The retired general thus shifts easily from the concept of separation, meant to ensure the safety of one's racial group under the apartheid regime, to that of a multicultural model respecting the particularities of each group. In both cases, he relies on a shopworn and essentialized view of blacks.

Conquering Equality

Freed from the colonial system, the new citizens can assert themselves as equals. Yet they meet with resistance in word or deed on the part of that system's former beneficiaries. How is one to convince the latter to relinquish their vision of the world? To what degree does the persistence of racist or neocolonial attitudes impinge upon the project of individual and collective emancipation for those who had been dominated?

What to Do with Racist Whites?

Multiracial democracy has yet to win over all South Africans. Even if many supporters of the old regime refrain from challenging the legitimacy of the new system, some show their reluctance to accept change through behaviors of avoidance and withdrawal, disparaging and contemptuous speech, and even acts of racist violence.

ANC militants deal with and analyze such resistance in various ways. Some seem to pursue their mission in the service of reconciliation, relying upon an "art of conviction" in their dealings with recalcitrant parties. By symbolically assuming the task of transmitting democratic values to the white community, black members of the ANC invert the relationship of domination that prevailed under apartheid, thereby reaffirming the moral superiority of the liberation movement. The grace shown by Nelson Mandela and the path laid out by the Truth and Reconciliation Commission (TRC) supply internationally renowned models. The spread of practices of forgiveness show that some persist in the spirit of clemency at their own level. Others, like Ibrahim, seem to adopt a more pragmatic approach. His remarks nevertheless conceal an irresistible satisfaction at finding oneself on the winning side. For this director of one of South Africa's leading institutions, the experience of encountering apartheid's holdouts is an occasion for feeling his superiority. This is confirmed by his choice of metaphor: "You can't make someone an enemy forever because if you treat these people like enemies forever, you will back them into a corner, and they will try to fight back. It's like cornering a rat. If you corner him, he'll leap at you. You have to leave him enough room to escape, leave the door open. In my opinion, you can't push these people, you can't take their humanity away. You can't say that they don't have a right to live. The war is over. We won."[29]

Some ANC ex-combatants betray a reluctance to see whites as like themselves, thereby revealing a discrepancy between the militant creed and the individual experience of economically disadvantaged blacks. The difficulty of establishing a new type of relationship vis-à-vis the former partisans of apartheid has two distinct sources. The first is the fear that whites still provoke among some black people. Disappointed with their leaders, a few ANC partisans continue to vote for Nelson Mandela's movement for fear that the whites will return to power. Fantasies regarding the former oppressor are still to be encountered among the least well-educated. A woman explained the uncontrollable discomfort she felt when mixing with whites during a trip to Belgium to visit her brother by reference to the fact that "apartheid runs in their veins."[30]

The second source of difficulty is the distrust or hostility that the former adversary still arouses. Accepting the Other amounts to granting him citizenship, particularly for economic reasons. Whites are believed to possess capital and skills that can be put to the use of South Africa. Frustration relating to the failure of living standards to improve thus sometimes fuels resentment toward the white community, which is accused of leaving the country and thereby slowing economic activity.

An unemployed former MK living in Soweto, Thami reflects on his own powerlessness to modify relations between blacks and whites, relations that concern the actors' objective attitude but are also a matter of perception: "Most white South Africans are arrogant. They still see us blacks as kafirs.[31] They don't see a human being when they look at us. They treat us without respect. They think we're stupid."[32] Thami perhaps bases these remarks on his run-ins with white police officers. They are also stoked by reports of violent crime in the country.[33] In fact, he has only sporadic contact with the beneficiaries of apartheid. While Thami lives in a liberated country, his ability to experience equality is limited. Unemployed and impoverished, he rarely leaves the township. Spatial and racial barriers render the question of coexistence purely theoretical. His social position precludes him from the possibility of frequent contact with whites. Yet, in order to convince oneself that the (former) adversary is like oneself, one must have contact with him. According to Thami,

> there's no reconciliation. Because us blacks who have been mistreated by the whites have to kneel down and beg them again. We're the only ones who want to reconcile . . . Our government tries, but there are only a handful of whites who are prepared to change. Go to Johannesburg! After 1994, blacks could legally buy apartments and set up their offices in town. What did the whites do? They fled to Sandtown[34] and elsewhere . . . What I know as a soldier, it's that some understand guns better than words. They understand better and a lot more quickly if you shoot.

Resisting what he sees as his people's excessive generosity, Thami is tempted to return to a language he knows well. Ultimately, this is also a way for him to emphasize his skills (the use of violence) and preserve his honor. Indeed, why stoop to begging one's oppressors, why speak the language of gentleness when one's adversary deserves the severity of arms? Isn't this a way of acknowledging one's weakness or admitting one's inferiority? If Thami resists the spirit of reconciliation extolled by South African elites, it is, among other reasons, because he perceives a series of concessions as humiliating. He nevertheless remains faithful to the discourse of the ANC, claiming that "this country's blacks and whites are all Africans, and all should work together to advance South Africa." Given the distance that continues to separate the black lower classes from other communities, support for reconciliation is above all a matter of loyalty to the country's political leadership and intellectual commitment to a humanist ideal.

When I asked him about the country's Indian community a little later, Thami expressed hostility toward what he saw as its members' racism. He referred to a scene he had witnessed in a supermarket during which he saw an

Indian child kicking his black servant: "Oh, the Indians think they're white!" In addition to reflecting his condemnation of the act, his exclamation seems to betray the idea that Indians indulge in attitudes that might be justified only among whites.

Convincing the Other: Algerian Hospitality and Table Manners in South Africa

The voyages made by pieds-noirs to Algeria provide an opportunity to examine relations between "Europeans" and "Muslims" and even sometimes between FLN and OAS ex-combatants. Pied-noir accounts supply evidence to this effect: the former inhabitants of French Algeria, including those who supported or participated in the activities of the OAS, are welcomed with open arms by the former colonial subjects. These voyages are sometimes an occasion for reunions with friends from one's youth. But Algerian warmth is apparent even outside groups bound by ties of mutual affection. Three former OAS members maintain that they were invited to visit Algeria by Yacef Saadi, leader of the nationalist side in the Battle of Algiers.[35] One of them claims to have accepted this invitation and to have received a very warm welcome. In my eyes, there is something enigmatic about the hospitality shown the pieds-noirs by Algerians. I will attempt to cast light on this phenomenon by considering it from the point of view of the exit from relations of domination.

Hospitality is of course a Mediterranean, Arabic, and Islamic tradition. Its roots run deep in Algeria, where it has been preserved thanks to an absence of mass tourism. This traditional hospitality largely explains the warm welcome received by foreigners visiting the country. In addition to these cultural considerations, a minority of Algerians seem to feel a form of regret concerning the choices taken by their country since independence. A Francophone and liberal segment of urban society associated with Europeans in the colonial era. It has been deeply disappointed by the regime's conservatism and the country's Islamicization. The civil war years only added to the disillusionment of this segment of the population. The existence of a European-origin minority in Algeria might have altered the rulers' choices and the balance of power among society's leaders. The encounter with pieds-noirs is thus an occasion for these Algerians to dream of another Algeria, one in which the pieds-noirs might have had a place.

This interpretation does not suffice to explain the attitude of Yacef Saadi, who, it is claimed, invited "deltas" originally from Bab-el-Oued and one of the OAS leaders in Oran. Nor does it explain that of Mehdi, who told me that he would gladly welcome the commune's former inhabitants, including those who had fought within an organization that had engaged in violence against his neighbors and compatriots.[36] For the pieds-noirs, are not these visits an occasion to experience equality with Algerians firsthand, something that a portion of them rejected upon leaving Algeria in 1962? As citizens of an independent state, the Algerians receive them as guests. This new relationship perhaps even sometimes inverts the situation of domination. The stakes are at once social and political.

In the course of our conversations, I repeatedly asked Mehdi—a man who claims to have never had a European friend—about why he was so eager to receive OAS pieds-noirs. Although his responses were evasive, he vaguely gestured toward his house. In their "racism," the "colonists" had seen him as little more than a "worthless native" (his words). It seems that he took pleasure at the idea of showing them his vast, two-story villa, which he had had built and stylishly decorated. His social advancement allowed him to imagine meeting with them from a position of self-confidence.

If one accepts with Axel Honneth that the individual ensures himself of recognition "via an expanding set of communication partners,"[37] it follows that Algerians are confronted with a structural problem stemming from the absence of partners, which prevents them from experiencing recognition. From this perspective, the sporadic visits of pieds-noirs thus constitute limited but novel occasions for experiencing equality. By traveling to Algeria, the country's former inhabitants accept its independence. As guests who have lost their bearings to some degree, they are obliged to behave courteously toward Algerians or at least abstain from showing contempt. Yet are these invitations to dine or drink together occasions for genuine exchange? And does not the warm welcome extended by Algerians reinforce Europeans in their belief that the colonial period was a time of harmony and mutual understanding?

Furthermore, welcoming former OAS combatants creates an opportunity to remind them of their defeat. Indeed, the vast majority of them refuse to return to Algeria—some because they worry that doing so would be too distressing, others because they see such visits as a form of surrender to the FLN.[38] In their view, traveling to Algeria when one has been defeated there is to sully one's honor. As one former OAS leader put it,[39] "I keep my dignity. I won't go to Algeria. The Algerians drove us out after all that we did for them. We built their country."

Athanase Georgopoulos claims to have accepted Yacef Saadi's invitation to visit Algeria. He explains this decision by telling the story of a party he attended, during which he apparently met an Algerian, an associate of Saadi, with whom he got along well. After consuming a fair amount of drink, Georgopoulos agreed to visit the two of them in Algeria. Sometime later, the intermediary convinced Georgopoulos to honor his promise by taunting him as follows: "So you are not a man!?" The former OAS leader thus decided to cross the Mediterranean. Shortly before he returned to France, he says, Yacef Saadi held a party. Among those invited were some women ex-combatants of the Battle of Algiers. Approaching the former OAS leader, they said, "So we won, you see?" Georgopoulos did not stay long, excusing himself on the grounds that he was tired.

In Algeria, it is a custom—indeed, a moral duty—to unconditionally grant protection. Perhaps this attitude supplies Algerians with a feeling of power. Or perhaps it is a further sign of their inability to discuss the colonial question. The explanations offered by Mohamed provide an opportunity to further explore these various possibilities:

—It's something that comes from the heart and is sincerely at the bottom of one's heart. It's part of our temperament. As soon as you are in a position of inferiority and are incapable of doing harm, ask me to do even nearly impossible things, and I will try to do them. I've seen people here who have harmed others and personally harmed me as well, I would never have dared knock them about or criticize them for anything as soon as they came here and are nearly defenseless. I can't send them away. And I was incapable of telling them, "Why did you do that?" . . . If one is dealing with a foreign man or woman, it is shameful to take advantage of one's superiority. It's base, even if [that person] is an enemy.

—So if they ring at your door, what do you do?

—If they want to come in, they come in. He comes in, he drinks some coffee. I would be delighted! Really, even if he has done harm. That's how it is with us. As soon as the fellow, even if he is seen as an enemy, is in a position of inferiority and he's the one who comes, it's absolutely forbidden in moral and religious terms to hurt him. It's forbidden. To the contrary, if you can help him, you help him despite whatever harm he has caused. Really, that's how it is, and you see it every day.

Mohamed sees these visitors as being in a position of inferiority. Perhaps he means that they now no longer possess the colonial status that assured them indisputable advantages. On this view, the pieds-noirs are doubly destitute: they have been deprived of their dominant status and are also foreigners. Hospitality, in this sense, serves to create distance.

A decade after the end of apartheid, 81 percent of South African blacks and 45 percent of South African whites claim never to have dined together.[40] Sharing food raises the question of the extent of interracial social interaction in post-apartheid South Africa. Communal exclusivity and the security it affords remain the dominant norm. Reluctance to cross the frontiers that separate one from other groups in particular stems from the disgust elicited by corporeal and hygienic norms. Among other things, apartheid guaranteed the frontiers between the country's various groups and minimized physical contact. For blacks and whites, the issue of "table manners" seems particularly salient. According to a navy colonel who began his career in the ranks of the PAC, white soldiers sought to impose their ways of behaving at the table on new black recruits. During my meetings with interviewees at restaurants, I had the impression that the new black bourgeoisie paid particular attention to the manner in which dishes were presented, served, and consumed. On each occasion, I observed that MK who had become businessmen or officials gave very specific instructions to waiters regarding the content of their orders and the manner in which they were to be presented. A native of Soweto who is now a company director asked to be given a new wine glass and criticized me for not holding my knife properly. These remarks are anecdotal in nature but perhaps indicate a desire on the part of socially successful blacks to assert themselves as experts at the table and thereby reverse a stigma.

Containing Equality

In South Africa, the beneficiaries of apartheid may today remain citizens of their country. In doing so, they must come to terms with the experience of equality with blacks. Powerless to challenge this universal principle, they criticize the government's chosen criteria and methods of application. By crossing the Mediterranean and becoming pieds-noirs, the Europeans of Algeria were deprived of interaction with Algerian citizens. Immigration has nevertheless revived questions of justice and equality as well as the triangular relationship between the French state, Arabs, and "us."

Affirmative Action: A Form of Reverse Discrimination?

None of those I met openly opposed equal rights. Nevertheless, the manner in which individuals view the apartheid regime casts light on their view of this abstract principle. A former chief of police, Lafras admits that apartheid was in some ways flawed and did not satisfy a part of the population. Yet he maintains that the system did not contravene the principle of equality. In the South African police force, according to him, promotion was based on merit, and the rules determining which blacks became officers were the same as those for other population groups. The fact that there were few black officers was in Lafras' view a matter of their personal abilities.

In the mind of this former police officer and many of his colleagues, apartheid was not a source of profound inequality; there is thus no reason to correct for it today. In this way of thinking, the white community is not indebted for the privileges it formerly enjoyed. The government's affirmative action policy is thus felt to be unjust punishment by many beneficiaries of apartheid. Lafras thinks that the inequalities produced by the new democracy—inequalities of which whites are the principal victims—are today the main obstacle to reconciliation: "I believe that whites are today in the same situation that blacks were in before. But this is something they had promised to change, the fact that there wasn't to be any more discrimination. Whites don't have equal opportunities . . . I believe that in the old system, they [blacks] had more opportunities than we have now."[41]

The former police chief's remarks are contradictory: he mentions the discrimination that existed under apartheid, but earlier denies that there was such a thing. The obvious incoherence of this type of discourse reflects a sort of inability to extricate oneself from a position of domination and concretely imagine the principle of equality being applied to the members of other communities. In the mind of the dominant party, the latter are still consigned to the margins of the legitimate political community and social contract.

Won over to democracy and rejecting the apartheid system, most white South Africans are nevertheless critical of affirmative action policies. They accuse the political elites of carrying out a "witch hunt" and of favoring ethnic criteria over individual merit. They thus remark upon the "waste of skill" and the fact that blacks occupy leadership positions for which they have not been properly trained. This attempt to correct inequalities, it is argued, has had harmful effects at the national level for the management of public affairs and the competitiveness of South African businesses.

Yet Afrikaners and Anglophones are not solely concerned about the future of their country. Their rejection of affirmative action is to be explained by the fact that this policy directly affects them or may someday do so. Failing to obtain a job or promotion is of course a source of disappointment. Yet the beneficiaries of apartheid feel the wound all the more keenly to the degree that it raises the question of their individual responsibility. Most deny any complicity with the old regime, particularly members of the younger generation, who reject the notion that they have a debt to repay. Paul, an Anglophone student pursuing a business degree at the University of Cape Town, thinks that the system of segregation was absurd. He feels comfortable in a multicultural society but hopes that the policy of affirmative action will have been ended once he begins to seek work. Today, he points out, 60 percent of university students are black. If injustices continue to exist, Paul sees no reason why he should personally suffer the consequences.[42]

Hein, an Afrikaner captain from the old army who remained in the ranks of its successor, explains that he supports nonracial democracy. He seeks to supply evidence of his commitment, recounting that he was present in the crowd to witness the presidential inauguration of Nelson Mandela and that he contributed to transforming his institution. Ideally, in Hein's view, the racial question will someday totally disappear from South Africa, and, in ten years, a white Afrikaner will be able to become president of a majority-black South Africa. According to this military man, South Africa would then be a "true democracy."[43] Most whites refuse to consider the colonial debt. The future must be constructed as if the past had never existed.

What Algerian Immigration Proves

Immigrants from Algeria do not go unnoticed by the pieds-noirs of the OAS. Although he sees Algerians as belonging to a "nasty race," Camille, like others, believes he has more in common with them than with the mainland French.[44] Such assertions of affinity above all serve to underscore one's distance from the French people of France. Distrust and resentment are preserved by the memory of the contempt with which one was greeted upon arriving on the northern shore of the Mediterranean and the belief that one has been misunderstood and demonized.

Some OAS militants reject the presence of these Algerians. They fear that France will be Islamicized, and accuse the immigrants of changing the social order. Their culture and their religion are said to be ultimately incompatible with those of the French. At the same time, their massive presence is said to prove that Europeans in Algeria "weren't so bad as all that." And some feel a kind of satisfaction in thinking that this is proof that the FLN has failed to meet the challenge of independence: "They've been independent for forty-two years now; do you think they live well? Why do they come here in France? . . . How is it possible that all these Algerians come here? It's because things aren't going well there; they've got nothing to eat."[45] The presence of Algerian immigrants is often perceived as an injustice. This is above all because, in the eyes of many, it is considered inconsistent with the FLN's nationalist choice to expel France and French people: "They have their country; let them stay there."[46]

Since OAS members and Harkis feel as if they are forbidden from visiting Algeria, moreover, some claim that the "free circulation" of Algerians is in conflict with the principle of equality. On their view, this policy of tolerance vis-à-vis Algerians goes hand in hand with France's perennial betrayal of the pieds-noirs. While the former are welcomed into the national community, the latter remain second-class citizens under a cloud of suspicion. Gabriel Anglade expresses this view: "I don't see why we should accept Algerian immigrants with Algerian citizenship coming here and taking French nationality. . . . And that's why I find it completely unfair that someone who isn't French shows up and all of sudden we make him French. Just like I find it unfair that we pieds-noirs should be obliged to prove that we're French by virtue of our parents. Otherwise, you have to make a special request in court so that you can be French. I find that really aberrant."[47]

For a segment of the pied-noir population, the impossibility of returning to Algeria and the forced renunciation of their native land are experienced as trauma. The private and collective pain of being torn from one's roots feeds envy and rejection of those who have the option of remaining in Algeria or coming to France. In the eyes of some, the old privileges have been inverted;

it is now Algerians who nearly exclusively enjoy the right of free movement. This frustration is not conducive to the process of recognition.

The Dilemmas of Recognition

The question of recognition mainly arises for formerly dominant parties. Admitting that a system in which one lived and participated was based on injustice provokes resistance. Recognizing the manner in which the Other has been injured requires that one perceive oneself, at least in part, as among those responsible for inflicting harm and contempt. The resulting efforts to rationalize the past can take several forms and indicate the path that individuals are ready to take. For formerly dominated parties, the ambivalence of the colonial context can sometimes weigh on them.

Hidden Ties

In the independent and nationalist Algeria of today, some of the relationships that were woven into the colonial context appear incomprehensible or illegitimate. Is it possible that one simultaneously fought colonialism and established intimate relations with its agents? Obviously so. By contrast, it is nearly impossible to speak of this.

I met Amel in the suburbs of Algiers. She is a doctor in her thirties who shows little patience for the various criticisms that might be made of her country. Through her, I met her mother, Linda. As her daughter sat in the next room, Linda recounted the following story.

Originally from a relatively well-off Algiers family, Linda intimates that her father was not in favor of independence. As a child, Linda was blonde and wore her hair in pigtails. She was often "better dressed than the little European girls" and attended the French school. After her middle school years, she trained as a nurse with the nuns. It was at this time that she was contacted by the FLN to transmit messages to its militants. Arrested by the French army, she was released thanks to the intervention of her school principal, who assured them of her innocence. Upon her release, Linda was punished by her father for participating in political acts and confined to the house. In the final months preceding independence, the FLN called upon Linda to treat the wounded. Obliged by the organization, her father allowed the apprentice nurse to go to a makeshift camp in Algiers. Linda's combat experience consisted in two types of task: transmission and care. Toward the end of her story, she lowered her voice somewhat. During the war, she was in love with a French soldier with whom she spent time. He wished to marry her. Linda was tempted but ultimately refused to take that step. She nevertheless continued to correspond with him after his return to France. After marrying an Algerian, she learned that he was in his turn in love with the daughter of a French colonel. The couple agreed to forget about their emotional past. It was only following the birth of his son and an ultimatum from Linda, however, that her husband ceased to correspond with the young French woman. Linda asked me to say nothing to her daughter about what she had told me about her past love life.

Seen from the perspective of intergenerational transmission, it is a striking account. Amel, whose nationalist sympathies are plainly apparent, portrays her mother as a "combatant" and "militant in the war of liberation." Linda was perhaps of assistance to the FLN at the local level, but it would be a stretch to characterize her relatively isolated actions as evidence of genuine political commitment. Moreover, what Linda really wanted to tell me about was her love affair with the French soldier, something she concealed from her daughter. Amel was also unaware of her father's past affair with a French woman he met during the war.

The government's rhetoric regarding the unity of the Algerian people requires that one adjust one's own experience to fit a nationalist norm. The concealment of personal experience or the impossibility of recounting it in a way consistent with the meaning one seeks to assign one's life are reflected in discursive lacunae. In the course of these interviews, disruptions of meaning revealed the disjunction between private experience and the abrupt political socialization that accompanied independence. In somewhat similar fashion, Rym was recruited by the FLN for her "European physique" and not as the result of a process of political socialization. A pretty young woman with blonde hair, she aroused no distrust among French soldiers or the Europeans of Algeria. Without supplying her with any political training, the FLN asked her to take advantage of her job in the administration to supply them with intelligence. Sometime later, she was thrown into direct action, placing three explosive devices in an Algiers bar. She appears to have never fully compensated for the fact that her actions were of little political significance to her. Though she draws upon nationalist arguments and vocabulary, they are completely out of sync with the personal experience she recounts: "At school, the teachers took me for a French girl. They were friendly. We didn't know anything. There was no racism. We spent time with one another. We danced together. There wasn't any racism. I don't know if Nicole was Jewish or Christian. No one worried about that."[48]

In Aïn Benian—before independence, a small, European-majority town near Algiers—I met Djamel, a man in his seventies who wanted to get in touch with the members of a family that left Algeria in 1962. According to Djamel, the mother of this family had nursed him when he was an infant. He claims that this woman had treated him like her own child, scolding him when he misbehaved and expressing pride when he succeeded. Djamel gives one to understand that he disowned this wet nurse and her loved ones during the war and would now like to send a message to them. He asked me to deliver it but simultaneously refused to give it to me. Djamel's account is a little confused; according to the village elders, he has been mad for some time. It is quite unlikely that a European woman would breastfeed a young Muslim child in the 1940s. But Djamel's story is perhaps more interesting if invented. It calls to mind the metaphor employed by an Islamic Salvation Front (ISF) leader who accused his country's Francophone intellectuals of having "imbibed the poisonous milk" of France.[49] Djamel avoids finishing his sentences, and his remarks are full of insinuations. His offense is perhaps twofold. He is a "son" of France—a sin from the perspective of Algerian Islamo-nationalism. And he seemed to be suggesting that he was a traitor: after having been fed and loved by a European woman and her family, he had turned his back on—and perhaps created trouble for—them. Djamel suggests that he failed to show the appropriate gratitude toward those who had displayed sincere and affectionate feelings toward him. The debt of the colonial relationship is thus inverted, but it remains impossible to avow.

Denying Injustice in Order to Proclaim One's Innocence

The failure to recognize the injustice of apartheid is partly a matter of defensiveness. Having occupied important posts under this regime, Lafras does not want to admit that he was a participant in an unjust system. As an ANC official remarked of several members of the Security Branch, "they don't want to reconcile if that means acknowledging they were at fault." A former police chief, Lafras recognizes the need to end apartheid. Like other privileged individuals in a colonial situation, he accepts that the principle of equality is legitimate but denies that the colonial system was based on an inequality in the status or relations between different communities. When admitting certain unjust aspects, he personally distances himself from them.

He wishes to prove that the system—and, above all, his own behavior—was free of racism.

It seems that individuals who enjoyed a legal status placing them in a situation of domination are incapable of realizing the nature of their relations with those dominated. Force of habit, their unconscious and/or bad faith, handicap their judgment. The inequality of relations does not preclude positive feelings from existing on either side. Those in a position of dominance, however, tend to confuse paternalism for generosity, submission for approbation. The absence of conflict may also be put forward as evidence of good relations when it is more the result of a profound disparity in the distribution of symbolic and material resources. Lafras maintains that interracial relations are no longer as good within the police force as they were in the time of apartheid. Today in a situation of formal equality, the institution's members are more likely to openly settle conflicts, and find it more or less difficult to adjust to the new rules governing their relations.

Moreover, the main argument advanced by South African whites and the Europeans of Algeria focuses on their indifference to politics. Noting that they themselves never cast a ballot in elections, some argue that the disparity in citizenship entailed by voting rights restrictions was a matter of little consequence. This stance seeks to clear them of responsibility and cast blame on politicians, institutions, and "important colonists." Police officers and soldiers present themselves as "neutral" officials, while most members of the OAS claim that they have never had any involvement in politics. Their carefree and harmonious life alongside Muslims supposedly rendered the system of domination invisible.

For example, after having presented the concerns of young people in Algiers, Gabriel Anglade attempted to demonstrate that his involvement in the OAS was apolitical:

—We were children. We were children in politics.
—Did you ever think at any point during or after the war that the inequality of status between Muslims and Europeans was unjust?
—No, because we didn't notice that in the towns. I have photos. It's too bad that I didn't bring them. I played soccer in the club. There were eleven of us. Well, I would have shown you the photo: there were two Jews, four Arabs, and the rest were Europeans. So we never had this problem. They had the same rights as I did, and I had the same rights as them. We didn't talk about politics or the *deuxième collège*. We lived

our daily lives. I tell you: we weren't politicized so we couldn't give a
shit. These Arabs, our mates, would never have thought to complain
that they were mistreated or that they were from the *deuxième collège*.
We didn't even talk about it!
—But the *deuxième collège*, for example, that didn't bother you?
—It never crossed our minds. It crossed our minds when politics got
involved—that is, when 1954 happened. Because, before 1954, no one
talked about the *collèges*. No one cared. . . .
—But in retrospect do you think that this inequality of status should
have been changed?
—But we never noticed the inequality of status. Because we never
talked about politics. That's what I said; we were apolitical. We weren't
interested in it.
—Yes, but once the events took place, you got involved in politics.
—I didn't get involved in politics, I got involved in the events. Like
here, I got into City Hall without being political.
—Yes, OK, but the OAS was a political undertaking of the FAF.[50]
—Yes, but it's the same thing. It's not politics; it's for French Algeria.
It's not at all the same; it was to defend a territory.

Anglade today recognizes the injustice but claims that it was invisible in
the colonial period. The good relations, sharing, and friendship that the pieds-
noirs of the OAS recall having existed among the inhabitants of Algeria
sharply contrast with their alarming analyses of the Islamic desire to con-
quer the world, the Arabs' warlike character, and international terrorism.
How could the Arabs have been one's mates from the neighborhood yesterday and be fundamentally violent individuals today? The key to this enigma
does not reside in the nature of the political order: in the eyes of some, Arabs
are good only when dominated.

Recognizing the Other Without Discrediting Oneself: Rereading History

As is the case for pieds-noirs who supported democracy, South African whites
today find it nearly impossible to defend the colonial system and its values.
Some thus modify their vision of the past to accommodate the contemporary
values of justice and equality. A few OAS members, for example, claim to have
supported the aim of integrating Muslims into the French Republic and

equality for all citizens. Referring to Ferhat Abbas, Jean-Jacques Susini thus regrets that France did not favorably respond to his political demands. If the former leader of OAS psychological and propaganda operations was unable to assert and disseminate his progressive ideas, it was because he was too young and marginalized by those he portrays as conservative colonialists: "Miss, as I told you, I was born on July 30, 1933. Calculate how old that made me in 1954: I was a twenty-one-year-old student; no one would have listened to me. At the time, politics in Algeria was Chevallier,[51] Suriny—those people, their habits, their way of seeing things. Even my friends and family resisted my discourse. Because they thought the past would endlessly repeat itself while improving over time. But what I had in mind was a revolution, after all. No one would have ever followed me."[52] This former OAS political leader attempts to present the liberals as conservatives lacking in vision. In 1960, however, he sought support from the leaders of Jeune Nation, a fascist and racist movement that wished to make Algeria a "white land once and for all." The revolution for which he called at the Barricades trial[53] sought to reconcile "the movement for social emancipation" with the "national phenomenon."[54]

In South Africa, several high-ranking soldiers present themselves as enlightened trailblazers who warned the country's politicians as to the inherent limits of relying on the forces of order to preserve the state. In their telling, they fought only in order to lay the best foundations possible for subsequent negotiations with the adversary.

The Pains of Recognition

Colonel Bernard served under apartheid and was at the time convinced that his country was threatened by the subversive forces of the ANC and PAC. Despite his support for the old system, he remained in the army after 1994. Colonel Bernard is one of the few who are willing to speak about the stages of their transformation. In contrast to the immense majority of his colleagues and members of his community, he admits that he had supported apartheid. The gradual realization that his world was based on lies and injustice was a painful ordeal.

Although he does not see himself as racist, Bernard claims that his education and socialization were entirely based on "white principles." As a child and, later, in the army, he never spent time in the company of blacks, nor did he question this separation: "When they called upon whites to join the army to defend the country, I joined the ranks to fight the enemy—or what was seen as the enemy, but which I now see as the government in exile. I joined the army to protect my country against impostors, the soldiers of the MK and APLA. We saw them as enemies. They were to be killed. We were supposed to hate them. . . . Blacks didn't have civil and political rights. They just had the right to work for whites. That's how I was brought up."[55] Bernard was sent to the front to fight along the border. The official objective was to repel the enemy, who was trying to infiltrate South Africa. Bernard did his job. If he joined the army, it was to go to war and use his weapon. Of course, once he was a father, he found it difficult to leave his children behind for months at a time, to miss out on the stages of their childhood, and he realized that it was difficult to speak with his wife after having been immersed in the atmosphere of combat. His first doubts emerged when he had to deploy inside the country, particularly the townships: was not the war already lost if the enemy was inside the country? It had thus been useless to fight at the border. Bernard recalls the various times he visited the parents of soldiers who had died in combat under his command.

Combat seemed at once costly and ineffective. Soldier Bernard had another shock. As a participant in the violent repression taking place within the townships, he met a poor black woman who offered him a piece of bread: "And with that, you begin—you couldn't talk to anyone about it—but it was damn painful to realize that they're not all bad, that some are good, and that all they want is to live in peace." Bernard met other township inhabitants in the course of a propaganda mission:

At first, when we arrived in a little house with a room and a kitchen— father, mother, and five children—I thought to myself that I had a house with three rooms. The first time, they didn't talk much. But when you visit them several times, they tell you. We asked them what they expected of life, and their response showed me that their expectations were exactly the same as mine. They wanted a job, money, a family, a house, and a car. Your head is in turmoil because you have all these contradictory messages. I went to war inside my country, so we lost the war. These people aren't so bad, even though that's what I had believed. They want peace and aspire to prosperity like me. I didn't know anymore.

Bernard was lost and, when President de Klerk submitted negotiations with the ANC to a referendum, he abstained. When the first democratic elections took place in 1994, he was dismayed by the results. Never would he have imagined that "the terrorist organization" would do so well. His most pessimistic evaluation put the number of whites in Parliament at 50 percent. Bernard thought of leaving South Africa. He nevertheless stayed and was assigned to a new duty. In 1996, he met military leaders from the national liberation movements for the first time. To learn that the MK had fought for an ideal, had suffered, and had aspirations similar to his own was for this white soldier a moving discovery:

> For the first time, I sat down with former members of the MK and APLA and asked them to tell me about their experience of the last forty years. It took me time—three years, from 1999 to 2002—to understand the blacks' political views, their aspirations, those of mixed-race people and Indians. I understood what had been denied them in the past. I understood what human rights, civil rights, the freedom of movement, were. Before 1994, if they didn't have a pass, they couldn't move freely. Mixed-race people and blacks didn't have the right to go to the whites' beach, and everything belonged to the whites. . . . I succeeded in really understanding my colleagues.

Colonel Bernard's evolution was not just intellectual; it was also a significant emotional upheaval. The white soldier was profoundly moved to discover the humanity of his former black enemies. He was also touched that they accepted him among themselves: "One day, I told myself: they really trust me, and I will try to never act contrary to this trust."

The colonel was sent to study at a British university. While pursuing a master's degree in political science, he attained an overarching understanding of the South African transition to democracy. Though he was already over forty, it was the first time he had spent time abroad. These various experiences and encounters allowed him to accept change and transform himself. Bernard underscores that not everyone is capable of following the same process. He mentions some of his colleagues and friends who joined the far right. One of them plotted against the government and was tried for treason. Bernard insists on the efforts he had to make to adapt, his desire to understand and rid himself of thirty-eight years' worth of conditioning. He admits that he was "liberated," not by the ANC, but by "all of the encounters" he had. Happy to live in a country enriched by its cultural differences, he nevertheless continues to think that interracial marriages are a mistake, since the children of mixed couples struggle to find their bearings. Despite these reservations, Bernard has changed a great deal.

Sociology has taken up the issue of recognition, albeit mainly from the perspective of those who demand it. There has been less discussion of what the process of recognition entails for the party granting it. Yet in interindividual and intercommunal processes of recognition, the denied subject and the solicited subject must each pass through many snares on the path to recognition. Bernard went through the steps of this path to the Other. Paul Ricoeur's exploration of recognition as a term[56] is based on the various definitions that the dictionary supplies of it. These "meanings [are] sometimes very far removed from one another." They "part ways at the outset but only do so in keeping with processes that—sometimes expanding upon the proper meaning, sometimes the metaphorical meaning—have nothing arbitrary or disorderly about them."[57] Ricoeur holds that disparities in meaning derive from what is implicitly left unsaid by earlier definitions. As identified by Ricoeur, the progression of meanings assigned the word "recognition" in Littré's dictionary corresponds to the steps that confronted Bernard in his process of recognition. The third definition of "to recognize" is thus given as "to succeed in knowing, to perceive, to discover the truth of something." The notion of truth is introduced, and Ricoeur underscores that the term "succeed" "insinuates a difficulty that takes the form of hesitation, delay, and resistance."[58] When sent to the township, Bernard makes two discoveries: he perceives that his country has not won the war against the ANC, and that blacks are not systematically bad. This confrontation with reality teaches him things of which he was formerly ignorant. Discerning these truths comes as a shock, since they contradict his earlier beliefs and representations of the world. Littré's subsequent definitions underscore the idea of truth but also that of reluctance: "to admit, to accept as true or indisputable."[59] Bernard was only able to accept the truth once he had gathered several indications or pieces of evidence of this reality. This involved significant reluctance and friction, since it called into question his knowledge of the world and, in so doing, was a source of suffering. The subsequent confirmation of his discovery (that blacks are not bad and have the same aspirations as he does) was no longer experienced as a total upheaval but required an intellectual effort: in order to fully admit the truth, it is necessary to have interpreted and understood its manifestations and abandoned the false truths to which one had formerly subscribed. The repercussions of his discovery nevertheless provoked an emotional response. Sharing duties with his new black colleagues moved Bernard to tears. Finally, one of the final definitions evokes the theme of confession: to recognize is to acknowledge "a misdeed, a debt, or a mistake."[60] Bernard recognized that he was wrong—because deceived by his government and its institutions—and committed himself to changing. In this respect, it can be argued that, for the person who carries it out, the act of recognition is at once a discourse regarding the past, in which the subject admits to having despised the Other, and a promise, to the degree that the subject makes a commitment to henceforth show him consideration. Bernard has remained in the army, where he works on behalf of the new South Africa under the orders of his new black hierarchical superiors.

Bernard is proud of the transformation he has already carried out. On the strength of his act of recognition, he hopes to be recognized in his turn as a nonracist white. The process of recognition repeatedly raises the issue of reciprocity.

*   *   *

Extricating oneself from a relationship of domination is a laborious and uncertain process that requires one to become aware of the unequal relations of the past and to desire to reform them. Two steps appear necessary to do so.

First of all, it is essential to encounter a member of the opposing community if one is to begin questioning one's former behavior and see the Other in a new light. The examples of Colonel Bernard and Athanase Georgopoulos demonstrate this: Bernard's exchanges with MK ex-combatants came as a revelation, and one may suppose that the OAS leader's visit with the mudjahid supplied him with a more flexible vision. Bernard's path was more painful to the degree that his encounter with the former enemy constituted a discovery. For Georgopoulos, by contrast, Yacef Saadi did not seem fundamentally foreign: in taking up what he claims was the latter's offer of hospitality, Georgopoulos accepted his defeat and initiated a dialogue. Of the two, the path followed by Bernard was more radical, since it entailed calling into question his political judgment and vision of the world. Georgopoulos, meanwhile, has kept some of his colonial certainties intact. Warm human relations do not suffice to purge the colonial debt; indeed, they tend to obfuscate it.

The ability to construct a common narrative is the second step that allows one to emancipate oneself from the old world. South African soldiers and police officers can find a place for themselves in the national narrative of reconciliation and make it their own. This allows them to avoid examining their consciences regarding their careers and participation in the apartheid system, but nevertheless to be part of the new South Africa. Several former OAS also attempt to position themselves as past supporters of a reform of the colonial system that would have benefited the natives. Yet this self-portrait is limited by fact that these same individuals today campaign for state recognition of France's overseas accomplishments.

Few people pursue the process of recognition to completion. The members of the OAS, for their part, fall far short of it. Their resistance to condemning the colonial system is explained by comparison with South African whites. First, the relative proximity of the Europeans of Algeria and that country's native population muddles their perception. The belief that one has had a "friendship" with an Arab hinders one's ability to recognize the latter's humiliation. In South Africa, the physical and social distance separating blacks from whites may help clarify the reality of the situation. Moreover, the exclusion (or self-exclusion) of OAS members from independent Algeria makes it impossible to construct a common narrative. In South Africa, the place reserved for those on the losing side allows them to preserve their self-esteem without falsifying their individual trajectories or diminishing their support for democracy. OAS activists, by contrast, are at home nowhere: though far from Algeria, they cannot identify with a French Republic that "betrayed" them. Seeing themselves as losers twice over, they prefer to continue relying on the honor of the defeated rather than call into question the political and moral legitimacy of their past. And, in contrast to the former defenders of apartheid, who can all claim to have been manipulated, their commitment to sever ties with the French state makes it more difficult to cast blame on that country's political and institutional structures.

Conclusion

While the postconflict order is based on the theme of reconciliation in South Africa and on that of victory in Algeria, in France it has its origins in obfuscation. Thus, while the country of Mandela has made room for the ex-adversary in the political community, and that of Boumediene exploits him as a symbol, he has vanished from metropolitan France. Though the ex-combatants of the ANC (African National Congress) have received little reward for their contribution to the struggle, South Africa's new rulers have seen to it that the apartheid-era forces of order are provided with the resources they need to integrate into the new society that is being constructed. The veterans of the FLN (National Liberation Front) have been elevated to the rank of heroes and, on the strength of the country's twofold rent (oil-producing and historical), have become a pampered social group and mainstay of the government. After having initially been condemned, OAS (Secret Army Organization) members have over time succeeded in winning various forms of rehabilitation. With little desire to examine its colonial past, the French Republic has granted at least some of the demands of those who were formerly the implacable partisans of French Algeria.

The narratives that the ex-combatants have developed are shaped by these political configurations but sometimes also clash with them. The existence or absence of measures to address past injustice and violence also determines the evolution of the combatants' stance. In South Africa, the creation of the Truth and Reconciliation Commission (TRC) gave the entire society access to precise, corroborated information regarding the major human rights violations committed by the apartheid regime and the abuses of the national liberation movements. In contrast to the attitude adopted by many French soldiers in regard to the army's practices in Algeria, the police officers of the Security Branch admit to having used torture and engaged in summary execution. Moreover, the TRC contributed to the emergence of a shared narrative centered on reconciliation and forgiveness. Although grassroots ANC militants struggle to embrace and personally experience it, and apartheid-era officials tend to twist it to their advantage, the invention of the South African narrative provides these old enemies with a shared framework of integration. Algeria and France have yet to come to terms with one another regarding their shared past of war and colonization. Algerian voices demanding apologies from France have rekindled the heat of battle, which has also been stoked by the deafness and blunders of the former colonial power.

The question of recognition is thus at the heart of the postconflict and postcolonial situation. In part, the protagonists' failure to publicly avow their participation in violence stems from their inability to identify relations of domination and the brutality they entail.

In South Africa, former officials accept their political and moral defeat, even if they individually seek to extricate themselves from it by distancing themselves from apartheid-era conceptions and giving their support to the new South Africa. The partisans of the OAS, by contrast, still believe in the moral legitimacy of their cause. Indeed, while fully accepting Algerian independence, a segment of French society today regards colonization as a "positive" phenomenon. Yet the expression of this opinion does not satisfy members of the OAS, who still resent the political left and the portion of France who accused them of being solely responsible for the wrongs of colonialism. For former OAS, there is no shared narrative; expelled from independent Algeria and stigmatized in France, they cling to their own. Taking advantage of France's refusal to take stock of the colonial question, some now seek to persuade the public of the validity of their vision of history.

In Algeria, the seizure of power drew its legitimacy from the history of the revolution against France. The FLN justifies its violence during the war by insisting on the heroic fight against a powerful and unrelenting adversary. The decision to exclude Europeans from the independent nation (or not keep them) helped lend credence to a binary and exclusive vision of history in which the Algerian people are presented as united in their fight against colonialism. This fiction is contradicted by ever more costly expressions of the "nation's gratitude" toward the "revolutionary family". The mujahideen have become a distinct social group. The obsession for legitimization is driven by their remuneration and the manner in which the group's contours are defined.

Able to count on the rent from oil and gas, the leaders of the FLN concluded that the European population contributed little in terms of economic know-how and skills. The revenue from fossil fuels allowed them to do without Europeans and subject the new society to their authoritarianism. Pursuing the struggle against the colonial undertaking, the Algerian government constantly engaged in nationalist escalation. By constantly seeking to uproot the colonial enemy's presence within the nation, Algeria's rulers deepened the contradictions within society. By Arabizing the school and university system without providing adequate resources while at the same time sending their own children to Francophone institutions or abroad, by denying the complexity of the colonial past, and by raising the specter of neocolonialism, they created gaping symbolic rifts within society. When the growth of social and economic inequality, moreover, revealed the discrepancy between the regime's discourse and practices, the protest movement spread. But despite their stated intention to overthrow a corrupt regime, the Algerian Islamists were incapable of freeing themselves from the founding myths of the Algerian state. The violence they unleashed on Algerian society reflected the madness to which their fantasy of impossible purity had given rise.

In South Africa, the leaders of the ANC developed a nonracial conception of the nation that made room for their former white enemies. They committed themselves to a democratic ideal and came to personify a new form of national liberation movement. Once they had come to power, their economic conservatism guaranteed white support for the regime and limited their emigration abroad. But the future of the South African model depends on the capacity of the country's elites to gradually integrate the nation's underprivileged population and reduce disparities of wealth.

As this comparison suggests, post-apartheid South Africa and independent Algeria represent distinct models: the first centers on forgiveness; the second relies on resentment. Yet by observing discourse and behavior in these countries, it becomes clear that, at a concrete, individual level, one's exchanges do not entirely reflect the regime's ideological stance.

In South Africa, the immense gaps separating blacks and whites, particularly in economic terms, are the main stumbling blocks to reconciliation. While interracial relations have significantly changed since the end of apartheid, it must be acknowledged that mistrust of the Other and intracommunal exclusivity remain the rule. Many South Africans, including the members of privileged circles where interracial socialization has taken place, prefer a moderate form of multiculturalism in which all can keep their identity and are free to choose the company they keep. For the poorest blacks, the end of the segregationist regime has changed little, and the absence of contact with whites contributes to distorted perceptions. Frightened by the growth of criminality, middle-class and well-off South Africans, who make up much of the country's white population, barricade themselves behind security systems. For some, black males, once seen as MK (Umkhonto we Sizwe) "terrorists," have been transformed into dangerous delinquents. Constrained by the new national narrative, blacks and whites have adopted a politically correct discourse that many are still incapable of putting into practice. In the public and private spheres, there thus remains considerable distance between blacks and whites and between opponents and supporters of the apartheid regime. The spirit of reconciliation is far from having permeated interracial social relations.

In Algeria, the rhetoric of the war of national liberation enjoys overwhelming support from the public. Yet some Algerians who can still recall the colonial period, a group that includes some former FLN combatants, have regular or occasional relations with former "colonists." Algerians and pieds-noirs alike recount emotional reunions. Although these encounters and discussions of old friendships are not free of contradiction and ambiguity, they nevertheless reveal the existence of a connection—or a desire for connection—that has survived the war and the subsequent separation of the two peoples.

In this respect, the comparison between South Africa and Algeria reveals something of a paradox. As in a mirror, the ideological and private registers stand in an inverted relationship to one another: where one shows forgiveness, the other expresses resentment. In Algeria, resentment toward "the colonial enterprise" is a mainstay of the government's rhetoric, but interindividual relations are characterized by much warmth. In South Africa, reconciliation supplies the regime's ideological foundation, but social relations continue to be dominated by distance and even distrust.

Notes

Introduction

1. In the 1950s, French soldiers did not specifically enlist to defend the Empire, even if the better part of their experiences subsequently brought them face-to-face with the colonial question; their choice of career was informed by other representations of the nation and the dangers that threatened it. Men who enlisted in the South African police or army, by contrast, were more clearly choosing to defend apartheid against regional and national threats or were at least aware of the central nature of this mission.

2. Comparative politics tends to focus on "big" objects of investigation such as the state or institutions and favors an approach that centers on a given geographical, cultural, or religious zone.

3. Nevertheless, several researchers have endeavored to produce a multinational comparative sociology: Michel Wieviorka reconstructed the trajectories of Basque, Italian, Peruvian, and Lebanese terrorist groups and the individual and collective dynamics informing their action (*Société et terrorisme* [Paris: Fayard, 1988]). Gilles Kepel tested his hypotheses regarding the Muslim world against Christian and Jewish forms of religious revival in Europe, the United States, and Israel (*La revanche de Dieu: Chrétiens, juifs et musulmans à la reconquête du monde* [Paris: Seuil, 1991]). Jacques Sémelin studied the intersection of individual and collective dynamics in the course of Jewish, Rwandan, and Bosniak massacres and genocides (*Purifier et détruire: Usages politiques des massacres et génocides* [Paris: Seuil, 2005]). See also Elizabeth Picard, "De la domination du groupe à l'invention de son identité: Les milices libanaises et les para-militaires nord-irlandais," in Denis-Constant Martin, ed., *Cartes d'identité: Comment dit-on "nous" en politique?* (Paris: Presses de la FNSP, 1994), 147–83.

4. Jean-François Bayart, in particular, puts paid to culturalist approaches, deconstructing traditional and modern categories of society in *L'illusion identitaire* (Paris: Fayard, 1996).

5. Todd Shepard, *The Invention of Decolonization: The Algerian War and the Remaking of France* (Ithaca, NY: Cornell University Press, 2006), 1.

6. Ibid.; and Sandrine Lefranc, *Politiques du pardon* (Paris: PUF, 2002), 24–25.

7. By studying the interrogations of German police from the 101st Battalion who participated in the summer 1942 massacre of Jews in Poland despite not being required to do so, Christopher Browning attempts to reconstruct the justifications for their choice. He writes: "It was a different time and place, as if they had been on another political planet, and the political vocabulary and values of the 1960s were helpless to explain the situation in which

they found themselves in 1942" (*Reserve Police Battalion 101 and the Final Solution in Poland* [New York & London: HarperCollins, 1992], 72).

8. Philippe Braud, *Violences politiques* (Paris: Seuil, 2004), 27–30.

9. Raphaëlle Branche, *La torture et l'armée pendant la guerre d'Algérie, 1954–1962* (Paris: Gallimard, 2001), 14.

10. Ibid., 22.

11. *Mujahid* is an Arab term that means "combatant"; *mujahideen* is the masculine plural; *mujahida* is the feminine singular, *mujahidat* the feminine plural.

12. Numa Murard, "La reconnaissance négative dans l'expérience de la vulnérabilité: La second liberté," in Jean-Paul Payet and Alain Battegay, eds., *La reconnaissance à l'épreuve: Explorations socio-anthropologiques* (Villeneuve d'Asq: Presses universitaires du Septentrion, 2008), 186.

13. Cornélius Castoriadis, *The Imaginary Institution of Society*, trans. Kathleen Blamey (Cambridge, MA: MIT Press, 1987), 163.

14. Notwithstanding Castoriadis' warning: "How are we to distinguish between the imaginary significations and the rational significations in history? . . . We are running the risk of introducing surreptitiously one rationality (our own) and making it play the role of rationality as such." Castoriadis, *The Imaginary Institution of Society*, 161.

15. Paul Ricoeur, *Soi-même comme un autre* (Paris: Seuil, 1990), 38.

16. Danilo Martuccelli, *Grammaires de l'individu* (Paris: Gallimard, coll. "Folio", 2002), 369.

17. Ibid.

18. Élise Féron and Michel Hastings, *L'imaginaire des conflits communautaires* (Paris: L'Harmattan, 2002).

19. Denis-Constant Martin, ed., *Cartes d'identité: Comment dit-on "nous" en politique?* (Paris: Presses de la FNSP, 1994).

Part I

1. Paul Veyne, "Foucault révolutionne l'histoire," in *Comment on écrit l'histoire* (Paris: Seuil, 1978), 203–42.

2. George L. Mosse, *Fallen Soldiers: Reshaping the Memory of the World Wars* (New York and Oxford: Oxford University Press, 1990).

3. Bruno Cabanes, *La victoire endeuillée* (Paris: Seuil, 2004), as well as Bruno Cabanes and Guillaume Piketty, "Sortir de la guerre: Jalons pour une histoire en chantier," *Histoire@Politique: Politique, Culture et Société* 3 (November–December 2007), www.histoire-politique.fr.

4. The Locarno Accords between Germany and the European allies were signed on 16 October 1925. They marked Germany's return to the diplomatic concert of nations.

5. John Horne, "Locarno et la politique de démobilisation culturelle: 1925–1930," *14–18 Aujourd'hui, Today, Heute*, Noésis (May 2002): 73–86.

Chapter 1

1. On the meaning of the rainbow symbol, see Dominique Darbon, "Le pays de l'arc-en-ciel," *Hérodote* 82–83: "La nouvelle Afrique du Sud" (1996): 5–7.

2. The ANC received 62.65 percent of votes at the national level, while the National Party (NP) received 20.24 percent and the Inkhata Freedom Party (IFP) 10.5 percent.

3. Richard Wilson, *The Politics of Truth and Reconciliation in South Africa: Legitimizing the Post-Apartheid State* (Cambridge: Cambridge University Press, 2001), 8.

4. François-Xavier Fauvelle-Aymar, *Histoire de l'Afrique du Sud* (Paris: Seuil, 2006); and Denis-Constant Martin, *Sortir de l'Apartheid* (Brussels: Complexe, 1992).

5. Daniel Bar-Tal and Gemma H. Bennink, "The Nature of Reconciliation as an Outcome and as a Process," in Yaacob Bar-Siman-Tov, ed., *From Conflict Resolution to Reconciliation* (Oxford: Oxford University Press, 2004), 17.

6. This is the interpretation of Patti Waldmeir, *Anatomy of a Miracle* (New York: Viking, 1997); and Allister Sparks, *Tomorrow Is Another Country: The Inside Story of South Africa's Road to Change* (New York: Hill and Wang, 1995). See, in particular, Sparks' parable, "The Tale of the Trout Hook," which recounts the first meeting between the two adversaries.

7. Sparks, *Tomorrow Is Another Country*, 186.

8. Leon, a fifty-four-year-old Afrikaner family man, interview by author, Pretoria, February 2004.

9. Wilson, *The Politics of Truth and Reconciliation*, 153.

10. Heribert Adam and Kogila Moodley, "The Purchased Revolution in South Africa: Lessons for Democratic Transformation," *Nationalism and Ethnic Politics* 3, no. 4, 113–27.

11. Ibid., 120.

12. The alliance included the ANC, labor unions under the umbrella of the Congress of South African Trade Unions (COSATU), civic organizations, and the Communist Party. See Tom Lodge, *Politics in South Africa: From Mandela to Mbeki* (Cape Town: David Philip, 2002; Oxford: James Currey, 2003).

13. Cyril Ramaphosa, a member of the mining union and general secretary of the ANC, became a board member of the Anglo-American Corporation. Cf. Adam and Moodley, "The Purchased Revolution in South Africa," 115. Neville Alexander identifies several radicals who converted to economic conservatism and political racketeering: Cyril Ramaphosa and Tokyo Sexwale became very rich. See Neville Alexander, *An Ordinary Country: Issues in the Transition from Apartheid to Democracy in South Africa* (New York and Oxford: Berghahn Books, 2003).

14. Benjamin Roberts, "'Empty Stomachs, Empty Pockets': Poverty and Inequality in Post-Apartheid South Africa," in John Daniel, Roger Southall, and Jessica Lutchman, eds., *State of the Nation: South Africa 2007* (Cape Town: HSRC Press, 2007).

15. The IFP was a political party that fought to defend Zulu identity. The apartheid regime, with which it had cooperated, used its supporters against ANC militants. Violence between the two organizations was particularly intense during the period of democratic transition.

16. Mandela attempted up till the last moment to convince him to participate in the 27 April 1994 vote, which Viljoen and Buthelezi agreed to do in extremis.

17. Sparks, *Tomorrow Is Another Country*, 182.

18. Adam and Moodley, "The Purchased Revolution in South Africa," 116–18.

19. Brian Frost, *Struggling to Forgive* (New York: Harper Collins Publishers, 1998), 10. The author repeats a quotation that appeared in the 25 November 1995 edition of the *Saturday Star*.

20. Michael H. Allen, *Globalization, Negotiation, and the Failure of Transformation in South Africa: Revolution at a Bargain?* (New York: Palgrave Macmillan, 2006), chap. 5.

21. Nelson Mandela, *Long Walk to Freedom: The Autobiography of Nelson Mandela* (Boston: Little Brown, 1994), 617.

22. Waldmeir, *Anatomy of a Miracle*, 67 and 74.

23. Lodge, *Politics in South Africa*, 126.

24. Tom Lodge, *Mandela* (Oxford: Oxford University Press, 2006), 212.

25. Mandela, *Long Walk to Freedom*, 449 and 450.

26. Frost, *Struggling to Forgive*, 12.

27. Afrikaans word meaning "people's state," with the people understood to consist of the Afrikaner community.

28. Allister Sparks, *Beyond the Miracle* (Johannesburg and Cape Town: Jonathan Ball Publishers, 2003), 131.

29. Mandela, *Long Walk to Freedom*, 559.

30. Waldmeir, *Anatomy of a Miracle*, 78.

31. Lodge, *Politics in South Africa*, 6.

32. Waldmeir, *Anatomy of a Miracle*, 68.

33. Sparks, *Tomorrow Is Another Country*, 229.

34. Heribert Adam, Fredererik Van Zyl Slabbert, and Kogila Moodley, *Comrades in Business* (Cape Town: Tafelberg, 1997), 123–24.

35. Fauvelle-Aymar, *Histoire de l'Afrique du Sud*.

36. Waldmeir, *Anatomy of a Miracle*, 275.

37. Lodge, *Politics in South Africa*, 13.

38. Ibid. Neville Alexander denounced the former supporters of apartheid who had abruptly converted to multiracial democracy. See Alexander, *An Ordinary Country*, 64.

39. According to Nader Carrim, the fact that race was passed over in silence was motivated by fear of losing the privileges of the past, continuing to be racist, or suffering racist discrimination. See Nader Carrim, "Critical Anti-Racism and Problems in Self-Articulated Forms of Identity," *Race, Ethnicity, and Education* 1 (2000): 25–44.

40. James Gregory, *Goodbye Bafana* (Paris: Robert Laffont, 2007).

41. Anthony Sampson, *Mandela: The Authorized Biography* (New York: Alfred A. Knopf, 1999), 522.

42. Roger Southall, "Black Empowerment and Present Limits to a More Democratic Capitalism in South Africa," in Daniel, Southall, and Lutchman, *State of the Nation*, 185.

43. Ibid., 177 and 170.

44. Michael Brookes and Timothy Hinks, "Le fossé 'racial': L'accès à l'emploi dans la nouvelle Afrique du sud," in Philippe Guillaume, Nicolas Péjout, and Aurelia Wa Kabwe-Segatti, eds., *L'Afrique du Sud dix ans après: Transition accomplie?* (Paris: Karthala; Johannesburg: IFAS Karthala, 2004), 59–61.

45. Percy Moleke, "The State of Labour Market Deracialization," in Daniel, Southall, and Lutchman, *State of the Nation*, 210.

46. Described by Sparks in *Beyond the Miracle*, chap. 6.

47. Cf. Adrian Guelke, *South Africa in Transition: The Misunderstood Miracle* (London: I.B. Tauris, 1999), 177; or consult the website www.anc.org.za.

48. Colin Bundy, "New Nation, New History? Constructing the Past in Post-Apartheid South Africa," in Hans Erik Stolten, ed., *History Making and Present-Day Politics: The Meaning of Collective Memory in South Africa* (Uppsala: Nordiska Afrikainstitutet, 2007), 80–81.

49. Thomas Blaser, "A New South African Imaginary: Nation-Building and Afrikaners in Post-Apartheid South Africa," *South African Historical Journal* 51 (2004): 179–98.

50. Ibid.

51. Heribert Adam and Kogila Moodley, "Race and Nation in South Africa," *Current Sociology* 48, no. 3 (July 2000): 51–69.

52. Ernest Renan, *Qu'est-ce qu'une nation?* (Paris: Mille et une nuits, 2004).

53. Ibid., 44.

54. Lodge, *Mandela*, 212.

55. Albert Grundlingh, "Reframing Remembrance: The Politics of the Centenary Commemoration of the South Africa War of 1899–1902," in Stolten, *History Making and Present-Day Politics*, 202.

56. Hans Erik Stolten, "History in the New South Africa: An Introduction," in Stolten, *History Making and Present-Day Politics*, 33.

57. Christophe Saunders, "The Transformation of Heritage in the New South Africa," in Stolten, *History Making and Present-Day Politics*, 190.

58. The text also mentions genocide, slavery, and the wars of resistance. For a description of the park, see the website www.freedom.org.za.

59. Annie E. Coombes, *Visual Culture and Public Memory in Democratic South Africa: History After Apartheid* (Durham, NC: Duke University Press, 2003), 36–37. The author refers to Andrew Unsworth, "Tokyo's Groot Trek," *Sunday Times*, 15 December 1996.

60. Martin Meredith, *Nelson Mandela* (London: Hamish Hamilton, 1997), 495.

61. Sampson, *Nelson Mandela*, 516.

62. Chris Hani, an ANC and Communist Party member who became chief of the general staff of the armed wing in 1987, was among those who still supported an insurrectional strategy. Moreover, twenty-four prisoners on Robben Island refused their release on the grounds that they did not wish to leave the island before a military victory had been achieved. Cf. Lodge, *Mandela*, 171.

63. Sparks, *Tomorrow Is Another Country*, 122–24.

64. Dale McKinley, *The ANC and the Liberation Struggle* (London: Pluto Press, 1997), 53; Alexander, *An Ordinary Country*, 47; and Hein Marais, *South Africa* (Rondebosch: UCT Press; London: Pluto Press, 1998), 74.

65. McKinley, *The ANC and the Liberation Struggle*, 50.

66. Stephen Ellis and Tsepo Sechaba, *Comrades Against Apartheid* (Bloomington: Indiana University Press, 1992).

67. McKinley, *The ANC and the Liberation Struggle*, 54–55.

68. Ibid., 63 and 74.

69. However, the meager results of the ANC's guerrilla war are not an obstacle to the construction of a heroic narrative of resistance. If one compares it with the Palestinian struggle, neither the operations carried out against Israel by the PLO from bases in Jordan or Lebanon nor the first Intifada changed power relations among the protagonists. Yet the Palestinian narrative emphasizes these armed exploits and the resistance of the Palestinians.

70. He was assassinated on 10 April 1993 by members of the South African far right.

71. Originally from Lithuania, Joe Slovo was one of the leaders of Umkhonto we Sizwe and the Communist Party. He was among the theoreticians of the ANC and participated in negotiations with the apartheid leaders. He became minister of housing in 1994 and died of cancer one year later.

72. See, for example, Mandela's speech to the 9th Congress of the SACP on 6 April 1995 on the official website of the ANC: www.anc.org.za.

73. See also his 10 May 1995 speech at the ceremony marking the first anniversary of the first democratic presidential election, which can be consulted at the official ANC website.

74. McKinley, *The ANC and the Liberation Struggle*, 132–34.

Chapter 2

1. By placing European particularism on the same level as others, colonial discourse suggested that these groups had no more to do with one another than they did with the French minority. See Michel Camau, *La notion de démocratie dans la pensée des dirigeants maghrébins* (Paris: CNRS, 1971), 29.

2. Camau, *La notion de démocratie*, 55.

3. Ahmed Rouadjia, *Grandeur et décadence de l'État algérien* (Paris: Karthala, 1994), 85.

4. Mohamed Harbi, *L'Algérie et son destin* (Paris: Arcantère, 1992), 23 and 36.

5. Omar Carlier, "Violence(s)," in Mohamed Harbi and Benjamin Stora, eds., *La Guerre d'Algérie, 1954–1962* (Paris: Hachette Littératures, 2006), 525.

6. Ibid., 525–28.

7. Camau, *La notion de démocratie*, 99.

8. Raymon Vallin, "Muslim Socialism in Algeria," in William Zartman, *Man, State, and Society in Contemporary Maghreb* (New York: Pall Mall Press, 1973), 62; and Mustafa Al-Ahnaf, Bernard Botiveau, and Franck Frégosi, *L'Algérie par ses islamistes* (Paris: Karthala, 1991), 24–26.

9. Monique Gadant, *Islam et nationalisme en Algérie, d'après "El Moudjahid," organe central du FLN de 1956 à 1962* (Paris: L'Harmattan, 1988), 11.

10. Camau, *La notion de démocratie*, 99.

11. Gilbert Grandguillaume, "L'arabisation en Algérie des 'ulamâ' à nos jours," in *Colloque: Pour une histoire critique et citoyenne: Le cas de l'histoire franco-algérienne, Colloquium, 20–22 June 2006, Lyon* (ENS LSH, 2007), http://colloque-algerie.ens-lyon.fr/rubrique.php3?id_rubrique=67.

12. Gilbert Grandguillaume, "Comment a-t-on pu en arriver là?," *Esprit* 208 (January 1995): 18.

13. John Entelis, *Algeria: The Revolution Institutionalized* (Boulder, CO: Westview Press, 1986), 91.

14. Ibid., 93.

15. Grandguillaume, "L'arabisation en Algérie."

16. Harbi, *L'Algérie et son destin*, 114.

17. Lucile Provost, "L'économie de rente et ses avatars," *Esprit* 208 (January 1995): 83.

18. André Nouschi, *L'Algérie amère, 1914–1994* (Paris: Maison des sciences de l'homme, 1994), 246.

19. Ibid., 85.

20. Carlier, "Violence(s)," 528.

21. Camau, *La notion de démocratie*, 35.

22. Ibid., 36–37.

23. Jean Leca and Jean-Claude Vatin, *L'Algérie politique* (Paris: Presses de la FNSP, 1975), 275.

24. *Programme de Tripoli*, "Vue d'Ensemble de la situation Algérienne," II, quoted by Camau, *La notion de démocratie*, 38.

25. Camau, *La notion de démocratie*, 39.

26. In 1961, 1,050,000 Europeans lived in Algeria. In August 1962, only 340,000 of them remained. Cf. Benjamin Stora, *La gangrène et l'oubli* (Paris: La Découverte, 1998), 216.

27. Stora, *La gangrène et l'oubli*, 162–63.

28. Some members of the ANC who had been forced by the police to collaborate (the "askaris") were recognized as victims by the Truth and Reconciliation Commission (TRC). They could simultaneously request amnesty for the operations in which they participated and be designated as victims by the TRC.

29. A wilaya is an administrative division corresponding to a region during the War of Independence (plural: wilayat).

30. Interview for the *Années algériennes*, quoted by Stora, *La gangrène et l'oubli*, 200.

31. In the majority of cases, they were agricultural laborers and unskilled urban workers. At most a handful worked as office employees. David Ottaway and Marina Ottaway, *Algeria* (Berkeley: University of California Press, 1970), 29.

32. In this connection, Pervillé raises the question of the implications of this large-scale coexistence for the war's conduct: was it "a factor of spontaneous confrontation or, to the contrary, was it necessary to rely upon strategies of provocation to separate the two communities and unify each of them around terrorist groups?" See Guy Pervillé, "Le terrorisme urbain dans la guerre d'Algérie (1954–62)," in Jean-Charles Jauffret and Maurice Vaïsse, *Militaires et guérilla dans la guerre d'Algérie* (Brussels: Complexe, 2001).

33. Gilbert Meynier, "Le FLN/ALN dans les six wilaya: Étude comparée," in Jauffret and Vaïsse, *Militaires et guérilla*, 155–56.

34. A caid was an Algerian notable, sometimes a tribal chief, who had been officially recognized by the French administration and carried out administrative and judicial functions.

35. These figures are reported by Ottaway and Ottaway, *Algeria*, 29, and are drawn from those supplied by the Charter of Algiers, which itself relied on a French estimate that appeared in the Plan de Constantine (1958).

36. According to a UN report quoted by Stora, *La gangrène et l'oubli*, 163.

37. Harbi, *L'Algérie et son destin*, 24.

38. Charles Tilly, ed., *The Formation of National States in Western Europe* (Princeton, NJ: Princeton University Press, 1975).

39. Ottaway and Ottaway, *Algeria*, 32.

40. Harbi, *L'Algérie et son destin*, 166.

41. Ibid., 154.

42. Ibid., 54. See also Camau, *La notion de la démocratie*, 58.

43. Harbi, *L'Algérie et son destin*, 54. See also Camau, *La notion de démocratie*, 58.

44. Gadant, *Islam et nationalisme en Algérie*, 10.

45. Jean Leca and Jean-Claude Vatin, "Le système politique algérien (1967–1978): Idéologie, institutions et changement social," *Annuaire de l'Afrique du Nord* 16 (1977): 19.

46. Jean Leca, "Paradoxes de la démocratisation: L'Algérie au chevet de la science politique," *Pouvoirs* 86 (1998): 20.

47. Ottaway and Ottaway, *Algeria*, 49. See also Jean Leca, "État et société en Algérie," in Basma Kodmani-Darwish, *Les années de transition* (Paris: Masson, 1990), 18.

48. Ottaway and Ottaway, *Algeria*, 33–34. See also Nouschi, *L'Algérie amère*, 242 and 265–66. According to Nouschi, it was city-dwellers who most profited from Boumediene's economic policy, with their incomes growing in an independent Algeria that continued to be characterized by rural stagnation.

49. William Quandt, *Revolution and Political Leadership: Algeria, 1954–1968* (Cambridge, MA: MIT Press, 1969), 275 and 268.

50. Ibid., 47.

51. In Algeria, this term refers to someone who lays bombs. Interview by author, Algiers, September 2006.

52. Gilles Kepel, *Jihad* (Paris: Gallimard, 2000), 176.

53. Charles-André Julien, *Histoire de l'Algérie contemporaine*, vol. 2, *De l'insurrection de 1871 au déclenchement de la guerre de libération* (1954) (Paris: PUF, 1979).

54. Carlier, "Violence(s)," 514.

55. Ibid.

56. Despite postwar efforts to improve literacy among Arabo-Berber populations, at independence 80 percent of the population was illiterate. See Monique Gadant, "Violence(s)," in Harbi and Stora, *La Guerre d'Algérie*, 44.

57. See Gilles Manceron and Hassan Remaoun, *D'une rive à l'autre* (Paris: Syros, 1993), chap. 5.

58. On this theme, see Chapter 10 in this book.

59. Carlier, "Violence(s)," 523. See also Nicolas Bancel, Pascal Blanchard, and Françoise Vergès, *La République coloniale* (Paris: Albin Michel, 2003).

60. The Front Populaire is a coalition of left parties which governed France between May 1936 and April 1938 and raised many progressive hopes.

61. Beginning in 1947, French Algeria featured an Algerian Assembly elected by two electoral colleges on the basis of universal suffrage. The first college consisted of French citizens, while the second was reserved for "French Muslims."

62. Carlier, "Violence(s)," 514–15. On the question of French deafness to the demands of Algerian society, see also Manceron and Remaoun, *D'une rive à l'autre*, 118–20.

63. On this point, see Stora, *La gangrène et l'oubli*, 156.

64. Pervillé, "Le terrorisme urbain," 452–53.

65. Ibid.

66. René Gallissot, "La guerre d'Algérie: La fin des secrets et le secret d'une guerre doublement nationale," *Le Mouvement Social* 138 (January–March 1987): 102 and 104.

67. Carlier, "Violence(s)," 507.

68. Harbi, *L'Algérie et son destin*, 100 and 106.

69. Described by Daho Djerbal in "*Mounadiline* et *mousebbiline*: Les forces auxiliaires de l'ALN du Nord-Constantinois," in Jean-Charles Jauffret, *Des hommes et des femmes en guerre d'Algérie* (Paris: Autrement, 2003), 290–91; and by Pervillé, "Le terrorisme urbain," 451–54.

70. Algerian notables who signed an appeal condemning "all violence whatever its source" were victims of an attack. See Pervillé, "Le terrorisme urbain," 452–63.

71. Stora, *La gangrène et l'oubli*, 145 and 167.

72. Three hundred villagers were massacred in Beni Ilman in May 1957 (an event known as the Melouza massacre); others were killed in Aïn Manaa, Wagram, and Honaïm in 1958. See Meynier, "Le FLN/ALN dans les six wilaya," 166. See also Stora, *La gangrène et l'oubli*, 166.

73. Jacques Valette, "Militants et combattants messalistes: 1954–1962," in Jauffret, *Des hommes et des femmes en guerre d'Algérie*, 320–41; and Stora, *La gangrène et l'oubli*, 142–44.

74. Carlier, "Violence(s)," 511.

75. Guy Pervillé, "La guerre d'Algérie: Combien de morts?," in Harbi and Stora, *La Guerre d'Algérie*, 706–8.

76. Harbi, *L'Algérie et son destin*, 165–66.

77. Ibid., 166.

78. Mohamed Harbi writes that "the historiography of the FLN blithely combines all forces of opposition under the term 'counter-revolution,'" in *L'Algérie et son destin*, 153.

79. To borrow Mohamed Harbi's expression; see *L'Algérie et son destin*, 155.

80. Azzedine, a seventy-five-year-old husband and father, had run a textile factory with his brothers and is now retired. Interview by author, Algiers region, September 2006.

81. Luis Martinez, *La guerre civile en Algérie* (Paris: Karthala, 1998), 26–32.

82. Democratic People's Republic of Algeria, *Projet de Charte pour la Paix et la Réconciliation Nationale*, August 2005, 10.

83. Ibid., 14.

84. I.e., kidnapped by the police. According to human rights organizations, nearly 18,000 people "disappeared" in this fashion.

85. "Is punished with three (3) to five (5) years imprisonment and a fine of between 250,000 DA and 500,000 DA anyone who, by his statements, writings or any other act, uses or exploits the wounds of the national tragedy to harm the institutions of the People's Democratic Republic of Algeria, weaken the state, cast aspersions on the honorability of its agents who served it with dignity or tarnish the image of Algeria on the international scene. Legal proceedings are compulsorily engaged by the public ministry." Article 46 of the edict promulgated on 27 February 2006.

86. Stora, *La gangrene et l'oubli*, 151, 149, and 150.

87. In July 1999, however, Abdelaziz Bouteflika rehabilitated the founding fathers of Algerian nationalism, Messali Hadj and Ferhat Abbas. See Benjamin Stora, "1999–2003: Guerre d'Algérie, les accélérations de la mémoire," in Harbi and Stora, *La Guerre d'Algérie*, 737.

88. Stora, "1999–2003," 229 and 230.

89. Benjamin Stora, "Algérie, absence et surabondance de mémoire," *Esprit* 208 (January 1995), 65.

90. Manceron and Remaoun, *D'une rive à l'autre*, 55–58.

91. Rouadjia, *Grandeur et décadence de l'État algérien*, 41.

92. Ibid., 36–37.

93. Lydia Aït Saadi, "Le passé franco-algérien dans les manuels scolaires d'histoire algériens," in *Colloque: Pour une histoire critique et citoyenne*.

94. Leca and Vatin, *L'Algérie politique*, 262–63.

95. Laetitia Bucaille, "La socialisation politique des jeunes en Algérie depuis octobre 1988" (master's thesis, Institut d'Études Politiques, 1990), 42.

96. Kamel, twenty-five years old, interview by author, Algiers, July 1990. Following independence, Kamel's Kabyle parents had moved from the countryside to a small commune neighboring Algiers. His father was a mujahid.

97. Toufiq, twenty-eight years old, interview by author, Algiers region, July 1990.

98. Selma Belaala, "Représentations de la violence politique chez les jeunes des quartiers populaires d'Alger" (DEA in political studies (Jean Leca, dir.), Institut d'Études Politiques, 1998), 50.

99. Jean Leca, "L'Algérie au chevet de la science politique," *Pouvoirs* 86 (1998): 18, in reference to the text by Fanny Colonna, "Radiographie d'une société en mouvement," *Monde Arabe Maghreb-Machreck* 154 (October–December 1996): 7.

100. Martinez, *La guerre civile en Algérie*, 292–300.

101. Kepel, *Jihad*, 177.

102. "L'armée (Extrait du programme officiel du FIS)," in Al-Ahnaf, Botiveau, and Frégosi, *L'Algérie par ses islamistes*, 121.

Chapter 3

1. Todd Shepard, *The Invention of Decolonization: The Algerian War and the Remaking of France* (Ithaca, NY: Cornell University Press, 2006), 1.

2. Frank Renken, "La guerre d'Algérie et la vie politique française (1954–2006)," *Colloque: Pour une histoire critique et citoyenne; Le cas de l'histoire franco-algérienne, 20–22 June 2006, Lyon* (ENS LSH, 2007), http://colloque-algerie.ens-lyon.fr/rubrique.php3?id_rubrique=67.

3. All figures cited here are presented and discussed by Guy Pervillé, "La guerre d'Algérie: Combien de morts?," in Mohamed Harbi and Benjamin Stora, eds., *La Guerre d'Algérie, 1954–1962* (Paris: Hachette Littératures, 2006), 693–716, with the exception of those for OAS deaths, which are supplied by Arnaud Déroulède, *OAS: Étude d'une organisation clandestine* (Hélette: Editions Jean Curutchet, 1997), 306.

4. Shepard, *The Invention of Decolonization*, 82.

5. Renken, "La guerre d'Algérie et la vie politique française."

6. Jean-Paul Sartre, "Les somnambules," in *Les temps modernes*, 1399, quoted by Shepard, *The Invention of Decolonization*, 194.

7. The term *barbouzes* was used to refer to the intelligence service agents sent to Algeria in 1961 to eliminate the OAS.

8. Estimates vary, ranging from 50 to 246 dead. See Jim House and Neil MacMaster, *Paris 1961: Les Algériens, la terreur d'État et la mémoire* (Paris: Tallandier, 2008).

9. According to Yves Courrière, *La Guerre d'Algérie* (Paris: Robert Laffont, 1990), 1062. On the various interpretations of the demonstration and repression, see Olivier Dard, *Voyage au coeur de l'OAS* (Paris: Perrin, 2005), 219–24.

10. Jean-Yves Sabot, *Le syndicalisme étudiant et la Guerre d'Algérie* (Paris: L'Harmattan, 1995).

11. Benjamin Stora, *La Gangrène et l'Oubli* (Paris: La Découverte, 1991), 110. See also Martin Evans, *The Memory of Resistance: French Opposition to the Algerian War (1954–1962)* (Oxford and New York: Berg, 1997).

12. Catherine Coquery-Vidrovitch and Charles-Robert Ageron, *Histoire de la France coloniale*, vol. 3, *Le déclin* (Paris: Armand Colin, 1991), 424–33.

13. Benjamin Stora, *La gangrène et l'oubli* (Paris: La Découverte, 1998), 83.

14. Shepard, *The Invention of Decolonization*, 11.

15. Ibid.; see Chapter 2, "Inventing Decolonization."

16. Stora, *La gangrène et l'oubli*, 19.

17. "L'Empire," in Vincent Duclert and Christophe Prochasson, *Dictionnaire critique de la République* (Paris: Flammarion, 2002), 481.

18. Nicolas Bancel, Pascal Blanchard, and Françoise Vergès, *La République coloniale* (Paris: Albin Michel, 2003), 11, 13, and 44.

19. Ibid., 43, 63, and 14.

20. Ibid., 33 and 46.

21. Pierre Bouretz, *La République et l'universel* (Paris: Gallimard, 2000), 17.

22. Bancel, Blanchard, and Vergès, *La République coloniale*, 69 and 31.

23. Shepard, *The Invention of Decolonization*, 70, 75–76, and 78.

24. Éric Savarèse, *Algérie, la guerre des mémoires* (Paris: Non-lieu, 2007).

25. Born in 1939 and formerly a member of the Socialist Party, Jean-Pierre Chevènement has on several occasions served as minister. In 1992, he left the Socialist Party and created the Mouvement des Citoyens (Citizens' Movement). It championed "sovereignist" positions, argued for strict secularism, and held that immigrants must assimilate.

26. Jean-Pierre Chevènement, in an article for *Le Nouvel Observateur*, quoted by Bancel, Blanchard, and Vergès, *La République coloniale*, 35.

27. Renken, "La guerre d'Algérie et la vie politique française."

28. Guy Pervillé, "L'Algérie des droites," in Jean-François Sirinelli, ed., *Les Droites en France*, vol. 2, Cultures (Paris: Gallimard, 1992), 625.

29. Renken, "La guerre d'Algérie et la vie politique française."

30. Éric Duhamel, "François Mitterand en guerre d'Algérie: Enjeu de pouvoir, enjeu de mémoire," in Serge Wolikow, ed., *Traces de la guerre d'Algérie* (Dijon: Éditions de l'Université de Dijon, 1995), 47.

31. An expression emphasizing the huge gap that existed between the discourse of the left and nationalist activity on the ground.

32. Shepard, *The Invention of Decolonization*, 193, 194–96.

33. Stora, *La grangrène et l'oubli*, 115 and 112.

34. Jean-François Sirinelli, *Les vingt décisives, 1965–1985: Le passé proche de notre avenir* (Paris: Fayard, 2007), 21, 29, and 31.

35. Henri Mendras, *La fin des paysans: Changement et innovation dans les sociétés rurales françaises* (Paris: Armand Colin, 1970) and *La seconde Révolution française: 1965–1984* (Paris: Gallimard, 1994).

36. Sirinelli, *Les vingt décisives*, 46 and 47.

37. Kristin Ross, *Fast Cars, Clean Bodies: Decolonization and the Reordering of French Culture* (Cambridge, MA: MIT Press, 1995), 5, 7, 11, 78, 150–51.

38. Stéphane Gacon, *L'Amnistie* (Paris: Seuil, 2002), 256–57.

39. Stora, *La grangrène et l'oubli*, 283.

40. Gacon, *L'Amnistie*, 259–62.

41. Henri Rousso distinguishes between four memorial sequences: mourning, repression, the return of the repressed, and obsession; Henri Rousso, *Le syndrome de Vichy* (Paris: Seuil, 1987).

42. A term referring to the French activists, many of whom moved in Francis Jeanson's circle, who decided to help the FLN during the war, mainly by raising money and supplying FLN members with forged papers.

43. Gacon, *L'Amnistie*, 285–86.

44. In the words of Deputy Louis Andrieux, session of 23 July 1920, *Journal Officiel*, 23 July 1920, 3042; quoted by Gacon, *L'Amnistie*, 355.

45. Gacon, *L'Amnistie*, 272–80.

46. In his book, General Challe wrote: "Besides, we did not want to be forgiven. We were the ones who had to do the forgiving." Maurice Challe, *Notre révolte* (Paris: Presses de la Cité, 1968), 304. In the 4 October 1982 number of the *Quotidien de Paris*, Hélie Denoix de Saint-Marc explained that he did not need to be forgiven or rehabilitated; quoted by Gacon, *L'Amnistie*, 275 and 314.

47. According to the term used by the PCF. See Gacon, *L'Amnistie*, 281.

48. Stéphane Gacon, "Histoire d'une amnistie, l'amnistie de la guerre d'Algérie," in Wolikow, *Traces de la guerre d'Algérie*, 22–23.

49. Gacon, *L'Amnistie*, 301.

50. Pervillé, "L'Algérie dans la mémoire des droites," 649.

51. Gacon, "Histoire d'une amnistie," 29.

52. Gacon, *L'Amnistie*, 273.

53. See François Mitterand, *Le coup d'état permanent* (Paris: Plon, 1964).

54. Renken, "La guerre d'Algérie et la vie politique française."

55. Duhamel, "François Mitterand en guerre d'Algérie," 57–58.

56. Stéphane Gacon writes: "These two laws exceeded the traditional framework of amnesty"; *L'Amnistie*, 297.

57. In other words, for six years spent on the run, an ex-activist can request to receive 30,656 euros. Some associations today require that the same principle be applied to those who received prison sentences in France.

58. Article 4 of the law held that "university research programs accord the place it deserves to the French presence overseas, particularly in North Africa. School programs, in particular, are to recognize the positive role played by France overseas, particularly in North Africa, and grant the eminent place that is their right to the history and sacrifices of French Army combatants from these territories."

59. This generational shift did not guarantee greater distance among the protagonists. Young academics and journalists inherited a "family history" relating to the Algerian War. This perhaps partly explains their interest in the Algerian War and French Algeria as objects of investigation. In this connection, the intergenerational transmission of Algerian War engagements remains to be studied.

60. Benjamin Stora, "1999–2003: Guerre d'Algérie, les accélérations de la mémoire," in Harbi and Stora, eds., *La Guerre d'Algérie*, 733, 735.

61. Savarèse, *Algérie*, 43.

62. Renken, "La guerre d'Algérie et la vie politique française"; Claude Liauzu, "Entre histoire nostalgique de la colonisation et posture anticolonialiste: Quelle critique historique de la colonisation?," in *Colloque: Pour une histoire critique et citoyenne*.

63. Gacon, *L'Amnistie*, 316–17.

64. The "Call of the Twelve," published by *L'Humanité* on 31 October 2000. The signatories of this petition included a number of men and women who had campaigned against torture during the Algerian War (Henri Alleg, Germaine Tillion, Pierre Vidal-Naquet, and Madeleine Rébérioux). It nevertheless called for discussion of the myths of republican identity and colonialism. On this subject, see also Neil Macmaster, "The Torture Controversy (1998–2002): Toward a 'New History' of the Algerian War?," *Modern & Contemporary France* 10, no. 4 (2002): 449–59.

65. E.g., Patrick Rotman, dir., *L'ennemi intime*, 2002.

66. Raphaëlle Branche, *La Guerre d'Algérie* (Paris: Seuil, 2005), 102–8.

67. Ibid., 56–57.

68. Law 94-488, 11 June 1998.

69. Emmanuel Brillet, "Scène juidiciaire et mobilisation politique: Les actions en justice des représentants de la communauté harkie," *Pôle Sud* 24 (January 2006): 45–58.

70. Note should also be taken of Jean-Luc Einaudi's book, *Octobre 1961: Un massacre à Paris* (Paris: Fayard, 2001).

71. Born in 1975, Jamel Debbouze is a widely popular French actor and comedian of Moroccan origin.

72. Macmaster, "The Torture Controversy (1998–2002)," 449–59.

73. Bancel, Blanchard, and Vergès, *La République coloniale*, 19.

74. Branche, *La Guerre d'Algérie*, 60–67.

75. Ibid.

76. This is the question raised by Valérie Rosoux, "Le travail de mémoire dans les relations franco-algériennes: Limites des retrouvailles," in Ohla Ostriitchouk, ed., *Mémoires de conflits, mémoires en conflits: Affrontements identitaires, tensions politiques et luttes symboliques autour du passé* (Brussels: Peter Lang, 2016), 209–26.

77. Branche, *La Guerre d'Algérie*, 96 and 109.

78. Ibid.

79. In Éric Savarèse's fine expression; Savarèse, *Algérie*, 69.

80. The work of Louis Crocq, an expert in the area of traumatic neurosis, laid the groundwork for the adoption of a 1992 decree recognizing the war neuroses from which Algerian War veterans suffered; Louis Crocq, *Les traumatismes psychiques de guerre* (Paris: Odile Jacob, 1999). See Branche, *La Guerre d'Algérie*, 102.

81. Sirinelli, *Les vingt décisives*, 266–71.

82. On the far right's time in the desert and subsequent reconstruction, see Pascal Perrineau, *Le symptôme Le Pen* (Paris: Faryard, 1997), 15–31.

83. Pervillé, "L'Algérie dans la mémoire des droites," 642–45.

84. Joseph Algazy, *L'extrême-droite en France (1965 à 1984)* (Paris: L'Harmattan, 1989), 262.

85. On the pied-noir vote, see Emmanuelle Comtat, "La question du vote Pied-Noir," *Pôle Sud* 24, no. 1 (2006): 75–88.

86. Benjamin Stora, *Le transfert d'une mémoire* (Paris: La Découverte, 1999), 53–68.

87. Pervillé, *L'Algérie dans la mémoire des droites*," 650.

88. Ibid., 96–88 and 288. See also Éric Savarèse, who seeks to "disentangle the complex ties that unite North African immigration and colonial history." By holding that history plays out as collective unconscious, he analyzes stereotypes regarding North Africans, examining and comparing the perceptions of indigenous populations during the colonial period with those of immigrants today. Éric Savarèse, *Histoire coloniale et immigration: Une invention de l'étranger* (Paris: Séguier, 2000).

89. As Guy Pervillé notes, the positions are here reversed: for the FN, integration is impossible, whereas the OAS promoted an assimilationist approach to French Algeria. See Pervillé, "L'Algérie dans la mémoire des droites," 652.

90. Dard, *Voyage au coeur de l'OAS*, 314–22.

91. Romain Bertrand, *Mémoires d'empire* (Paris: Éditions du Croquant, 2006), 68–75.

92. Gilles Manceon, *Marianne et les colonies, Une introduction à l'histoire coloniale de la France* (Paris: La Découverte, 2003), 20.

93. Yann Scioldo-Zürcher mentions Kleber Mesquida. See Yann Scioldo-Zürcher, "Existe-t-il une vision pied-noir des rapports franco-algériens?," *Colloque: Pour une histoire critique et citoyenne.*

94. Quoted by Yann Scioldo-Zürcher, in "Existe-t-il une vision pied-noir des rapports franco-algériens?," who refers to the JORF, "Débats parlementaires," National Assembly, session of 7 July 1987, 3720.

95. JORF, "Débats parlementaires," 4839 and following.

96. For a discussion of the position adopted by the Indigènes de la République, see Savarèse, *La guerre des mémoires*, chap. 1; and Bertrand, *Mémoires d'empire*, 147–66.

97. Nicolas Sarkozy, *Journal du Dimanche*, 11 December 2005.

98. "Mémoire et histoire, examen critique ou repentance: Le débat fait désormais rage," *Le Monde*, 13 December 2005, 4; quoted by Bertrand, *Mémoires d'empire*, 135–36.

99. I borrow this distinction between the various types of conflict from Sandrine Lefranc, who discusses it in "Les politiques du pardon: La continuation du conflit par d'autres moyens," in Elise Féron and Pierre Hastings, eds., *L'imaginaire des conflits communautaires* (Paris: L'Harmattan, 2002), 265.

100. See also the typology developed by Valérie-Barbara Rosoux, who speaks of "memory work," "over-emphasis on the past," and the "obliteration of the past" in regard to South Africa, Algeria, and France in *Les usages de la mémoire dans les relations internationales* (Brussels: Bruylant, 2001).

101. In December 1970, Willy Brandt, chancellor of the German Federal Republic, kneeled before the monument to the Warsaw ghetto; speaking before the Knesset, Polish president Lech Walesa presented his excuses on behalf of his fellow citizens for the wrongs they committed against Jews during the Second World War. In July 1995, French president Jacques Chirac recognized the responsibility of the French state in deporting Jews. On behalf of the Catholic Church, Pope John Paul II apologized to Jews and American Indians, among others. On this question, see Philippe Moreau-Desfarges, *Repentance et réconciliation* (Paris: Presses de FNSP, 1999).

Part II

1. Bruno Cabanes, "Les vivants et les morts: La France au sortir de la grande guerre," in Stéphane Audoin-Rouzeau and Christophe Prochasson, eds., *Sortir de la grande guerre Le monde et l'après-1918* (Paris: Tallandier, 2008), 28.

2. Ibid., 28–29.

3. Antoine Prost, *Les anciens combattants, 1914–1939* (Paris: Gallimard, 1977), 159.

4. A notion first developed by Bruno Cabanes, *La victoire endeuillée: La sortie de guerre des soldats français (1918–1920)* (Paris: Seuil, 2004).

5. My approach resembles that adopted by Norma Kriger, *Veterans in Zimbabwe: Symbolic and Violent Politics, 1980–1987* (New York: Cambridge University Press, 2003).

Chapter 4

1. In August 1990, Nelson Mandela's political grouping halted the armed struggle. Profiting from the policy of amnesty, the first combatants returned from exile a year later.

2. Janet Cherry, John Daniel, and Madeleine Fullard, "Researching the 'Truth': A View from Inside the Truth and Reconciliation Commission," in Deborah Posel and Graeme Simpson, eds., *Commissioning the Past: Understanding South Africa's Truth and Reconciliation Commission* (Johannesburg: Witwatersrand University Press, 2002).

3. Ian Liebenberg, "The Integration of the Military in Post-Liberation South Africa: The Contributions of Revolutionary Armies," *Armed Forces and Society* 24, no. 1 (1997): 108. See also Jaclyn Cock and Laurie Nathan, eds., *War and Society: The Militarization of South Africa* (Cape Town: David Philip, 1989); Philip Frankel, *Pretoria's Praetorians: Civil-Military Relations in South Africa* (Cambridge: Cambridge University Press, 1984); Noel Stott, *From the SADF to the SANDF: Safeguarding South Africa for a Better Life for All?* Centre for the Study of Violence and Reconciliation, Violence and Transition Series, vol. 7 (2002), 13–15; http://www.csvr.org.za/papers/papvtp7.htm.

4. Stott, *From the SADF to the SANDF*, 33.

5. These were the Transkei, Bophuthatswana, Venda, and Ciskei Defense Forces (TBVC).

6. *Demobilization and Its Aftermath II*, ISS Monograph Series, no. 61 (August 2001), 43. See also Lephophotho Mashike and Mafole Mokalobe, *Reintegration into Civilian Life: The Case of Former MK and APLA Combatants*, Center for Conflict Resolution, vol. 12, no. 1, (September 2003), 11.

7. Ian Liebenberg, "The Integration of the Military in Post-Liberation South Africa, 117–18.

8. British Military Advisory and Training Team (BMATT).

9. Department of Defense, *Final Integration Report* (2003), 3.

10. Frankel, *Pretoria's Praetorians*, 25 and 48.

11. Fifteen hundred new infections are said to take place each day, with South Africa numbering 5 million infected individuals. Cf. Stott, *From the SADF to the SANDF*, 55.

12. While 18 percent of blacks say they do not trust the army, 62 percent do. By contrast, only 27 percent of whites trust the army, while 41 percent do not. Cf. Stott, *From the SADF to the SANDF*, 62.

13. Lephophotho Mashike, "'Some of Us Know Nothing Except Military Skills': South Africa's Former Guerrilla Combatants," in Sakhela Buhlungu, John Daniel, Roger Southall, and Jessica Lutchman, eds., *State of the Nation: South Africa* (Cape Town: HSRC Press, 2007), 13.

14. Interview by author, Soweto, February 2004.

15. Stott, *From the SADF to the SANDF*, 30.

16. Gregory, thirty-six years old, an unemployed father of two who is separated from his wife. Interview by author, Soweto, February 2004.

17. Frankel, *Pretoria's Praetorians*, 92–94; *Demobilization and Its Aftermath II*, 47.

18. A thirty-seven-year-old resident of Soweto, Ronald joined the ANC when he was still a high school student. In 1986, he traveled to Angola to join the MK. On his return to South Africa in 1993, he had to fight to be included on the list of MK eligible for integration into the army and obtain an "honorable" rank. He is taking evening courses to complete his last year of high school. Interview by author, Soweto, March 2004.

19. Frankel, *Pretoria's Praetorians*, 94–95.

20. Department of Defense, *Final Integration Report* (2003), 3.

21. Interview by author, Pretoria, March 2005.

22. Interview by author, Pretoria, February 2004.

23. *Demobilization and Its Aftermath I*, 68.

24. Mashike, "Some of Us Know Nothing Except Military Skills," 15.

25. *Demobilization and Its Aftermath II*, 54.

26. Condemned to long sentences, activists who met in prison often took advantage of these years to study. By contrast, those who remained for long periods in Angolan training camps returned without diplomas. The ANC is said to have offered members who joined it in exile—particularly the youngest among them—the choice of pursuing their studies or undergoing military training. Many, it seems, preferred to "make war," but the offer was not systematically extended.

27. This was, for example, the case of Tokyo Sexwale. After a period as governor of Gauteng province, he left politics and became an extremely wealthy businessman. The new president, Jacob Zuma, nevertheless recalled him to government in 2009.

28. Interview by author, Johannesburg, February 2005.

29. A hip and rather mixed neighborhood in Johannesburg.

30. Mashike and Mokalobe, *Reintegration into Civilian Life*, 17. Estimates of the unemployment rate in South Africa range from 29 percent to 36 percent.

31. Liebenberg, "The Integration of the Military in Post-Liberation South Africa," 304–5.

32. Mxolise, an impoverished thirty-seven-year-old former MK, recounts: "When I returned, my parents asked me, 'What do you bring?' They didn't have any money to pay for me and they didn't understand. They told me, 'Sort it out yourself!'" Interview by author, Johannesburg, February 2004.

33. Mashike, "Some of Us Know Nothing Except Military Skills," 20.

34. Heribert Adam and Kogila Moodley, "The Purchased Revolution in South Africa: Lessons for Democratic Transformation," *Nationalism and Ethnic Politics* 3, no. 4 (1997): 114.

35. I here discuss the trajectory of two police officers, but former soldiers also fall under the category of "new democrats," including General Leon, who was discussed above (Chapter 1), and Colonel Bernard (this chapter). Interview by author, Pretoria, February 2006.

36. The rank of brigadier is located between that of colonel and that of major general. In the NATO system of equivalent ranks, it was considered the first rank of general officer.

37. Interview by author, Pretoria, March 2004 and March 2005.

38. Colonel Eugene de Kock was head of the Vlakplaas unit. Nicknamed "Prime Evil" by the media, he was prevented from receiving amnesty by the scale of his crimes and in 1996 he was sentenced to 212 years in prison for the murder of eighty-seven opponents of apartheid. In 2015, he was released on parole in 2015 for the sake of "national reconciliation."

39. Nicolas, a forty-five-year-old Afrikaner family man and financial analyst. Interview by author, Cape Town, March 2004.

40. A diminutive referring to one of these units' central missions: reconnaissance. The first commando unit (1 Recce) was formed in 1972. The Special Forces conducted attacks and support actions in Angola, Mozambique, and Namibia.

41. The reconnaissance units recruited many black Africans in order to go unnoticed in their fields of intervention.

Chapter 5

1. Mujahid (pl. mujahideen): an Arab term that is in this context equivalent to "combatant."

2. A word formed in reference to the signing of the Evian Accords on 19 March 1962. The same month, the "Marsiens" joined the FLN's struggle.

3. William Zartman, "L'armée dans la politique algérienne," in *Annuaire de l'Afrique du Nord* 6 (1967): 269; and Jean Leca and Jean-Claude Vatin, *L'Algérie politique* (Paris: Presses de la FNSP, 1975), 382.

4. Leca and Vatin, *L'Algérie politique*, 383.

5. Ibid., 386.

6. David Ottaway and Marina Ottaway, *Algeria* (Berkeley: University of California Press, 1970), 181.

7. Leca and Vatin, *L'Algérie politique*, 386 and 389. Boumediene promoted young technicians as tank unit commanders in place of mujahideen. Cf. William Zartman, *Man, State, and Society in the Contemporary Maghrib* (New York: Praeger Publishers, 1973), 275.

8. Leca and Vatin, *L'Algérie politique*, 392.

9. Ibid., 386 and 393.

10. Ottaway and Ottaway, *Algeria*, 305.

11. Zartman, *Man, State, and Society*, 276.

12. Leca and Vatin, *L'Algérie politique*, 396.

13. Zartman, *Man, State, and Society*, 392.

14. Ibid., 267; Leca and Vatin, *L'Algérie politique*, 392.

15. André Nouschi, *L'Algérie amère, 1914–1994* (Paris: Maison des Sciences de l'Homme, 1995), 262.

16. Luis Martinez, *La guerre civile en Algérie* (Paris: Karthala, 1998), 250.

17. Omar Carlier, "Gestuelle du pouvoir et modèle de souveraineté: Les figures présidentielles de l'autorité dans l'Algérie indépendante, 1962–1988," in Michel Camau, *Changements politiques au Maghreb* (Paris: CNRS, 1991), 116.

18. Zartman, *Man, State, and Society*, 266.

19. Martinez, *La guerre civile en Algérie*, 241 and 231.

20. Ottaway and Ottaway, *Algeria*, 98; and Zartman, *Man, State, and Society*, 276.

21. Leca and Vatin, *L'Algérie politique*, 387, 395, 389, and 397.

22. Ibid., 397.

23. Martinez, *La guerre civile en Algérie*, 250 and 251. This claim calls for a more nuanced sociological examination of the profiles of officer corps candidates.

24. Editorial in *El Moudjahid*, no. 1, June 1956, vol, 1, pp. 8 and 9, quoted and discussed by Monique Gadant, *Islam et nationalisme en Algérie, d'après "El Moudjahid" organe central du FLN de 1956 à 1962* (Paris: L'harmattan, 1988), 23.

25. Gadant, *Islam et nationalisme en Algérie*, 88.

26. Martinez, *La guerre civile en Algérie*, 33.

27. René Galissot, *Maghreb-Algérie: Classes et nation* (Paris: Arcantère, 1987), 77–88.

28. According to the official records of the mujahideen, women make up 3 percent of all veterans. For the most part, women saw to administrative tasks, such as supplies, housing, and support for combatants. They also served as liaison agents, guides on the borders of the casbah, secretaries, and nurses. See Gilbert Meynier, "Les femmes dans l'ALN/FLN," in Jean-Charles Jauffret, *Des femmes et des hommes en guerre d'Algérie* (Paris: Autrement, 2003), 309–17. See also Djamila Amrane, *Les femmes algériennes dans la guerre* (Paris: Plon, 1991); Monique Gadant, *Le nationalisme algérien et les femmes* (Paris: L'Harmattan, 1995). See also Ryme Seferdjeli, "Les femmes dans l'Armée de libération nationale: Le mariage et/ou l'action?," *Colloque: Pour une histoire critique et citoyenne; Le cas de l'histoire franco-algérienne, 20–22 June 2006, Lyon* (ENS LSH, 2007), http://colloque-algerie.ens-lyon.fr/rubrique.php3?id_rubrique=67.

29. Zartman, *Man, State, and Society*, 213.

30. Omar Carlier, "Le moudjahid, mort ou vif?," in Anny Dayan Rosenman and Lucette Valensi, *La Guerre d'Algérie dans la mémoire et l'imaginaire* (Paris: Éditions Bouchène, 2004), 65.

31. Ibid., 64.

32. Ibid., 67–68.

33. Smail Goumeziane, *Le mal algérien* (Paris: Fayard, 1994), 34.

34. Ibid., 62.

35. According to information collected in the field.

36. Ministry of Information, *La dette de la nation: Les anciens moudjahidine et victimes de la guerre* (Constantine: 1969), 10–16.

37. The intermediary levels are 27,000, 32,000, and 52,000.

38. Ministry of Information, *La dette de la nation*, 20–27.

39. Carlier, "Le moudjahid, mort ou vif?," 65–66.

40. The question of rights once again arose in 2007, with some associations in particular demanding a retirement pension equal to three to five times the inflation-adjusted minimum wage, the status of mujahida for chahid widows, and the provision of housing. "Algérie: Nouvelle campagne pour débusquer les faux moudjahidine?," *La Voix de l'Oranie*, 26 February 2007.

41. Carlier, "Le moudjahid, mort ou vif?," 66.

42. Interview by author, Aïn Benian, June 2009.

43. Goumeziane, *Le mal algérien*, 130.

44. Mohamed Harbi, *L'Algérie et son destin: Croyants ou citoyens* (Paris: Arcantère, 1992), 109.

45. Carlier, "Le moudjahid, mort ou vif?," 66.

46. Remarks reported by Gilbert Meynier, *Histoire intérieure du FLN* (Paris: Fayard, 2002), 288–89.

47. Carlier, "Le moujahid, mort ou vif?," 66–67.

48. Zahir Boukhelifa, "Algérie: De l'usage de l'antisémitisme," "Rebonds," *Libération*, 17 December 2007.

49. "Algérie: Nouvelle campagne?"

50. Rachida, a sixty-year-old divorced and retired nurse, interview by author, Algiers, September 2006.

51. Carlier, "Le moudjahid, mort ou vif?," 71–73.

52. The following information is all drawn from the biography of Louisette Ighilahriz, *Algérienne*, an account assembled by Anne Nivat (Paris: Fayard/Calman-Levy, 2001), and from my own interviews with her in October 2005, September 2006, and June 2009. The quotations are taken from my interviews.

53. Post–high school Brevet d'Études Primaires Supérieures (Advanced Primary Education Diploma), subsequently renamed the BEPC, and the Certificat d'Aptitude Professionnelle (Professional Aptitude Certificate), or CAP.

54. We will consider the torture inflicted on Louisette Ighilahriz in Chapter 9.

55. Interviews by author, Algiers region, September 2006 and June 2009.

56. In her book, Louisette Ighilahriz describes her father reacting in exactly the same way when she showed him a villa where she thought of settling with her family. Her father, however, offered different reasons: "'So your sole aim in fighting was to have a villa, that's it?,' he began to shout. 'And the martyr's children, where do you think they will live?'" Ighilahriz, *Algérienne*, 31.

57. Interview by author, Algiers, June 2009.

58. Interviews by author, Algiers, October 2005 and September 2006.

Chapter 6

1. Work on the OAS is nearly exclusively historical and only superficially addresses the post-1962 period. The exception is Vincent Quivy's book, the last three chapters of which are devoted to this issue. See Vincent Quivy, *Les soldats perdus: Des anciens de l'OAS racontent* (Paris: Seuil, 2003).

2. Unless otherwise indicated, the careers of the OAS members described in this chapter are based on the accounts they supplied in our interviews.

3. Éric Savarèse, *Algérie, la guerre des mémoires* (Paris: Non-lieu, 2007), 91.

4. Évelyne Lever, "L'OAS et les pieds-noirs," in Charles-Robert Ageron, ed., *L'Algérie des Français* (Paris: Seuil, 1993), 228.

5. Pierre Vidal-Naquet, *Face à la raison d'État: Un historien dans la guerre d'Algérie* (Paris: La Découverte, 1989), 170–86.

6. Arnaud Déroulède, *OAS* (Hélette: Editions Jean Curutchet, 1997), 311–13. The author offers a detailed presentation of the methods used to capture OAS members: infiltrated soldiers, information collected from the FLN, and strong-arm interrogation of the protagonists.

7. According to Arnaud Déroulède, the court handed down 1,085 sentences, including 18 death penalties; Déroulède, *OAS*, 315.

8. Following an appeal submitted by a defendant's lawyers, the Council of State overturned the order establishing this special court. Cf. Anne-Marie Duranton-Crabol, *Le temps de l'OAS* (Brussels: Complexe, 1995), 235–36.

9. In Pierre Viansson-Ponté's words. See Pierre Viansson-Ponté, *Histoire de la République gaullienne, mai 1958–avril 1969* (Paris: Robert Laffont, 1984), 294.

10. The state security court handed down 29 death sentences (including 13 in 1963), 33 life sentences, and 1,952 terms in prison with lesser sentences. Déroulède, *OAS*, 316.

11. The four "delta" commando leaders I interviewed are Gabriel Anglade, Joseph Rizza, Edouard Slama, and Quentin. These interviews took place in Cagnes-sur-Mer, Nice, and the Toulon region in July 2004 and January 2005. The man's romantic dimension also became apparent over the course of these interviews: Degueldre was a man whose "dream was to retire, get a little boat, and go fishing." While hiding out in Fort de l'Eau, he once asked one of his commando leaders to prepare mussels for his pregnant companion.

12. Duranton-Crabol, *Le temps de l'OAS*, 124–25.

13. Yann Scioldo-Zürcher, "Devenir métropolitain" (PhD diss., EHESS, 2006), 386.

14. Interview by author, cited. See also Olivier Dard, *Voyage au coeur de l'OAS* (Paris: Perrin, 2005), 273.

15. Each organized a new assassination attempt targeting General de Gaulle, the first in the fall of 1963, the second at Mont Faron in August 1964. They did not join the National Council of the Resistance (CNR) that was established in the spring of 1962, although they shared its objective: to punish the president of the Republic. Under the leadership of Georges Bidault, Jacques Soustelle, and Colonel Argoud, the CNR failed to unite the various branches of the OAS. See Duranton-Crabol, *Le temps de l'OAS*, 227–32; and Dard, *Voyage au coeur de l'OAS*, 271–77.

16. Dard, *Voyage au coeur de l'OAS*, 269–71.

17. Ibid., 271.

18. Quivy, *Les soldats perdus*, 171.

19. Rémy Kauffer, *OAS* (Paris: Seuil, 2002), 382; Quivy, *Les soldats perdus*, 172.

20. Interview by author, Cannes, 2004.

21. Kauffer, *OAS*, 391–94; Dard, *Voyage au coeur de l'OAS*, 271.

22. On 7 February 1962, an explosive charge intended for André Malraux wounded a four-year-old girl, Delphine Renard. The attack shocked public opinion.

23. Todd Shepard, *The Invention of Decolonization: The Algerian War and the Remaking of France* (Ithaca, NY: Cornell University Press, 2006), 185 and 193.

24. On the term *pied-noir*, see Clarisse Buono's book, *Pieds-noirs de père en fils* (Paris: Balland, 2004), in particular 58–59; and Éric Savarèse, *L'invention des pieds-noirs* (Biarritz: Séguier, 2002).

25. Shepard, *The Invention of Decolonization*, 89 and 122.

26. Jean-Jacques Jordi refers to the departmental archives of Bouches du Rhone; Jean-Jacques Jordi, *1962* (Paris: Autrement, 1995), 26.

27. Benjamin Stora, *La gangrène et l'oubli* (Paris: La Découverte, 1991), 256.

28. Interior Ministry figures cited by Michèle Baussant, *Pieds-noirs* (Paris: Stock, 2002), 352 and 365–69.

29. Kauffer, *OAS*, 309–10; Paul Henissart, *Les combattants du crépuscule* (Paris : Grasset, 1970), 498; Jordi, *1962*, 54.

30. Buono, *Pieds-noirs de père en fils*, 79.

31. Interview by author, Béziers, 2005.

32. Michèle Baussant also mentions the testimony of pieds-noirs regarding their difficulties in obtaining license plates; Baussant, *Pieds-noirs*, 414–15.

33. Interview by author, region of Sète, 2005.

34. Shepard, *The Invention of Decolonization*, 221–23.

35. Baussant, *Pieds-noirs*, 351. Later portions of her book contain a discussion of the term "repatriate," see 396–411, and Savarèse, *L'invention des pieds-noirs*, op. cit., 227–53.

36. Scioldo-Zürcher, "Devenir métropolitain," 499–501.

37. Ibid., 414.

38. Ibid., 408–9.

39. Ibid., 416–40.

40. Dard, *Voyage au coeur de l'OAS*, 310 and 312.

41. Ibid., 441–45.

42. Scioldo-Zürcher, "Devenir métropolitain," 490.

43. Dard, *Voyage au coeur de l'OAS*, 349.

44. In Mayenne, for example, the pieds-noirs thus "gradually melted into the local population. For a portion of them, integration into the metropolitan civil service clearly played a role but perhaps also—and paradoxically—did the absence of a local representative body for repatriates, which allowed them to avoid communitarian withdrawal." Michel Dloussky, "Les dimanches leur semblent longs: Les Français d'Algérie en Mayenne," in Raphaëlle Branche and Sylvie Thénault, eds., *La France en guerre* (Paris: Autrement, 2008), 452–53.

45. Michèle Baussant, *Pieds-noirs. Mémoirs d'exil*, 379 and 415.

46. Buono, *Pieds-noirs de père en fils*, 82 and 93.

47. Scioldo-Zürcher, "Devenir métropolitain," 434–36.

48. Rémi Kauffer mentions the case of Gabriel Anglade and Joseph Rizza; Kauffer, *OAS*, 310 and 352. Alexander Harrison, for his part, reports testimony indicating that Edouard Slama "made a vain attempt to get into organized crime in Toulon" after losing his position with Olivetti; Alexander Harrison, *Challenging de Gaulle* (New York: Praeger, 1989), 11.

49. Interview by author, Nice, March 2005. Quivy, *Les soldats perdus*, 195.

50. Of which Michel Barouin became president in 1974.

51. Interview by author, Toulon, June 2004.

52. The RPR, or Rassemblement pour le République (Rally for the Republic), was a French political party that claimed to represent the legacy of General de Gaulle. It existed from 1978 to 2002 and then became Union pour un Mouvement Populaire (UMP).

53. On the FURR, see Alain Rollat, *Les hommes de l'extrême droite* (Paris: Calmann-Lévy, 1985), 214–17; Benjamin Stora, *Le transfert d'une mémoire* (Paris: La Découverte, 1999), 58.

54. Dard, *Voyage au coeur de l'OAS*, 307–8; Quivy, *Les soldats perdus*, 200–202.

55. Rollat, *Les hommes de l'extrême droite*, 214. The association's website is not very clear, referring to 750 members, among them 600 former prisoners and 600 benefactors.

56. See the website of the Ligue des Droits de l'Homme (LDH), http://www.ldh-toulon .net/spip.php?article747.

57. Adimad has two Internet sites: www.adimad.fr and www.adimad-oas.com. Formerly divided between ADIMAD South and ADIMAD Paris Region, in 2003 the two organizations merged into a single structure presided over by Jean-François Colin, a former city councilman for the National Front in the town of Hyères.

58. Dard, *Voyage au cœur de l'OAS*, 307.

59. Quivy, *Les soldats perdus*, 227.

60. Scioldo-Zürcher, "Devenir métropolitain," 501.

61. Yann Scioldo-Zürcher, "Existe-t-il une vision pied-noir des rapports franco-algériens?," *Colloque: Pour une histoire critique et citoyenne; Le cas de l'histoire franco-algérienne, 20–22 June 2006, Lyon* (ENS LSH, 2007), http://colloque-algerie.ens-lyon.fr/rubrique.php3?id _rubrique=67.

62. Gilles Manceron, "Passé colonial: Les propos inquiétants de Nicolas Sarkozy," on the website of the Toulon Human Rights League, http://www.ldh.toulon.net/spip.php?article2019.

63. Raphaëlle Branche, *La guerre d'Algérie* (Paris: Seuil, 2005), 26.

64. Scioldo-Zürcher, "Devenir métropolitain," 482; see also Jean-Philippe Ould Aoudia, *La bataille de Marignane* (Paris: Éditions du Tirésias, 2006), 93–106. Steles celebrating the "martyrs" of the OAS also exist in Théoule-sur-Mer, Paris (Saint-Nicolas du Chardonnet) and Pérols (Hérault). In Toulon, there is a monument to the Porte d'Italie (constructed in 1980) as well as to the "Salan crossroads" (2001). The controversy elicited by a "stele of the executed" in Marignane led the project to be abandoned.

65. Quoted by Stora, *Le transfert d'une mémoire*, 67.

66. As Clarisse Buono has shown in regard to the pieds-noirs, memory endures precisely because it is conflictual. See Buono, *Pieds-noirs de père en fils*, 78–79.

Part III

1. By "violence," I am here referring to the violation of the other's physical integrity, whether by way of torture or a specific or blind attack, leading to the reduction (wounds) or death of the target.

2. Antoine Prost, *Les anciens combattants* (Paris: Gallimard, 1977), 13, 26–28.

Chapter 7

1. Vamik Volkan, *Blood Lines: From Ethnic Pride to Ethnic Terrorism* (Boulder, CO: Westview Press, 1997), chap. 3.

2. Florence Passy and Marco Giugni, "Récits, imaginaires collectifs et formes d'action protestataire: Une approche constructiviste de la contestation antiraciste," *Revue Française de Science Politique* 55, no. 5/6 (October–December 2005): 893.

3. Jean-Michel Chaumont, *La concurrence des victimes. Génocide, identité, reconnaissance* (Paris: La Découverte, 1997).

4. A psychiatrist working in 1950s Algeria, Frantz Fanon joined the FLN. Considered to be one of the leading theoreticians of the emancipation of subjugated peoples, he produced foundational analyses of relations within colonial societies and the decolonization process.

5. Frantz Fanon, *Les damnés de la terre* (Paris: Gallimard, 1991), 92.

6. Ibid., chap. 5, "Guerre coloniale et troubles mentaux."

7. Feminine plural of the term *mujahid*.

8. Interview by author, region of Algiers, September 2006.

9. Ghassan, seventy-one years old, interview by author, Algiers region, September 2006.

10. Nelson Mandela, *Long Walk to Freedom* (Boston: Little Brown, 1994), 324–25 and 329–30.

11. This is the argument offered by Gail M. Presbey, "Fanon on the Role of Violence in Liberation: A Comparison with Gandhi and Mandela," in Lewis R. Gordon, T. Denean Sharpley-Whiting, and Renée T. White, *Fanon* (Oxford and Cambridge, MA: Blackwell Publishers, 1996), 283–96.

12. In the 1960s and 1970s, the MK set its sights on symbolic or economic targets and carried out acts of sabotage. According to the terms of the TRC report, very few "human rights violations" took place at this time. In 1978, the military command created elite units in order to accelerate the armed struggle. Beginning in 1983, MK members carried out bomb attacks—evidence of disagreement or a breakdown of command within the organization. They attacked the security forces as well as "enemy agents" thought to be traitors. In the late 1980s, increased recruitment in the townships of young people lacking real political or military training led to an augmentation of the brutality of the actions that were carried out. See *Truth and Reconciliation Commission of South Africa, Report* (Bath: Bath Press, 1998), 2:8–36.

13. *Truth and Reconciliation Commission of South Africa, Report* (Bath: Bath Press, 1998), 2:290.

14. Albert Luthuli, *Liberté pour mon peuple* (Paris: Buchet Castel, 1963).

15. Yunis, a former member of the MK and today a lawyer and father, interview by author, Johannesburg, March 2004.

16. On 20 May 1983, a bomb exploded on Church Street in Pretoria, killing 11 people and wounding 217 more. The explosive device targeted the security forces but was prematurely detonated. Another sadly famous event was the attack against the Magoo Bar in Durban on 14 June 1986, which killed 3 people and wounded 69. Eight other attacks were carried out by the MK between 1985 and 1988, killing 20 people, among them 3 police officers and 2 soldiers. The ANC declared that these actions were the result of misunderstanding on the part of activists in the field. Between 1985 and 1987, the ANC planted mines in rural zones with the aim of striking military patrols. These led to the death of 23 people, among them 2 MK as well as a number of black agricultural workers and members of their families. *Truth and Reconciliation Commission*, 2:328–35.

17. The "civil war" in Kwazulu-Natal is said to have led to the death of 3,653 people between July 1990 and June 1993. The pace of killing further accelerated the following year. *Truth and Reconciliation Commission*, 2:584–85.

18. Erick Erickson, *Gandhi's Truth: On the Origins of Militant Nonviolence* (New York: Norton, 1969), 437.

19. Between 1984 and 1989, 700 people are said to have died after being subjected to necklacing. See *Truth and Reconciliation Commission*, 2:389.

20. Established in 1993, the Motsuenyane Commission was created on the orders of Nelson Mandela to investigate the abuses committed in training camps by the ANC against its own members. It concluded that failures of judgment had afflicted investigations of agents accused of being enemy infiltrators as well as the manner in which rebels were treated. See *Truth and Reconciliation Commission*, 351.

21. Lyn S. Graybill, *Truth and Reconciliation in South Africa* (Boulder and London: Lynne Rienner Publishers, 2002), 61–89.

22. ANC, "Statement at the Truth and Reconciliation Commission," August 1996.

23. Graybill, *Truth and Reconciliation in South Africa*, 90.

24. I possess no data that would confirm or quantify the extent of such consultation. The frequency of this observation is perhaps partly due to the way in which I was guided during my visits to the field. In any case, the projects I encountered for reintegrating veterans or addressing violence drew upon the services of psychologists. Moreover, in the chapter of the TRC report containing recommendations, it was specified that "the Commission recommends that priority be given to mental health as a national concern." *Truth and Reconciliation Commission*, 5:337.

25. In the context of the Algerian War and the years preceding it, the term *liberal* was used to refer to a group of Europeans composed, among others, of intellectuals and prominent figures who denounced the injustice of the colonial system. Though they did not support or join the FLN, the liberals spoke out against repression and torture. They were often targeted by the OAS.

26. Camille, a seventy-four-year-old native of Oran and member of a "colline" (armed unit in Oran), interview by author, Nice, November 2004.

27. Barbouzes: members of the French intelligence services sent to Algeria in 1961 to eliminate the OAS by means of expeditious measures.

28. Todd Shepard, *The Invention of Decolonization: The Algerian War and the Remaking of France* (Ithaca, NY: Cornell University Press, 2006), 106.

29. In the 1994 elections, the National Party received 20 percent of the vote. In 2004, it only obtained 1.65 percent. The party was disbanded, and its leaders joined the ANC.

30. On the denials of Frederik de Klerk or Pietr Botha, see Graybill, *Truth and Reconciliation in South Africa*, chap. 4.

31. A now retired sixty-seven-year-old Afrikaner father, interview by author, Pretoria, March 2004.

32. Major-General H. D. Stadler, with the collaboration of other retired South African police officers, *The Other Side of the Story: A True Perspective* (Pretoria: Contact Publishers, 1997).

33. The church to which most Afrikaners belong, it supported the doctrine of apartheid.

34. "National victim," a category created by Desmond Tutu. See Tom Lodge, *Politics in South Africa* (Cape Town: David Philip, 2002; Oxford: James Currey, 2003), 184.

35. The first term of this expression and those that follow refers to the protagonists' subjective perception, while the second refers to the objective reality of the power struggle.

36. Stéphane Audoin-Rouzeau and Annette Becker, "Violence et constentement: 'La culture de guerre' du premier conflit mondial," in Jean-Pierre Rioux and Jean-François Sirinelli, *Pour une histoire culturelle* (Paris: Seuil, 1997), 254.

Chapter 8

1. Antoine Prost, *Les anciens combattants* (Paris: Gallimard, 1977), 14.

2. Stéphane Audoin-Rouzeau and Annette Becker, "Violence et consentement: 'La culture de guerre' du premier conflit mondial," in Jean-Pierre Rioux and Jean-François Sirinelli, *Pour une histoire culturelle* (Paris: Seuil, 1997), 258 and 270.

3. Jean Hatzfeld, *Une saison de machettes* (Paris: Seuil, 2003).

4. Audoin-Rouzeau and Becker, "Violence et consentement," 257–58.

5. On the various forms of denial, see Stanley Cohen, *States of Denial: Knowing about Atrocities and Suffering* (Cambridge: Polity Press, 2001).

6. Cohen, *States of Denial*, chap. 1.

7. Philippe Braud, *Violences politiques* (Paris: Seuil, 2004), 96. A clear example of the denial of others' suffering is revealed in the responses of Kobus, who was questioned by the TRC in regard to a prisoner he tortured and the effects this had on the prisoner: "Mister President, I could not tell whether it affected him. All that I observed was that Mr. X was a very aggressive individual and that he took a very negative attitude towards the questions we asked him. If I had to make an assessment, I would say that suffocation had absolutely no effect on him." http:www.doj.gov.za/trc/.

8. Rym, a seventy-year-old retired secretary in the civil service, interview by author, Algiers, September 2006.

9. See his portrait in Chapter 4.

10. Xavier Crettiez, *Violence et nationalisme* (Paris: Odile Jacob, 2006), 216–17.

11. Audoin-Rouzeau and Becker, "Violence et consentement," 260–61.

12. Mehdi, a retired, seventy-two-year-old customs officer and family man, interview by author, Algiers region, September 2006.

13. See the section in Chapter 7 entitled "OAS: Between Vengeance and Resistance."

14. On this point, see in particular Christopher Browning, *Ordinary Men* (New York: Harper Collins, 1992), 128.

15. Wolfgang Sofsky, *L'ère de l'épouvante: Folie meurtrière, terreur, guerre* (Paris: Gallimard, 2002), 34–35.

16. Nicolas, a forty-five-year-old family man and financial analyst, interview by author, Cape Town, March 2004. See his portrait in Chapter 4.

17. John, an Anglophone in his fifties, is a veteran of the C1 unit that specialized in tracking members of the ANC (Vlakplaas). He today works as a risk analyst for a diamond-mining company in the Democratic Republic of Congo. He requested and received amnesty for eight different affairs. Interview by author, Pretoria, March 2005.

18. Gabriel Anglade, interview cited.

19. Auguste, a sixty-nine-year-old native of Oran, interview by author, Toulon, June 2004.

20. On OAS violence against Muslim civilians, see Anne-Marie Duranton-Crabol, *Le temps de l'OAS* (Brussels: Complexe, 1995), 216–19.

21. Joanna Bourke, *An Intimate History of Killing: Face-to-Face Killing in Twentieth-Century Warfare* (London: Granta Publications, 1999); see in particular the first chapter, "The Pleasures of War."

22. Sofsky, *L'ère de l'épouvante*, 17–18.

23. A diminutive referring to one of these units' central missions: reconnaissance.

24. The 32nd Battalion was created in 1975 by Colonel Jan Breytenbach. An infantry unit composed of Angolan recruits captured by the South African Army during the civil war, the unit was modeled on the French Foreign Legion and focused on bush warfare and counter-guerrilla operations in Angola and, later, Namibia. The unit disbanded in 1992, and its foreign members were excluded from the integration process within the new South African Army. Some of them subsequently joined mercenary companies.

25. Johann, a forty-seven-year-old family man and Afrikaner, interview by author, Cape Town, March 2004.

26. Teddy the lion became the mascot of one of the Special Forces units. His photograph is featured on the Internet site of the Recces association.

27. Prost, *Les anciens combattants*, 33.

28. In the clinical cases described by Fanon, he mentions the case of a French army soldier who opened up to the psychiatrist about symptoms of anxiety relating to his daily use of torture. He asked Fanon to treat him in such a way as to allow him to continue his work without suffering from these troubles. Cf. Frantz Fanon, *Les damnés de la terre* (Paris: Gallimard, 1991), 319–22.

29. Louis Crocq, *Les traumatismes psychiques de guerre* (Paris: Odile Jacob, 1999), 340.

30. Bourke, *An Intimate History of Killing*, 239–40.

31. Crocq, *Les traumatismes psychiques de guerre*, 342.

32. Ibid., 342–45.

33. "The apologists of the therapeutic society have a habit of re-baptizing the guilty as victims," writes Wolfgang Sofsky, *L'ère de l'épouvante*, 25. In a discussion of American torture "chicks," Coco Fusco also mentions how the American media presented them as victims; Coco Fusco, *A Field Guide for Female Interrogators* (New York, London, Melbourne, Toronto: Seven Stories Press, 2008), 38–39.

34. In their book, Don Foster, Paul Haupt, and Marésa de Beer mention the case of a member of the Special Forces who refused to request amnesty for his past actions, maintaining that his fate would have to be decided by a court of justice. This case is exceptional. See Don Foster, Paul Haupt, and Marésa de Beer, *The Theatre of Violence: Narratives of the Protagonists in the South African Conflict* (Cape Town: Institute for Justice and Reconciliation and HSRC Press; Oxford: James Currey, 2005).

35. See Chapter 6.

36. Interview by author, Kwazulu-Natal, March 2005.

37. South African Press Association, *Brian Mitchell Released After Receiving Amnesty*, 10 December 1996, http://www.justice.gov.za/trc/media/1996/9612/s961210.htm.

38. Emphasis mine.

39. See his portrait in Chapter 4.

40. Thami is too young to receive a veteran's pension—one must have been more than thirty-five years old in 1994. If he succeeds in proving that his illness stems from his time with the ANC, he will be eligible for a special pension.

41. By contrast, physical distance and a lack of visual confirmation have the effect of reducing feelings of guilt. As John Glenn Gray notes, air force pilots and artillery troops can kill many men without feeling the least regret. See John Glenn Gray, *The Warriors* (New York: Harcourt, 1959), 173.

42. Now in his forties, Michael is a married ex-MK. After a time in the civil service, he started his own company. Interviews by author, Pretoria, March 2005 and March 2006.

43. Members of the OAS and the South African security forces speak of drinking with FLN and ANC activists, respectively.

Chapter 9

1. Jacques Sémelin, *Purifier et détruire* (Paris: Seuil, 2005).

2. Raphaëlle Branche, *La torture et l'armée pendant la guerre d'Algérie* (Paris: Gallimard, 2001); Marnia Lazreg, *Torture and the Twilight of Empire* (Princeton, NJ: Princeton University Press, 2008).

3. Coco Fusco, *Field Guide for Female Interrogators* (New York, London, Melbourne, Toronto: Seven Stories Press, 2008).

4. Ibid., 47–57.

5. Henri Pouillot, *La Villa Susini* (Paris: Éditions Tiréisas, 2001); Jean-Pierre Vittori, *On a torturé en Algérie: Témoignages recueillis par Jean-Pierre Vittori* (Paris: Éditions Ramsay, 2000); Bernard Sigg, *Le silence et la honte* (Paris: Messidor, 1989).

6. Christiane Chaulet-Achour, "La question de la torture en Algérie," in Véronique Bonnet, ed., *Conflits de mémoire* (Paris: Karthala, 2004), 263–66.

7. Henri Alleg, *La question* (Paris: Editions de Minuit, 1958); Pierre Vidal-Naquet, *L'affaire Audin* (Paris: Minuit, 1958); Vidal-Naquet, *La torture dans la République* (Paris: Minuit, 1972); Simone de Beauvoir and Gisèle Halimi, *Djamila Boupacha* (Paris: Gallimard, 1962).

8. Numa Muraud refers to a survey carried out by INSEE and DREES. See Catherine Cavalin, "Les violences subies par les personnes âgées de 18 à 75 ans," *Études et Résultats* 598 (September 2007). Numa Muraud, "La violence dans les entretiens biographiques" (talk, Congress of the Association Française de Sociologie, April 2009).

9. Michael Pollak and Nathalie Heinich, "Le témoignage," in *Actes de la Recherche en Sciences Sociales* 62, no. 1 (1986): 4.

10. Vincent Romani, "Quelques réflexions à propos des processus coercitifs dans les Territoires occupés," *Études Rurales* 1–2, nos. 173–74 (2005): 262.

11. See his portrait in Chapter 5.

12. Thus Tahar, calling into question the Harkis' methods, explained the harm they inflicted: "Us, our traditions, our mores, for example, um . . . I would rather die than show myself naked to my mother or father. So they [the Harkis], when they enter a family like that, in a house in Kabylie or anywhere: 'Everyone get your clothes off!' Everyone! The Harkis!" Interview by author, Algiers region, September 2006.

13. Lazreg, *Torture and the Twilight of Empire*, 1 and 130.

14. Michael Pollak and Nathalie Heinich underscore this problem in regard to concentration camp survivors who may have "compromised themselves" with the kapos, or camp leaders. Pollak and Heinich, "Le témoignage," 6.

15. Lazreg, *Torture and the Twilight of Empire*, 136–41.

16. Gillian Slovo, *Poussière rouge* (Paris: Christian Bourgois, 2001); Jann Turner, *Southern Cross* (London: Orion Books, 2002).

17. Odette Marinez employs this expression in discussing her documentary, *L'île de Celo*, in which she interviews an anti-Franco combatant; presentation at a CERI seminar on women combatants, 20 May 2009.

18. The term *askari* designates a combatant of the national liberation movements who, after being captured, was forced to collaborate with and join government forces.

19. Christiane Chaulet-Achour, among others, has made this observation; Chaulet-Achour, "La question de la torture en Algérie," 266. This point of view was also expressed by Raphaëlle Branche in the course of a conference on "war's end" (14 June 2007) organized by Bruno Cabanes and Guillaume Piketty at the Centre d'Histoire de Sciences-Po.

20. Ghassan, a seventy-one-year-old family man who worked as a taxi driver before becoming a FLN leader. He was later elected to the wilaya assembly, a position from which he resigned in 1972 to create a small transportation business. He is now retired and receives a pension as a "cadre de la nation," a sort of high-ranking category among the mujahideen. Interview cited.

21. Lazreg, *Torture and the Twilight of Empire*, 138–39.

22. Louisette Ighilahriz with Anne Nivat, *Algérienne* (Paris: Fayard/Calman-Lévy, 2001).

23. On this theme, see also the case of Sami, a Palestinian Fatah militant who explains how to keep control of oneself during torture. Laetitia Bucaille, "Armed Resistance and Self-Esteem: Ex-Combatants in Palestine and South Africa," *International Political Sociology* 5 (2011): 65.

24. Yunis, a forty-four-year-old family man and lawyer, interview by author, Jonnesburg, March 2004.

25. Popo, a forty-five-year-old former MK who spent ten years in prison at Robben Island. Today, he is a family man and ministry official. Interview by author, Johannesburg, March 2005.

26. Pollak and Heinich, "Le témoignage," 16.

27. An ex-MK, Dipuo is today a fifty-four-year-old mother separated from her husband. Under threat, she fled the country and joined the ANC in southern Africa. Upon returning from exile, she joined the army as a sergeant. Interview by author, Soweto, February 2004.

28. Michael, a forty-three-year-old ex-MK, businessman, interview by author, March 2006.

29. I interviewed Michael on two occasions in 2005. I met him again in 2006, and, on that occasion, he asked me to hear him out.

30. Christopher, a fifty-five-year-old father of two who divorced following a car accident that rendered him paraplegic. He receives a 700-rand handicap pension each month. When he left the police in 1993, he received a 250,000-rand compensation package. Interview by author, township in the Pretoria region, 2006.

31. Ighilahriz, *L'algérienne*, See her portrait in Chapter 5.

32. In particular, at a September 2000 Festival of Humanity and during her testimony at the June 2003 trial of General Schmitt. See Sylvie Durmelat, "Revisiting Ghosts: Louisette Ighilahriz and the Remembering of Torture," in Alec G. Hargreaves, ed., *Memory, Empire, and Postcolonialism* (Lanham, MD: Lexington Books, 2005), 142–59.

33. Interviews by author, Algiers, November 2005 and September 2006.

34. Interview cited.

35. Interview cited.

36. Lee Taft, "Apology Subverted: The Commodification of Apology," *Yale Law Journal* 109, no. 5 (March 2000): 1137.

37. Of the three soldiers she accused, only General Massu admitted that the French army had engaged in torture, though he maintained that he did not know or recall Louisette Ighilahriz. He added: "In her case, things seem to have gone very far. Perhaps her account is a little excessive but it is not necessarily so and, in that case, I truly regret it. All of that was part of the climate in Algiers at that time." Florence Beaugé, "Le général Massu exprime ses regrets pour la torture en Algérie," in Florence Beaugé, *L'Algérie de la guerre à la mémoire Paris-Alger: Quel avenir ?* (Paris: Éditions du Cygne, 2008), 17. General Bigeard, for his part, denied everything. See his interview with Florence Beaugé, 15–16. Captain Graziani died in the course of a military operation in Kabylie in 1959.

38. Nicholas Tavuchis, *Mea Culpa* (Stanford, CA: Stanford University Press, 1991).

39. Sylvie Durmelat, "Revisiting Ghosts: Louisette Ighilahriz and the Remembering of Torture," in Hargreaves, *Memory, Empire, and Postcolonialism*, 148.

40. Mohamed Harbi, *L'Algérie et son destin* (Paris: Arcantère, 1992).

41. Jean-Michel Chaumont has shown how, after initially feeling shame at their status as victims, those who escaped the Nazi genocide eventually came to see it as a source of pride. Jean-Michel Chaumont, *La concurrence des victimes* (Paris: La Découverte, 1997).

42. Quoted by Durmelat, "Revisiting Ghosts," 154.

324 Notes to Pages 231–235

Part IV

1. For an overview of the various approaches to reconciliation, see Valérie Rosoux, "Reconciliation as a Peace-Building Process: Scope and Limits," in Jacob Berkovitch, Victor Kremenyuk, and William Zartman, *The Sage Handbook of Conflict Resolution* (Los Angeles: Sage Publications, 2009).

Chapter 10

1. These are defined as murder, kidnapping, torture, and other blatant abuses, as well as inciting, instigating, or ordering them.

2. The first date corresponds to the Sharperville Massacre, which took place on 21 March 1960 when the government repressed a demonstration against pass laws, killing 79 people and wounding 178 others. The regime's brutality subsequently led the ANC to resort to violence and form an armed wing. The second date is when Mandela took office.

3. Jacques Derrida, "Versöhnung, ubuntu, pardon: quel genre?," in Barbara Cassin, Olivier Cayla, and Philippe-Joseph Salazar, *Vérité, Réconciliation, Réparation*, special issue of *Le Genre Humain*, November 2004, 141.

4. Among others things, Dominique Darbon cites the arrival of the first colonists, who were compared to the chosen people, with the myth of blood river interpreted by the Boers as a pact with God, and the rainbow symbolizing the alliance between God and the South African people. See Dominique Darbon, "La Truth and Reconciliation Commission: Le miracle sud-africain en question," *Revue Française de Science Politique* 48, no. 6 (December 1998): 713–14.

5. Although he was not particularly religious, Nelson Mandela presented himself as a Christian (he was Methodist). Frederik de Klerk was for his part convinced that God had called upon him to save the peoples of South Africa. Brian Frost, *Struggling to Forgive: Nelson Mandela and South Africa's Search for Reconciliation* (New York: Harper Collins, 1998), 15 and 76.

6. On this question and for a comparison with the Chilean and Argentine cases, see Sandrine Lefranc, *Politiques du pardon* (Paris: PUF, 2002). See also Antoine Garapon, "La justice comme reconnaissance," in Cassin, Cayla, and Salazar, *Vérité, Réconciliation, Réparation*, 184–86.

7. As in the 1995 law creating the TRC, a postscript entitled "National Unity and Reconciliation" stipulated that past injustices were to be addressed in such a way as to advance a "need for understanding but not for vengeance, a need for reparation but not retaliation." Richard Wilson, *The Politics of Truth and Reconciliation in South Africa* (Cambridge: Cambridge University Press, 2001), 8.

8. Alex Boraine, *A Country Unmasked* (Oxford: Oxford University Press, 2000), chap. 4.

9. After having been abused, ignored, and despised by the state, many survivors in Chile, Sri Lanka, and South Africa have vouched for the curative powers of testimony. See Elizabeth Kiss, "Moral Ambition Within and Beyond Political Constraints: Reflections on Restorative Justice," in Robert I. Rotberg and Dennis Thompson, eds., *Truth v. Justice* (Princeton, NJ: Princeton University Press, 2000), 71 and following.

10. The methods of infiltration, recruiting collaborators, and elimination practiced by the police could cast some anti-apartheid activists into disrepute within their community. See Wilson, *The Politics of Truth and Reconciliation*, 143–50.

11. On this point, see Kiss, "Moral Ambition Within and Beyond Political Constraints," 90.

12. See Piers Pigou, "False Promises and Wasted Opportunities? Inside South Africa's Truth and Reconciliation Commission," in Deborah Posel and Graeme Simpson, *Commissioning the Past* (Johannesburg: Witwatersrand University Press, 2002), 37–65.

13. Lyn S. Graybill, *Truth and Reconciliation in South Africa* (Boulder and London: Lynne Rienner Publishers, 2002), 49.

14. This is the point of view of Graeme Simpson, director of the Centre for the Study of Violence and Reconciliation (CSVR), as well as that of Jeffrie G. Murphy and Jean Hampton, *Forgiveness and Mercy* (Cambridge: Cambridge University Press, 1988), 80, 90, and 149.

15. On this theme, see Thomas Brudholm, "Revisiting Resentments: Jean Améry and the Dark Side of Forgiveness and Reconciliation," *Journal of Human Rights* 5, no. 1 (January 2006): 7–26.

16. Interview by author, Soweto, April 2003.

17. In its report, the TRC recommended four types of reparation: community reinsertion programs to promote reconciliation; symbolic measures of reparation (burials, commemorations, and so on); institutional reforms to prevent human rights violations from recurring; and individual reparations. The proposal consisted in paying sums varying between 17,000 and 23,000 rands (or between 2,000 and 2,800 euros on the basis of a 0.122 exchange rate) per year for a period of six years.

18. François du Bois, "Reparations and the Forms of Justice," in François du Bois and Antjie du Bois-Pedain, *Justice and Reconciliation in Post-Apartheid South Africa* (Cambridge: Cambridge University Press, 2008), 125–27.

19. Or 3,660 euros.

20. Graybill, *Truth and Reconciliation in South Africa*, 152.

21. David Crocker, "Forgive and Not Forget," in Elazar Barkan and Alexander Karn, *Taking Wrongs Seriously* (Stanford, CA: Stanford University Press, 2006).

22. Graybill, *Truth and Reconciliation in South Africa*, 88–89.

23. Or 998 requests for amnesty from the ANC, and 293 from the state and security forces.

24. This attack killed 19 people and wounded more than 200 others. *Truth and Reconciliation Commission of South Africa, Report* (Bath: Bath Press, 1998), 5:261.

25. Abu Bakr Ismael, fifty-one years old, interview by author, Pretoria, April 2005.

26. James Gibson, *Overcoming Apartheid* (Cape Town: HSRC Press, 2004), 99.

27. Other countries that have established truth commissions have favored collective amnesty.

28. Kiss, "Moral Ambition Within and Beyond Political Constraints," 77.

29. Graybill, *Truth and Reconciliation in South Africa*, 40.

30. Garapon, "La justice comme reconnaissance," 190.

31. According to a lawyer who defended several dozen members of the forces of order; interview by author, Pretoria, April 2006.

32. André du Toit characterizes the TRC in terms of "truth as acknowledgement" and "justice as recognition." See André du Toit, "The Moral Foundations of the South African TRC," in Rotberg and Thompson, *Truth v. Justice*, 122–40.

33. Barbara Cassin, "Amnistie et pardon: Pour une ligne de partage entre éthique et politique," in Cassin, Cayla, Salazar, *Vérité, Réconciliation, Réparation*, 50.

34. Interview by author, Pretoria, March 2005.

35. Lefranc, *Politiques du pardon*, 17.

36. Graybill, *Truth and Reconciliation in South Africa*, chap. 3.

37. Desmond Tutu, *No Future Without Forgiveness* (London: Rider, 1999), 35.

38. Brian Frost, *Struggling to Forgive: Nelson Mandela and South Africa's Search for Reconciliation* (New York: Harper Collins Publishers, 1998), 24.

39. Graybill, *Truth and Reconciliation in South Africa*, 41.

40. Allister Sparks, *Tomorrow Is Another Country* (New York: Hill and Wang, 1995), 91–92.

41. Frost, *Struggling to Forgive*, 72–76. See also Antjie Krog, *La douleur des mots* (Arles: Actes Sud, 2004), 144–49.

42. Pumla Gobodo-Madikizela, *A Human Being Died That Night: A South African Story of Forgiveness* (Boston: Houghton Mifflin, 2003), 102–3.

43. Interview cited. See Oscar's portrait in Chapter 4.

44. Gobodo-Madikizela, *A Human Being Died That Night*, 98. The author presents the testimony of Pearl Faku as she addresses the former leader of an anti-insurrectionary unit, the Vlakplaas, guilty of murdering her husband: "I couldn't control my tears. I heard him but I was submerged by the emotion and I nodded my head, as if to say, I forgive you. I hope that he saw my tears. He knew that they weren't only tears for our husbands but tears for him, too . . . I would like to take him by the hand and show him that there is a future and that he can still change" (15).

45. "If you love those who love you, what benefit is that to you? For even sinners love those who love them. And if you do good to those who do good to you, what benefit is that to you? For even sinners do the same. And if you lend to those from whom you expect to receive, what credit is that to you?" Luke 6:32–34.

46. Lefranc, *Politiques du pardon*, 161.

47. Marie-Thérèse Nadeau, *Pardonner l'impardonnable* (Montreal: Mediaspaul, 1998), 42.

48. "I wanted to meet the man who killed my friends and wounded me. I wanted to meet the man who threw this grenade in an attitude of forgiveness and hope that he will also be able to forgive me for whatever reason." Statement by Beth Savage, reported by Boraine, *A Country Unmasked*, chap. 4.

49. See Ginn Fourie, "A Personal Encounter with Perpetrators," in Charles Villa Vicencio and Wilhem Verwoerd, *Looking Back, Reading Forward* (Cape Town: University of Cape Town Press, 2000), 145–60; Ingrid Martens' SABC television documentary; and my February 2003 interview with Letlapla Mpaphele in Johannesburg.

50. Gibson, *Overcoming Apartheid*, 158.

51. Guy Pervillé, "La guerre d'Algérie cinquante ans après: Le temps de la mémoire, de la justice, ou de l'histoire?," *Historiens et Géographes* 388 (October 2004): 237–46.

52. The plaintiffs were the Ligue des Droits de l'Homme, Le Mouvement contre le Racisme et pour l'Amitié entre les Peuples (MRAP), and Action des Chrétiens pour l'Abolition de la Torture.

53. Paul Aussaresses, *Services spéciaux Algérie (1955–1957)* (Paris: Perrin, 2000).

54. Garapon, "La justice comme reconnaissance," 194.

55. Yacef Saadi, interview by author, Algiers, September 2005.

56. Guy Pervillé, "L'histoire immédiate de la relation franco-algérienne: Vers un traité d'amitié franco-algérien?" (paper delivered at the "Bilan et perspectives de l'histoire immédiate" colloquium held in Toulouse by the Groupe de Recherche en Histoire Immédiate [GRHI], 5 and 6 April 2006), http://www.communautarisme.net/L-histoire-immediate-de-la-relation-franco-algerienne-vers-un-traite-d-amitie-franco-algerien_a766.html.

57. Ibid.

58. The case of Japan's apologies to South Korea demonstrates the limits of this policy. Despite the serial expression of regrets, reconciliation is far from achieved. See Lionel Babicz, "Japon-Corée: De vaines excuses?," *Raison Publique* 10 (May 2009): 17–28.

59. France's ambassador, Bernard Bajolet, declared at Guelma's 8 May 1945 University that the days of May 1945 "were an insult to the founding principles of the French Republic and left an indelible stain on its history." He further underscored that "already, and however hard the facts, I can tell you that France does not intend, no longer intends, to hide them. The time of denial is over"; "We must have done with denying the injustices, errors and crimes of the past."

60. In a 5 December 2009 speech in Constantine, Nicolas Sarkozy paid tribute to the "innocent victims of blind and brutal repression," referred to the "errors and crimes of the past," describing them as "unforgivable," and denounced "the injustice of the colonial system."

61. Florence Beaugé, *Algérie de la guerre à la mémoire* (Paris: Éditions du Cygne, 2008), 149.

62. Elazar Barkan and Alexander Karn, "Group Apology as an Ethical Imperative," in Elazar Barkan and Alexander Karn, *Taking Wrongs Seriously* (Stanford, CA: Stanford University Press, 2006), 7–8.

63. Jean-Michel Chaumont, *La concurrence des victimes: Génocide, identité, reconnaissance* (Paris: La Découverte, 1997).

64. *Le Quotidien d'Oran*, 27 August 2005.

65. Quoted by Pervillé, "L'histoire immédiate de la relation franco-algérienne."

66. Mehdi, seventy-two-year-old family man and retired customs officer; interview by author, Algiers region, September 2006.

Chapter 11

1. Georges Balandier, *Sociologie actuelle de l'Afrique noire* (Paris: PUF, 1982).

2. Nadia, a seventy-three-year-old retired nurse and divorced mother, interview by author, Algiers, September 2006.

3. Tahar, a retired sixty-six-year-old. See his portrait in Chapter 5.

4. Richard Wright, *Black Boy* (New York: Harper & Brothers, 1945), 202.

5. Dominique Vidal, *Les bonnes de Rio* (Villeneuve d'Ascq: Presses Universitaires du Septentrion, 2007), 192–93.

6. Ibid., 197–98.

7. Éric Savarèse, *Algérie* (Paris: Non-lieu, 2007), 125.

8. Marie Cardinal, *Au pays de mes racines* (Paris: Grasset, 1980), 111.

9. Assia Djebar, *La disparition de la langue française* (Paris: Albin Michel, 2003).

10. Interview by author, Cannes, June 2004. Tassou is his nickname.

11. Éric Savarèse, "Après la guerre d'Algérie: La diversité des recompositions identitaires des pieds-noirs," in Laetitia Bucaille, *Recomposition identitaires dans les sociétés postconflictuelles: Ex-combattants, héros, exilés,* special issue, *Revue Internationale des Sciences Sociales* 58, no. 189 (2006). Savarèse draws upon Pierre Nora's account in *Les Français d'Algérie* (Paris: Julliard, 1961).

12. Etienne, a sixty-four-year-old native of Oran and member of a "colline," blew up the port of Oran before his departure. A married family man, he is today retired from a career as a factory director. He explains that his parents, who remained in Algeria until 1963, were saved by Algerians. Interview by author, Sète, January 2005. In Assia Djebar's novel, the narrator,

armed with an axe during a protest and "ringleader of an army of boys letting off steam after the gray years," forced his way as part of a crowd into the apartment of a European family. Among them, he recognized a schoolmate: "It's Popaul! A schoolmate! Don't touch him! Holding my axe, I posted myself in the space between the frightened ones, turning my back to them, and my group. I firmly repeated: He's a mate of mine! Then, holding my weapon, I led the others out." Djebar, *La disparition de la langue française*, 144–46.

13. Azzedine, a seventy-five-year-old family man who formerly ran a textile factory with his brothers and is now retired. Interview by author, Algiers region, September 2006. A pied-noir woman and native of the same locality explained to me that her mother protected Arabs while her brother, a member of the OAS, attacked them.

14. See Mohamed's portrait in Chapter 5.

15. James Gregory, *Goodbye Bafana* (Paris: Robert Laffont, 2007).

16. This trajectory presents similarities with the biography of Rudyard Kipling, which has been studied by Ashis Nandy. She discusses "the cruelty of his first encounter with England at the end of an idyllic childhood in India"; Ashis Nandy, *L'ennemi intime* (Paris: Fayard, 2007), 79 and 111–18.

17. David, a fifty-eight-year-old ex-MK who worked in the provincial government between 1995 and 2003 before becoming a businessman; interview by author, Johannesburg, February 2004.

18. Wright, *Black Boy*, 399–400.

19. Interview by author, Pretoria, February 2005.

20. Karl, a forty-six-year-old family man; interview by author, Pretoria region, March 2005.

21. Albert Memmi, *Portrait du colonisateur* (Paris: Gallimard, 1985), 106–7.

22. Vidal, *Les bonnes de Rio*, 195.

23. Luca, a forty-nine-year-old former Recce and family man who has since gone into finance; interview by author, Cape Town, March 2005.

24. "If a white man had sought to prevent us from getting a job or enjoying our civil rights, we would bow our heads without protesting. But if he had tried to deprive of us of ten cents, the blood would have flowed. For this reason, every moment of our daily life was so intimately related to an immediate and trivial objective that capitulating when we were provoked was the same thing as purely and simply giving up on existence. Our anger was like the anger of children, passing quickly from one petty grievance to another, from the memory of one slight wrong to another." Wright, *Black Boy*, 392.

25. Married and in his seventies, he spends his retirement on the coast; interview by author, Sedgefield, March 2005.

26. Interview by author, Sedgefield, March 2005.

27. Jeremie, an eighty-two-year-old family man who runs a soft-drink factory; interview by author, Marseille region, May 2005.

28. Interview by author, Pretoria, February 2006.

29. Interview by author, Pretoria, April 2006.

30. Dima, a sixty-five-year-old mother and inhabitant of the Katlehong township; interview by author, Johannesburg, February 2004.

31. A pejorative term designating blacks in South Africa.

32. Interview by author, Soweto, February 2004.

33. The case of the white farmer who had one of his black field-hands devoured by lions in 2005 scandalized public opinion at the same time that it threw a harsh light on relations

between blacks and whites in the countryside a decade after the end of apartheid. See *Le Monde*, 1 October 2005.

34. A rich suburb north of Johannesburg that rapidly grew in the 1990s and is mainly populated by whites.

35. This version was not confirmed by the person concerned. The discussion is thus based on the account of the OAS members.

36. Interview by author, Algiers, August 2006.

37. "Intégrité et mépris: Principes d'une morale de la reconnaissance," in Jean-Michel Chaumont and Hervé Pourtois, "Souffrance sociale et attentes de reconnaissance: Autour du travail d'Axel Honneth," *Recherches Sociologiques* 30, no. 2 (1999): 13.

38. Of my sample of sixteen people, only two of them had returned to visit Algeria. The others refuse to consider doing so.

39. Marcel Ronda, interview by author, Nice, November 2004.

40. Gibson, *Overcoming Apartheid*, 138.

41. Interview by author, Pretoria, March 2004.

42. Student, interview by author, campus of Cape Town University, March 2005.

43. Hein, a forty-two-year-old SANDF captain and former member of the SADF; interview cited.

44. Interview cited.

45. Joseph Rizza, interview cited.

46. Marcel Ronda, interview cited.

47. Gabriel Anglade, interview by author, Cagnes-sur-Mer, March 2004.

48. Interview by author, Algiers, September 2006.

49. See Slimane Zeghidour's interview with Ali Benhadj, in *Politique Internationale*, Fall 1990, 156, quoted by Gilles Kepel, *Jihad* (Paris: Gallimard, 2000), 177.

50. Front de l'Algérie Française, the short-lived precursor of the OAS (June–December 1960).

51. Jacques Chevallier was the former liberal mayor of Algiers, who advocated a federation between France and Algeria.

52. Interview by author, Paris, 2006.

53. The "Week of the Barricades" refers to the January 1960 uprising in the course of which a segment of Algiers' pied-noir population demonstrated against what was perceived as a softening in French policy toward Algeria. The week resulted in the death of protesters and police alike. The ringleaders were tried in November 1960.

54. Anne-Marie Duranton-Crabol, *Le temps de l'OAS* (Brussels: Complexe, 1995), 52–53.

55. Interview, Pretoria, February 2004.

56. Paul Ricoeur, *Parcours de la reconnaissance* (Paris: Stock, 2002), introduction.

57. Emile Littré, quoted by Ricoeur, *Parcours de la reconnaissance*, 17.

58. Ibid., 19–20.

59. Ibid., 20–21.

60. Ibid., 21.

Acknowledgments

I would like to warmly thank everyone who read and discussed earlier versions of this text and offered me their criticism and suggestions. Particular thanks are due to Thomas Blaser and Agnès Villechaise for their thoughtful remarks. Comments from Bibiane de La Roque, Alexandra Poli, and Valérie Rosoux were also a great help.

In the process of publishing the English version of this book, I am grateful to Dale Eickelman, who provided considerate and efficient help. I am also thankful to Peter Agree, who showed receptivity, temerity, and great support for this project. Thanks are also due to different institutions that made the translation possible: my university, Institut national des langues et civilisations orientales (Inalco), the Centre d'Études en Sciences Sociales sur les Mondes Africains, Américains et Asiatiques (CESSMA), the Centre de Recherches Moyen-Orient Méditerranée (CERMOM), and the Institut de Recherche Interdisciplinaire en Sciences Sociales (IRISSO). I will not forget the patient work of Ethan Rundell. And I thank as well Lucy McNeece for her fruitful remarks.

As I conducted my research, many people assisted me by sharing their experience and contacts. In South Africa, Dipuo and Thami showed me great generosity. John Daniel and Madeleine Fullard also taught me a great deal. On many occasions, I benefited from the warm hospitality of Safy Nezam, Shervin, Ashkan, and Christophe Le Du. To all of them as well as Thabile and Nthabiseng I wish a happy life. In Algeria, I would like to express my gratitude to Meriem Belaala and Ghania Ibrouchene for their assistance. Their humor and warmth always lent my stays in the country particular meaning and zest. In France, I would like to thank François Margolin, who helped me make my first contacts with members of the OAS.

Finally, I would like to express my deep gratitude to all of those who, in South Africa, Algeria, and France, shared with me their experiences as ex-combatants.